Thomas Hirzel, Nanny Kim (Eds.)

Metals, Monies, and Markets in Early Modern Societies: East Asian and Global Perspectives

BUNKA
WENHUA

Tübinger Ostasiatische Forschungen
Tuebingen East Asian Studies

herausgegeben von/edited by

Klaus Antoni, Viktoria Eschbach-Szabo,
Robert Horres, Achim Mittag,
Gunter Schubert, Hans Ulrich Vogel

Band/Volume 17

LIT

Metals, Monies, and Markets in Early Modern Societies: East Asian and Global Perspectives

Monies, Markets, and Finance in China and East Asia

Volume 1

edited by

Thomas Hirzel and Nanny Kim

LIT

Printed with the support of the Association of the Friends of the University of Tübingen (Vereinigung der Freunde der Universität Tübingen – Universitätsbund e. V.) and the China Society of Baden-Württemberg for the Advancement of Scientific and Technical Cooperation with the People's Republic of China (Baden-Württembergische Gesellschaft zur Förderung der Zusammenarbeit mit der Volksrepublik China e. V.)

Bibliographic information published by the Deutsche Nationalbibliothek
The Deutsche Nationalbibliothek lists this publication in the Deutsche Nationalbibliografie; detailed bibliographic data are available in the Internet at http://dnb.d-nb.de.

ISBN 978-3-8258-0822-8

A catalogue record for this book is available from the British Library

Auslieferung/Verlagskontakt:
Fresnostr. 2 48159 Münster
Tel. +49 (0)251–62 03 20 Fax +49 (0)251–23 19 72
e-Mail: lit@lit-verlag.de http://www.lit-verlag.de

Distributed in the UK by: Global Book Marketing, 99B Wallis Rd, London, E9 5LN
Phone: +44 (0) 20 8533 5800 – Fax: +44 (0) 1600 775 663
http://www.centralbooks.co.uk/acatalog/search.html

Distributed in North America by:

Transaction Publishers
New Brunswick (U.S.A.) and London (U.K.)

Transaction Publishers
Rutgers University
35 Berrue Circle
Piscataway, NJ 08854

Phone: +1 (732) 445 - 2280
Fax: + 1 (732) 445 - 3138
for orders (U. S. only):
toll free (888) 999 - 6778
e-mail:
orders@transactionspub.com

Contents

Acknowledgments

The articles of this volume present the majority of papers presented on the First International Workshop of the research group "Monies, Markets and Finance in China and East Asia, 1600–1900" held 12 to 16 October 2006 at the Institute of Chinese Studies of the University of Heidelberg. The workshop was funded by the German Research Foundation (Deutsche Forschungsgemeinschaft), the German Asia-Pacific Business Association, and the German – East Asian Forum of Sciences and Humanities (Deutsch-ostasiatisches Wissenschaftsforum) of the Universities of Tübingen, Hohenheim and Stuttgart. We would like to express our deep gratitude to these institutions, whose support enabled us to organize a thoroughly agreeable conference. The publication of this volume was made possible by special funding provided by the Association of the Friends of the University of Tübingen (Vereinigung der Freunde der Universität Tübingen – Universitätsbund e.V.), the China Society of Baden-Württemberg for the Advancement of Scientific and Technical Cooperation with the People's Republic of China (Baden-Württembergische Gesellschaft zur Förderung der Zusammenarbeit mit der Volksrepublik China e.V.), and the Institute of Chinese and Korean Studies of the University of Tübingen.

Professors Mark Elvin, Arturo Giraldez, Jan Lucassen and Nakayama Shigeru, who attended the workshop both as presenting participants and as members of the research group's advisory board, provided invaluable guidance through generously sharing scholarly insights and contributing methodological focus. The editors are particularly indebted to Jane Kate Leonard, Professor Emerita of Chinese History, University of Akron, Ohio, whose intellectual generosity, culminated in providing an introduction to this volume, greatly enhanced the focus of the workshop and this publication. Special thanks for help with the organization of the workshop are due to Prof. Barbara Mittler, Anne Labitzky-Wagner, Lucia Banholzer, Shan Kunqin, Huang Xuelei, Shi Yun and Verena Birkhold. Thomas Hirzel and myself consider ourselves privileged to have profited from much collegial collaboration and stimulation both during the workshop and the preparation of this volume. We would like to express heartfelt thanks to all participants of the workshop and to all contributors to this volume in particular, who patiently bore with us our first attempt at editing, as well as to Tony Howes, who equally patiently helped with copy-editing.

The thematic focus of the volume is defined by the research group 'Monies, Markets and Finance in China and East Asia, 1600–1900.' The group, directed by Hans Ulrich Vogel, consists of seven core projects funded by the German Research Foundation and some forty associated projects and began its work in October 2005. Information on the group is available under http://www.monieseastasia.uni-tuebingen.de. A number of projects concentrate on the exploration of concrete aspects in the production and circulation of small currencies in Qing China, Tokugawa Japan, Choseon Korea and the Ryukyu kingdom, with others on financial and administrative structures, global trade networks, living conditions and demography, mentalities, ideologies and religion providing wider comparative perspectives. The group defines itself by an empirical approach, often based on hitherto unused archival material, with competences in the fields of social, technological and cultural history, geography and economics combined in collaborative exchange. The aim of this volume was to provide a substantial and readable introduction to the fields of research involved, and to the extend in which we succeeded we thank the support of all involved.

Nanny Kim

About the Contributors

Werner Burger is a specialist in Chinese monetary history, with a special interest in numismatics. He received his PhD in 1976 for his book *Ch'ing Cash until 1735*. In addition to this work, he published widely on the subject of Qing coinage. His present project in the framework of the research group is the completion of his long-standing numismatic project, namely the continuation of his former work on Qing cash by extending the period covered from 1736 to 1911.

Stefan Dieball studied geography at Tübingen and Durham and graduated in 2004 with a diploma thesis on the development of traffic in the Tübingen area and possibilities of achieving sustainable traffic development. His special areas are Geographical Information Systems (GIS), statistics and Applied Geography. He presently works as junior lecturer at Tübingen University and as research associate with the project 'Cartography and GIS-based Analyses.'

Mark Elvin took his BA in history at Cambridge in 1959, learned the rudiments of literary Chinese and then went Harvard for two years to study under John Fairbank. His PhD (Cambridge 1969) was a study of the first functioning formally democratic local government in China. He is best known for *The Pattern of the Chinese Past* (Stanford UP 1973), the *Cultural Atlas of China* (Facts on File 1983) with Caroline Blunden, *Sediments of Time* (Cambridge UP, New York, 1998), edited with Liu Ts'ui-jung, and *The Retreat of the Elephants* (Yale UP 2004). He is Emeritus Professor of Chinese History in the Australian National University and an Emeritus Fellow of St Antony's College, Oxford. His main interests are the interplay of environmental and economic factors in the history of premodern China, though he has written in a number of other fields, notably the history of premodern Chinese science.

Josephine Fox studied Chinese language and modern history at the University of Melbourne, at Nankai University, Tianjin and at the Australian National University, Canberra. The main focus of her personal research has been early modern Chinese labour history, on which she is preparing a book. In 2002 she joined forces on a part-time basis with Mark Elvin in the Project on the Historical Demography of Premodern China funded by the Chiang Ching-Kuo Foundation and later by the Australian Research Council.

Arturo Giraldez is Professor at the University of the Pacific, California. His work concentrates on monetary history, precious metals and the formation of global economic systems in the early modern and modern periods. With his colleague Dennis O. Flynn he has published articles on precious metals trade during the Modern Era and about globalization. He is also the general co-editor of a collection of volumes entitled "The Pacific World: Lands, Peoples and History of the Pacific, 1500–1900." Aldershot (UK): Ashgate/Variorum.

Bettina Gramlich-Oka works currently in the research group 'Monies, Markets and Finance in China and East Asia' on the project 'Money and Monetary Policies of the Shogunate and Domains in Late Tokugawa Japan: Discourses and Practices.' She received her PhD in 2006 from the Institute for Japanese Studies, Tübingen University. Based on her dissertation is her main publication *Thinking Like a Man: Tadano Makuzu (1763–1825)* (Leiden: Brill, 2006). Her fields of research are intellectual and women's history as well as the history of economic thought.

Roger Greatrex is Director of the Centre for East and South-East Asian Studies at Lund University in Sweden. He received his PhD in Sinology at Stockholm University in 1987, and was appointed Professor in Chinese Studies at Lund University in 2000. Greatrex served between 1996–2001 in Beijing as Director of the EU-China Higher Education Cooperation Programme. He currently works in the field of the social history of law, and concurrently in contemporary Chinese trademark law. Within the framework of the project 'Monies, Markets and Finance in China and East Asia', Greatrex is working on the topic of counterfeit coinage and counterfeiters in the eighteenth century.

Thomas Hirzel studied Chinese studies and philosophy in Tübingen and graduated in 2003 with a MA thesis entitled "Aspects of Corruption in the 18th Century in China: Selected Sources about the Case of the Provincial Treasurer Qian Du." His research interests are economic, social and administrative problems during the Qing-dynasty. In the research group 'Monies, Markets and Finance in China and East Asia' he presently works on his PhD project on 'Mint Metal Procurement for Jiangsu and Zhejiang in the 18th and 19th Centuries: An Inquiry into the Organisational Capacity of the Qing State.'

Elisabeth Kaske majored in Chinese studies in Berlin, Beijing and Heidelberg and has since done extensive research in late Qing and early Republican history. Major publications are: *Bismarcks Missionäre: Deutsche Militärinstrukteure in China 1884–1890* (Wiesbaden: Harrassowitz, 2002) and Georg Baur: *China um 1900: Aufzeichnungen eines Krupp-Direktors* (edited and commented; Weimar: Böhlau, 2005). In 2006, she completed her PhD at Heidelberg University with a thesis entitled *The Politics of Language in Chinese Education, 1895–1919* (Leiden: Brill, 2007). She was appointed Junior Professor at Frankfurt University in October 2006. Within the research group 'Monies, Markets and Finance in China and East Asia' she studies the sale of offices and military finance during the Qing period.

Nanny Kim is a China historian who has been working on Chinese transport history since 2001. In this project, she concentrates on the transport of mint metals from the mines in Southwestern China to the metropolitan mints in Beijing. Her special interest is the investigation of technologies in overland and water transport through Chinese history, relating them to infrastructure, the density of transport and economic systems, and to ecological change. She received her MA in 1994 with a study on the illustrated magazine *Dianshizhai huabao* and her PhD in 2000 with a thesis on images of Korea in Chinese writings during the late nineteenth and early twentieth centuries.

Jane Kate Leonard is Professor Emerita of History at the University of Akron and a specialist in Qing thought and institutions. Her major publications include: *Wei Yuan and China's Rediscovery of the Maritime World* (Council on East Asian Studies, Harvard University, 1984); *Controlling* *from Afar: The Daoguang Emperor's Management of the Grand Canal Crisis, 1824–1826* (Center for Chinese Studies, University of Michigan, 1996); co-editor with John R. Watt, *To Achieve Security and Wealth. The Qing Imperial State and the Economy, 1644–1911* (East Asia Program, Cornell University, 1992); and co-editor with Robert J. Antony, *Dragons, Tiger, and Dogs. Qing Crisis Management and the Boundaries of State Power in Late Imperial China* (East Asia Program, Cornell University, 2002).

Hans-Joachim Rosner is a physical geographer who specializes on applying Geographic Information Systems (GIS) in analyses of changes in cultural landscapes, climates and geostatics. He received his MA in geography with a thesis on recent changes of the cultural landscape of Trisuli-Langtang/Nepal and his PhD with a study on the regional climatology in the Black Forest/Germany, using digital image processing. Since 1993 he has been working as Senior Lecturer at the Department of Geography of Tuebingen University. In the research group 'Monies, Markets and Finance in China and East Asia' he directs the project 'Cartography and GIS-based Analyses.'

Gregory Smits is an historian of Japan and East Asia who has made a specialized study of the Ryukyu Kingdom. In this project he focuses on monetary policy and currency in Ryukyu during the seventeenth and eighteenth centuries. He received his PhD in 1992 and is the author of *Visions of Ryukyu: Identity and Ideology in Early-Modern Thought and Politics* (Hawaii, 1999).

Rüdiger Specht graduated in geography, Chinese studies and anthropology from the University of Freiburg. Since 1993, he has participated in several projects on nature conservation and environmental education. His interests centre on landscape ecology and its cultural and historic aspects. As research associate in the project 'Cartography and GIS-based Analyses' he focuses on the preparation of data from Chinese sources.

Hans Ulrich Vogel was appointed Professor for Chinese History and Society at the Institute of Chinese and Korean Studies of Tübingen University in 1994. His work concentrates on the economic, social and cultural history as well as the history of sciences and technology of pre-industrial China. He has widely published on the history of mining, salt production, monies, weights and measures, on urban history, and on physical exercises namely kickball. He is the director of the research group 'Monies, Markets and Finance in China and East Asia, 1600–1900.'

Harald Witthöft received his PhD at Göttingen University in 1959, spent two years as research assistant and lecturer at Melbourne University and held the chair in economic and social history and didactics of history at Siegen University until becoming an Emeritus Professor in 1996. His publications concentrate on the history of trade and industry, especially of salt, commerce, transport and communications, the monetary history and history of metrology with a geographic focus on Northern Germany, Northern Europe and the Hanse, spanning the time period of the early middle ages to the 19th century. His research interest led to his being elected General Secretary and President of the Comité International pour la Métrologie Historique (1983/1986–1996) and Vice-President of the Commission Internationale d'Histoire du Sel (1988).

Introduction

Jane Kate Leonard

The research papers in this volume contain a rich variety of scholarly analyses whose topical breath, archival depth and careful interpretations deepen our understanding of monies, markets and finance in East Asia in the early modern period. Collectively, they suggest two major themes. The first highlights the centrality of the coppercoinage system to the Qing dynasty's governing mission; the second demonstrates the diverse ways that global and regional silver flows snaked in and around East Asian trading networks and interacted with the monetary systems and domestic economies of this region's constituent polities, revealing in many cases that discrete local circumstances determined the impact of these flows on domestic economic conditions. Finally, these papers demonstrate important new methodological approaches that facilitate archeological, geographical and demographic analyses of issues related to the production and circulation of monetary metals. They also contain cautionary tales about the perils of over-generalization and uncritical reliance on Eurocentric interpretive models to explain East Asian historical realities.

Studies of the Qing copper coin, or cash, reveal how determined the Qing state was to harness its bureaucratic and fiscal resources to provide a stable and useful currency to facilitate payments for government work and commercial exchange in China's many diverse local economies. The control and management of the Chinese monetary system had been a pivotal responsibility of imperial government since the early empire because it was held to be essential to generating prosperity and conditions of peace and stability on which the Confucian moral mission depended.[1] Confucian moralizing about the need to improve society was founded on the practical proposition that economic well-being was a precondition of individual and societal moral advancement. In practical terms, then, copper coin provided a useful medium for government payments and the market exchange of agricultural and craft commodities, while silver served as a measure of value for fiscal accounting,

1 King 1965, von Glahn 1996, 15–47; Vogel 1987, 1–52.

tax collection, and large-scale domestic and commercial transactions.[2] While Chinese demand for silver in its trading networks in maritime Asia had an important impact on global and regional circulation of silver,[3] the money that served the vast population and domestic markets of interior China was copper coin.

In a very real sense, copper coinage and its sister institution—the empire-wide system of grain supply that expressed the government's responsibility for guaranteeing food grain accessibility—were two crucial branches of imperial government on which state and society depended.[4] For this reason, the Board of Revenue, that administered both the monetary and grain supply system, was singled out by the compilers of the 1826 collection of statecraft essays as second only to the Board of Civil Office in its importance to imperial government "under the six boards."[5] Notwithstanding the Board of Revenue's pride of place in imperial government, the structure of Qing administration was limited in its vertical reach to department and county government, which represented the outer boundaries of direct bureaucratic administration. Qing government was further limited by the stingy allocation of bureaucratic and fiscal resources at every level of regional government.[6] Both of these factors reduced the force and presence of imperial government at the local level and compromised its ability to undertake administrative reform or respond to emergencies and crises; however, at the same time, it may be suggested that this thin veneer of government mitigated the potential for fiscal extortion and state interference in social-economic activities in the sub-county community.

The management of the copper coinage and grain-transport was also unique among the various branches of imperial government because their operations penetrated deeply into the sub-county arena; both had to rely on the collaboration of bureaucratic, sub-bureaucratic, and extra-bureaucratic organizations to carry out their yearly tasks. However, in contrast to the grain transport system that was assisted by a cadre of special grain officials

2 Von Glahn 1996, 18–23.

3 Giraldez in this volume.

4 Leonard 1996, 66–77.

5 He Changling and Wei Yuan 1826, 1:15b.

6 Wang 1973; Zelin 1984.

and two military-labor organizations (*caobiao* 漕標 and *hebiao* 河標) in the performance of its many supervisory and operational tasks, copper production required managers, artisans and semi-skilled laborers with special technological expertise in mining, smelting and minting of monetary metals. It was up to regional and local officials to recruit and organize these various private groups into stable efficient collaborations to assure the on-going production and minting of monetary metals.[7] Equally daunting was the organization of transport and porterage of metal and coin along thousands of miles of road and riverine routes to the capital and provincial mints—distances far greater than those in the yearly transport of tax-grain shipments. Such a vast undertaking should not have worked, given the limited bureaucratic and fiscal resources available to imperial government. The fact that it operated at all attests to the tremendous will and organizational capacity of Qing government.

In the seventeenth century, the newly established Qing dynasty re-cast Ming coins on a large scale, as well as importing Japanese copper and forcibly buying up bronze and brass utensils. When the Tokugawa regime imposed strict limitations on copper exports in the early eighteenth century, the Qing undertook a massive effort to develop and exploit copper, zinc, and lead deposits required for copper cash production in the remote southwestern border regions, recently pacified and in the midst of political reorganization that drew the provinces of Yunnan and Guizhou firmly into the Chinese political orbit. Political integration was paralleled by massive investments in the development of communications infrastructure and the opening of the region to Han immigration to dilute the multi-ethnic population of aboriginal groups and Chinese Muslims.[8]

With the decision to exploit metal deposits in the southwest, even greater efforts were made to develop roads, riverine routes, and tracking paths on the rivers in northern Yunnan that created a transit corridor to the metal storage depot at Luzhou, Sichuan, the gateway to the Yangzi River passage to interior China and to the Beijing and provincial mints.[9] The development of routes into and out of northern Yunnan to speed the transport of copper was

7 Schulman 1989; Sun 1967; 1968, 835–845; 1971, 132–148; Vogel 1983.

8 Atwill 2002, 245–271.

9 Kim in this volume.

paralleled by great efforts to found and maintain state-private collaborative enterprises, planted deeply in the local setting of Yunnan, to mine and smelt monetary metals for the production of copper coin. Although directed from the top by the inner court and the Board of Revenue and guided by the elastic regulatory framework spelled out in the Qing code, the really daunting tasks of recruiting merchant capital, managers, craftsmen and transport labor fell to a thinly spread layer of regional civil and military officials.

We get a glimpse of the difficulties they faced when we consider the time, energies, and resources devoted to overcoming the geographical barriers to shipping copper through the northern prefectures of Yunnan on the route to Luzhou on the Yangze River. We can also measure Qing will and determination by the laborious efforts that low-level civil and military officials made to lead and escort copper shipments to the Zhejiang/Jiangsu provincial mints.[10]

Although it appears that these individuals and their deputies were drawn from the low-level civil and military bureaucracy, or from the ranks of expectant officials waiting for appointment,[11] one must assume, however, that they had a modicum of bureaucratic know-how, experience, and prestige to carry out this seemingly impossible task.[12] The case of sea transport of tax grain in 1826 and the creation of bureaus (*ju* 局) in Shanghai after the Opium War suggests the importance of expectant officials whose numbers increased in the Jiaqing and Daoguang reigns due to increases in the sale of office, which provided a pool of bureaucratic talent to call on during emergencies.[13]

In the case of copper shipments, the officials in charge had to meet fixed deadlines in order to collect their pay, and they faced dangers en route from weather, bandits, recalcitrant mule-team drivers, and boatmen. The faces of these transport managers are all but invisible in the archival record. Little information survives about the journeys other than the reports of their arrivals and departures from the mines and mints and their fiscal accounts.[14] But

10 Hirzel in this volume.

11 *houbu guan* 候補官, *houbu reyuan* 候補人員.

12 Antony 2002, 28–42; Leung 2002, 68–75.

13 Kaske in this volume; Leonard in this volume; Leung 2002, 68–75.

14 Hirzel in this volume.

it was precisely these modest actors that the Qing depended on for the successful delivery of monetary copper. Geographical Information Systems (GIS) mapping techniques may enable us to plot their travel routes with precision,[15] but we are just beginning to learn about the people that actually did the work, the deals they struck, and the compensation they received for carrying out this crucial shipping task.[16]

The growing body of scholarly literature on the Qing monetary system draws our attention to the importance of ad hoc state collaborations with private, extra-bureaucratic organizations that the Qing recruited to perform extremely important strategic tasks associated with the production and transport of copper cash. How were these joint ventures organized, managed and funded? Given the Qing dependence on the special technical, managerial and capital resources of these organizations, how much leverage did the state actually have over the groups that carried out the specialty functions of mining, smelting, minting and transport of monetary copper, or for that matter, over those merchant groups responsible for the import of Japanese copper, or those who transported tax grain in 1826? How did the collaborations in both monetary copper production and grain transport contribute to long-term environmental degradation, such as deforestation in Yunnan and soil erosion and siltation in the Grand Canal and Huai-Huang riverine networks, respectively?[17]

One can appreciate the attractiveness of these collaborations to the Qing leadership. They were cheap compared to the costs of permanently extending bureaucratic government; they were infinitely malleable according to time, place and task; and they could be created or dissolved at a moment's notice. But, the more important question is, how did the temporary, ad hoc character of these collaborations affect the performance of high-priority governing tasks associated with maintaining a stable monetary system or capital grain supply? What was in it for the private collaborators? Each state-private col-

15 Rosner et al. in this volume.

16 Much detailed information can be gleamed from a handbook entitled *Tongyun shengguan jue* 銅運升官訣 (The formula for official advancement through transporting copper). The manuscript was unearthed by Hans Ulrich Vogel in the library of the Academy of Sciences, Beijing. For a first reconstruction of the practical side of organizing a copper shipment based primarily on this source, see Kim (forthcoming).

17 Vogel in this volume.

laboration tells a unique story, and much more research is needed in order to determine a profile of the different categories of collaborations and to judge their role in Qing governance.[18]

A consideration of the nature of collaborations inevitably leads to the question of compensation and corruption in the performance of government work. The Qing codes lay out categories and amounts of payments for various tasks, such as hiring price, rations and salaries, and they warn of the need to adjust compensation to prevailing market conditions. Administrative codes and memorial reports also comment on special surcharges (*jintie* 津貼), "gifts," brokerage fees and other transactional costs, as well as the impact of counterfeiting on local market stability. But, in the highly fluid context of ad hoc collaborations that operated within a culture of gift-giving, what constitutes compensation, gifts, corrupt exactions and extortion, and to what extent did all the collaborating parties participate in each? Should a distinction be made between "functional" corruption that greased the machines of collaborative work, on the one hand, and "dysfunctional" corruption that jammed them up, on the other? How do the corrupt exactions of private merchant and labor organizations compare to the corruption of officials and sub-bureaucratic clerks, runners, and brokers? Should counterfeiting be viewed as a crime, or as a logical and sometimes useful response to shortages of copper coin?[19]

Finally, how important were ad hoc collaborations in Qing governance? Do they hold the key to understanding the organizational capacity of the Qing state under the six boards? It is difficult to assess their role in government because each collaboration had its own narrative and operational profile. Much more research is needed to address these questions. Nevertheless, in the case of copper-coin production and government grain transport, state-private collaborations were certainly crucial to the performance of operational tasks at the sub-county level.

Japan's monetary history from the mid-sixteenth to early seventeenth centuries is complicated by the political transition from domain autonomy in the

18 Significant strides have been made in analyzing the collaborations in the production of official Qing handicrafts, the construction of government buildings, and in the Beijing mint workshops. See Vogel, Moll-Murata, Song 2005.

19 Burger in this volume; Greatrex in this volume.

Muromachi period to the Tokugawa unification (1600–1868) and also by the simultaneous technological advances in the mining of silver, gold and copper.[20] These metals were minted in the Tokugawa period for use in a complex tripartite monetary system comprised of gold, silver, and copper coins that rested on a rice-based agricultural economy and fiscal system. All three played a role in the shogunate's management of Tokugawa domains and its restriction of foreign trade at the port of Nagasaki, as well as facilitating domain finances and economic activity. The founding shogun, Ieyasu, rationalized the coinage system, producing high quality gold and silver coins that remained the standard for the remainder of the shogunate. Tax grain was converted to currency to fund the shogunal and domain governments. Gold and silver were used for government and large-scale commercial transactions while copper coins facilitated small-scale commercial exchanges, all of which fueled Japan's expanding commercial economy. As one commentator has noted, the Tokugawa monetary system "was remarkably complex and unwieldy but [it] accommodated society's needs as long as Japan had minimal contact with foreign monetary systems."[21] Yet, severe strains appeared in the monetary system by the mid-eighteenth century, due to the depletion of Japan's gold, silver, and copper mines and to the simultaneous occurrence of natural disasters. In this complicated monetary environment, the Tokugawa shoguns struggled to fund the bakufu with tax grain revenues collected from their private domains, and they resorted to such measures as increasing grain production, tapping the commercial economy and manipulating the money supply through currency debasement, the re-minting of old coins, and, for example, the introduction of new silver coins.[22] Although often less than effective, these initiatives reflected the practical Confucian tradition of balancing the fiscal needs of the shogunate with those of the domains and, at the same time, insuring the stability of the commercial economy.[23]

The case of early modern Korea from 1600 to the mid-nineteenth century reveals how the economic policies of the state played a critical role in agri-

20 Nakayama MMF 2006; Scherer MMF 2006.

21 Totman 2000, p. 249.

22 Gramlich-Oka in this volume.

23 Totmann 2000.

cultural development and proto-industrial cotton production.[24] The state invested heavily in communications and hydraulic infrastructure, and it protected land rights and a system of partible, non-gendered inheritance that fostered a booming land market and paved the way for rural prosperity based on agricultural productivity and female production of cotton products. This prosperity, centered in rural markets where both coin and kind served as media of exchange, remained relatively unaffected by global and regional circulation of silver, or even by the domestic circulation of copper coin in Korean urban markets! This case shows that Korean prosperity in general and rural prosperity in particular cannot be measured by the price of rice, denominated in either silver or copper cash, because monetary media in rural Korea included rice and cotton products as well as coin. This case presents a cautionary tale about the limits of using prices, accounted in silver or copper coin, to compute the per capita prosperity of early modern Korea, or to compare it to that of European and other East Asian countries.

Occupying a niche between China and Japan, Ryukyu created a copper-coin currency that reflected the influence of both of its powerful neighbors.[25] During the unification of the state from the early fifteenth to early sixteenth centuries, the Okinawan kings embarked on the minting of copper coin primarily to mark the advent of their reigns and the ritual celebration of Chinese investiture. Even though the coins could not be used in the China trade because of their poor quality, they may have served as a medium of exchange in Ryukyu's growing domestic economy. From the seventeenth century until its colonization by Japan in the 1870s, when Ryukyu served as a political-economic conduit between China and the Japanese domain of Satsuma, they created a copper cash currency for its domestic economy by reminting various types of used Japanese coins. While of little use in foreign trade, copper coin production symbolized the emergence of the Okinawan state and its complicated web of relationships with both China and Japan.

From the perspective of larger global trading networks in the early modern period, studies suggest that the circulation of silver and other monetary metals was shaped by a variety of factors from climate change to the dramatic expansion of South American silver production, technological innova-

24 Jun MMF 2006.
25 Smits in this volume.

tion, political upheavals and China's unrelenting demand for silver. Take the case of silver production in Potosí, Peru: As the value of silver declined from the mid-sixteenth to early seventeenth centuries, it sparked a series of fiscal and economic disasters in Spain and its empire that generated upheavals in global trade and contributed to the collapse of Peruvian silver production. Yet, even in this case, local conditions in Peru, such as a failing hydraulic infrastructure, poor technology, local counterfeiting and corruption and the harsh Spanish repression of local political and economic elites responsible for silver production also contributed the decline of the Potosí mines.[26]

Similarly, in the domestic economies of East Asia, discrete local conditions and traditions seem to have muted the disruptive effects of global market fluctuations in the price of silver and other monetary metals, compared to their impact on the urban commercialized economies of Europe.[27] The reasons seem to lie in their common Confucian approach to the role of the state in their respective economies and their assumption of responsibility for controlling the monetary system and other key functions that supported and stabilized the agricultural prosperity, such as investment in roads, hydraulic infrastructure, and the maintenance of peace and order.[28] In the early modern period, the governments of China, Japan, and Korea all continued these traditions while adapting flexibly to commercial expansion and the growing role of local customary law and private economic organizations in the management of local markets and ports, the mediation of economic disputes and the collection of commercial taxes for the state. Their relative immunity to fluctuations in the global and regional supply of silver seems to have lain in the spatially discrete character of rural markets where local agricultural and craft goods as well as different kinds of copper coin, some of it counterfeit, served as media of exchange.[29] Silver served primarily as measure of value in the accounting of wages, taxes, and trade balances.[30]

26 Giraldez in this volume.

27 Jun MMF 2006.

28 Gramlich-Oka in this volume; Jun MMF 2006; Von Glahn 1996, 7–47, 142–172, 255–257; Vogel 1987, 1–52.

29 Burger in this volume; Greatrex in this volume; Jun MMF 2006.

30 Burger op. cit.; Moll-Murata MMF 2006; Von Glahn 1996, 253–257.

These various uses of copper coin, silver and other monetary media in discrete local settings helps to shed light on complex issues, such as wage history and the growth of wage labor in government and private enterprises. Investigations of government craft workers, cotton-cloth calenderers and paper makers in the Qing period show that different enterprises in diverse local settings shaped the terms and conditions of work, and they also highlight the relations between merchant and labor organizations and the nature of state-private collaborations.[31] More studies of this kind will help scholars figure out the relationship between wage labor, prices and living standards, and ultimately to make comparative judgments about these issues with respect to Europe and other Asian economies.

New methodological approaches to the study of mining transport, technology and mint metallurgy serve to expand our understanding of monies, markets and finance in East Asia. Geographers at Tübingen University have begun an ambitious project to construct a GIS database on copper transport routes in the Qing period. This multi-source database draws on Chinese archival sources and historical maps, modern Soviet-era and U. S. military maps, various other modern maps, and the valuable Harvard University "China Historical GIS," which has data sets for 1820, 1911, and 1990;[32] and it will enable scholars to analyze and visualize the transport process in general and make component maps for discrete parts of Qing copper transport routes.[33] A new statistical approach to reconstructing rates of marriages, births, and deaths in the lower Yangzi valley will enable scholars to develop a more precise picture of demographic change that affected markets and economic conditions in this region.[34]

Similarly, Japanese scholars engaged in a five-year project on artifact production during the Edo period (1600–1868) have developed an approach to archaeo-materials science that uses X-ray fluorescence spectrometry to analyze materials, such as mining slag, waste and tailings, unearthed at archeological sites connected to mining and smelting of gold, silver and copper from the Iwami and other mines. These methods shed light on different

31 Moll-Murata MMF 2006.

32 China Historical GIS (CH-GIS). http://www.fas.harvard.edu/~chgis/.

33 Rosner et al. in this volume.

34 Elvin and Fox in this volume.

technological aspects of the smelting process and the mineral content of the ores mined at specific locations, which will enable scholars to trace the origin and flow of coins in Asian markets in the early modern period.[35]

The studies of silver flows continue to raise important questions about the nature and significance of the global and regional circulation of silver in the critical years between 1600 and 1900. Was its value a reflection of its role as a commodity, a money of account or a medium of exchange for large-scale commercial and government transactions and transfers? Moreover, are the changing ratios of silver to other monetary metals, such as copper and gold, determined by their "intrinsic" worth or by the interplay of supply and demand? Is there a universal relationship between the value of silver and gold,[36] or does silver merely serve as a convenient bookkeeping tool as a money of account? More practically speaking, was it the intrinsic value of silver *per se*, or the enduring quality and utility of the Spanish/Mexican dollar during the explosive expansion of global trade, in particular, that explains the reasons for its importance and continued use in global and regional trade from the sixteenth to nineteenth centuries? While the impact of silver and the global trade it fostered on world history cannot be overestimated, studies of monies, markets and finance in the economies of East Asia in the early modern period seem to suggest that practical issues about the nature and function of monetary media are best understood by investigating their role and operation in discrete local economies.

Bibliography

Antony, Robert J. (2002). "Subcounty Officials, the State, and Local Communities in Guangdong Province, 1644–1911." In Antony and Leonard (eds.), pp. 27–59.

Antony, Robert J. and Jane Kate Leonard (eds.) (2002). *Dragons, Tigers, and Dogs. Qing Crisis Management and the Boundaries of State Power in Late Imperial China. Ithaca*. NY: East Asia Program, Cornell University.

Atwill, David G. (2002). "Trading Places: Resistance, Ethnicity, and Governance in Nineteenth-Century China." In Antony and Leonard (eds.), pp. 245–271.

35 Nakayama MMF 2006.

36 Witthöft in this volume.

Burger, Werner (2007). "Coin Production during the Qianlong and Jiaqing Reigns (1736–1820): Issues in Cash and Silver Supply." In Hirzel and Kim (eds.), pp. 171–189.

CH-GIS (China Historical-Geographic Information Systems). http://www.fas.harvard.edu/~chgis/.

Elvin, Mark and Josephine Fox. (2007). "Local Demographic Variations in the Lower Yangzi Valley during Mid-Qing Times." In Hirzel and Kim (eds.), pp. 333–378.

Giraldez, Arturo. (2007). "China and Counterfeiting in 1650 Potosí." In Hirzel and Kim (eds.), pp. 15–43.

Gramlich-Oka, Bettina. (2007). "Shogunal Administration of Copper in the Mid-Tokugawa Period (1670–1720)." In Hirzel and Kim (eds.), pp. 65–105.

Greatrex, Roger. (2007). "Layers of Deception: Counterfeiting Cases in the Mid-Qing" In Hirzel and Kim (eds.), pp. 309–331.

He Changling and Wei Yuan. (comps.). (1826). *Huangchao jingshi wenbian* (Essays on Qing Statecraft).

Hirzel, Thomas (2007). "Mint Metal Procurement for Jiangsu and Zhejiang during the Qianlong Period (1736–1795): An Inquiry into the Central Government's Expectations and the Provinces' Strategies of Implementation." In Hirzel and Kim (eds.), pp. 221–236.

Hirzel, Thomas and Nanny Kim (eds.) (2007). *Metals, Monies, and Markets in Early Modern Societies: East Asian and Global Perspectives*. Monies, Markets and Finance in China and East Asia, 1600–1900, vol. 1.

Huangchao jingshi wenbian 皇朝經世文編 (Collected Essays on Statecraft in the Qing Dynasty). He Changling 賀長齡 (comp.). 1826. 120 *juan*. Reprint. Taibei: Shijie, 1965.

Jun, Seong Ho (2006). What Korean Prices, Productivity, Money Supply, and Population from 1392 to 1900 Tell [sic] Us: Adam Smith or Malthus or Monetarist? MMF 2006.

Kaske, Elisabeth (2007). "The Price of an Office: Venality, the Individual and the State in 19th Century China." In Hirzel and Kim (eds.), pp. 281–308.

Kim, Nanny (2007). "Copper Transports out of Yunnan, ca. 1750–1850: Transport Technologies, Natural Difficulties and Environmental Change in a Southwestern Highland Area." In Hirzel and Kim (eds.), pp. 191–220.

_________ (forthcoming). "'Traue nicht den Nachwächtern, halte dich bei Tempelfeiern zu Ehren des Stroms zurück:" Zu praktischen Bedenken von Kupfertransportbeamten auf der Fahrt durch die Drei Schluchten des Changjiang und ihrem Verhältnis zu angeheuerten Schiffern und Mannschaften.' In Martina Eglauer and Clemes Treter (eds.), *Reisen: Tagungsband der Deutschen Vereinigung für Chinastudien*. Wiesbaden: Harrassowitz.

King, F.H.H. (1965). *Money and Monetary Policy in China*. Cambridge, MA: Harvard University Press.

Leonard, Jane Kate (1996). *Controlling from Afar. The Daoguang Emperor's Management of the Grand Canal Crisis, 1824–1826*. Ann Arbor: Center for Chinese Studies, University of Michigan.

________ (2002). "Negotiating Beyond the Boundaries of State Power: Organizing the 1826 Sea Transport Experiment." In Antony and Leonard (eds.), pp. 183–211.

________ (2005). "Timeliness and Innovation. The 1825 Revision of the Complete Book on Grain Transport (*Caoyun quanshu* 漕運全書)." In Vogel, Moll-Murata et al. (eds.), pp. 449–464.

________ (2007). "Stretching the Bureaucracy. Ad Hoc Agencies and Recruitment in the 1826 Sea Transport Experiment." In Hirzel and Kim (eds.), pp. 255–279.

Leung, Yuen-sang Philip (2002). "Crisis Management and Institutional Reform: The Expectant Officials in the Late Qing." In Antony and Leonard, (eds.), pp. 61–77.

MMF 2006. "First International Workshop on Monies, Markets and Finance in China and East Asia, 1600–1900." Institute of Chinese Studies, University of Heidelberg. Heidelberg, Germany. 10–12 October, 2006.

Moll-Murata, Christine (2006). Wage Payments in the Qing Period: Problems and Solutions. MMF 2006.

Nakayama, Shigeru (2006). An Introduction to the History of Japanese Gold and Silver Mines during the Edo Period. MMF 2006.

Rosner, Hans-Joachim, Stephan Dieball, Rüdiger Specht (2007). "Reconstruction of Copper Transportation Routes in Qing China—A Multi-Source Approach." In Hirzel and Kim (eds.), pp. 237–254.

Scherer, Anke (2006). Japanese Copper Production in the Tokugawa Period. MMF 2006.

Schottenhammer, Angela (2006). The Role of Copper in Qing Period Maritime Trade with Japan. MMF 2006.

Schulman, Anna See Ping Leon (1898). Copper, Copper Cash, and Government Controls in Ch'ing China (1644–1795). Ph.D. diss. University of Maryland.

Smits, Gregory (2007). "Money in the Kingdom of Ryukyu." In Hirzel and Kim (eds.), pp. 107–117.

Sun, E-tu Zen (1967). "Mining Labor in the Ch'ing Period." In *Approaches to Modern Chinese History*. Albert Feuerwerker, Rhoads Murphey, Mary C. Wright (eds.). Berkeley: University of California Press.

________ (1968). "Ch'ing Government and the Mineral Industries before 1800." *Journal of Asian Studies* 27, 4: 835–845.

________ (1971). "The Transportation of Yunnan Copper to Peking in the Ch'ing Period." *Journal of Oriental Studies* 9: 132–148.

Totman, Conrad (2000). *A History of Japan.* Malden MA: Blackwell Publishers.

Vogel, Hans Ulrich (1983). Chinese Central Monetary Policy and Yunnan Copper Mining in the Early Qing (1644–1800). Ph.D. diss. University of Zurich.

________ (1987). "Chinese Central Monetary Policy." *Late Imperial China* 8, 2:1–52.

________ (2005). "Unrest and Strikes at the Metropolitan Mints in 1771 and 1816 and Their Economic and Social Background." In Vogel, Moll-Murata et al.

________ (2007). "Copper Smelting and Fuel Consumption in Yunnan, Eighteenth to Nineteenth Centuries." In Hirzel and Kim (eds.), pp. 119–170.

Vogel, Hans Ulrich, Christine Moll-Murata, and Song Jianze (eds.) (2005). *Chinese Handicraft Regulations of the Qing Dynasty: Theory and Application.* Munich: Iudicium.

Von Glahn, Richard (1996). *Fountain of Fortune. Money and Monetary Policy in China, 1000–1700.* Berkeley: University of California Press.

Wang, Yeh-chien (1973). *Land Taxation in Imperial China, 1750–1911.* Cambridge, MA: Harvard University Press.

Witthöft, Harald (2007). "Perception and Numeric Order: An Analysis of Northern European Monetary Sources from Carolingian Times to the Era of Mercantilism." In Hirzel and Kim (eds.), pp. 44–63.

Zelin, Madeleine (1984). *The Magistrate's Tael: Rationalizing Fiscal Reform in Eighteenth-Century Ch'ing China.* Berkeley: University of California Press.

China and Counterfeiting in 1650 Potosí

Arturo Giraldez

to Andre Gunder Frank, in memoriam

The paper shows how China was at the centre of the relationships between local events in Potosí (Peru) and the global silver market. The largest counterfeiting fraud in the history of the Spanish Empire was related to the decline in the price of silver due to the Price Revolution in Europe and the convergence of monetary ratios throughout the world. The role of China as the demand side in the silver market is linked to what otherwise seem to be merely anecdotal events in Potosí.

Introduction[1]

> All attempts to account for or explain local, national, or regional ripple developments primarily in terms of their respective supposedly cultural or class determinants are too limited in their purview. They neglect the fundamental world economic sea change, of which the local ones often are only superficial ripples and manifestations. In short, all attempts to account for features and factors of development on the basis only or even primarily of local antecedents and in the absence of their function in the world economy/system can result only in the neglect of factors that are essential to any satisfactory explanation.[2]

In 1650 a series of dramatic events took place in Potosí, the mining center of the Vice-Royalty of Perú. In January the captain Francisco Gómez de la Rocha —a rich and powerful businessman— was garroted and his corpse hung up in the central plaza "as a public example." Felípe Ramírez, one of the assayers of the mint, suffered the same fate.[3] The executions were or-

1 The international currency of the Spanish Empire was the piece-of-eight, or *peso* of eight *rials*. Each piece-of-eight contained 25.56 grams of silver. The *ducat* and the *maravedi* were moneys of account in the sixteenth and seventeenth centuries. 1 *ducat* = 11 *rials* or 375 *maravedis*; 1 piece-of-eight = 272 *maravedis*. 1 million *pesos* were roughly equivalent to 51 tons of silver. Translations to English are mine.

2 Frank 1998, 326–327.

3 Bakewell 1995, 42.

dered by Francisco de Nestares Marín, a former inquisitor acting as an inspector. The inspection was caused by universal complaints about the quality of the pieces-of-eight minted in Potosí, which had prompted the Imperial administration to adopt forceful measures to restore confidence in the Spanish peso. The Peruvian coinage was devalued and *pesos* with a new design replaced the old ones, at great cost to the Peruvian economy and Imperial finances. The local series of events was essentially related to the finances of Imperial Spain, the Chinese economy and, in the final analysis, the global silver market. "The rise and fall of the Spanish Empire is best viewed in the context of a Sino-centered world economy."[4] The micro-history of Potosí — the "superficial ripples and manifestations" (in the words of A. Gunder Frank)— was embedded in the global trends of the seventeenth century.[5]

The sixteenth century witnessed the beginnings of a global economy driven by silver from America and Japan on the supply side, and with China as the main customer. The benefits produced by the trade financed the military machine of the Spanish Empire, which was involved in wars all over the world during the seventeenth century. Across the Pacific in China, the fall of the Ming dynasty opened a period of social disturbances and economic hardships with repercussions of a global nature. A "silver line" connected such disparate processes and events.

Wars and revolutions were not the only calamities which affected people in the seventeenth century. Rural societies were afflicted by harsh weather, due to the "Little Ice Age" that resulted in poor agricultural yields, disrupted commerce and brought about waves of epidemics that decimated populations. Hence the counterfeiting of Peruvian coins and the measures taken by the Spanish government took place in a context of economic difficulties and in an Empire that required ever-increasing financial resources.

4 Flynn and Giraldez 1996, 311.

5 Frank 1998, 326.

The origins of a global world

The foundation of Manila in 1571 inaugurated a direct route between the mining economies of America and the Chinese Empire. The "sangleys," the Chinese merchants in the Parian, exchanged silk and porcelain for Peruvian and Mexican silver brought yearly by the galleons crossing the Pacific between Acapulco and the Philippines. According to Henry Kamen:

> For the first time in history, an international empire integrated the markets of the world, as vessels from the St. Lawrence, the Rio de la Plata, from Nagasaki, Macao, Manila, Acapulco, Callao, Veracruz, Havana, Antwerp, Genoa and Seville criss-crossed in an interminable commercial chain that exchanged commodities and profits, enriched merchants and globalized civilization. African slaves went to Mexico, Mexican silver to China, Chinese silks to Madrid.[6]

A global economy was established and the processes that today are called globalization were initiated. "Globalization began when all heavily populated land masses began sustained interaction in a manner that deeply linked them all through global trade."[7] The reverberations of such processes were immense. As David Christian writes: "The new level of creative synergy generated by linking the two largest world zones —Afro-Eurasia and the Americas— was and remains perhaps the most powerful single level of change in the modern world."[8]

The commodity most responsible for this global economy was American and Japanese silver. Harry E. Cross calculates that American production between 1500 and 1800 amounted to 80 per cent of the world output of this precious metal.[9] The metal traveled from an area of high pressure, the Vice-Royalties of Peru and Mexico —called New Spain in these centuries— and Japan to, in the words of Vitorino Magalhaes Godinho, the Chinese "suction pump."[10] In the first decades of the seventeenth century the admiral Don Gerónimo de Bañuelos y Carrillo gave a picturesque assessment of the pow-

6 Kamen 2003, 296.

7 Flynn and Giraldez 2006, 235.

8 Christian 2004, 365.

9 Cross 1983, 397.

10 Godinho 1984, IV, 34.

power exercised by the Ming economy: "The King of China could build a palace with the silver bars from Peru which are carried to his country."[11] In the Chinese world map by Mateo Ricci, in South America three of the five regions mentioned were *P'o-lu* (Perú), "Golden *Ka-hsi-la* (Castilla), so-called for the great quantities of gold and silver it produces", and *Pei-tu-hsi* (Potosí), which is geographically misplaced, but for which the indication that "there are many silver-mines in these mountains" is true.[12]

In Canton during the sixteenth century until the beginnings of the seventeenth century, the gold-silver ratio ranged between 1:5.5 and 1:7, while in Spain it was between 1:12.5 and 1:14.[13] According to Richard von Glahn "the gold/silver ratio hovered around 1:12 in Europe, 1:10 in Persia, and 1:8 in India."[14] For example, silver in Genoa was less valuable than in Istanbul, hence Persia attracted Ottoman silver and relinquished it to other markets. Fernand Braudel writes: "So during the sixteenth and seventeenth centuries there circulated throughout the vast Asian continent source of spices, drugs, and silk, precious gold and above all silver coins minted at Venice, Genoa, or Florence, and later the famous Spanish silver pieces-of-eight."[15] The Portuguese in Goa who brought their silver to China and to Nagasaki and Macao carried on a brisk trade propelled by Japanese mines until they were expelled from Japan.

Profits in Asian markets —in which the Chinese tributary system occupied a central place— were much larger than in Europe. "Divergent bimetallic ratios created tremendous prospects for profitable arbitrage trade."[16]

A Chinese author remarked intelligently on the relationship between silver and the economic transactions in 1680: "The value of all goods under Heaven, whether great or small, cheap or dear, is measured in terms of silver... Silver indeed is the lever by which the treasures of the earth are controlled."[17] This statement is almost an echo of a letter written by a French businessman in the times of Philip II, referring to the precious metals carried

11 Blair and Robertson, vol. 29, 71.

12 Giles 1919, 24–25 and 27.

13 Chuan 1969, 2.

14 Von Glahn 1996, 127.

15 Braudel 1972, I, 464.

16 Flynn and Giraldez 2001, 144.

17 Quoted in von Glahn 1996, 216.

by the galleons to Seville: "We will be only liberated of this anguish when we know that the fleet is secure, because it is a matter that serves as the rule of the world."[18]

The influx of large quantities of precious metals into the global markets affected economies in different degrees. In Europe and adjacent markets, like the Ottoman Empire, there was a price increase without precedent, which Earl J. Hamilton has labeled the "Price Revolution". In China, imported silver resulted in modest inflation: "grain prices in China rose slowly before 1630."[19] Jack Goldstone has advanced the hypothesis that because taxes were set in terms of fixed quantities of silver in Ming China, price increases in the precious metal contributed to the crisis of the Empire.[20]

During the centuries we are considering, many bureaucrats and businessmen knew the role played by the Chinese Empire in the precious metals trade. Such was the case of Francisco López de Caravantes discussing the proposal to import Chinese mercury through the Pacific. The matter was forwarded to the Council of the Indies, the governing body of American and Asian territories. Some of the councilors opposed the idea, afraid of great quantities of silver leaving America in the Manila galleons, but another group argued:

> Silver going to China by that route is of little consequence, because the silver that arrives in Spain from the Indies leaves by trade with France, Italy, England, Flanders and Germany and the northern provinces, as well as Turkey and Persia, until it reaches India, from which, with less fineness it goes by the same trade to China, where it is collected and hoarded (God knows to what end), because the Chinese only trade their harvest and manufactures with the Tartars, Japanese and Portuguese who have houses and factories in Macao and Canton, on the borders of China, and they trade with Malaca, Goa and Lisbon and with the Castilian merchants of Manila who take the merchandise to New Spain by permission of his Majesty.[21]

One of the main entities profiting from the global silver market was the Spanish Empire. Without American silver the Spanish Empire is inconceivable. A well-known Spanish historian, Antonio Domínguez Ortíz, comments

18 Quoted in Domínguez Ortíz 1977, 291.

19 Von Glahn 1996, 255.

20 Goldstone 1991, chap. 4.

21 López de Caravantes 1985–1989, 226–227.

on the significance in strategic and financial terms of silver arrivals in Seville: "When there was a delay in the arrival of the fleets the silver premium rose by enormous proportions, trade stopped and remittals to armies and allies were impossible."[22]

Philip IV and crisis in the Empire

When Philip the IV (1621–1665) became King, the financial situation was disastrous and the Imperial bureaucracy was searching for new means to increase revenue. The royal accountant, Gilimón de la Mota, told the recently-crowned king that "all your state sold to the public was worth less than one hundred thousand *ducats*, because all your revenues are mortgaged in perpetuity or already spent years ahead."[23] As an example to encourage his subjects to support the Royal Treasury in a critical moment, Philip IV sent his silver plates and the lions of the throne to be melted down and minted.[24] "Two years after Philip IV's accession, in 1623, the total public debt had risen to 112 million *ducats* — the equivalent of at least ten years' revenue: Two years after his death, in 1667, the debt stood at 180 million."[25]

In order to improve royal finances, in 1626 the first minister, the Count-Duke of Olivares, promulgated the "Unión de Armas", a fiscal policy that eliminated fiscal exemptions in all Imperial territories and required them to contribute proportionally to the central treasury. The Imperial authorities risked the unpopularity of the measures because of the urgent need to finance the armies involved in the beginnings of the Thirty Year War, as well as because of renewed conflict with the Netherlands in 1621 after the failure of the truce. To make matters worse, the French declared war in 1635, and at the same time Catalonia revolted, supported by Cardinal Richelieu. Then Portugal sought independence, and the Duke of Medina Sidonia and the Marquis of Ayamonte tried to separate Andalusia from Castille. High taxation and increased food prices were behind popular upheavals that were followed in 1647 by the Masianello revolt in Naples and Sicily. "From the end

22 Domínguez Ortíz 1959, 335.
23 Ibid., 311.
24 Ibid., 335.
25 Parker 1979, 189.

of 1640 Spain and Spain's international power were visibly crumbling."[26] In 1648 Spain accepted Dutch independence in the Treaty of Munster. The Spanish Empire in Europe finished in effect with the Treaty of Westphalia (1648), but war expenditures remained high due to war with France until the Treaty of the Pyrenees (1659), and Portugal's independence through the Treaty of Lisbon (1668).

Philip IV greatly increased fiscal pressure throughout the Empire under a variety of devices —new taxes, forced gifts, the sale of noble titles, public offices and pardons to criminals, etc.— but the most unpopular measure was the re-coinage of copper money called *vellón* in Spain. The name of this coinage came from a Roman coin with an engraved sheep. Beginning with Philip III the Crown had manipulated the value of copper, with economic and social disruptions of enormous proportions. So large was the amount of *vellón* issued under Philip III and Philip IV that it caused a period of prosperity in Sweden, the main European supplier of copper.

A Spanish historian has characterized the relationship between royal finances and copper coinage in a dramatic fashion: "Without the resource of *vellon*, Castille never could have prolonged its agony."[27] With Philip IV the manipulation of *vellón* reached its peak in the years between 1634 and 1656, coinciding with the revolutions of 1640 and the military campaigns in Europe. For instance, in 1651 the king ordered that the small copper coins of 2 *maravedis* were to have a face value of 8 *maravedis*.[28] Profiteers took advantage of the situation and large quantities of counterfeit copper coins entered Spain to be exchanged for silver and gold. In 1621 the profits from such illegal trade reached 500%.[29]

In spite of the damage to the Spanish economy, Philip IV's monetary policy was an efficient way to finance Imperial policy.[30] The re-minting of copper coin in 1636 produced 4,700,000 *ducats*, 10,000,000 in 1641; 6,000,000 in 1643 and 11,000,000 in 1651.[31]

26 Elliot 1970, 470.

27 Serrano Mangas 2000, 569.

28 Reglá 1970, 403.

29 Hamilton 1975, 95.

30 For the monetary decisions of the Spanish Habsburgs see Flynn and Giráldez 2000. The article tries to explain how copper coinage was linked to Habsburg imperial policy.

31 Domínguez Ortíz 1960, 272–273.

Surprisingly, the manipulations of copper coinage affected only the inhabitants of the Spanish peninsula, because "the Empire's money was silver: Armies, embassies and subsidies of foreign princes were paid in silver."[32] In America, until the first half of the sixteenth century, only New Spain and the small island *La Española* minted copper. In Mexico, cocoa beans were the fractionary money.[33]

Perú in the seventeenth century

At the beginning of the seventeenth century a merchant wrote in an anonymous report addressed to the government of the Netherlands:

> The Imperial City of Potosí, the happiest and most fortunate of all known cities in the world for its wealth [...]; has a large amount of business with Lima, and many merchants go to Lima, Mexico and Seville. Likewise Potosí sends many very rich men to live in Spain. [...] Every year they mint six or seven thousand bars of silver, worth on average one thousand *pesos* each. They also make large amounts of *rials* and use a large amount of silver to make dinner services. This mine was discovered eighty years ago and the quantities of silver extracted now and in the past are infinite.[34]

The economic center of the Vice-Royalty was the city of Potosí, located at 4,000 meters above sea level with the famous *cerro* 400 meters high above it. At Arica, the official port of Potosí, 640 km away, ships arrived carrying mercury for the mines and the galleons that transported the silver. Almost nothing grew around the Imperial City, but beyond a radius of forty kilometers fruits, vegetables, wheat and corn were cultivated in the surrounding valleys. There were also pastures for animals. In 1603, according the *Las descripciones geográficas del Perú* (Geographical Descriptions of Perú), 40,000 llamas carried general supplies including the indispensable coca leaves, and another 60,000 carried food for the "mitayos" —the indigenous workers forced to labor— of the mine.[35]

32 Domínguez Ortíz 1963, 150.

33 Serrano Mangas 2000, 569.

34 Anonymous 1958, 99 and 101.

35 Cited in Cobb 1949, 32.

The wealth in the city was fabulous. The expenditures by the city to celebrate the coronation of Philip II are estimated to have been 8 million *pesos*. Many women spent between twelve and fourteen thousand *pesos* in clothing and jewels. It is known that one woman bought five hundred *pesos* of pearls. The indigenous inhabitants of the city participated in the extravagant festivities, displaying clothing embroidered with pearls and precious stones.[36]

During the first years of mining operations it was quite common that an indigenous merchant selling supplies could earn between 25,000 and 40,000 *pesos* of gold in a single day of trade.[37] These extraordinary profits persisted until 1640. In fact, the attraction exercised by the Peruvian market was so powerful that other places in the Americas were deprived of foreign products, these going instead to Potosí, where a profit of 1,000% could be earned.[38] There are numerous anecdotes about the extraordinary wealth of Potosí. For example, a rich man could pay 10,000 *pesos* for a single fish. Dowries of 100,000 *pesos* were common, while in 1597 a bride brought to her husband a dowry of 2,000,300 *pesos*.

Another indication of the powerful mining economy was the population of Potosí. In the middle of the seventeenth century the number of inhabitants reached a high of 160,000, falling to 145,000 by 1660.[39] According to Peter Bakewell, each year about 50,000 indigenous people, the "mitayos" and their families, arrived in Potosí, and at the beginning of the seventeenth century another 37,000 indigenous people not belonging to the "mita" lived in the city.[40]

For the modern era these figures are astonishing, given the isolation of Potosí, the arduous routes to it and the inhospitable conditions of the place. During the first fifty years of the city not a single newborn baby was able to survive, and the Spanish mothers went to the surrounding valleys to give birth, remaining there until the babies reached six months to one year of age.[41]

36 Cobb 1945, 54.
37 Ibid., 52.
38 Cobb 1949, 45.
39 Mangan 2000, 165.
40 Bakewell 1984, 133.
41 Cobb 1945, 54.

The Spaniards had known about Potosí since 1545, and the mercury from Huancavelica became available after 1563. From then on, the Spanish miners possessed both silver ore and the mercury to implement the amalgamation process used to produce silver. The new technology and the institutional reforms introduced by the Viceroy Francisco de Toledo resulted in a prodigious increase in silver production. When the mercury from Huancavelica was not enough, the government brought supplies from Almadén in Spain or from Idria in Slovenia, which was conveniently located in Habsburg territories. The mercury from Idria was mainly employed in the mining camps of Mexico, mainly between 1621 and 1645, the year in which the Spanish Crown discontinued purchases.[42]

Amalgamation was not the only process for producing silver. For instance, in Mexico, in the camps of Zacatecas and Sombrerete, smelting was used at the end of the seventeenth century. Nonetheless, amalgamation was the most efficient process for extracting silver, and there was a direct relation between mercury consumption and silver production.[43]

Following the reforms of Toledo in 1570 that brought about an abundant supply of mercury and a massive influx of *mitayos*, the Potosí output reached quantities previously unknown. 70% of all Peruvian silver was produced at Potosí, representing 50% of total American production. Both the advantage and the risk of Potosí "resided in its concentrated area, which permitted economies of scale and easy access to capital."[44] This outstanding production initiated in the sixteenth century continued until 1627 —Philip IV's first year in power— when a downward trend began, this becoming more pronounced after 1680.[45] The extraordinary initial benefits were achieved by applying the amalgamation process to the tailings, but the necessity to excavate longer shafts into the sides of the hills and deeper galleries required large amounts of capital that increased the costs of mining.

In fact, the silver produced in Perú was inferior in quality to that of Mexico, and the mining operation costs were higher in Potosí when compared to New Spain. Mercury was a royal monopoly and the Crown charged a higher

42 Bakewell 1984, 122.

43 Brading and Cross 1972, 556 and 570.

44 Ibid., 574 and 576.

45 Garner 1988, 228; Brading and Cross 1972, 574.

price in Perú than in Mexico, while also silver taxes were higher in the Andes region. Until 1736 the government in Potosí collected the royal *quinto* (a 20% tax on silver production), but in New Spain the tax rate was lower. Total mining costs associated with payments to the government were about 20% in Mexico, but reached 35% in Perú.[46] The concentration of mining operations in Potosí made it easy to collect taxes, which explains the different taxation regimes in New Spain and Perú.

Financial crisis and fraud

The tributary pressure in Perú increased under Philip IV. Following the "Unión de Armas" scheme in 1627, Perú was required to pay 350,000 *ducats* yearly for the next fifteen years.[47] Several measures were promulgated to improve fiscal revenues, but with little success. In addition to increasing the fiscal pressure in these ways, the monarchy also required *donativos*, gifts to the Crown, and "loans".

During the Viceroy Chinchón's tenure, petitions were repeated with such frequency that a friar, Buenaventura Salinas, openly preached against the government in the Cathedral of Cuzco. "The insistent demand of gifts implied indirectly a prejudice against the Royal Treasury and negatively affected the social stability of the Vice-Royalty."[48] In spite of difficulties and opposition, in 1639 the Viceroy sent 2,400,000 *pesos* to Spain, while his successor the Marquis of Mancera increased the quantity to 2,600,000 *pesos*. From 1636 to 1644 remittances were uniformly above 2,000,000 pesos.[49] Nevertheless, this success was only a partial solution to the King's woes. The silver leaving America did not reach Spain in the same amount, because it was necessary to deduct the *situados* (the subsidies to support fortresses and the local administration), the expenditures for the fleets, as well as other payments of a diverse nature.

In moments of extreme need the Crown confiscated silver consigned to merchants in exchange for copper monies (*vellón*) and annuities. This prac-

46 Garner 1988, 906.

47 Lynch 1969, 164.

48 Báncora Cañero 1959, 77.

49 Báncora Cañero 1959, 85–86.

tice meant in effect that the merchants made involuntary loans to the Crown. In 1621 Philip IV confiscated American silver and paid with copper at an interest rate of 8% to the merchants and 5% to others. In 1622 the King confiscated the silver rescued from the galleon Santa Margarita, with the owners receiving nothing in return. When in 1628 the Dutch captured the silver fleet from Mexico, the King decided to take 1,000,500 *pesos* from the fleet from Perú.[50] In 1629 the amount collected in this way was one million *ducats*, and in the years 1635 and 1637 two million more were exchanged for copper. The practice continued during the 1640s, and in 1649 the amount confiscated was one million *ducats*. In 1652 the Crown sent agents to collect the silver arriving in Seville: "Suddenly and without a preconceived plan and no visible leader, (in May of 1652) the so-called *El Motín de la Feria* (The Mutiny of the Fair) exploded. After this upheaval the government cancelled the confiscation."[51]

The merchants rejected copper or annuities because as the only monetary substance with universal value silver was essential for their business transactions; "giving up their silver as lost, they sold the annuities below their nominal price, with great damage to their capital."[52] Added to the fiscal pressure in Perú and the possibility of confiscation was the need for the merchants to pay for the fleets' costly military protection, known as the "avería". Clarence Haring, quoting Vieitia Linaje's well-informed seventeenth century treatise, has noted that under this scheme passengers on the fleets paid 20 *ducats* for themselves and the same amount for each of their companions, servants, slaves, etc. For merchandise a percentage of its value was paid.[53] With wars, the amount of the *avería* increased until 1644, when Philip IV promised that goods coming from the Indies would only pay 12% of their value, and that the government would take care of the difference between military costs and the taxes collected.[54]

50 Suárez 1995, 78–79.

51 Domínguez Ortíz 1956, 372.

52 Báncora Cañero 1959, 77.

53 Haring 1964, 76; Joseph Vieitia Linaje, *Norte de la Contratación de las Indias Orientales*, (Seville 1672).

54 Ibid., 78.

In this situation of increased tributary pressure and lower silver value, fraud became a structural component of the Empire's economic life. The mining industry had transformed the Vice-Royalty's economic geography. New cities emerged in previously unpopulated regions, as was the case for Potosí in the district of Charcas. New agricultural activities were added to local production, such as wine in coastal Perú and Chile and animal husbandry in Argentina. Textile and other manufacturing activities also supplied new population centers. An active transportation network connected these industries and agricultural production.[55] In Perú, "el Callao", the port of Lima, was the center of trade for distributing local products and European merchandise throughout the Vice-Royalty. El Callao was part of a network of more than twenty-four ports along the Pacific Ocean coast.[56] From the Cuzco region, a trade route took coca leaves to Potosí; following a southern branch it continued on to Tucumán, Córdoba and Buenos Aires. This route was used to supply the Vice-Royalty with mules, horses, hides and slaves.[57] There was also an active trade with Mexico and the Philippines. Commerce with Asia was extremely profitable too. During the seventeenth century the average profit of trade with Spain is estimated to have been between 20% and 30%, and 35% for commerce with Mexico, where Acapulco received the "ship from China".[58] In a memorandum to the King in 1621, a royal functionary warned:

> Since the goods from China began to arrive in the times of the King our Lord, the father of your Majesty, God rest his soul, and considering attentively the richness of the land and that, after opening the door to this commerce, they were taking money from the Indies, and in its place the merchants were bringing such an amount of goods to the Americas that the colonies had no further need of Spain.[59]

The economic development of Perú escaped Imperial regulation. The mercury industry —a strategic product for mining— is a clear example. Huan-

55 Bethell 1984, 108–109.

56 Suárez 2001, 201 and 209.

57 Ibid., 224.

58 Suárez 2001, 238.

59 "Pedro Hurtado de Alcocer a Felipe IV" in *Colección de Documentos Inéditos para la Historia de España y sus Indias* (MCXXII) T V, 172.

cavelica belonged to the king, but businessmen, "asentistas", took care of its exploitation and transportation to the mining camps. In the beginning of the seventeenth century, large quantities of mercury were not taxed, with the illegal trade reaching enormous proportions, and it was used to produce silver outside Royal control. "In Tacna and Arica there were special places to receive illegal mercury and silver that were afterwards shipped to Lima."[60]

Furthermore, the religious orders did not pay taxes on merchandise arriving at Lima, and local merchants took advantage of this loophole to make illegal business deals with churchmen. "In 1650 there was a great scandal when the *curaca* of Surco, Don Juan Tanta Chumbi, and his sentinels discovered a clandestine circuit to export silver based on the hacienda villa property of the San Pablo Jesuit school."[61]

The ecclesiastics, merchants, landowners and Imperial bureaucrats that constituted the vice-regal elite transformed the colonial pact. This new equilibrium was reflected in lower remittances to Spain and lesser financial involvement by American territories in the Imperial wars in Europe.[62] Public functions like collecting the *avería* and other taxes were farmed out to the powerful merchants of the *Consulado*, giving them a privileged business position in the Vice-Royalty.[63] The government finally acknowledged the widespread fraud and established the practice of "indulto" —a negotiated payment to the government for illegal business activities— in the second half of the seventeenth century, which implies that the legal framework had virtually disappeared.[64]

Fraud was present in every instance of the colonial trade system. In the Callao merchants paid a fee of 4% of their silver to embark it unregistered. In Panamá and Portobelo the rate was 2%. In Portobelo in 1652, the merchants used to pay to the royal officers 8% of the silver if they allowed them to remove it from the official ledger, and the illegal transportation fee was 4 or 5%. Silver entered two different trade networks according to whether

60 Suárez 2001, 301.
61 Ibid., 206.
62 Lynch 1969, 195.
63 Suárez 2001, 302–303.
64 Suárez 2001, 260.

silver was registered or unregistered. Profits were 30 to 40% higher in the clandestine trade.[65]

Panama was the strategic link between el Callao and Seville and a prominent location for fraud. In 1654, the president of the *Audiencia* —a judicial institution with general administrative powers— Pedro Carrillo de Guzmán, received 400,000 *pesos* as bribe for 6,000,000 unregistered *pesos*.[66] Due to military expenditures, large amounts destined to the King remained in Panama. Investigations in 1656, 1659 and 1660 indicated that royal functionaries defrauded the treasury on the soldiers' salaries and supplies.[67]

Once the silver had been loaded on board, the fraud continued. It was a known fact that the admirals and generals of the fleets participated actively in contraband, but in spite of this their appointments were consistently renewed. For example: Nicolás Judici received a fine of 22,480 *ducats*, Jerónimo Gómez de Sandoval and Carlos de Mencos 20,000 each, and Valencegui, 6,100. "The fines were considered a discount to make up for the illicit gains earned by their positions."[68] The clergy also participated in the fraud. When the bishop Juan Pérez de Espinosa died, the Royal Treasury confiscated from his estate 414,700 *rials* of silver, 62 gold bars and several gold and silver objects because none of them had been registered.[69] In a memorandum to the King, a royal officer, Hortuño de Urizar, wrote that as soon as the fleets reached the Peninsula:

> It would be appropriate if before the arrival of the first galleons a knowledgeable and honest person is nominated to be present in San Lúcar in charge of conducting all the silver and gold to Seville, because fraud has reached such proportions that without unloading the silver they pass a large quantity of it to foreign ships that are there waiting for it.[70]

At Cadiz and San Lúcar —in the mouth of the Guadalquivir— foreign merchants transferred merchandise illegally to the fleets plying the Atlantic re-

65 Ibid., 304.

66 Ibid., 360.

67 Ibid., 361.

68 Domínguez Ortíz 1956, 328.

69 Domínguez Ortíz 1969, 56.

70 "El proveedor Hortuño de Urizar A la Junta," in *Colección de Documentos Inéditos para la Historia de España y sus Indias* (MCXXII) T V, 506.

ceiving payment in silver and gold on the fleet's return. Fraud became a semi-professional activity carried on by the so-called "metedores." These were junior members of aristocratic families who acted as intermediaries in the business. The governor, the major of Cadiz and the sentinels in the ramparts participated in this lucrative enterprise. Clarence Haring quotes these facts from a 1691 French report, which indicates that the same activities took place in both the sixteenth and seventeenth centuries.[71] Payments to the *metedores* were calculated at 1% of the merchandise value, but during the second half of the seventeenth century the fraudulent practice was a way to avoid 23% in taxes and 45 to 50% of the same value in insurance, freight and storage.[72] Fernández de Rebolledo, a businessman in 1650, indicated that to introduce money illegally the payment was 3% in all the Spanish ports.[73] In 1626 an informer wrote to the King from Lima: "On the occasion of the fleet it came to my knowledge that foreigners living in this kingdom under the pretense of being from Seville are taking 2 million and they are sons of Dutch, Flemish and merchants of different nations."[74]

Antonio Merlo de la Fuente, an official inspector to Potosí, wrote that in 1650 these illegal business practices were a common occurrence.

> The amount of unregistered silver is eight times that registered, and without being unloaded in Spain it goes from the merchant vessels to the foreign ships [...] that are waiting for them in the ports of Cadiz and San Lucar; they take it to foreign kingdoms and bring the merchandise for the fleets without paying taxes for entering or leaving; the damage to the Royal treasury amounts to more than 2,000,000 [*pesos*] each year.[75]

The port of Cadiz competed successfully with Seville from the sixteenth century, but in the second half of the seventeenth century the decline of Seville was so pronounced that the fleets could only load there a third of the cargo space available, with the rest being loaded in Cadiz.[76] Finally, in 1660

71 Haring 1964, 112.

72 Bernal 1992, 278.

73 "Fernández de Rebolledo's memorandum" edition, with an introduction in Giraldez 2006a, 181.

74 Quoted in Suárez 1995, 87.

75 See the "Alonso Merlo de la Fuente's memorandum" edition, with an introduction in Giraldez 2006b, 200–201.

76 Haring 1964, 12.

the Crown decided to allow the arrival of precious metals without registration, and the cost of *avería* was negotiated with the *Consulados* of merchants in America and Seville.

The structural reason behind the illegal trade was the commercial capacity of foreign merchants —"they provided the departing fleets with five-sixths of the cargo"[77]— because the ruined Spanish manufacturers could not fulfill the American demand. In fact, foreigners controlled trade between Seville and the Vice-Royalties, with a direct exchange with foreign ships taking place in many American ports from 1625, and the French, Dutch and British establishing themselves in the Caribbean islands unoccupied by the Spaniards.

At the beginning of the seventeenth century an average of 200 ships sailed from Portugal with cargoes of textile products for the Vice-Royalty of Peru. A route through Buenos Aires, which served as the port of Potosí and Tucumán, reached the Andes. Soon an economic exchange between the silver mining regions of the Andes and the areas producing foodstuffs and cotton and with pasture for animals like cows and mules was established.[78] This was also the entry point for manufactured products and slaves.[79] In Buenos Aires two monetary regimes coexisted: The local commerce was based on barter and foreign trade was carried out in silver.[80]

Beginning with the sixteenth century many Portuguese merchants entered the Vice-Royalty. The process accelerated under Philip IV after they made a loan of 3.24 million pesos. Portuguese businessmen in Peru had agents in Seville and were engaged in the Atlantic economy and the profitable slave trade. In 1623 "slave profits could be substantial since their selling price delivered to Buenos Aires averaged about 140 *pesos*; [while] in Peru they sold for at least 500 *pesos*."[81] The animosity against this group of merchants, who had converted from Judaism, culminated in the Inquisition trials between 1635 and 1639 called the *Complicidad Grande,* accusing them of practicing Judaism in secret. These trials were actually instigated by the

77 Ibid., 113.
78 Canabrava 1944, 17.
79 Ibid., 67.
80 Canabrava 1944, 93.
81 Cross 1978, 155.

Peruvian merchants to eliminate powerful competitors. "The Inquisitors did not hide the fact that their primary objection to the Portuguese was economic rather than religious."[82] One casualty of these events was Juan de la Cueva, the owner of a bank that suffered bankruptcy in 1635, with losses calculated at 1,000,000 *pesos*.[83] The Inquisition unsuccessfully urged the establishment of a tribunal in Buenos Aires to prosecute heretics. The *Audiencia*, a Royal Tribunal in charge of controlling contraband, lasted only a decade after 1663[84], and fraud in the Rio de la Plata estuary continued unabated.

Counterfeiting in Perú

The famous pieces-of-eight (also known as the Spanish dollar) was the basis of the Spanish Empire's monetary system. The coin was equal to 8 *rials*, or 272 *maravedís,* with 25.56 grams of silver. The same quantity of precious metal remained almost unaltered in twentieth century Mexican *pesos*. During all these centuries the amount of silver in the pieces-of-eight suffered a reduction of only 5.9% by weight.[85] "Under Philip II the piece-of-eight is already the Spanish coin *par excellence*."[86]

This coin circulated widely "from the Gobi desert to the Amazon's banks and from the Great Wall of China to the Australian continent."[87]. Notwithstanding the coin's global success in the sixteenth and seventeenth centuries, the quality of the *rials* was very low. According to Humberto F. Burzio, a famous historian of American numismatics, the Peruvian pieces-of-eight "were the product of a primitive and defective monetary technology. They were manufactured by hammering, and it shows in the imperfect figures and poorly engraved legends."[88] The assayers of the refined silver were incom-

82 Ibid., 162.

83 Ibid., 161. The Viceroy Conde de Chinchón gave this figure in a letter to the king on the 17 of May 1635. Quoted in Suarez 1995, 48.

84 Haring 1965, 118.

85 McMaster 1959, 372.

86 Reglá 1970, 320.

87 Pérez 1955, 54.

88 Burzio 1945, 55.

petent and fuel for the minting operations was very expensive. The faulty technology facilitated counterfeiting.

Carlo Cipolla wondered why "such an ugly coin, of such a poor mintage, easy to counterfeit, and whose intrinsic value was difficult to ascertain, was in such a high demand and accepted all over the world." The answer he provided was that the large amounts of coins allowed the extraordinary development of international trade during the sixteenth and seventeenth centuries.[89] João dos Santos, a Portuguese Dominican friar, wrote in 1609: "In India pieces-of-eight and four-*rial* coins coming from Portugal circulated widely." Another Portuguese friar from Manila in the years 1637 and 1638 described how the Chinese merchants remarked "in badly pronounced Spanish, *Plata es sangue*" (silver is blood).[90] The silver came in pieces-of-eight to Manila. In Bantam, on the island of Java, in 1604 the counterfeiting of pieces-of-eight was punishable with death.[91] All these anecdotes indicate the widespread use of the coin.

Despite the importance of the *rial* in the global market and Perú's position as the main silver producer of the modern era, the monetary situation in the Vice-Royalty was quite different from that of the legal monetary system. According to André Sayous, the larger monetary commodity was the silver bar, of about 1,000 *pesos*, used for large transactions. For everyday life all kinds of coinage were in use, from small silver coins alloyed with lead to supposedly illegal small gold coins stamped with a crown in the environs of Quito.[92] In 1650 a memorandum of Antonio Merlo de la Fuente describes a much more heterogeneous monetary panorama than in the legal monetary system. The general population used fragments of silver and gold, gold powder, silver bars, silver paste, and the same precious metal in various degrees of refinement. In 1637, thirteen years before Merlo de la Fuente, the Viceroy, Count of Chinchón, lamented in a letter to a relative that he received part of his salary in silver paste and not in coins.[93]

89 Cipolla 1996, 73–74.

90 Quoted in Boxer 1970, 463.

91 See Scott 1943–1944, 110–121.

92 Sayous 1928, 1310 and 1314.

93 Bronner 1981, 67.

In addition to the precious metals in a variety of forms, indigenous people used the so called *monedas de la tierra* —tobacco, *mate*, nails, etc.— to pay their taxes, as indicated in a 1618 royal document.[94] This monetary regime can be explained as being due to the inhabitants of the Vice-Royalty wanting to avoid paying minting taxes. Coins and bars were used in the foreign trade.

If the minting quality in Peru during those centuries was low, it declined markedly after 1633. In that year a royal order arrived in Lima complaining of the low fineness of the *pesos*, and another memorandum from the Council of the Indies to the Viceroy indicated that "there is not a single piece of eight *rials* that does not contain two *rials* of copper."[95] Gerónimo Garabito, a representative of Potosí refiners, wrote in 1636 that silver extraction had declined and that the minting quality had declined noticeably. In subsequent years the situation became even worse. In a memorandum to the King summarizing his findings in Perú, the doctor Alonso Merlo de la Fuente writes that the technological level was deplorable, and that "there is no assayer to be found in the mint nor at any Royal House where silver bars are melted who knows how to assay." Merlo de la Fuente recounts how on his visit to the mint at Potosí he found the workers mixing silver with large quantities of copper, giving this fraudulent coinage in return for the silver brought by miners, with the pieces-of-eight having a copper color. Obviously a great portion of royal taxes went uncollected.[96]

The low technical level and overall corruption of the assayers at the mint in Potosí was proved when the *Council of the Indies* required them to witness in Seville the assaying of Peruvian *pesos*. Two remained in the Americas, one in Oruro and the second in Havana. The third assayer agreed with the assessment made in Seville ascertaining the fineness of the silver. The usual practice of selling public offices by the King contributed to the monetary fraud. The assayers paid 60,000 pieces-of-eight for their positions and the *mercaderes de la plata,* or silver traders, had to pay a considerable fee, so they all expected to be able to recuperate their investment. The Council of

94 Burzio 1945, 37.

95 Bakewell 1995, 38.

96 Merlo de la Fuente's memorandum in Giraldez 2006b, 194 and 195–196.

Castille acknowledged that this was an encouragement to engage in counterfeiting.[97]

Early in Philip IV's reign, large quantities of silver arrived in Seville in the form of bars valued on average at 1,000 *pesos* or as *piñas* (lumps of silver not completely refined). Before minting, the assayers ascertained the metal quality. The results varied from small mistakes to obvious fraud, and there were even cases of copper bars with only a coating of silver. After 1640 fraud became generalized.[98] In Seville in 1638 the first assayer of the Mint warned of the low weight and fineness of large quantities of Potosí's *pesos*. Férnandez de Rebolledo, an assayer in Seville, wrote in 1650 that in the last six years in which he had assayed Peruvian coins, the reduction in weight and fineness averaged 30%. Other official tests estimated the percentage of fraud in fineness as between 18% and 50%.[99]

Treasury Council documents show that merchants supplying the fleets in Seville complained about the large quantities of counterfeited *pesos* that they received in payment.[100] Outside the Spanish Empire, references to the low quality of Peruvian coins were widespread. In 1630 and 1640 British merchants in India and the Dutch in Indonesia complained about this state of affairs.[101] In Genoa, one of Europe's primary financial centers, the circulation of Peruvian pieces-of-eight was forbidden. Milan in 1648 and Koenigsberg in 1651 took similar measures.[102] In Flanders, Peruvian coins were not accepted during that time, with the result that the financial system of the Spanish army was in serious jeopardy. The *Cour des Monnaies* in France took measures to impede the circulation of such coinage in 1646 and 1650. The infamous pieces-of-eight were retired in 1650 from circulation in the territories of Navarra, Aragón and Valencia, belonging to the Spanish monarchy, and only after assaying and weighing were they accepted in Italy and Flanders in the same year.[103] In 1651 the accounts of a hospital in Seville showed a loss of 576 *rials* out of a total of 3,204 Peruvian *rials* that had to

97 Domínguez Ortíz 1963, 148.

98 Ibid., 144–145.

99 Hamilton 1975, 82–83.

100 Domínguez Ortíz 1963, 146.

101 Boxer 1970, 465–466.

102 Cipolla 1996, 71–72.

103 Hamilton 1975, 82.

be melted down and re-coined because no payments could be made with them.[104]

The Crown had long known about the technological limitations of the coinage and about the illegal monetary regime in Perú, but when the fraud in the Potosí mint went beyond certain limits the Imperial authorities reacted with unusual decisiveness. Francisco Nestares Marín, a priest and a jurist with a career as an inquisitor in Galicia and Valladolid in Spain, was dispatched to Potosí. Initially, the Council of the Indies decided to impose large fines on the miscreants, with the hope that they would mend their ways and continue minting and financing the miners and refiners. Adding the fines and the silver confiscated, the figure was 1,500,000 *pesos*, a sum larger than the total amount that Potosí paid annually in silver taxes.[105] But Nestares Marín's actions went beyond those of the Council. The assayer Felipe Ramírez Arellano was executed, and Francisco Gómez de la Rocha, accused of trying to poison the *visitador* (inspector), suffered the same fate, already described at the beginning of this essay, in 1654. The accusation of poisoning against Gómez de la Rocha was plausible in the context of a violent colonial Potosí. In his 1650 memorandum, Merlo de la Fuente wrote that an inspector to Potosí decided to replace the mint's assayer, and appointed a new one who demanded a higher fineness for the silver. He was threatened and "some people thought that he escaped, and others that he was killed."[106] In 1661 the King sent a friar, Francisco de la Cruz, to Potosí. It seems that he antagonized the miners and was consequently poisoned.[107]

To put the Imperial policy in the social context of the Vice-Royalty it is necessary to know the highlights of Francisco Gómez de la Rocha's life. He was a *mercader de la plata*, or silver trader. These businessmen were few in number and occupied a crucial position in the Vice-Regal mining economy. They bought raw silver from the owners of the mills that processed the ore and took it to the mint. The quality of the silver was tested and coins were struck. Silver traders oversaw the process to avoid fraud. They also provided credit to miners and refiners. These businessmen received the lion's share of

104 Ibid., 83.

105 Bakewell 1995, 41.

106 Merlo de la Fuente's memorandum, in Giraldez 2006b, 194.

107 Mangan 2005, 165.

the mining profits. Peter Bakewell adds: "Perhaps this was partly because they had, as the saga of the Potosí mint in the 1640's shows, excellent opportunities for profitable fraud for which they were prosecuted only when they carried it to extremes, as Gómez de la Rocha and his companions had done."[108]

De la Rocha was extremely rich and apparently enjoyed royal favor. In 1645 the king sent him a personal letter acknowledging a loan without interest and thanking him for paying one hundred and fifty soldiers for the war in Chile against the Araucanos.[109] The king made de la Rocha a knight of a military order, but he was executed before he could receive the honor. Arzáns de Orsúa y Vela, a famous chronicler of Potosí, wrote of Francisco Gómez de la Rocha's fabulous wealth: "He had a personal fortune of 7,000,000 *pesos* in coin and 1,000,000 more in jewels and household furniture, ate his meals on gold plates, and his twenty horses used silver horseshoes instead of the common iron ones."[110]

The monetary measures taken were no less severe. The government decided that the pieces-of-eight minted before 1649 should circulate for a time with the value of 6 *rials* or 75% of their value, and coins produced in the following years were assigned 93.7% of their value.[111] Arzáns de Orsúa y Vela considered the monetary devaluation a catastrophe comparable to the civil war in Potosí between two groups of Spaniards, the *vascongados* and *vicuñas*, and to the destruction by a severe earthquake of the artificial water reservoirs that propelled the mills used for processing silver ore. The rich and the poor, Spaniards and indigenous, all suffered losses in their wealth. Good examples were the Indian sellers in the Potosí market. "There was an Indian woman (the ones that sell food supplies) who had about 40,000 *pesos*, and the other women more or less, and all of them lost half of their capital."[112]

A royal document in 1650 authorized the minting of a new coin called "columnaria" because the column of Hercules was engraved on its tail, and

108 Bakewell 1995, 46–47.

109 Ibid., 41

110 Arzáns de Orsúa y Vela 1965, II, 132.

111 Domínguez Ortíz 1963, 148; Bakewell 1995, 43.

112 Arzáns de Orsúa y Vela 1965, II, 124.

with symbols of the mint and the assayer. The mintage of these new coins began in 1652 but it took some time to restore confidence. In Spain on the 23rd of September 1653 a royal order informed the public that the Peruvian *pesos* imported that year were like the ones minted in Castille, with the only difference being the design.[113] In 1654 the Acapulco authorities rejected 5,000 of these new coins and Portugal required a decree from the Crown to enforce their circulation. In 1665 the Dutch already carried the new Peruvian *pesos*.[114]

The consequences of such devaluations were extremely hard on the Peruvian economy because they followed a series of economic catastrophes, including the bankruptcy in 1635 of Juan de la Cueva, the most important Peruvian banker, as well as the disruption created by the prosecution of the Jewish merchants between 1635 and 1639. Only three merchants of silver out of the previous twelve remained after the Nestares' inspection, because the minting of the new coinage was an uneconomical proposition now that it required a high degree of fineness.

In 1654 the merchants of Lima complained to the king that the devaluation had caused 4,000,000 *pesos* in direct losses, to which they added another 2,000,000 *pesos* in loans to merchants in Potosí and Chile that they couldn't recover.[115] In Spain the devaluation was followed by disturbances in Córdoba, Seville and other cities in southern Spain. Losses to the Royal Treasury and the general population have been estimated at 2,000,000 *ducats*.[116]

Conclusion

Expensive engineering —longer shafts and deeper galleries— was necessary to extract the mineral, and the costs of crushing the ore and refining silver were more expensive in the second half of the seventeenth than in the previous century. Simultaneously, the value of silver was decreasing due to the massive inflation which was the consequence of the "Price Revolution." But

113 Hamilton 1975, 84.

114 Boxer 1970, 469.

115 Suárez 2001, 308.

116 Domínguez Ortíz 1963, 154.

adding further to costs and inflation was yet another tectonic movement in the silver market. In China, in 1635 thirteen ounces of silver were needed to purchase one ounce of gold. Fifty years before only six ounces of silver had been needed.[117] In his *The Wealth of Nations* Adam Smith wrote: "Between 1630 and 1640, or about 1636, the effect of the discovery of America in reducing the value of silver, appears to have been completed, and the value of that metal seems never to have sunk lower in proportion to that of corn than it was about that time."[118] Richard von Glahn describes the same phenomenon: "The value of silver in terms of gold declined steadily throughout the first half of the seventeenth century, finally falling to the prevailing international level exactly at the moment the Ming dynasty fell."[119] Consequently the benefits of "arbitrage" disappeared. "This latter period contrasts sharply with the explosive pre-1640 arbitrage phase characterized by above-normal profits and the associated trade frenzy that accompanied the opening of global trade opportunities."[120]

The years that Adam Smith referred to coincided with the twilight years of the Spanish Empire in Europe and the crisis and fall of the Ming dynasty. This context of high prices and declining benefits explains the widespread contraband in the Spanish Empire. The authorities tried to adapt to the situation by negotiating the level of taxation, with however economic agents fully aware that their ability to increase tributary pressure was becoming increasingly limited. Given this context it could be expected that the monarchy would accommodate the powerful businessmen of Potosí. However, the fraudulent activities of de la Rocha and his accomplices were endangering the business of the Spanish Empire and the financial means of the Crown. In 1650, a memorandum to the King strongly recommended maintaining the fineness and weight of the pieces-of-eight:

> In other words do not allow fraud. In no way should the old pieces-of-eight and four-*rial* coins be devalued in fineness or weight, because they are used for the commercial trade and contracts throughout the far reaches of the world

117 Geiss 1979, 165.
118 Smith 1937, 192.
119 Von Glahn 1996, 242.
120 Flynn and Giraldez 2001, 156.

> and are the basis of large profits to the Royal taxes and the earnings of merchants and traders who are subjects of Spain.[121]

Obviously, it was necessary to stop the fraud. The "ripples and manifestations" in Perú were interconnected with the ocean swells and tectonic movements of the first global market. "The fact that Spain's empire owed its financial foundation to distant Ming China is a forceful reminder that much of what passes for local history in the early modern period can only be understood in terms of world history."[122] The local and the global are two abstractions of a single dynamic world.

References

Anonymous. *Descripción del Virreinato del Perú. Crónica inédita de comienzos del siglo XVII.* de Boleslao Lewin (ed.). Rosario: Universidad Nacional del Litoral Santa Fe, 1958.

Arzans de Orsua y Vela, Bartolomé. *Historia de la villa Imperial de Potosi.* Lewis Hanke y Gunnar Mendoza (eds.). Providence (RI): Brown University Press, 1965.

________ *Tales of Potosí.* R.C. Padden (ed.). Providence (RI): Brown University Press, 1975.

Bakewell, Peter (1995). Silver and Entrepreneurship in Seventeenth-Century Potosí. The Life and Times of Antonio López de Quiroga. Dallas: Southern Methodist University Press.

Báncora Cañero, Carmen (1959). "Las remesas de metales preciosos desde el Callao a España en la primera mitad del siglo XVII." *Revista de Indias*, XIX.75: 35–88.

Bernal, Antonio-Miguel. (1992). *La financiación de la Carrera de Indias (1492–1824).* Sevilla: Fundación El Monte.

Bethell, Leslie (1984). "Mining in Colonial Spanish America" Chapter 4, in *The Cambridge History of Latin America*, vol 2, *Colonial Latin America*, pp. 105–151. Cambridge: Cambridge University Press.

Blair, E.H. and J.A. Robertson (eds.) *The Philippine Islands*. 55 vols. Cleveland: A.H. Clark.

Brading, D.A. and Cross, Harry E. (1972). "Colonial Silver Mining: Mexico and Peru." *Hispanic American Historical Review*, 52.4: 545–579.

121 Fernández de Rebolledo's memorandum in Giraldez 2006a, 172.

122 Flynn and Giraldez 2001, 156.

Boxer, Charles R. (1970). "'*Plata es Sangre*': Sidelights on the Drain of Spanish American Silver in the Far East, 1550–1700." *Philippine Studies*, 18: 457–478.

Bourdon, Léon (1955). *Mémoires Inédits de Duarte Gomes Solis (Décembre 1621).* Lisbonne: [s.n.]

Braudel, Fernand (1972). *The Mediterranean and the Mediterranean World in the Age of Philip II*. 2 vols. New York: Harper and Row.

Bronner, Fred (1981). "Advertencia privada de un virrey peruano del siglo XVII a su presunto sucesor." *Revista de Indias*, XLI.163–164: 55–77.

Burzio, Humberto F. (1945). *La ceca de la villa Imperial de Potosí y la moneda colonial*. Buenos Aires: Peuser.

Canabrava, A.P. (1944). *O Comércio Portugûes no Rio da Prata (1580–1640)*. São Paulo: University of São Paulo.

Cipolla, Carlo M. (1996). *Conquistadores, pirati, mercatanti: La saga dell'argento spagnuolo*. Bologna: il Mulino.

Cobb, G. Ballantine (1945): "Potosí, a South American Mining Frontier." In *Greater American Essays in Honor of Herbert Eugene Bolton*. Berkeley & Los Angeles: University of California Press, pp. 39–57.

________ (1949). "Supply and Transportation for the Potosi Mines, 1545–1640." *The Hispanic American Historical Review*, February part. 1: 25–45.

Colección de Documentos Inéditos para la Historia de España y de sus Indias. (MCXXXII), t. V. Madrid: Academia de Estudios Histórico-Sociales de Valladolid.

Christian, D. (2004). *Maps of Time: An Introduction to Big History*. Berkeley, Los Angeles: University of California Press.

Cross, Harry E. (1978). "Commerce and Orthodoxy: A Spanish Response to Portuguese Commercial Penetration in the Viceroyalty of Peru, 1580–1640." *The Americas*, XXXV.2: 151–167.

________ (1983). "South American Bullion Production and Export, 1550–1750." In J. F Richards (ed.), *Precious Metals in the Later Medieval and Early Modern Worlds*. Durham: Carolina Academic Press, pp. 397–423.

Dominguez Ortiz, Antonio (1956). "Los caudales de Indias y la política de Felipe IV." *Anuario de Estudios Americanos*, 13: 311–383.

________ (1963). "La falsificación de moneda de plata peruana a mediados del siglo XVII." In *Homenaje a Don Ramón Carande*. Vol. II, Madrid: Sociedad de Estudios y Publicaciones, pp. 143–155.

________ (1968). "Las remesas de metales preciosos de Indias en 1655." *Anuario de historia económica y socia*, l n.2, pp. 562–581.

________ (1977). *El Antiguo Régimen: Los Reyes Católicos y los Austrias*. Fourth edition. Madrid: Alianza Editorial.

Elliot, J. H. (1970). "The Spanish Peninsula 1598–1648." In *The Decline of Spain and the Thirty Years War 1609–1648/59*. Vol. IV of *The New Cambridge Modern History*. Cambridge: Cambridge University Press, pp. 453–473.

Flynn, D. O. and Arturo Giraldez. (2006). "Globalization Began in 1571." In Barry K. Gills and William R. Thompson (eds.), *Globalization and Global History*. London and New York: Routledge, pp. 232–247.

________ (2001). "Latin American Silver and the Early Globalization of World Trade." In Mercedes F. Duran-Cogan and Antonio Gomez Moriana (eds.), *National Identities and Sociopolitical Changes in Latin America*. London and New York: Routledge, pp. 140–159.

________ (1999). "Imperial Monetary Policy in Global Perspective." In Antonio M. Bernal (ed.), *Dinero moneda y crédito en la Monarquía Hispánica*. Madrid: Marcial Pons, Ediciones de Historia, Fundación ICO, pp. 385–404.

Frank, Andre Gunder (1998). *ReOrient: Global Economy in the Asian Age*. Berkeley, Los Angeles: University of California Press.

Garner, Richard (1988). "Long-Term Silver Mining Trends in Spanish America: A Comparative Analysis of Peru and Mexico." *American Historical Review*, XCIII. 4: 898–935.

Geiss, J. P. (1979). "Peking under the Ming, 1368–1644." Ph.D. diss., Princeton University.

Giles, Lionel (1919). "Translations from the Chinese World Map of Father Ricci (Continued)." *The Geographical Journal*, 53/1: 19–30.

Giraldez, Arturo (2006a). "Falsificación monetaria en el siglo XVII: Un memorial de 1650." *eHumanista*, 6: 153–168.

________ (2006b). "La primera globalización y un inquisidor en el Potosí de 1650: El Memorial de Don Alonso Merlo de la Fuente." *eHumanista*, 7: 172–206.

Goldstone, Jack (1991). *Revolution and Rebellion in the Early Modern World*. Berkeley: University of California Press.

Hamilton, Earl J. (1975). *El tesoro americano y la revolución de los precios en España, 1501–1650*. Barcelona: Ariel.

Haring, Clarence H. (1964). *Trade and Navigation between Spain and the Indies in the Time of the Habsburgs*. Gloucester (Mass.): Peter Smith.

Kamen, Henry (2003). *Empire: How Spain Became a World Power 1492–1763*. New York: Harper and Collins.

López de Caravantes, Francisco, Introducción Guillermo Lohmann Villena ed. Maria Helmer y Jose María Pérez-Bustamante (1985–1989). *Noticia general del Perú*. Madrid: Atlas. Biblioteca de Autores Españoles (Continuación), pp. 292–293, and pp. 295–298.

Lynch, John (1969). *Spain Under the Habsburgs*. Vol. 2, *Spain and America 1598–1700*. New York: Oxford University Press.

Mangan, Jane E. (2005). *Trading Roles: Gender, Ethnicity, and the Urban Economy in Colonial Potosi*. Durham: Duke University Press.

Magalhaes Godinho, Vitorino. (1984). *Os Descobrimentos e a Economia Mundial*. Second edition. 4 vols.. Lisboa: Editorial Presença.

McMaster, John (1959). "Aventuras asiáticas del peso mexicano." *Historia Mexicana*, VIII.3: 372–399.

Perez, S. Gilbert (1955). "Manila Galleons and Mexican Pieces-of-eight. Mexico's Contribution to the Financial and Commercial Development of the Philippines." *Numisma. Revista de la Sociedad Iberoamericana de Estudios Numismáticos*, VI. 18: 39–51.

Parker, Geoffrey (1979). *Spain and the Netherlands, 1559–1659*. New Jersey: Enslow Publishers.

Reglá, Juan (1970). "Edad Moderna." In Antonio Ubieto, Juan Reglá, José María Jover, Carlos Seco, *Introducción a la Historia de España*. Barcelona: Teide, pp. 265–506.

Sayous, André E. (1928). "La circulation de metaux et monnais au Perou pendant le XVIe Siécle." *Reveu d'economie politique*. 42: 1300–1317.

Scott, Edmund (1943–1944). "An Exact Discourse of the Subtilties [...] of the East Indians." In *The Voyage of Sir Henry Middleton to the Moluccas 1604–1606*. London: Hakluyt Society, pp. 110–121.

Serrano Mangas, F. (1999). "El papel del vellón." In Antonio M. Bernal (ed.), *Dinero moneda y crédito en la Monarquía Hispánica*. Madrid: Marcial Pons, Ediciones de Historia, Fundación ICO, pp. 567–574.

Smith, Adam (1937). *An Inquiry into the Nature and Causes of the Wealth of Nations*. New York: Random House.

Suárez, Margarita (1995). *Comercio y Fraude en el Perú colonial. Las estrategias mercantiles de un banquero*. Lima: Banco Central de Reserva del Perú Fondo Editorial, Instituto de Estudios Peruanos.

________ (2001). *Desafíos transatlánticos: mercaderes, banqueros y el estado en el Perú virreinal 1600–1700*. Lima: Pontificia Universidad Católica del Perú, Instituto Riva-Agüero, Fondo de Cultura Económica, Instituto Francés de Estudios Andinos.

Vilar, Pierre (1974) *Oro y Moneda en la Historia (1450–1920)*. Third edition. Barcelona: Ariel.

Von Glahn, R. (1996). *Fountain of Fortune: Money and Monetary Policy in China 1000–1700*. Berkeley, Los Angeles: University of California Press.

Perception and Numeric Order: An Analysis of Northern European Monetary Sources from Carolingian Times to the Era of Mercantilism

Harald Witthöft

When the EURO as currency was finally installed in 2002[1], 1200 years of European monetary history were widely celebrated, commemorating the reforms of Charlemagne of about 793/794 AD as a European event[2]. How much, however, do we actually understand about the formation of money and the monetary order in Europe? While the more recent history of markets and money in Northern Europe is well explored, the earlier periods between the eighth and the turn of the sixteenth to the seventeenth centuries still raise many questions. When Michael North published his study on money and its history he let it commence with the monetisation of the economy and the commercial revolution of the twelfth and thirteenth centuries.[3] In commenting on the preceding centuries he left some controversial cultural aspects unresolved.[4] This paper addresses some issues that go back to Charlemagne (768–814 AD).

The problem to be discussed here—economic change as a change in cultural patterns or mentality—is a historical phenomenon of long duration *(longue durée)*. Especially when intercultural, intercontinental aspects are taken into consideration, the *longue durée* offers promising perspectives. Methodologically, my concern is a critical interpretation of medieval documentary evidence, which in my opinion has hitherto been insufficiently understood. On tracing key terms and concepts through several centuries, it can be shown that a fundamental cultural change provides the only historically

1 Pohl 2001, 8ff. I would like to thank Nanny Kim for her critical remarks on the manuscript. For polishing my English I am indebted to Tony Howes.

2 Witthöft 1984 and 1997a.

3 North 1994, 15ff.

4 See, for example, Fried 1994, 262–324 ('Ordnung des Reiches'), 737–766 ('Fernhandel und Städte'), 766–808 ('Kirche und Frömmigkeit') 808–852 ('geistige Kultur'); Britnell and Campbell 1995; Emmerich 2004.

adequate explanation. Indeed, after early indications of theological, philosophical and intellectual reactions to these changes in the medieval scholastic era, monetary matters and the economy as a whole finally became publicly and politically relevant and extensively debated only in early modern times and the era of mercantilism.

Monies and markets in Carolingian times (around 800 AD)

Let me set the scene by presenting two *capitularies* (imperial statutes) and a chronicle providing information on money and economy in the Carolingian age. The '*Capitulare Saxonicum*' of 797 tells us how certain regional monies or monetary units such as oxen, bushels of grain (*scapila* of oats or rye) and silver pennies (*denarii*) used to be compared by means of whole numbers in relation to a *solidus* (shilling), equalling 12 *denarii*:[5]

region	money of account or unit of weight	number	unit or weight/ measure	substance, object
Empire	1 *solidus* (Ag)	12	*Denarii*	silver
Saxony	1 *solidus* (Ag)	1	1 year old	ox
Bortrini	1 *solidus* (Ag)	40	*Scapili*	oats
ditto	ditto	20	*Scapili*	rye
Septemtrionales	1 *solidus* (Ag)	30	*Scapili*	oats
ditto	ditto	15	*Scapili*	rye

Similarly, the Frankfurt Capitulary from 793/794 makes use of fixed ratios for bushels of different types of grain (*modii* of oats, barley, rye or wheat) and silver pennies ('*denarii*') on the one hand, and for grain, different types of bread ('*librae*') and silver pennies ('*denarii*') on the other.[6] No doubt here we encounter 'money' in its original meaning—objects or goods serving as reliable regional monetary media of exchange.

Another item of documentary evidence—the Fulda Annals in two different versions, written in Mainz (A) and Regensburg (B), and reporting on a

5 *Monumenta Germaniae Historica*, LL, vol. V (1875–1879), 92f.; Witthöft 1984, 12, 138ff. and 148; also 1997a, 235f.; 1991, 11f.

6 Witthöft 1984, 114 ff.; 1997a, 230 ff.

tribute paid to the Vikings in 882 AD—appears to be the 'missing link' in our chain of arguments. These texts provide the decisive clue for arriving at a rational understanding of an underlying numeric system of handling gold and silver as currency in the early middle ages:[7]

Fulda Annals, version A	
"*Nam thesauros aecclesiarum, qui propter metum hostium absconditi fuerant, abstulit,* ***et auri purissimi atque argenti****, ad confusionem sui totuisque exercitus qui illum sequebatur; libras 2412 eisdem dedit inimicis*."	- **pure gold and silver**; - the enemies are given 2412 *librae* [of gold and silver]
Fulda Annals, version B	
"*Munera autem talia erant:* ***in auro et argento*** *duo mille libras et octoginta, vel paulo plus****;*** *quam libram viginti solidos computavimus expletam*."	- 2080 *librae* and a bit more **in gold and silver**; - the *libra* is reckoned 20 *solidi*

Most intriguing in both versions of the Annals is the phrase "*in auro et argento.*" How much was actually paid in gold, and how much in silver? The contemporaries seem to have understood without further explanation. In fact, gold and silver as money had been reckoned since antiquity in a stable numeric standard ratio of 1:12 by weight.[8] Hence the evidence of 882 AD is neither accidental nor singular.[9]

The definition of a *libra* added in the Regensburg version (B) confirms our assumption—1 *libra* equals 20 *solidi*. This relation or comparison or—in modern understanding—this definition has turned out to be a key to the reconstruction of a rational system of monetary units used in Northern European written sources of the seventh to ninth centuries. We discover a numeric system of gold-silver units for reckoning *inter aurum et argentum* and/or paying *in auro et argento,* based on a stable ratio of 12:1, with, in turn, a gold-*libra* being worth 20 gold-*solidi* by weight. All units, coined or

7 Witthöft 1979, 318ff.; 1983, 459–464; 1985, 29 f.

8 Witthöft 1991, 15; Patterson 1972, 229.

9 Witthöft 2002, 341–343.

uncoined, were equivalent to a systematically defined weight of gold or silver and understood to represent their real, immutable and intrinsic 'value'.[10]

Reckoning *inter aurum et argentum*

GOLD→	*SOLIDUS*$_{Au}$	*LIBRA*$_{Au}$
	= 1/20 *libra*$_{Au}$	= **20 *solidi*$_{Au}$**
	= 1/72 (standard) *libra*	
[Roman standard:		*sol*$_{Au}$ *= 4.5479 g*
		(libra = 327.450 g ; libra$_{Au}$ *= 90.958 g)]*
[Carolingian standard (since 793/794):		*sol*$_{Au}$ *=* ***4,5360 g***
		(libra = 326.592 g ; libra$_{Au}$ *=* ***9.,710 g)]***

GOLD+SILVER→	*LIBRA*$_{Au+Ag}$
	= 12 *librae*$_{Au}$
	= **240 *solidi*$_{Au}$**
	= 2 *pondera*$_{Au+Ag}$
[Carolingian standard 'inter aurum et argentum':	
	lb$_{Au+Ag}$ *=* ***1088.640 g*** *= 2 pd*$_{Au+Ag}$ *à* ***544.320 g]***

SILVER→	*DENARIUS*$_{Ag}$	*SOLIDUS*$_{Ag}$	*PONDUS*$_{Ag}$	*LIBRA*$_{Ag}$
	= 1/12 *solidus*$_{Ag}$	= **12 *denarii*$_{Ag}$**	= 120 *denarii*$_{Ag}$	= **240 *denarii-*** $_{Ag}$
			= 10 *solidi*$_{Ag}$	= 20 *solidi*$_{Ag}$
			= ½ *libra*$_{Ag}$	

[Carolingian monetary standard (since 793/794):
den$_{Ag}$ *=* ***1.701 g****; sol*$_{Ag}$ *= 20.412 g; pd*$_{Ag}$ *=* ***204.120 g****; lb*$_{Ag}$ *=* ***408.240 g]***

10 Witthöft 2001b, 407–409; 1984; and 1985, 20–29.

↓ ***LIBRA, PONDERA*** (STANDARD weights)

			10 *solidi*$_{Ag}$	**=120 denarii$_{Ag}$**	[= **204.120** g]
→**12 *unciae***	=	**72 *solidi*$_{Au}$**	→	= 192 *denarii*$_{Ag}$	[= **326.592 g**]
		75 *solidi*$_{Au}$	→	= 200 *denarii*$_{Ag}$	[= 340.200 g]
			20 *solidi*$_{Ag}$	**=240 *denarii*$_{Ag}$**	[= 408.240 g]
			24 *solidi*$_{Ag}$	= 288 *denarii*$_{Ag}$	[= 489.888 g]
			25 *solidi*$_{Ag}$	= 300 *denarii*$_{Ag}$	[= 510.300 g]
		120 *solidi*$_{Au}$	→	= 320 *denarii*$_{Ag}$	[= 544.320 g]
		240 *solidi*$_{Au}$	→	= 640 *denarii*$_{Ag}$	[= 1,088.640 g]

[Carolingian standard and gold/silver- weights (since 793/794):
uncia = 27.216 g; sol$_{Ag}$*= 20.412 g; sol*$_{Au}$*= 4.536 g; den*$_{Ag}$*= 1.701 g]*

Based on the above, the tribute paid to the Vikings in 882 can be worked out as follows:[11]

	2083⅓ *libra*$_{Au}$	(*libra*$_{Au}$ Carolingian standard = 90.71 g)	= 189 kg gold
or	2083⅓ *libra*$_{Ag}$	(*libra*$_{Ag}$ Carolingian standard = 1088.64 g)	= 2268 kg silver.

We may conclude that the early medieval basic monetary and economic order in the Franconian Empire was ideally based on numerical ratios of physical phenomena, natural objects and goods, i.e. on the real 'value' of money. At the same time, there are indications that in case of necessity the ratio of exchange for goods in demand, i.e. the 'prices', could, and did, vary. Such practice, however, was liable to be perceived as violation of law—and might be denounced or even punished as usury.

Carolingian metrology and the Imperial monetary system (793/794–1871)

Written and material sources allow the reconstruction of Franconian weights, measures and monies and the definition of their basic units in metric terms. This is of help for a systematic analysis of the Imperial monetary system up until 1871. It is important to keep in mind that any European monetary order since Charlemagne generally depended on the material substance and right

11 Witthöft 1983, 461–464; 1985, 29–30.

of coinage, the organisation of minting, and on the control of monetary systems as well as its success in deterring contraventions.[12]

In our context, the material substance of coined money since the Middle Ages can be defined by the KIND OF METAL (gold, silver, copper), the MONETARY UNIT (denarius, penny, floren, Taler etc.), its internal NUMBER OF DIVISION in a system of reckoning (1 libra = 20 solidi à 12 denarii = 240 denarii; 1 Mark = 160 Pfennige; 1 Mark = 8 Taler etc.), the MONETARY STANDARD, i.e. its fineness (such as an alloy of 1:16 etc.), its external NUMBER OF COMPARISON (1 $libra_{Au}$ = 12 $libra_{Au+Ag}$; 6 mark Cologne = 5 mark Vienna etc.), and its relevant BASIC MONETARY WEIGHT, i.e. the standard weight of any unit (by traditional numerical comparison or metric definition).[13]

Any material monetary order appears to be reconstructable as a rational network of systems and subsystems of their respective units and numbers. Each of these may have experienced changes for different reasons over the course of time, due to variations in basic weights and/or the ratios of whole numbers of division and comparison. Such complex monetary systems developed over centuries and have been of long duration—from the reforms of Charlemagne (793/794) to the final introduction of the decimal metric system in the German Empire on its founding in 1871/1872.[14]

The following table provides an overview of basic monetary units, standards and weights in gold and silver, with structural comparisons, divisions and ratios by number from 793/794 to 1871/1872:

12 Witthöft 1993a, 47.

13 Witthöft 1993a, 49–55, 59–67; 1993b, 2–5; 2003, 58–69.

14 Witthöft 1997a, 234–235; 1993a, 68: Table of the ratios of selected basic units in gold and silver (lb. = libra; M. = mark; pd. = pound; Pfd. = pound). Following the monetary standard of the Bohemian 'Joachimstaler' the Spanish King and German Emperor Charles I. (1516/1519–1556) let the first 'Peso de à ocho' be minted as 'Taler' of 8 Reales (Fengler, Gierow and Unger 1977, 279f.). In 1535 the coinage of the 'pieces of eight' began in Mexico too. This peso was due to circulate "extensively in both hemispheres" in the following centuries (see the contribution of Arturo Giraldez in this volume).

basic units			
Origin (metal/alloy) r=raw,gross;f=fine,net	>(numeric comparison/ratio)< metric value/ratio	monetary standard, basic weight (in g)	identity of basic weight
793/794:			
Denar (rAg) Charlemagne	**1.7010g→** → ↓ ↓	x120= **204.120 g** (*Au:Ag = 12:1*)	½ pondus A Charlemagne
11th–13th centuries:	(7:6)<		
Pfennig/Sterling (rAg) England/Köln	**1.4580g** ↓	x120= 174.960 g x160= **233.280 g**	½ pd.Troy M. London + Köln A
	(11:40)<	x40 = 212.0725g	M. Sicily
1231:	5.3019g ↓	x48 = 254.487 g	M. Nürnberg B
Augustalis (rAu) Frederick II.	>(8:25) 5.3156g ↓	x40 = 212.625 g x48 = **255.150 g**	½ pd. Sweden M. Nürnberg A
1252:	(3:2)<		
Floren (rAu) Florence	←**3.5345g**→ ↓ ↓	x96 = 339.316 g x66 = 233.280 g	lb. Florence M. Köln A + London
1284:	(134:135)<		
Ducat (rAu) Venice	3.5609g ↓	x67 = 238.581 g	M. Venice
1385/1386:	>(3:2)		
rhein.Gulden (rAu) Rhenish electors	**3.5437g** ←	x66 = **233.8875 g** x72 = 255.150 g	M. Köln B M. Nürnberg A
1518:	↓		
Guldengroschen (Ag) Saxony, Joachimsthal	(4:33)< ↓ **29.160g**(r) >(10:77) → **27.216g**(f) ↓	x8 = 233.280 g x8 = 217.728 g	M. Köln A + London ½ pondus B

1559:			>(72:66)		
Goldgulden (rAu) German Empire			↓ 3.248g	x72=233.8875g (*Au:Ag=11.44:1*)	M. Köln B
	←	>(4:33)	→		
1566:		↓	>(3:22)		
Reichs-Speziestaler (Ag) German Empire		**29.235g**(r)	↓	x8 = 233.8875 g	M. Köln B
			25.987g(f)	x9 = 233.8875 g	M. Köln B
	(67:66)< ↓				
Ducat (Au) German Empire	**3.4908g**(r)			x67= 233.8875 g	M. Köln B
	(72:71)< ↓				
	3.4423g(f)	↓		x67= **230.6390 g**	M. Köln C
1750:		>(14:8)			
Reichstaler (fAg) Prussia etc.		**16.706g** ↓		x14= 233.8875 g	M. Köln B
1838:		>(~1:1)			
Reichstaler (fAg) German Customs Union		16.704g ↓		x14= **233.8555 g**	½ Pfd.Köln in Prussia
1857:		>(~1:1)			
Vereinstaler (fAg) German Customs Union, Austria		**16.666g** ↓		x30= **500.000 g**	1 Zollpfd.
1871/1872:		>(1:3)			
1 Mark (fAg) German Empire		**5.555g**		x90= 500.000 g	1 Pfund
		>(20:31)		(*Au:Ag=15½:1*)	
10 Mark (fAu) German Empire		**3.5842g**		x139½=500.000 g	1 Pfund

The development of markets and money (eleventh – sixteenth/ seventeenth centuries)

A rapidly growing population stimulating rising demand as well as increasingly intensive trade connecting more customers, interlinked with an increase in the supply of goods—such facts describe a combination of forces behind the development of markets and money in a changing economic culture between the eleventh and fourteenth centuries.[15]

In this momentous transformation, weights, measures and monies were elementary media of commercial communication and economic exchange. They displayed striking stability. Fundamental numeric traditions were based upon immutable, stable qualities of physical phenomena. They tended to persist, even when the specific practices changed—the only result being an increasing fragmentation of units. In the changing economic order, however, another, a second quality of coined and uncoined metal as money came to the fore: It could not only be used in accordance to its real, traditionally stable ratio of metals, but also according to its nominal 'value', i.e. as virtual media for non-permanent, unstable, dynamically adaptable 'values' of goods and services, which also could be expressed by means of numbers of comparison.[16]

The ratio or exchange-rate of gold and silver itself began to experience noticeable market fluctuations—and the market consequently also began to exert growing influence on the minting policies of sovereigns. But while coinage could be evaluated according to its metal-content, that did not solve the increasing problem of debasement.

While a more dynamic practice developed and money acquired, in effect, a double meaning from the eleventh century onwards, the ratio between gold and silver of 12:1 nevertheless continued to underpin monetary thinking and the idea of currency until the at least the sixteenth century. Hence, the coexistence of more than one economy and different mentalities or cultures in different regions or territories within the German Empire need to be recognised.[17]

15 See, for example, Britnell and Campbell 1995.

16 Witthöft 1993a, 49–59; 2002, 337–339.

17 Witthöft 2001a, 21–25.

The persisting tradition: A monetary order based on numerical ratios of physical phenomena

Only once the obvious and deliberate debasement of the coinage had become practice common throughout Europe did it finally come to be regarded as a disturbing economic problem. From the late fifteenth century onwards, we find evidence for such a change in the sources, both in terms of financially motivated political intervention influencing the monetary system, and in increasing public concern and reaction. Documents illustrate a 'clash of cultures,' that is, a conflict between traditionalists and modernists, between theoreticians and practitioners, concerning right vs. false money, or intrinsic vs. nominal value. Nevertheless, a stable gold-silver-ratio of 12:1 was considered a precondition for sound monetary policy until at least the late sixteenth century, as can be demonstrated for England, France, Germany and Poland.[18]

In 1549 Sir Thomas Smith, the influential Secretary to the Royal English Court, wrote his '*Discourse of the Common Weal*', followed in 1562 by '*The Wages of a Roman Footsoldier*' or '*A Treatise on the Money of the Romans*'. Basing his work on "classical allusions to the value of money" he demonstrates his acquaintance "with the works of Budé, Georgius Agricola, Erasmus, Melanchthon, and Turnstall on coinage."[19] In the '*Discourse*', as well as in the '*Treatise*', Smith comments on the debasement of coinage in his time. He regarded price increases and debasement as interrelated, arguing that the King could never balance losses caused by debasement with profits from minting.

Smith reminded his readers that "the proportion of silver and gold in the coinage was a fixed unalterable ratio of 12 to 1. The *Discourse* states:

> [The relation] '... of silver towardes gold, I thinke, cannot be altered by the auctoritie of anie prince ... Plato ... in his dialouge called Hipparchus, shewethe that the said proportion was in his time betwene silver and gold; and

18 See Witthöft 1993a, 56–59; 2001a, 26–31, 38–42; 1991, 7–15.

19 Dewar 1966, 389 f.; see also Witthöft 1984, 28 f. Summarising a long lasting debate on the publication of "W. S. Gentleman" from 1581, Dewar 1966, 397–399, convincingly argues in favour of Sir Thomas Smith as author and his son William Smith as editor. On the question of contemporary writings and the development of mercantilist ideas see e.g. Stafford 1581/1895, XI–XVIII, and Witthöft 2008b.

> the same is now still, for XII oz. of silver is worthe but one oz. of pure gold at this daye'."[20]

Aristotle (384–322 BC) had regarded money as the general measure of all things. Asking how in Flanders brass-money, made from a cheap alloy, pure silver und pure gold could be traded in the same monetary circuit, Smith assured his readers that it worked by maintaining an adequate ratio between the metals, with, for example, brass and silver as 100:1, silver and gold as 12:1.[21]

In Saxony in Germany, in Poland and in France, we find a similar debate going on. When in 1526 and 1528 Sigismund I., King of Poland (1506–1548), tried to unify the monetary systems of Poland, Lithuania and his Prussian provinces, the decisions were regarded as conforming with the ideas of Nicolaus Copernicus (1473–1543) and based on his gold-silver ratio of 12:1.[22]

A little later, in 1568, Jean Bodin (1530–1596) wrote: "aussi il ne se trouve point de prince qui change la proportion de l'or à l'argent, qui est quasi comme d'un à douze, gardèe en toute Europe."[23] It is worth pointing out that Bodin regarded this gold-silver ratio as a Europe-wide practice.

While rates of exchange of gold and silver on selected markets in the sixteenth and seventeenth centuries certainly did experience some fluctuation, this took place within a comparatively narrow range, so narrow, in fact, that it seems unlikely that pure market forces of demand and supply are reflected here.[24]

20 Dewar 1966, 391 f. In his 'Discourse' he also wrote: "*A man may chaunge the name of thinges but the valew in anie wise ye cannot, to indure for anie space*", and in his 'Treatise': "*Let prince heighten or diminish the coine as they liste. For there is a certain proportion in nature betwixt the raritie and excellence of gold and silver and the plentifulnesse and necessitie of all things which is universall through the whole world and hath and will be so in all ages. Th'estimation which princes give to their coine beside that is an imaginary and vaine thinge and can no long while endure but the longer it doth tarrie after it is spied, the more it turneth to their owne losse. Of the which thinge Englande of late hath had too much experience*" (ibidem, 392).

21 S[tafford] 1581/1895, 111 f.; see also Witthöft 1991, 10.

22 Copernic (1522–1526), XVIII ff.; see also Witthöft 2006, 471 f.; and 1991, 10. For an example from Saxony see below.

23 Bodin 1568, 142; see Metz 1990, 5; also Witthöft 1991, 10.

24 See e.g. the examples given by Metz 1990, 1–53 etc.

In the light of this evidence it is worth noticing that even today a German scholar writing on monetary matters in English will still find it difficult to translate the term 'Währung'. The German meaning encompasses something like 'right money' in a 'durable reliable order', the word still displaying a persistence of the tradition of concepts of 'real', 'intrinsic value.' This is distinctly different from the English meaning of 'monetary order' and 'current money', which goes back to the Latin '*moneta*' or coin.

Fundamental change: dynamic concepts of monetary and economic thinking

Since the shift of the European philosophic-theological centre from Cordoba to Paris and the learned scholastic debates of the twelfth and thirteenth centuries, and up until the reformation of the early sixteenth century, a more rationally abstract economic and monetary thinking had begun to accompany the developing dynamic markets.[25] The older, static and material concept of economic and monetary order had been challenged by an 'artificial', intellectual concept of 'value'.

We know the result: the rise of a modern monetary order embedded in a dynamic market-economy of increasing dominance, which was finally decisively promoted by political economic interest in the period of mercantilism during the seventeenth/eighteenth centuries. But what about the evidence in our context?

An early relevant indication of change in mentality may be detected in the Ebstorf World Map from about 1235. Separate from the image of two walled blocks of buildings representing the Lüneburg Castle and the neighbouring Monastery of St. Michael, we find in writing 'fontes saline' and a drawing of a square structure possibly symbolizing the well and/or a boiling hut. This is the first example of a map of the world, traditionally a representation of Biblical and learned ancient historical content, which reflects the material existence of a Northern German industry. The Benedictine Ebstorf

25 See e.g. Langholm 1992. Authors such as Krings 1982, 11941 not yet reflect the crucial cultural and even theological developments and changes in the middle ages.

Monastery, some 25 km south of Lüneburg, in fact held shares in the Lüneburg saline, from which it drew a considerable income paid as rent.[26]

The change in mentality in how economic matters are represented and reflected in social and religious life, becomes even more evident when exploring the terms used to describe the problem of price changes in times of poor harvests. Such events were a constant threat throughout the period, with hunger the inevitable consequence. In daily life, grain most probably was sold at differing prices depending on a surplus or deficiency ever since Carolingian times.[27] However, the concept of *Teuerung*, conveying the experience of 'dearness' for the phenomenon we would nowadays economically define as 'price increase', is a term that first occurs in sources of the thirteenth century as 'caristia'.[28] Prior to that it was experienced as, and called, hunger ('fames').

Rainer Albertz has kindly confirmed that Martin Luther (1483–1546) translated *Theurung* (dearness) for the Greek word meaning 'hunger' or 'famine'. "The editors of the Bible have meanwhile recognized that Luther's phrasing was influenced by contemporary perception and terminology". A revised edition of the *Old Testament* from 1964 replaced 'Teuerung' (dearness) with 'Hungersnot' (famine), with the *New Testament* following suit from 1984.[29] Costs and prices had considerably increased during the fifteenth and sixteenth centuries, leading to a higher sensitivity to causes and consequences of dearness, as well as to the changing values of precious metals and the debasement of coinage.[30]

About the same time in Saxony, the problem of debasement had led to a debate on 'real' or 'nominal value', i.e. on 'right money' (*rechtes Geld*). In 1530 two pamphlets appeared—thesis and antithesis.[31] The '*Gemeine Stym-*

26 Witthöft 2008a. Even the most recent publication of Kugler 2006 does not comment on this important detail in the representation of the material world—to be found in no other than the Ebstorf world map.

27 Witthöft 1984, 131, 136, 140 ff.; see also Fuhrmann 1996, 126 f., and especially Siems 1992, 384–394 ('Pretium, Preisangaben und Geld') and 749–764 ('Preissetzungen und Steuerung des Handels in Notzeiten').

28 Witthöft 1984, 131.

29 Letter of Rainer Albertz (Siegen, now Münster/Westfalen) of December 20th 1994.

30 Witthöft 2006, 471–479; 2001a, 26–31.

31 Witthöft 1991, pp. 8f.; 2001a, 26–28.

men Von der Müntze' (Common Voices on Coinage) argued, "that the value of a coin, like all other goods made from metal ... has to be measured exactly by its content in silver and metal. .... Eternally like nature, a grain or an ounce of silver remain what they are".[32] *'Die Müntz Belangene'* (Regarding Coinage) responded that "an appeal to the Word of God ... appears to be a cunning argumentation", since "the price of silver under debate for coins of full value has been voluntarily agreed upon by all parties".[33]

In Saxony the interests of merchants and mining-corporations (Berggewerke) stood against the interests of the sovereign, and the idea of a divine, natural reason for a stable exchange rate against the demand for a new, fluctuating and dynamic evaluation of gold and silver in conformity with the market. The arguments advanced in this context already display a predominance of economic and political over philosophical or theological thinking. These texts may be regarded as two of the earliest on monetary theory in Germany; and are certainly among the first documents on mercantilist thoughts within a German territory.[34] They are documents from a period during which German Imperial legislation, in the Coinage Acts from 1561/1566, finally decided on gold and silver as parallel currencies—a fundamental change to the monetary order.[35]

32 Lotz 1893, 10 f. "*Deshalb ist darauf Acht zu geben, daß der Wert der Münze, wie aller aus Metall verfertigter Waren - ja noch mehr denn aller anderen, da es um den allgemeinen Wertmaßstab sich hier handelt - genau nach dem bemessen werde, was die Münze selbst an Silber und Metall enthält. [...] Denn die bloße Prägung oder auch der jeweilige Verkehrskurs der Münze genügt nicht als Grundlage der Wertschätzung und ist vergänglich wie alle anderen Dinge, die auf unbedachter Willkür oder Gewohnheit der Menschen beruhen, der von Gott geschaffenen Natur aber entgegen sind. Ewig wie die Natur bleibt ein Grän oder ein Lot Silber das, was es ist*" (ibid., transferred into modern standard German).

33 Lotz 1893, 24, 26 f., 55, 57. "*Die Einführung des göttlichen Wortes als Grundlage in der Vorrede und die deutsche Kaufmanns- oder Marktschreierpredigt im Verlaufe des Büchleins, ..., kommt einem billig wie schlaue Berechnung vor: [...].*" "*Erstlich ist durchaus keine geringe, sondern billig eine vollwertige Münze in Aussicht genommen, welche nach dem Silberpreis sich richtet. [...] Dieser Preis ist ein freiwillig von den Parteienl vereinbarter und [...] nicht durch gewinnsüchtige Auswucherung oder listigen Eigennutz seitens der Landesherrn verursacht worden*" (ibid., transferred into modern standard German).

34 Lotz 1893, 11 f.; Witthöft 1991, 8 f.; 2001a, 26–28.

35 Witthöft 1993a, 52, 56–59.

In order to trace the links between changes in economic structures and mentality or culture, in this paper I have been looking methodically for an explanation of an apparently trifling but puzzling issue in the terminology of early medieval documents. In pursuing evidence through centuries, a slow fundamental cultural change appears to offer the only adequate explanation. Indeed, after early indications of theological and philosophical reactions to these changes in the medieval scholastic era, monetary matters and the economy as a whole finally became publicly and politically relevant only in early modern times.

A final example from the early seventeenth century has less to do with economics than with culture in its widest sense. In 1615 and 1616 Johannes Kepler (1571–1630) published two studies on the measurement of the wine-barrel.[36] The first treatise, his *Nova Stereometria Doliorum vinariorum,* is a mathematical one. Written in Latin it demonstrates the reliability of the Austrian technique of gauging vessels (*Visierkunst*) "by means of geometric demonstrations according to the art of science" (*mit Geometrischen Demonstrationibus nach art der kunst*).[37] The second, *Außzug auß der Vralten Messe Kunst Archimedis,* written in German, is a traditional post-humanist metrological treatise, tying the Austrian wine-barrel and the metrology of Linz and Lower Austria respectively to a Roman and Greek numeric tradition; referring to Archimedes and the ancient knowledge concerning specific weight, as well as to relevant data.

Hence Kepler wrote two books on the same general topic, addressing two obviously still separate cultures—the *artes liberales* and the *artes mechanicae*—for readers of different social groupings. Both were literate. The dividing line is not between the 'bright and intelligent' on the one hand and the 'dull and stupid' on the other, but between 'art/science' and 'trade/craft', between an 'intellectual' and a 'material culture'—which still existed alongside each other in the seventeenth century![38]

36 Kepler 1615 and 1616.

37 Witthöft 1997b, 116.

38 Witthöft 1997b, 121 "*damit also ein jeder/ nach seinem verstand und glegenheiten/ das Lateinische oder das Teutsche Exemplar/ oder beyde zusamen erkauffen und gebrauchen könde: Verhoffend/ beydes glehrte und Idioten werden mit meinem wolgemeinten fleiß zufriden sein/ und dessen geniessen beim Oesterreichischen külen Wein*" (ibid., p. 116).

Summary

Distinguishing between subsistence and monetary economy, material and intellectual culture, between real/intrinsic and abstract, perception and cognition, acting and thinking, practice and theory, static and dynamic mentality—a discussion of 'function' and 'structure' does indeed lead us to a better understanding of facts and developments of the European economy and monetary matters since Carolingian times.

In medieval and early modern Northern Europe more than one kind of money and economy co-existed at the same time. In the history of culture, we need to recognise that a change in mentality took place from the eleventh century as far as monetary and economic thinking and acting are concerned—a development from a relatively static towards a more dynamic perception and cognition, from a predominantly material culture (*materielle Kultur, civilisation matérielle*) towards a predominantly intellectual culture (*geistige Kultur*). Long-lived traditional notions of the intrinsic values of substances and goods were very gradually replaced by functional conceptions, based on abstract economic thinking.[39]

We may add that the medieval material order remained present in practice beyond the era of mercantilism, far into modern times. But as time went by it appears to have been of different importance for different periods, regions and social-economic strata in Northern Europe, leading to differing standards of development. At the same time, a new economic order gained more abstract 'intellectual' substance, creating a new and increasingly scientific economic terminology.

A dialectic concept of enquiry brings to light a distinct earlier medieval development of money and the economy, whereas up to now history is still being written as a story of the success of a market economy since Roman times. When from the late fifteenth century onwards Europeans began to discover a wider world, they still applied a fundamentally material understanding of monetary and economic matters, deeply rooted in the first millennium AD. Traces of this understanding can be found as late as merchants'

39 See Witthöft 2006, 438–442, 476–479; 2001a, 19–25, 48–52; 1997a, 220–226, 234–237; and especially Braudel 1979.

handbooks of the eighteenth and nineteenth centuries.[40] A cultural dualism and a tension between material and abstract conceptions of values became, and still remain, a characteristic of European thinking.

References

Bodin, Jean (1568). "La response de Maistre Iean Bodin Advocat en la Cour au paradoxe de Monsieur de Malestroit, touchant l'encherissement de toutes choses, & le moyen d`y remédier", Paris. In J.-Y. Le Branchu, *Écrits Notables sur la monnaie XVIe de Copernic a Davanzati.* (Collection des principaux Économistes. Nouvelle Édition), vol. I, Paris 1934, p. 142.

Braudel, Fernand (1979). *Civilisation matérielle, économie et capitalisme. XVe-XVIIe siècle.* Paris.

Britnell, Richard H., and Bruce M. S. Campbell (eds.) (1995). *A Commercialising Economy. England 1086 to c. 1300.* Manchester and New York.

Copernic, Nicolas (1522–1526). "Discours sur la Frappe des Monnaies [= Monete Cutende Ratio]." In J.-Y. Le Branchu, *Écrits Notables sur la monnaie XVIe de Copernic a Davanzati.* (Collection des principaux Économistes. Nouvelle Édition), vol. I, Paris 1934, p. XVIIIff..

Dewar, Mary (1996). "The Authorship of the 'Discourse of the Commonweal'." *Economic History Review* 19: 389ff..

Emmerich, Bettina (2004). *Geiz und Gerechtigkeit. Ökonomisches Denken im frühen Mittelalter* (Beiheft zur Vierteljahrschrift für Sozial- und Wirtschaftsgeschichte 168), Wiesbaden.

Fengler, Heinz, Gerhard Gierow and Willy Unger (1977, [1]1976). *Lexikon der Numismatik*, 2nd ed. Berlin.

Fried, Johannes (1994). *Propyläen Geschichte Deutschlands.* Vol. 1, *Der Weg in die Geschichte. Die Ursprünge Deutschlands bis 1024*, Frankfurt/M. and Berlin (ibid. 'Ordnung des Reiches', pp. 262–324; 'Fernhandel und Städte', pp. 737–766; ,'Kirche und Frömmigkeit', pp. 766–808; 'geistige Kultur', pp. 808–852).

Fuhrmann, Horst (1996). "Der 'schnöde Gewinn' oder das Zinsverbot im Mittelalter." In idem, *Überall ist Mittelalter. Von der Gegenwart einer vergangenen Zeit.* München, pp. 123–149.

Kepler, Johannes (1615). *Nova Stereometria Doliorum vinariorum, in primis Austriaci, figurae omnium aptissimae; et usus in eo virgae cubicae compendiosissimus & plane singularis. Accessit Stereometriae Archimedeae Supplementum.* Linz (Johannes Kepler, Gesammelte Werke IX = Mathematische Schriften, bearb. v. F. Hammer, München 1960, pp. 1–133).

40 Witthöft 2003, part I, 81–113.

Kepler, Johannes (1616). *Außzug auß der Vralten Messe Kunst Archimedis Vnd deroselben newlich in Latein außgegangener Ergentzung, betreffend Rechnung der Cörperlichen Figuren, holen Gefessen vnd Weinfässer, sonderlich deß Oesterreichischen.* Linz.

Krings, Hermann ([1]1941, [2]1982). *Ordo. Philosophisch-historische Grundlegung einer abendländischen Idee.* Second revised edition. Hamburg.

Kugler, Hartmut (ed.) (2006). *Die Ebstorfer Weltkarte.* 2 vols. Berlin.

Langholm, Odd (1992). *Economics in the Medieval Schools. Wealth, Exchange, Value, Money and Usury according to the Paris Theological Tradition 1200–1350.* (Studien und Texte zur Geistesgeschichte des Mittelalters 29), Leiden, New York and Köln.

Lotz, Walther (ed.) (1893). *Die drei Flugschriften über den Münzstreit der sächsischen Albertiner und Ernestiner um 1530* (unter Mitwirkung von Dr. K. F. Jötze) (Sammlung älterer und neuerer Staatswissenschaftlicher Schriften des In- und Auslandes 2), Leipzig.

Metz, Rainer (1990). *Geld, Währung und Preisentwicklung. Der Niederrheinraum im europäischen Vergleich: 1350–1800* (Schriftenreihe des Instituts für bankhistorische Forschung 14), Frankfurt.

Monumenta Germaniae Historica, LL, vol. V, Hannover 1875–1879, reprint 1965.

North, Michael (1994). *Das Geld und seine Geschichte vom Mittelalter bis zur Gegenwart.* München.

Patterson, C. C. (1972). "Silver Stocks and Losses in Ancient and Medieval Times." *Economic History Review* XXV,2 : 205–236.

Pohl, Manfred (2001). "Das Symbol für Freiheit und Stabilität—die D-Mark 1948–2001." In C.-L. Holtfrerich, H. James and M. Pohl, *Requiem auf eine Währung. Die Mark 1873–2001.* Stuttgart and München, pp. 7–59.

S[tafford], W[illiam] (1581/1895). "Eine kurz gefaßte Prüfung von gewissen alltäglichen Beschwerden verschiedener unserer Landsleute in diesen unseren Tagen: ... ." London. In: Emanuel Leser (ed.) and Dr. Hoops (transl.), *William Stafford's Drei Gespräche über die in der Bevölkerung verbreiteten Klagen.* (Sammlung älterer und neuerer Staatswissenschaftlicher Schriften des In- und Auslandes), Leipzig 1895, pp. III–IX, 11–150.

Witthöft, Harald (1979). *Umrisse einer historischen Metrologie zum Nutzen der wirtschafts- und sozialgeschichtlichen Forschung. Maß und Gewicht in Stadt und Land Lüneburg, im Hanseraum und im Kurfürstentum/Königreich Hannover vom 13. bis zum 19. Jahrhundert* (Veröffentlichungen d. Max-Planck-Instituts f. Geschichte 60,1 and 2), 2 vols., Göttingen.

Witthöft, Harald (1983). "Maß und Gewicht im 9. Jahrhundert. Fränkische Traditionen im Übergang von der Antike zum Mittelalter." *Vierteljahrschrift für Sozial- und Wirtschaftsgeschichte* 70,4 : 457–482.

Witthöft, Harald (1984). *Münzfuß, Kleingewichte, pondus Caroli und die Grundlegung des nordeuropäischen Maß- und Gewichtswesens in fränkischer Zeit* (Sachüberlieferung u. Geschichte. Siegener Abhandlungen z. Entwicklung d. materiellen Kultur 1), Ostfildern.

Witthöft, Harald (1985). "Die Rechnung und Zahlung mit Gold und Silber nach Zeugnissen des 6. bis 9. und 13./14. Jahrhunderts." *Hamburger Beiträge zur Numismatik* 30/32 (1976/1978): 9–36.

Witthöft, Harald (1991). "Gold.Silber..Gold...Geld.... Vom Grunde eines uralten Vertrauens." *Geld (Diagonal. Zeitschrift der UGH Siegen)*, Siegen, pp. 7–16.

Witthöft, Harald (1993a). "Die Münzordnungen und das Grundgewicht im Deutschen Reich vom 16. Jahrhundert bis 1871/72." In E. Schremmer (ed.), *Geld und Währung vom 16. Jahrhundert bis zur Gegenwart*. (Beiheft z. Vierteljahrschrift für Sozial- und Wirtschaftsgeschichte 106), Stuttgart, pp. 45–68.

Witthöft, Harald, u.a. (1993b). *Handbuch der historischen Metrologie*. Vol. 2, *Deutsche Maße und Gewichte des 19. Jahrhunderts. Nach Gesetzen, Verordnungen und autorisierten Publikationen deutscher Staaten, Territorien und Städte*, part 1 (= *Die Orts- und Landesmaße. Mit ausgewählten Daten und Texten zur Vereinheitlichung und Normierung von deutschen Maßen und Gewichten seit dem 16.Jahrhundert*), St. Katharinen.

Witthöft, Harald (1997a). "Denarius novus, modius publicus und libra panis im Frankfurter Kapitulare. Elemente und Struktur einer materiellen Ordnung in fränkischer Zeit." In R. Berndt (ed.), *Das Frankfurter Konzil von 794. Kristallisationspunkt karolingischer Kultur*. (Quellen und Abhandlungen zur mittelrheinischen Kirchengeschichte 80), Teil I = Politik und Kirche, Mainz, pp. 219–252.

Witthöft, Harald (1997b). "Johannes Kepler über Messen und Wiegen—metrologische Aspekte einer geistigen und materiellen Kultur in Zeiten des Wandels (1605–1627)." In H.-J. Gerhard (ed.), *Struktur und Dimension. Festschrift für K. H. Kaufhold* 1. (Beiheft z. Vierteljahrschrift für Sozial- und Wirtschaftsgeschichte 132/1), Stuttgart, pp. 111–137.

Witthöft, Harald (2001a). "Die Währung in sich wandelnden Wirtschaftsordnungen im Fränkischen und Deutschen Reich zwischen dem 8. und dem 16./17. Jahrhundert." In J. Schneider (ed.), *Öffentliches und privates Wirtschaften in sich wandelnden Wirtschaftsordnungen.* Stuttgart, pp. 19–52.

Witthöft, Harald (2001b). "Maß und Gewicht [zwischen Römerzeit und Mittelalter]." *Reallexikon der Germanischen Altertumskunde* vol. 19, second edition, Berlin and New York, pp. 398–418.

Witthöft, Harald (2002). "Münzfuß [im frühen Mittelalter]." *Reallexikon der Germanischen Altertumskunde* vol. 20, second edition, Berlin and New York, pp. 337–350.

Witthöft, Harald, u.a. (2003). *Handbuch der historischen Metrologie*. Vol. 5, *Johann Christian Nelkenbrechers Taschenbuch eines Banquiers und Kaufmanns in zwanzig Auflagen, Berlin 1762–1890. Ein synoptisches Handbuch. Maß und Gewicht ausgewählter Finanz- und Handelsplätze,*

Territorien und Staaten Europas 1762–1890, part 1 (= *Der 'Nelkenbrecher' und die kaufmännische Metrologie. Einrichtung und Inhalt, Würdigung und Kritik des Taschenbuchs.* Mit Übersichten und Tabellen von K. J. Roth, erweitert um bibliographische Daten und ausgewählte Titelblätter durch H. Homann), St. Katharinen.

Witthöft, Harald (2006). "Über Korn und Brot—Geld und Münze. Rechte Zahl und *aequalitas* als gerechter Preis in Mittelalter und Neuzeit." *Vierteljahrschrift für Wirtschafts- und Sozialgeschichte* 93,4: 438–479.

Witthöft, Harald (2008a). "Lüneburg in Saxony: A Medieval Saline in Northern Europe in its Changing Cultural and Economic Setting (10th–14th century)." In Shuicheng Li and Lothar von Falkenhausen (eds.), *The Ancient Salt Industry of the Sichuan Basin in Comparative Perspective* (Salt Archaeology in China 2), [in print].

Witthöft, Harald (2008b). „Merkantilistische Vorstellungen bei Georgius Agricola? Von Gütern und Geld, Handel und Preisen aus Perspektiven langer Dauer und kurzer Zeiten." In Angelika und Ekkehard Westermann (eds.), *Wirtschaftslenkende Montanverwaltung—fürstlicher Unternehmer—Merkantilismus.* (3. Internationale Bergbautagung, Steinhaus 2007), [in print].

Shogunal Administration of Copper in the Mid-Tokugawa Period (1670–1720)

Bettina Gramlich-Oka

Economic thought of the Tokugawa shogunate (1600–1868) is not well documented and thus not well studied. In the paper, I use foreign trade policies to deduce the economic thinking behind shogunal policies. Historians commonly divide the policies into three stages: expanding volume of imports under the first shogun, then taking greater control of the import trade under the third shogun, and last the time of gradual restriction and limitation beginning around 1670 until the end of the Tokugawa reign. The reason for the latter policy of curtailment is in general attributed to the fear of depleting the country of its precious metals through their excessive export, which suggests that the shogunate was following the economic idea of negative mercantilism. In the following I investigate the shogunal copper policies between 1670 and 1720 in order to offer some new insights into the historical perception of shogunal economic thought.

1. Foreign trade regulations and copper exports

During the Tokugawa period (1600–1868) the political economic views of the shogunate in regard to foreign trade varied depending on the domestic and external political and economic conditions. Historians commonly divide the policies into three stages: expanding volume of imports under the first shogun Ieyasu 家康 (1542–1616), then taking greater control of the import trade under the third shogun Iemitsu 家光 (1604–1651), and last the time of gradual restriction and limitation which would begin around 1670 and last until the end of the Tokugawa reign. The reason for the latter policy of curtailment is, in general, attributed to the fear of depleting the country of its precious metals through their extensive export. As a countermeasure, by achieving self-sufficiency the trade should be reduced. Simply put, the rhetoric of autarky and bullionism are used to explain the economic thought behind shogunal policies from around 1670 until the end of the Tokugawa period.[1] Self-sufficiency was never achieved, however. The scale of silk

1 For this view, see, for instance, Shimada 2006, 61 or Nakai 1988, 111.

imports in the seventeenth century was replaced with cotton, sugar, and silver in the eighteenth and early nineteenth century.[2] The trade volume, first fixed in 1685, too, designated rather a particular point in time than a policy that would be continued until the fall of the Tokugawa shogunate. Over the subsequent 150 years, trade through Nagasaki would at times expand and at times decrease.[3] At the same time, the main articles of export trade changed. What was first mainly silver was replaced with gold and copper in varying proportions, and also with other commodities such as camphor, porcelain, and especially sea products, until the late mid-nineteenth century.[4] Perhaps, bullionism and in particular self-sufficiency do not satisfactorily explain policies of the shogunate in regard to its Nagasaki trade over time.[5]

Another view identifies the logic behind shogunal policies as a means to support the economy of the city of Nagasaki and to maintain and control political relations with foreign countries. As Robert L. Innes has pointed out, the interest in foreign trade by the shogunate first and foremost was defined by issues of political control. He distinguishes between four objectives of the shogunate: the continuation of trade to supply the shogunate with its desired supplies of silk, medicine, and other sundries, the preservation of domestic order, the assurance of national security, and the enhancement of Tokugawa legitimacy (by cutting out other lords from the involvement and profits in the trade conducted through Nagasaki). These four objectives at times conflicted but all were mostly concerned with imports.[6]

The reason for these assumptions about underlying shogunal policies results from the lack of explicit sources about economic thought among the high officials who ordered these regulations. What we can distinguish after

2 See Innes 1980, Chapter 5, which deals with silk and sugar. In particular in regard to sugar, see 504–518. For instance, sugar imports were raised in the Shōtoku regulations of 1715 from 3,500,000 *kin* to 4,500,000 *kin*. Higuchi 1956, 309. For units see Appendix.

3 In the Jōkyō regulation of 1685 the trade was limited for the first time by quantity: the Dutch East India Company (VOC) was allowed to trade 3,000 *kanme* and the Chinese merchants 6,000 *kanme*. For trade regulations and units see Appendix.

4 The devastating Meireki fire (1656) in Edo may have enhanced the worry of depleting metals. During the fire the gold and silver reserves kept in the Edo castle melted.

5 See for instance Suzuki 2004. See also Hellyer 2005, 84.

6 Innes 1980, 217. Here and in the following I deal only with Nagasaki, which was a shogunal city. The other three windows to foreign countries, Satsuma, Tsushima, and Matsumae, were under domainal jurisdiction.

1670 is the period of greater involvement by the government in foreign trade, when the shortage of Chinese supply due to the *qianjie* 遷界 (move the frontier) order of 1661 led to price inflation of imported goods. In response, in 1672 the shogunate changed trade regulation from a more liberal regulation to the so-called Market Trade System (*kamotsu shihō* 貨物市法 or *Taxatie Handel* in Dutch).[7] In this system, the most noticeable change from the former policies is that now the transactions of the imports were supervised by the office of the magistrate of Nagasaki in order to prevent overbidding. This was the first step of the shogunate to intervene in the pricing of all goods.[8] The wholesalers of the five shogunal cities, Osaka, Kyoto, Sakai, Edo, and Nagasaki, were permitted to participate in auctions, put in their bids, and the lowest would be chosen to be presented to, and hopefully be approved by, the magistrate's office. The price would then be posted openly to prevent speculation and presented to the foreigners who could either accept the offer and the transaction would take place, or reject in which case it was canceled. In order to be able to participate in bidding, one had to be a member of a guild, which limited the number of participants. The office of the five chambers of the city (*gokasho kaisho* 五ヶ所会所) would then actualize the trade.[9]

In general this new regulation is interpreted as having a second aim, not only to react to the rather free trade transactions of the former rules that caused price inflation, but also to halt the outflow of bullion.[10] This view is based on the fact that the shogunate faced reduced production of precious metals concurrent with the extensive outflow of bullion. As indicated in Table 1, in particular silver outflow increased drastically after 1658, reaching its peak in 1661.

7 Innes 1980, 306.

8 A different type of intervention was the shogunal practice of purchasing large amounts of silk to manipulate the domestic yarn price. Innes 1980, 255–256.

9 Innes 1980, 305–309.

10 Certainly, the shogunate had its merchants in Nagasaki who were also privileged to purchase for the shogun silk, medicine, books etc., before other wholesalers were permitted to trade. This is different though from direct government involvement.

Table 1 Silver Exports 1640–1672

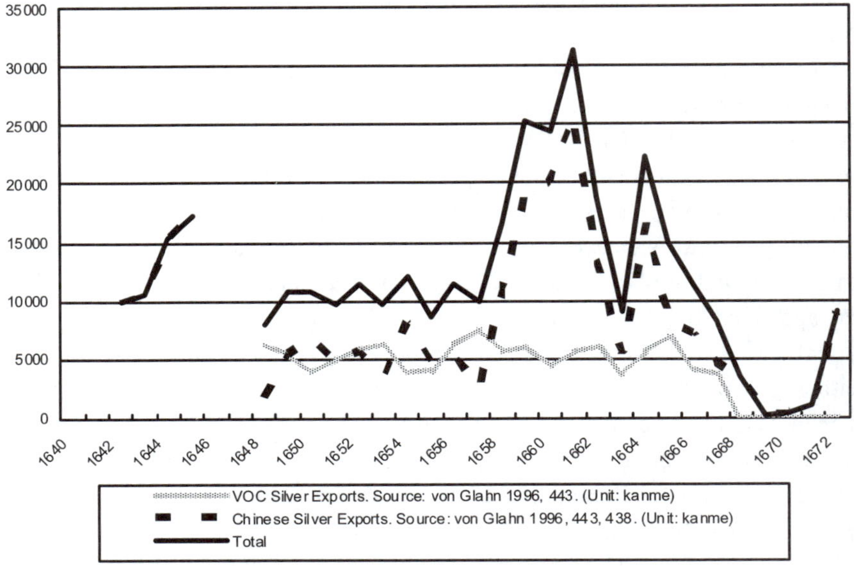

Even if in the higher ranks of the shogunate the notion of bullionism developed, to put it into practice was a different matter. Some of the policies would seem inconsistent if not contradictory. For instance, the shogunal worry over depleting silver advanced the idea to abolish the prohibition of gold exports in 1664.[11] The outflow of silver was much higher because it fetched a better price in Asia, thus silver was the main concern of the shogunate. Since the success was minimal, in 1668 the shogunate decided to ban the export of silver, which caused protests from the foreigners, most strongly from the Chinese merchants. While the Dutch East India Company (VOC)

11 Innes 1980, 302. The exchange rate of silver and gold on the various Asian markets is the significant factor. The ban of gold exports was promulgated in 1641, since gold/silver price ratio equalized throughout East Asia and the Dutch had thus a greater interest in exporting gold. Other reasons, Innes conjures, was the intention of the shogunate to strike gold coins and to demonstrate that gold was superior to silver. By exporting silver, the price of gold would rise. Innes 1980, 591.

had already seen an opportunity to make profit with gold coins (*koban* 小判), the Chinese merchants insisted on silver due to its favorable price on the Chinese market.[12] Under pressure from the Chinese traders, perhaps, silver export recommenced in 1671.[13] At the same time, the new shogunal intervention into the actual trade by limiting the number of Japanese merchants and representing the middlemen between the two parties of merchants was supposed to further hinder the outflow of silver and gold. In lowering the prices of the import goods artificially, less bullion volume was expected to be exported.[14]

Table 2 VOC Gold Exports 1665–1753

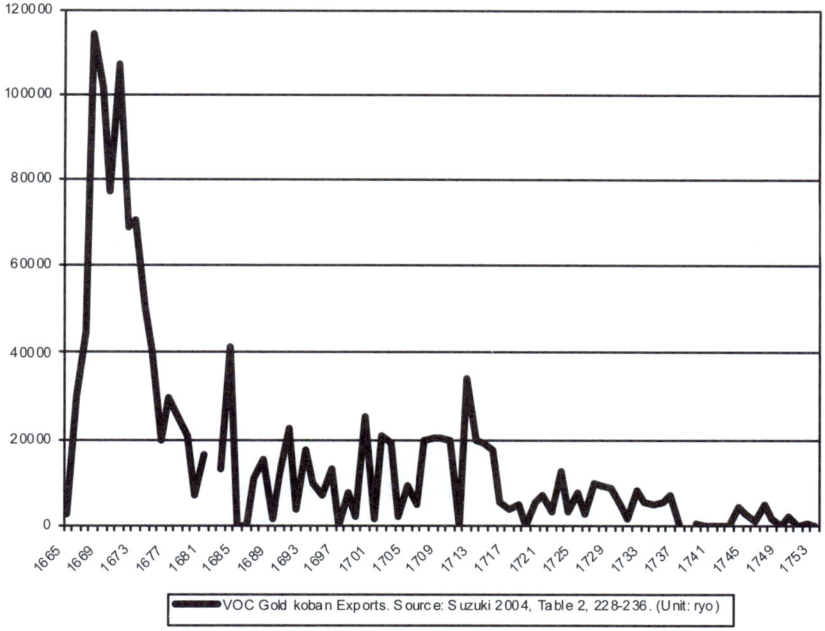

12 See Innes 1980, 410. For the Dutch, see Suzuki 2004, chapter 5, which deals with the Japanese gold coins (*koban*) on the Asian market. See also Glamann 1953, 45, where he explains that the loss of Formosa in 1665 interrupted the gold purchases from the Chinese.

13 See Yao 1998, 58.

14 Yamawaki 1964, 36–39.

While positive results were achieved, they remained limited. Since there was no intention to limit trade per se, the main problem was that the Japanese side had no goods to offer as an alternative to bullion to sustain the same trade volume. As a result, the outflow of silver and gold continued. This was to change however. Copper was to become the commodity that catered to foreign demands as well as demonstrated the convenience to be available in great quantities for supply. In the following I will outline the copper administration in order to see if we can identify a leading economic thought behind the shogunate's policies.

2. Copper, the substitute export commodity

Copper is a different medium than gold or silver. Though part of the trimetallic currency system in Tokugawa Japan, its value was low and it was not considered a precious metal. For instance, Arai Hakuseki 新井白石 (1657–1725), who is often (though undeservedly) branded as the father of bullionist thought, mentions the importance of gold and silver, but disregards copper:[15]

> Past generations in that country have regarded gold and silver, of all things between heaven and earth, as most like the bones of the body. Although injured, blood, flesh, skin, and hair reproduce again and again. ... Once broken and lost, however, there is no such thing as a bone growing again. Gold and silver are the bones of nature.[16]

In the famous quote Hakuseki excludes copper from the comparison that defines gold and silver as irreplaceable and precious. This becomes all the more evident when he continues that Tokugawa Ieyasu's last testament "praised Japan's gold and silver as superior to that of all other nations and

15 See, for instance, Shimada 2006, 61, who calls Hakuseki the first bullionist.

16 Translation by Innes 1980, 298. Out of *Honchō hōka tsūyō jiryaku* 本朝宝貨通用事略 in *Hakuseki zenshū*, vol. 3, 673–674. Certainly, there are also times, when Hakuseki refers to all the five metals, or gold and silver together with copper. Yet, from the overall statements, Hakuseki, as well as other thinkers of his time, observed that copper is not valued the same as gold and silver.

stressed that the nation's treasure should be hoarded forever after."[17] Gold and silver were considered—by Hakuseki and others—as a treasure, whereas copper was regarded as a medium of exchange.[18] When we consider the trade regulations, in particular, we can discern how copper was indeed regarded inferior to gold and silver.

Officially, the administration of a copper mine was similar to that of gold and silver mines. Mines were considered as belonging to public interest (*kōgi* 公儀), which was represented by the shogunate. Yet the mines on domainal lands were under the individual public authority of the lord. The balance of these two claims of authority was not constant, and in particular in case of gold and silver mines the Tokugawa shogunate from early on emphasized its political weight. Copper mines, however, developed mostly later.[19] Copper mines were subjected to the same regulations, including the necessity of shogunal approval for the opening and closing of mines, irrespective of whether they were located on shogunal or domainal land. The shogunal interest, however, was not as invested, since copper was not considered as a source of wealth.[20] As Shimada Ryuto has shown, interest in opening copper mines was less pronounced than silver or gold mines until the demand for copper in various countries in Asia, was brought to the attention in Nagasaki, beginning more overtly in the 1660s.[21] Prior to this period,

17 Innes 1980, 299.

18 Scholars before and after Hakuseki describe how society engages in hoarding gold and silver, but not copper or iron. Perhaps the fact that copper coins have been long used on the archipelago as money may play a role in this perception.

19 Often copper mines were formerly gold and/or silver mines.

20 About mining see Kobata 1968, 8–14. About 'public interest', see Nakai 1988, 129–131. Minting of copper coins, too, was handled similarly like a stepchild of the shogunate. In the case of silver and gold early on, the shogunate minted its own currency and opened the semi-official operations of the *kinza* 金座 and *ginza* 銀座 (gold and silver monopoly functioning as agency and mint). The *kinza* (gold mint) was opened in 1594 by Tokugawa Ieyasu for his minting of gold coins. The *ginza* (silver mint) was opened in 1601 in Fushimi and moved in 1608 to Kyoto where it remained until 1800. Another *ginza* was opened in Sumpu, later moved to Edo. During the Genroku period the *ginza* came under the supervision of the commissioners of finance (*kanjō bugyō*). All these offices were semi-official. The minting of shogunal copper coins, however, was initially undertaken by a domain mint (Mito) in 1636. By the 1650s sixteen copper coin mints (*zeniza* 銭座) were permitted to strike shogunal coins *Kan'ei tsūhō* 寛永通宝.

21 Shimada 2006, 14.

copper had been exported either in the form of copper coins (domestic and foreign), or more commonly as refined copper, in form of staffs (*saodō* 棹銅).[22] The export of staff copper began in 1646, after the shogunate had lifted a nine year long ban of copper exports. Between 1638 and 1646, the government, in order to secure the procurement of copper for the minting of a new copper coin, had banned the export of copper; a ban that according to Imai Noriko was lifted owing to petitions by copper merchants and refiners.[23] From 1646 onwards, it was left up to these copper merchants to directly sell to the Dutch and Chinese. The copper trade was run, as the trade in camphor and other commodities, by specialized merchants.

Another landmark in favor of the leading copper merchants was the decree, which was promulgated sometime between 1646 and 1650, by the Nagasaki magistrate that all export copper was to be processed by Osaka refiners whose performance demonstrated an efficient refining technique to extract as much silver as possible from the copper ore.[24] As a result of this decision copper refining came to be concentrated in Osaka and the group of refiners limited. Since the 1650s the copper trade in refined copper expanded and the group of specialized copper merchants—most famously the Izumi-ya 泉屋 (Sumitomo) family—became increasingly visible in the sources.

Similar to requests of the licensed cartel of silk traders, the shogunate's responses to the copper merchants' requests were usually positive. For instance, as part of sumptuary laws against luxury, the Nagasaki import and export was drastically reduced, including a second ban of copper exports, postulated in 1668/3, as part of a larger set of prohibitions including the export of silver.[25] However, the ban on copper was lifted the following year, since the price of copper went down and the smelters complained to the sho-

22 About the export of copper coins by the VOC, see for instance Innes 1980, Table 35, 531: almost 27 million pieces in 1665 and 20 million pieces in 1666.

23 Imai 1999, 193. The shogunate permitted the city of Nagasaki to cast coins designated for trade from 1659 to 1685, also called 'Nagasaki trade coins', to avoid the export of its new copper currency the *Kan'ei tsūhō*. Munro 1904, 156. The earlier copper ban (from 1638 until 1646) concerned not copper per se but copper coins (which were exported to Central Vietnam by *shuin-sen* ships and the VOC) because the minting of the new coin, *Kan'ei tsūhō*, from 1636–1670. Yoon 1995, 124.

24 Innes 1980, 594–595.

25 One edict can be found in *Ofuregaki Kampō shūsei*, 970. See Yao 1998, 60, for the varying sources that list the prohibited items. For convention of dates see Appendix.

gunate that their business was jeopardized.[26] Due to a combination of the ban of silver exports in 1668, the artificially maintained exchange rate,[27] and the rise in available copper for export, the copper merchants achieved increasing profits. In particular, the Dutch were now more interested in purchasing copper than expensive gold. Accordingly, the number of merchants involved in the copper trade increased. The trade in Nagasaki was certainly of concern to the shogunate, but as long as some degree of control seemed secured the interests of those involved, such as the Nagasaki citizens or guild merchants, were given priority.[28]

Copper was the second largest export product after silver but it was not until the time period between 1668 and 1684 that the export of copper had multiplied from 1.1 million to 4.9 million *kin*. While copper began to replace silver and later gold for export, the metal was a commodity produced mainly for export.[29] As mentioned above, with the new regulation of 1672 the shogunate reached a degree of success in reducing silver exports.[30] Tables 1 and 3 show that the volume of copper export to Chinese merchants doubled, while the export of silver dropped from 15,082 *kanme* in 1672 to 9,982 *kanme* in 1682. This effect probably was connected with renewed warfare in southern China, since only 26 Chinese ships called on Nagasaki harbor in 1682, while in sharp contrast to the 43 ships that had dropped anchor in 1672. (Table 1) As a result, however, we can assume that the export of silver was reduced by about thirty percent.[31] In regard to Dutch gold exports, too,

26 *Taigaikankeishi sōgō nenpyō*, 672, Izumi-ya received already two months later, 1668/5/6, the permit to trade copper as before.

27 In fear that the import prices would rise, the shogunate, as part of the new regulations of the Market Trade System, decided in 1672 that the Dutch, who could only trade in gold, had to change 1 *ryō* (1 *koban*) gold for 68 *monme* silver, and the Chinese who were permitted to trade in silver again since 1671 were allowed to exchange according to the market rate of 1 *ryō* for 56 *monme*. Kobata 1957, 30–41. See also Glamann 1953, 45. Dutch made high profits with the gold coin at the Coromandel Coast, in particular since its former supply of Chinese gold through Formosa was lost in 1665, while for the Chinese merchants the gold price in China was cheaper than in Japan and thus not profitable to import.

28 Yoon 1995, 116. Ōta 1992, 144–146.

29 Yoon 1995, 126. For units see Appendix.

30 This can be said only for Nagasaki. See about the silver export through Tsushima to the Korean Peninsula, Tashiro 1970, 88–114.

31 Ōta 1992, 236–237. For units see Appendix.

the amount was reduced from 5,964.000 *kanme* in 1668 down to 1,436.636 *kanme* in 1679.[32] (Table 2)

The Jōkyō 貞享 regulations of 1685 were intended to further consolidate and regulate this trend in the configuration of foreign trade. With the fixation of the trade volume (ceiling trade *jōdaka* 定高) the shogunate meant to further stall the export of precious metals through Chinese and Dutch merchants. The ceiling was set at 9,000 *kanme* (6,000 *kanme* for the Chinese and 3,000 *kanme* for the VOC), which is based on the amount traded in the previous years and functioned as the indicator of how much was necessary and desirable to be traded. Not the volume itself but the kind of payment should be changed and thus, what had been paid for in silver and gold before now was to be exchanged for refined copper and other products, mainly sea products such as sea cucumber, dried abalone, shark fillets, and seaweed.[33]

The true reasons for the ceiling regulation, however, remain a conjecture since there are no sources that allow for a concrete conclusion. The common argument is that the trade ceiling was implemented because of the fear that trade could get out of control when in 1684 the Qing government renounced the 1661 ban on sea traffic after the unification of the Qing empire was achieved. In 1684 the government announced the *zhanhai* 展海 (expand to the sea) order and Nagasaki could anticipate a higher volume of Chinese ships calling on its harbor.[34] That the ceiling trade regulation was not a well-structured and sound plan can be surmised from the fact that already in 1688 the shogunate had to reconsider its policy and make adjustments with the system of *waritsuke* 割付 (allotment) for the Chinese merchants. In 1685, twelve Chinese vessels had to be turned away, since the volume of 6,000 *kanme* had been reached with the first 73 ships. In 1688, the peak number of Chinese ships was reached, with 192 vessels, of which 75 had to be turned away. The shogunate therefore limited the number to seventy ships, divided by port of origin, season of the year, and individual ceilings, hence

32 Innes 1980, 527.

33 Ceilings were also set for Tsushima (1,080 *kanme*), and Ryukyu (804 *kanme*).

34 Hall 1946, 452. Hall mentioned that the "Emperor himself ordered the Amoy and Foochow authorities to fit out thirteen junks with cargoes of sugar and silk for Japan" in 1685. See also Ōba 1980, 30–32 or Ōba 1996, 52. See Appendix.

waritsuke.[35] The Japanese side meant thereby to insure receiving the variety of products it desired. Furthermore, the shogunate declared another important change in the trade pattern for both Dutch and Chinese merchants, the quota of imports. One third of the value of total imports had to be silk yarn, one third silk fabrics, and one third medicinal drugs and sundries. Again, it appears that the quotas were based on the amount of imports from previous years.[36]

Considering the reduction in the export of precious metals the ceiling trade system was certainly efficient and a success. In 1686 only 597 *kanme* of silver were exported by the Chinese, in 1694 as little as 65 *kanme* (Table 1). The total between the years of 1685 and 1697 was 3,973 *kanme*, on average about 305 *kanme* annually, while in the twelve preceding years, under the market trade regulation, about 6,000 *kanme* left Nagasaki each year.[37] The Dutch, who were no longer allowed to export silver from 1668, also took less gold coins than before owing to the new regulations.[38] (Table 2)

Nevertheless, the ceiling trade still caused problems that may not have been foreseeable. The ships that were not able to sell their goods returned home or, more often, engaged in smuggling. While the Dutch trade was already tightly regulated through the establishment of Deshima, the Chinese trade appears to have been subjected to only limited control. Since their trade was decentralized and a third of the trade was conducted through innkeepers doubling as brokers, with the opening of the Chinese quarter (*tōjin yashiki* 唐人屋敷) in 1689 smuggling was theoretically undermined, as at least the innkeepers now were kept from a direct contact with Chinese merchants.[39] Another reason for opening the Chinese quarter, Yamawaki Teijirō conjures, was that by keeping the merchants together it became possible to consolidate the price of copper.[40]

35 Innes 1980, 322–323.

36 Innes 1980, 508. Yamawaki 1964, 55.

37 Numbers are rounded, Yamawaki 1964, 57. In the following years approximately 2 *kanme* per junk was exported which makes annually about 160 *kanme*.

38 About 5,087 *ryō* were exported which breaks down annually to about 120 *ryō*. The highest amount is about 20,000 *ryō*. Ōta 1992, 468–469.

39 Yamawaki 1964, 73–75. See Chang 1970, 142.

40 Yamawaki 1964, 77–78. For instance, for the year 1699, we have the price posting to the gate of the Chinese settlement as 100 *kin* of copper for 104.4 *monme*.

Table 3 Copper Exports 1640–1818

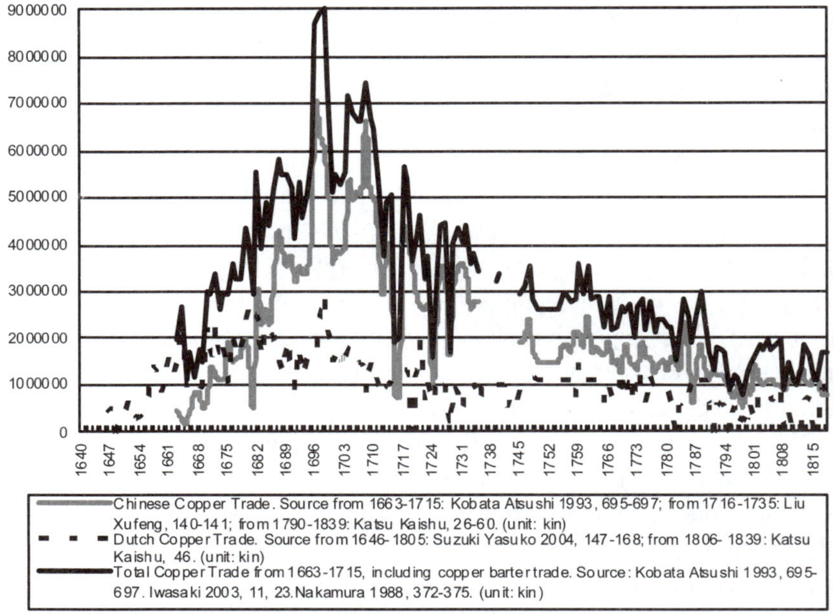

Copper had replaced silver and gold as an export product, and the regulations show that there was no intention on the part of the shogunate to stop its outflow. Rather, copper export was encouraged. After the implementation of the artificial exchange rate of gold versus silver and the prohibition of Dutch silver exports, copper export increased (Table 3). With it increased also the need for organization. After a petition to the Osaka city magistrate, sixteen copper businesses (including merchants, refiners, and miners) were chosen to form a licensed cartel or guild of copper traders (*dōfukiya nakama* 銅吹屋仲間) in 1678.[41] With the new regulations of 1685, various other mer-

41 The meaning of the guild was not to regulate all the copper merchants in the country. Rather the group petitioned to the shogunate in order to become stronger against other copper merchants. Basically, only these sixteen members or those who received from them a share were allowed to conduct the Nagasaki copper trade, but according to Imai Noriko, there were still copper merchants in Edo or Nagasaki who received a license, such as in 1697. While the cartel had to cope with it, realistically without its help the delivery to Nagasaki was not possible. Imai 1999, 193; and Imai 1989, 11.

chants from the shogunal cities and copper refiners came up with plans to conduct the export trade as well, but the guild protested. The shogunate granted their petition, and contracted even the copper of the Ashio mine to be refined by the guild.[42] This decision confirmed the refiners' guild dominance over other copper merchants, at least for the time being.

There is much room for doubt if the shogunate had a clear economic view on how to conduct its export policies beyond a general intention to halt the export of precious metals. Trial and error seems to have dictated a rather practical path of policies. In this context, currency reforms which began in 1695 seem to have importantly influenced decisions. Already in the 1660s the goldsmiths had petitioned to the shogunate that the ratio of the precious metals for coins should be depreciated and in 1692 the silversmiths repeated their petition.[43] With the debasement of the currency the interest of foreign merchants to trade their goods for the new currency sank. This made copper the more attractive form of payment. The debasement thus impacted foreign trade while the reason for the debasement cannot directly be related to the trade itself.[44] In general it is argued that silver and gold mines' output was in decline, thus the shortage of newly available gold and silver may have led to the debasement. Nevertheless, it has also been argued that the need for a larger quantity of money supply due to increasing economic transactions and the anticipation of shogunal revenues for the depleted treasury were likely reasons as well.[45] The Genroku 元禄 debasement was the first in Japanese history and while Chinese sources may have given the officials in charge some blueprints about what to expect, the experience was certainly untested and experimental.

42 Imai 1989, 11.

43 *Ofuregaki Kampō shūsei* (no. 1757), 892.

44 The exchange of the old with the new currency took place mainly between 1696 and 1697, for foreigners it began in 1698.

45 See in general for numbers, Kobata 1968, 196, and Innes 1980, 562, for the Ikuno silver mine from 1683–1715. See Innes 1980, Table 36, 557, for Sado mine's silver and gold output from 1602–1715.

3. Copper barter trade

While the shogunate was interested in cutting down exports of precious metals, it saw in copper the ideal commodity to maintain foreign trade and therefore promoted its export.[46] This is particularly supported by the shogunal response to a petition in 1695 to permit a copper barter trade (*dō shiro-monogae* 銅代物替). The shogunate was petitioned by Fushimi-ya 伏見屋, a merchant house from Edo, to arrange an unofficial copper trade, since due to the new trade limitation abundant amounts of copper were available. As a voluntary business levy the merchant offered a certain percentage of his profit.[47]

As Ōta Katsuya argues, it is important to recognize that the ceiling trade cannot simply be reduced to the political intention to avoid metal exports, but was a search for a new way to pay for imports.[48] Even if the shogunate was interested in cutting the export of silver and gold and the trade ceiling of 1685 is decisive, it permitted barter trade soon after, which did not reduce but actually expanded trade. The additional amount of copper used in barter emphasizes that the government had found the commodity that could replace silver and gold while being acceptable for both parties of the trade (Table 4).

These conditions did not last long, however. As with the regulations of 1685, repeatedly the shogunate had to reconsider its former regulations. The merchant house Fushimi-ya, which was not part of the copper guild, already by the following year encountered difficulties to finance and supply Nagasaki with the fixed amount of copper. Thus, in the eighth month of 1697 the shogunate ordered its new assessment.[49] In the reform edict of 1697/8 (Ōta calls it the Genroku Foreign Trade Reform), the shogunate fixed the barter trade to 5,000 *kanme* (4,200 *kanme* worth of copper could be sold to

46 In 1685/9 Osaka copper merchants mentioned in their petition to the Osaka city magistrate Kai Masachika 甲斐正親 that there were fifty copper mines delivering to them and annually they received about 9,000,000 *kin*. From this they refined 1,000,000 *kin* for domestic use and the remainder of about 8,000,000 *kin* would be shipped to Nagasaki.

47 The source of the petition is reproduced by Ōta 1992, 345–346. Fushimi-ya offered to pay royalties of 1,500 *ryō* per 1,000 *kanme* of copper sold.

48 Ōta 1992, 414.

49 The edict was pronounced a couple of months later by the Nagasaki city magistrate to the city elders of Nagasaki (1697/12). The edict is reproduced in Ōta 1992, 371–372; *Tokugawa kinreikō*, 414.

the Chinese merchants and 800 *kanme* to the VOC), with a fee, or royalty (*Nagasaki unjōkin* 長崎運上金), to the shogunate of 45,000 *ryō*, from which 10,000 *ryō* were to go to the city of Nagasaki.[50] (See Table 5) Three merchants from Edo were made responsible for the transport of copper over the next seven years. In the following year, after having raised the official trade volume of 9,000 *kanme* to 14,000 *kanme*, Edo decided that 8,902,000 *kin* of copper (2,500,000 *kin* for the VOC and 6,402,000 *kin* for the Chinese) for export should be provided, based again most probably on the amount delivered the previous year. This amount has to be understood as the total of official trade and copper barter trade. A little less than half of the copper was used in barter and was thus outside of the 9,000 *kanme* ceiling cap. The copper delivered was now regarded as shogunal copper (conspicuously called 'shogunal copper', *goyōdō* 御用銅), regardless of whether it was sold under the official trade or barter trade and royalties had to be paid for all the copper exported. With this system the shogunate was able to secure a higher amount of the newly established license fee.

Table 4 Copper Barter Trade 1695–1715

Year	Chinese Copper Barter Trade. Source: *Sen'oku sōkō* 18, 28–29 and 124–125. (Unit: *kin*)	VOC Copper Barter Trade. Source: Suzuki 2004, 186. (Unit: *kin*)	Total
1695	701,758	308,639	1,010,397
1696	4,577,823	462,963	5,040,786
1697	4,225,352	733,945	4,959,297
1698	3,925,234	704,846	4,630,080
1699	3,903,950	701,754	4,605,704
1700	2,957,361	672,834	3,630,195
1701	2,755,304	672,834	3,428,138
1702	3,613,513	670,578	4,284,091

50 Ōta 1992, 425 and 447. Of the 9,020,295 *kin* exported in 1698, about half of the copper, 4,630,080 *kin*, was part of the sanctioned barter trade, the other half was traded under the ceiling.

1703	3,710,247	670,578	4,380,825
1704	4,416,961	0	4,416,961
1705	3,997,350	399,495	4,396,845
1706	4,416,961	0	4,416,961
1707	3,708,222	672,834	4,381,056
1708	4,291,157	0	4,291,157
1709	3,677,758	672,834	4,350,592
1710	3,415,061	672,834	4,087,895
1711	3,082,854	168,208	3,251,062
1712	1,851,852	50,251	1,902,103
1713		81,699	81,699
1714		121,556	121,556
1715		121,556	121,556

Yet the problems were not solved. With the amount of copper of 8,902,000 *kin* a peak was reached that could not be repeated. Already in 1699, the year following the new edict, the three merchants had difficulties to transport the copper to Nagasaki on time. By 1700 and 1701, the merchants were not able to deliver the amount that the shogunate anticipated.

Ōta Katsuya remarks that with the permission to Edo merchants the supply system was disrupted. The Osaka copper guild, formerly firmly in control of the copper trade, now saw their privileges taken away. Why the shogunate decided to permit first Fushimi-ya and then three other Edo merchants to conduct the copper barter trade is unknown. Ōta speculates that the connection between Fushimi-ya and the shogun's chamberlain Yanagisawa Yoshiyasu 柳沢吉保 (1658–1714) was not unimportant. The fact that by including new merchants the government could more easily impose the new license fee is certainly another motivation.[51] As a result, Edo undermined the privileges of the guild, causing an impractical situation for the large refiners were all located in Osaka and were members of the guild.

Providing the capital for shipping was another problem that the three Edo merchants failed to solve. In 1698 the guild was ordered to take over the shipping and financing. However, in the following year, the guild, too, could

51 Ōta 1992, 448.

only deliver 5,126,415 *kin*. As indicated in Table 3, the peak of copper delivered to Nagasaki was in 1696 and 1697, but already in 1698 the figures fall, with marked decline setting in by 1700. In 1699, in order to investigate the matter more fully, the superintendent of finance (*kanjō bugyō* 勘定奉行) Ogiwara Shigehide 荻原重秀 (1656–1713; superintendent since 1696), who is one of the key figures for economic reforms during the Genroku period, led an inspection. Shigehide went to Nagasaki via Osaka to investigate the situation himself. After fourteen days he departed leaving two officials behind,[52] and soon after drafted a new edict regarding copper and the *Nagasaki unjōkin*. The edict declares anyone was permitted to undertake shipments of official copper.[53]

There was an increase in demand for copper but the supply soon posed a problem. Not only the transport of copper to Nagasaki, but also its procurement from the mines, when considering the amount that was now annually expected, became problematic. Worried that the most important export commodity might not remain available for long, the shogunate began actively to call upon domains and its own lands to encourage mining. So for instance in the edict of 1698:

> Within the bakufu and domain lands there should be a search for gold, silver, and copper mines. Their development should be reported. Especially in the case of domain mines, daimyo should administer them carefully. If mines are in temple or shrine land, the bakufu deputy in the bakufu land, and the daimyo in the domain land, should manage them.[54]

The interest in mining was—mildly put—low. The fact that copper was mainly intended for export, since the domestic supply was at the time only a tenth of the whole production, plays an important role in the lack of response. The profits made from the export for those directly involved were not high enough to be attractive.

52 Ogiwara Shigehide convened with the Chinese for three days. Since the Chinese had paid 7 *monme* silver as tax (*kōsen* 口銭) for 100 *kin* of copper (1 *monme* went to the interpreters, and 1 *monme* to the rent for the Chinese Quarter), Shigehide decided to reduce the fee by 2 *monme* so the shogunate received only 5 *monme* per 100 *kin*. Kobata 1980, 134, and Ōta 1992, 419–420.

53 The edict (1699/6/15) is reproduced in Ōta 1992, 423.

54 Translation by Yoon 1995, 137. Citation from *Ofuregaki Kampō shūsei* (no. 1765). The first edict (no. 1759) pointed out the lack of enthusiasm on the part of the domains.

4. The opening of the Nagasaki Accounting House

With the 1697/8 reform edict that sanctioned barter trade the shogunate became more directly involved in the Nagasaki export trade. Not only through receiving royalties of the barter trade (*unjōkin*), but also through the opening of a new office that should deal with its affairs in Nagasaki, namely the *Nagasaki kaisho* 長崎会所 (Nagasaki Accounting House) or, as the Dutch called it, the *Geldkamer*.[55] The office was run by local authorities appointed by the magistrate of Nagasaki.[56] In addition to purchasing all Chinese and Dutch imports, the agency also deducted the expenditures of the Dutch before returning the remainder. It thus took over the administration and accounting of the Dutch factory.[57] Since all trade went now through its office, the city, too, came under closer supervision of Edo.[58] From the gross profits, after paying its expenses and the city of Nagasaki, the office sent the

55 Ōta 1992, 412. In 1699 the *Nagasaki unjōkin* became official, but actually according to Ōta, the *Nagasaki kaisho* already collected it previously. In his analysis, Ōta determines that the term *unjōkin* does not appear in the reform edict of 1697/8, but it is evident that the shogunate already secured the profit of which a part went as support to the city of Nagasaki. The shogunate placed an overseer in control of the trade in 1695. The next year this overseer, Takagi Hikoemon, became the controller of the copper barter trade. The *Nagasaki kaisho* was most likely established a couple of months after the edict, probably in the twelfth month of 1697. Therefore, the edict and the opening of the *kaisho* cannot be separated. The *Nagasaki kaisho* was supposed to manage the royalties for the shogunate from the beginning, and not as for instance Yamawaki argues, that there is a gap between the year of the edict and the year the shogunate established the barter trade in 1699 and thus the *Nagasaki kaisho* only later began to manage this task. Takagi became head of the Nagasaki kaisho, in which all financial accounting took now place. *Itowappu* (yarn guild) became a subsidiary organ on its own premises. Ōta 1992, 381, and 416–417.

56 Among the officials were ward elders, Nagasaki *itowappu* elders, the inspectors, the paymasters, the subordinate officials and the experts. See Yao 2000, 60.

57 According to the *Deshima Diary* of 1708/July 1, a reorganization of the *Nagasaki kaisho* took place whereby from now on, the Dutch had to ask for permission to have their allowance. For instance, when they needed money for expenses, such as their annual journey to Edo, they had to put in a request. The *Deshima Diaries*, 564.

58 The maximum the city would receive from trade, rent, etc. was set at 110,000 *ryō*, plus and extra 70,000 *ryō* (or 4,200 *kanme*) as deposit. The remaining profit would be used for salaries and other expenses. See Nagazumi 2000, 63.

proceeds to the shogunate. Its establishment marked a new phase in the series of trade regulations.[59]

The importance of the office becomes more concrete when we consider the amount the *Nagasaki kaisho* paid to the Osaka reserve. As Table 5 indicates the *unjōkin*, initially only applied to the copper barter trade, but soon extended to all copper exports, became a significant source of revenue to the shogunate.

Table 5 *Unjōkin* (License Fee) for Copper[60]

Year	Unit: *ryō*	Year	Unit: *ryō*
1695	1,500	1702	66,024
1696	10,000	1703	67,057
1697	35,000	1708	50,000
1701	60,000	1714	76,234

Perhaps triggered by the opening of the copper mine of Besshi in 1691, the shogunate assumed that a constant supply of export copper would be available. The decision of the shogunate to reopen two copper mints in 1697 and 1700 that consumed masses of raw copper strengthens this interpretation.[61] Yet, the amount of metal needed for minting became difficult to supply, as the amount exported was about 8,000,000 *kin*, while the official total production for these years was only about 8,900,000 *kin*.[62] In 1700 only

59 With the office, the rank of the Nagasaki magistrate (*Nagasaki bugyō*), too, rose. From 1700 onwards the office was ranked higher than that of the other shogunal cities. Innes 1980, 341; and see also Ōta 1992, 365.

60 Ōta 1992, 433–434. From 1715 onwards the *Nagasaki kaisho* sent a fixed amount of 70,000 *ryō* annually to the Osaka treasury. After 1723: 50,000 *ryō*; 1733: 35,000 *ryō*; after 1736 only when some profit was made and the Osaka reserve had to supply some funding. The *unjōkin* was abolished in 1742 but resumed in 1761 when the *kaisho* sent 15,000 *ryō*. Yamawaki 1964, 86 and 282. See also Yamawaki 1986, 564.

61 Yamawaki 1986, 603. For instance, the copper mint Kameido in Edo used annually between 1697 and 1703 1,750,000 *kin* of copper and the Kyoto mint under the control of the *itowappu* used annually between 1700 and 1703 550,000 *kin*.

62 Some data for mining output of copper: 1668: 9,000,000 *kin* produced; 1698: 10,000,000 *kin*; 1700: 8,900,000 *kin* (of which about 72% of production was exported); 1714: 6,400,000 *kin* (about 65% exported); 1715 and 1716: 5,000,000 *kin*; 1717: 4,000,000 *kin*; 1718: 5,000,000 *kin*; 1719: 4,410,000 *kin*; 1722: 7,335,000 *kin*; 1760s: 4,000,000 *kin*

5,124,415 *kin* of copper were shipped to Nagasaki, since difficulties with transport and a decline in the mines' productivity led to delays.[63] This is less than the amount the shogunate envisioned to be traded in Nagasaki, when we consider that for the years 1696–1698 annually over 8.5 million *kin* were exported (8,669,768, 8,908,178, 9,020,295 *kin* respectively). (Table 3) Up to this point the merchants were in charge, and had been increasing in number, but the results dissatisfied the government. As a response to the bumpy, but quite lucrative, copper business, the shogunate decided to establish its own agency in Osaka, where it would closely oversee and control the transactions. In 1701 the shogunate opened a copper office (*dōza* 銅座) directly in Osaka, which was to ensure the procurement and transport to Nagasaki, as well as the supply of copper to the mints.

5. *The first shogunal copper office: Genroku dōza*

The issue at the turn of the seventeenth century was not the shortage of copper, but the problem of logistics and, in all likelihood, of cooperation, which is indicated in the frequent shogunal requests to open new metal mines as mentioned above. While the shogunate could not do much more than remind domains and officials of shogunal holdings to search with more enthusiasm for new mines, with regard to the organization of copper procurement the government experimented with various approaches. As I have shown above, in 1678 the shogunate allowed sixteen members to form a copper guild that was responsible for the purchase, refinement, and transport of copper to Nagasaki. In 1695 this monopoly ended. Permitting the Edo merchant Fushimi-ya to conduct the copper barter trade, and then extending this privilege in 1698 to three Edo merchants, and one year later, in 1699, even to everyone interested, the shogunate curtailed the privileges of the copper guild. With the establishment of the *dōza* a sort of compromise was achieved. The eighteen members of the copper guild at the time (copper wholesalers, large

(about 56% exported); 1764: 5,000,000 *kin*; 1767: 612,600 *kin*; 1770s: 4,000,000 *kin* (about 54% exported). Sources: Sasaki 1983, 181.

63 Yao 1998, 76.

and small refiners) were bound by oath to the *dōza*.[64] They oversaw the copper transport from the mines, the refinement, and the sale of domestic and foreign export copper. The guild was therefore placed underneath this organ and must have been pleased, while the shogunate secured for itself a key position that would decide the copper price at the mines, both in shogunal and domainal land, and ensured new revenue (*unjōkin*).[65]

In 1701/1/15 the *dōza* (copper office) was opened in Osaka under the supervision of the *ginza* (silver monopoly), which was a semi-shogunal agency.[66] Three elders (*toshiyori* 年寄) from the Edo *ginza* and one from the Kyoto office were supposed to take turns to oversee the new agency.[67] The salaries came from the Osaka city magistrate. With this central organ the purchase and shipping troubles should be taken care of. The start-up money came from the *Nagasaki kaisho*: 1,500 *kanme*, which the *dōza* could use as an initial revolving fund. Afterwards it was to support itself from the turnover of buying and selling the copper. The copper produced in the mines was bought by the wholesalers or other copper merchants and taken to Osaka, where it was purchased by the refiners. Each month the refiners submitted their records to the *dōza* with the amount received, the date, and the name of the refiner.[68] The *dōza* purchased from the refineries the copper for export (*goyōdō* 御用銅), which compared to the copper for domestic use (*chiuridō* 地売銅) was by far the larger amount.[69] Initially the *dōza* paid 105 *monme* per 100 *kin*, which was below the market price.[70] (Table 7) The payments of the export copper were settled when the guild of refiners and merchants had delivered the copper to Nagasaki.[71] The *Nagasaki kaisho* would make the

64 Imai 1989, 14.

65 Imai 1989, 11. The *dōza* was responsible for delivering the wooden chests for the staff copper.

66 Kobata 1980, 72 and 88.

67 Also officials from the *Ōsaka machi bugyō*, according to Nagazumi 1960, 414.

68 Ōta 1992, 448–52; Nagazumi 1960, 409.

69 Nagazumi 1960, 409.

70 Kobata 1980, 143.

71 Imai 1988, 50; Ōta 1992, 452–453.

payment to the *ginza*, which in turn would pay the money for the staff copper to the refiners and merchants.[72]

The delay of payment, however, brought financial difficulties for refiners and merchants. In addition, the fixed price of the export copper was, it was argued, too low to cover the costs for mining, refining, and transport, making it difficult to procure the necessary amount of copper. In the *Deshima Diaries*, the Dutch, who were not aware of the new copper agency, comment that there were rumors that it was the refiners' fault, that their prices were too high so that it was not worth transporting copper to Nagasaki.[73] When we consider that the copper fetched a much better price on the domestic market—by 1701 about 121 *monme* per 100 *kin* had to be paid while the VOC paid only 115.9 *monme*—we can suspect that not the delay in payments, but other issues as well caused the decline in the supply of export copper. (Table 7)

Superintendent of Finance Ogiwara Shigehide, who was disappointed with the results of the copper business, again, began an investigation.[74] In one of the meetings with the head of the *dōza* and members of the guild he requested surveys of the active mines. These were delivered in 1702 and an extended survey was completed in 1703, which listed 211 copper mines in the country.[75] From 1703 onwards we see a rise in exports. The pressure by the shogunate and the establishment of the *dōza* was, in its initial stage, a success. This success, however, was only temporary. The copper mints, located in Edo (Kameido) and Kyoto respectively, were active until 1708. Also, continuous debasements of the silver coins from an original silver content of 80 per cent and copper of 20 per cent brought about a reverse silver/copper ratio by 1710, resulting in accordingly increased amounts of copper required. In addition, various earthquakes ruined buildings, which

72 In Nagasaki, officials of the *dōza* sat in the negotiations between the Chinese merchants and the copper merchants. In particular in the beginning the rank of these officials was low. Imai 1989, 4–5.

73 *Deshima Diaries*, 129; and 131–132.

74 Innes 1980, 342–243; Kobata 1999, 85.

75 *Shokoku dōzan oboegaki* 諸国銅山覚書, included in *Sumitomo shiryō sōsho* 4. The first list mentioned 130 mines. The difference might be explained by the fact that in Northern Japan refinement took place at the mines and thus they were not included in the earlier survey. Imai 1989, 15.

needed to be repaired with copper roofs, and the productive Besshi mine with an approximate annual output of about 1,000,000 *kin* had to halt all production for one year in 1708 due to an earthquake.

Table 6 *Genroku Dōza*: Copper Purchases from the Mines[76]

	Export Copper (Unit: *kin*)	Domestic Copper (Unit: *kin*)
1708	6,120,200	1,337,640
1709	7,164,000	1,115,890
1710	5,592,000	1,851,274
1711	2,668,433	1,053,660
1712	55,600	1,002,457

Even if it appears that the Japanese side had difficulties with keeping up the copper production and in particular with the copper transportation to Nagasaki, there were also logistical problems on the side of the buyers. The VOC had its problems with the heavy and bulky substitute for gold. A vessel could hold approximately 4,000 chests of staff copper (400,000 *kin*) without being overloaded. When the purchase was more than 1,500,000 *kin* of copper, however, four ships were needed. Was this cost-effective for the VOC? Apparently not, since already in 1696 the headquarters in Batavia wrote to the Dutch factory in Deshima that only 16,500 chests of copper should be purchased. The vessels were not new and the possibility of shipwrecks was high. Sending out more than four ships, on the other hand, was deemed too expensive.[77] The following two years Batavia had to send six ships, but that was not in the company's interest. As Yao Keisuke shows, the Dutch decline in copper exports in the late seventeenth century can thereby also be explained by the decision of the VOC not to provide more ships to sail to Japan.[78]

While copper may have been an important export commodity, there were also other desired commodities that took up space on Dutch vessels. In 1685,

76 Sources: Nagazumi 1960, 410; Kobata 1980, 105. (Source: *Genroku dōza no dōkaiage-daka* 銅買上高.)

77 Yao 1998, 106–112.

78 Yao 1998, 101.

under the ceiling trade regulation, the Dutch were allowed to have 400 *kanme* of private trade (*wakini* 脇荷), which became an important part for the VOC's overall trade.[79] In the case of the Chinese, where the distance was much shorter and the ships smaller, it was up to the shogunate to reconsider its former limit of seventy ships. In 1698 Edo allowed eighty ships to enter the harbor of Nagasaki.[80]

Different currencies and exchange rates between them also played a role in the trade with the foreigners. In the period of highest debasement, between 1704 and 1710, the VOC took more copper than gold, while they exported gold in large quantities between 1700 and 1703 (and again between 1707 and 1715), to the headache of the shogunate.[81] When in 1711 Edo requested Japanese merchants to pay for the merchandise from the Dutch with the greatly debased gold coin, *Hōei koban* (minted in 1700), the Dutch flatly refused to sell their goods. As a means to pressure the Dutch the Japanese told them that only 1,000,000 *kin* of copper were available. The Dutch still refused and took only copper, thereby incurring the financial loss of not selling all their merchandise that trading season.[82]

From the *Deshima Diaries* we learn how each year tough negotiations took place, which reminds us that the trade in Nagasaki was, after all, business transactions. Therefore a reduced volume of export copper can mean various things: not enough copper might have been available in Nagasaki, or other products might have appeared more profitable to the buyers. The negotiations between the parties were not only about copper, but also about other commodities, and transactions depended on what promised higher profits in Asia, Europe, and domestic Japan.[83]

79 Private trade had probably always existed, but was now officially sanctioned. The trade was abolished in 1721 but reestablished under a different name with an increase of 25% trade volume. Initially, the trade amounted to 400 *kanme*, and from 1721 on, it was 250 *kanme* of the new currency, which was worth 500 *kanme* of the old currency. In 1737 the private trade was reinstalled under its old name *wakini* but again abolished in 1743. See Yao 2006, 3f.. Some of the products were copper products, porcelain, and lacquer ware. Even when official trade decreased, private trade continued.

80 See Appendix.

81 Yao 1998, 93.

82 Yao 1998, 118–119. Between 1712 and 1715, when the reminting of the gold coin to higher purity began, the VOC received about half the amount of copper and half gold.

83 Yao 1998, 152–153, and 132.

Table 7 Copper Prices (Average per 100 *kin* in Silver *monme*)[84]

	Cost of Export Copper	Chinese Price	VOC Price	Domestic Market Price
1691		104.4	107	
1693		100	106	
1695		98.3	105	
1697	ca. 92	104	106	
1698		107	110.5	
1700		113.5	115.9	
1701	103–105		115.9	121
1702			116.4	
1704	103–132	113.2		
1708				136
1711			115.9	191–193.5
1712		135	116.4	251–253
1713			119.4	
1714		135.5	120.4	
1715			120.4	
1717	141–174			195–240

Various problems undermined the success of the *dōza*'s enterprise. In 1711 officials of the *dōza* complained that the transport of copper to Nagasaki was simply not possible. Soon after, the government issued an edict which asked the copper merchants to deliver copper as fast as possible to Nagasaki.[85] The *dōza* was not capable of managing this task, and in 1712/3, after months of investigations in Edo, Osaka, and Nagasaki, the shogunate reached the decision to close the office. After only eleven years the *dōza*

84 For VOC and Chinese copper price, see Kobata 1980, 30, and 64. For more details on VOC prices, see Yao 1998, 140–141, who lists the copper prices for the VOC from 1691–1725. He compares three different sources with different amounts. Table 7 lists the refiners' price for the VOC not including other costs, such as taxes and levies. For domestic prices, see Imai 1988; 52–53; Kobata 1980, 106f..

85 Kobata 1957, 147–148.

ceased to exist. Its main task had been to secure enough copper for export and, if possible, to increase the trade volume. Its purpose was not to generate revenue for the shogunate, since this came from the *unjōkin* in Nagasaki. Since the *dōza* was founded on very little capital and probably not much merchant support, it failed.

From then on, the purchase and transport to Nagasaki was contracted out by the Osaka city magistrate to the copper guild of now seventeen members, which established an administrative trading station, or factory, called *Osaka dōkaisho* 大阪銅会所 or *dōfukiya kaisho* 銅吹屋会所.[86] The monopoly of the guild was reassured. As during the time of the *dōza*, the guild's duty was to purchase and transport the export copper as before, but it was no longer charged with selling the staff copper to the *dōza*.[87] Edo required a minimum of 5,000,000 *kin* to be sent to Nagasaki. To ensure the implementation of this new policy, the shogunate decreed in the sixth month of 1713 that all copper had to be shipped to Osaka.[88] Moreover, having learned from its former mistakes, the shogunate subsidized the merchant office with premiums and advances. In addition, the purchase price of unrefined copper as bought by the refiner was increased from 103–105 *monme* per 100 *kin* to 134–35 *monme*, which was more profitable and thus attractive to the mining operations.[89] (Table 7) With these regulations the goal of five million *kin* was reached in the years 1713 and 1714.[90] However, since the refined export copper was purchased at a lower price than the purchasing price of unrefined copper and eventually sold to an even lower price to the foreigners in Nagasaki, someone had to cover the deficit.[91] The *Nagasaki kaisho* carried the

86 Kobata 1980, 152. The members changed over the years. Primary sources for the time after the first *dōza* are available in print in the *Sumitomo shiryō sōsho*.

87 What also continued was the guild's purchase of the various types of copper for domestic use, receiving used copper. Imai 1989, 22.

88 Iwasaki 1997, 356. Because of this the transport to Osaka became more expensive. *Ofuregaki Kampō shūsei* (no. 1865).

89 The regulation was repeated in 1713/6. Kobata 1980, 166. According to Imai, the copper was purchased from the producers for the same price as domestic copper. Imai 1988, 51.

90 1713: 4,909,199 *kin*; 1714: 5,049,915 *kin*. See Table 3.

91 Chinese merchants bought 100 *kin* per 130–135 *monme*, and the Dutch even paid only ca. 116–120 *monme* per 100 *kin*.

loss, since it was also the *Nagasaki kaisho* that made the profits from the overall trade.[92]

6. Shōtoku regulations of 1715

The shogunate certainly was interested in finding better solutions for the trade in Nagasaki for many reasons. Various activities of high-ranking officials, such as Ogiwara Shigehide, demonstrate the importance of the economic and political issues that came together in the distant port of Nagasaki. For this reason it is not surprising that parallel to the conundrums with the procurement of export copper even the shogun began to investigating the matter. The newly invested shogun Ienobu 家宣 (1663–1712; r. 1709–12) asked Arai Hakuseki in 1709/2 about his opinion on economic conditions and how the Nagasaki trade could be improved. Soon after, Hakuseki submitted a proposal. Following some of his recommendations, the shogunate promulgated a new set of regulations in 1710/3.[93] The new system included

92 List by Kobata 1980, Tables 3 and 4, 162. Kobata Atsushi demonstrates with two examples the deficit of the *Nagasaki kaisho* with copper exports. In 1712, the *Nagasaki kaisho* purchased 3,535,213 *kin* of copper from the copper guild for 4,998,656.51 *monme*. Then the kaisho sold it for 4,717,259.15 *monme* to the Dutch and Chinese merchants. The deficit accounts for 281,397.36 *monme*. The same in 1715, when the *Nagasaki kaisho* bought 5,000,000 *kin* for 6,968,764.43 *monme*, sold it to the foreigners for 6,687,100.891 *monme*, which resulted in a loss of 281,663.539 *monme*.

93 Hakuseki wrote in 1709/3/22 a letter to grand chamberlain (*soba yōnin* 側用人) Manabe Akifusa 間部詮房 (1667–1720), called *Nagasaki omote no koto o-fumi* 長崎表の事御文. He further investigated with the Nagasaki magistrate who was at the time residing in Edo (3/29) and two months later turned in a report that is called *Hakuseki jōsho* 白石上書, reproduced in *Tsūkō ichiran* 4, 615, 383–390. The memorandum was basically about three points: the extent of metal export was so high that after another hundred years the country would be without any precious metals. Second, *unjōkin* and taxes should be stopped. The last point was concerned with the amount of trade itself: less Chinese ships would be enough, even if it meant fewer goods, because the goods that are imported were not necessary for daily life anyway, and the city of Nagasaki was too rich. He suggested that the entire merchandise should be bought off by the shogunate to avoid smuggling and the limit of the volume should be fixed for each ship. This would reduce the number to about six to seven ships a season. Basically, Hakuseki was interested in stopping trade with the exception of medical supplies. By making a turn to a current problem of the shogunate, Hakuseki argues that if there was more bullion in the country, there would be no shortage of currency. In the following months notes were circulating from

twelve points, mainly concerning the reduction of the number of foreign ships received in Nagasaki and of trade volume. The plan was to halve the ceiling of trade volume: 4,500 *kanme* (which is about 65% less, and from that about 75% less for the Chinese, than what was decided in 1685). Hakuseki's goal was to restore the currency and for that aim export trade had to be cut. But the Nagasaki city magistrate rejected the new trade pattern arguing that it would neither be realistic nor pragmatic.[94] In regard to pricing the magistrate responded that the current regulations were fine and work well, if the shogunate interfered further it would do more harm than good.[95]

After the regulations were rejected, Hakuseki continued to investigate the matter of Nagasaki by making inquiries to officials. One of them was Ōoka (Bizen no kami) Kiyosuke 大岡清相 (1679–1717), who had become Nagasaki magistrate in 1711.[96] In his first response (1713/2/4) to Hakuseki, the magistrate mainly discussed the setting of the prices. In an undated letter from around the same time, Kiyosuke concentrated on the copper exports, which interests us here.[97]

The magistrate explained that a quota of 5,000,000 *kin* of copper was necessary for export. The amount of 8,902,000 *kin* set in 1698 had been exported only in one year. Two years earlier, when the copper could not be delivered on time, the Chinese ships had not been able to leave until the following spring. Last year, in 1712, again the staff copper shipments had not arrived in time and the ships had to wait until this month (1713/2). Last month, the city elder reported that it was impossible to load the copper onto the ships on time. Instead silver was offered, but the Chinese declined. Some of the merchants were willing to take other goods.[98] The bill from last year

various magistrates. Hakuseki meant to get individual responses from the four magistrates about the condition in Nagasaki. He compiled in the end about five volumes, which have not survived in their entirety. A variety of excerpts from these volumes are extant. Ōta 1992, 454–482.

94 Ōta 1992, 519.

95 Ōta 1992, 502–504.

96 Ōoka Kiyosuke was Nagasaki magistrate from 1711–1717.

97 See Nakai 1988, 111–114, where Nakai also explains that Hakuseki should not be regarded as the architect of the new regulations, *Shōtoku shinrei* of 1715. For one of Ōoka Kiyosuke's memorandum, see *Tsūkō ichiran* 4, 398–407.

98 Probably the debasement plays an important role why the Chinese rejected silver.

to the copper refiners was not settled yet, and it was not clear how to pay for this year's shipment. One possibility, the magistrate suggested, was that the *Nagasaki kaisho* could advance the fees from its profits. There is the general worry that if the refiners were not paid the copper would never reach Nagasaki. So far, from last year to this spring, only 3,500,000 *kin* had left port. When copper had been insufficient previously, the magistrate had paid the refiners in advance to devoid delays, sometimes without notifying the shogunate. Kiyosuke thought that this practice should be officially permitted.[99] Hakuseki's response to Kiyosuke's letter is unknown, but the suggestions do not envision a trade curtailment.

Meanwhile, Ienobu had died after a short reign of only three years and his successor, child shogun, Ietsugu 家継 (1709–16; r. 1712–16) also ruled for only a few years. But it was under the latter's rule that the new regulations *Shōtoku shinrei* 正徳新令 concerning the Nagasaki trade were proclaimed. The main points of the regulations concern trade in general, copper exports, the management of the city of Nagasaki, Chinese interpreters, the China trade, the Dutch trade, and last year's trade.[100] The contents, which were proclaimed in 1715/1/11 and pronounced in Nagasaki in 2/23, employ

99 Ōta 1992, 528–529. Another major concern was smuggling. In the magistrate's opinion, the general argument, that if not enough copper is exported, smuggling will occur, does not hold up, since, for instance, even if seven to eight million kin of copper were exported, smuggling occurred. While, on the other hand, so far only 3,500,000 *kin* have been shipped, no incident of smuggling has been reported. It was strict laws and their persecution that mattered. This was an issue that needed to be taken up more seriously. Smuggling was a concern that both men shared. Hakuseki wrote in his autobiography: "First, the approximate annual production of gold, silver, and copper, and the amount destined for foreign countries should be calculated and compared so that a yearly quota can be determined for Nagasaki, the designated port for overseas trade. Next, the carrying capacity of the foreign ships should be estimated, and then both the number of vessels and volume of goods fixed. Since all the commodities imported will be purchased, our country's treasure will not be lost because of smuggling as has been the case till now, and foreigners will no longer scorn the laws of our land. Our country's stature will spread over ten thousand miles and the nation's wealth will suffice for myriad generations." *Arai Hakuseki zenshū 3*, 168. Translation by Innes 1980, 352.

100 There were also many administrative changes: the shogunate decided to keep an inspector (*metsuke*) in the city who would report directly to Edo. Also only one magistrate would reside in Nagasaki instead of two.

some of the two visions of Hakuseki and Kiyosuke.[101] For instance, while Hakuseki meant to cut the trade volume in half, the Shōtoku version returned to the Jōkyō ceiling of 9,000 *kanme*, which is more along the lines of Kiyosuke's proposal. While Chinese merchants were allowed to trade with value worth of 6,000 *kanme*, only thirty ships were permitted to enter Nagasaki harbor.[102] Two ships and 3,000 *kanme* was the limit of the VOC, and in addition private trade of 400 *kanme*.[103] Barter trade—copper and sea products—was suspended.[104] As far as copper trade was concerned, the *Shōtoku shinrei* probably came as no surprise to the Chinese and Dutch, since the amount delivered had been in decline for several years. In the end, the trade returned to its volume of 1685 with the exception that the volume of the copper exports was now limited to 4 to 4.5 million *kin*, depending on availability, of which Chinese merchants were allotted three million *kin* and the VOC 1.5 million *kin*. The numbers again reflect reality rather than a future goal.

A development rarely mentioned in textbooks is that already in the following years the regulations were changed and adjusted, certainly for pragmatic reasons. First, the number of Chinese ships was raised to forty in 1717, while the trade volume went up to 8,000 *kanme*; in 1719, this decision was

101 The text can be found in *Tsūkō ichiran* 4, 413; and in *Tokugawa kinreikō*, 417. For more details on the various manuscripts, and print versions, see Ōta 1992, fn. 7, 586.

102 The captains of the ships received a permit (*shinpai* 信牌) which they had to show when entering the following year and all trade had to be conducted via the system of *negumi* 直組 (price agreement). With this the foreigners were obliged to pay the price determined by the merchants, after the imports' quality was appraised, or to take the goods back home. The *Deshima Diaries*, April 27, 1715, mention "[The Chinese] trade will be limited to 600.000 taels. Only thirty junks will be allowed to trade. These will be given shogunal passes. This is a heavy blow to their trade. In the meantime thirty smugglers have been apprehended." The Dutch did not know at that time that their trade regulations were to change as well. Another diarist wrote April 9, 1715, "if the Chinese behave themselves they will be allowed to live in the city."

103 The *Deshima Diaries* mention on October 16, 1715, "1. Only two ships are to be allowed to trade annually. 2. Our trade will be limited to 300.000 taels. 3. We will have to exchange the kobans at a rate of 6.8 taels. 4. Our annual copper quota will be set at 15.000 chests..."

104 The barter trade of sea products was already abolished in 1708, since hardly ever filled. The copper barter trade went on until 1715, although for the Dutch, it hardly was executed, due to the problems discussed above. Suzuki 2004, 188.

revoked, restoring the original number of thirty ships and a trade volume of 4,000 *kanme*. The amount of copper exported declined over the following years. Soon after, more adjustments were undertaken. (See Appendix) Innes observes that the new limitations brought again more profit to the shogunate, since the *Nagasaki kaisho* could sell the import goods at a higher price. Because the amount set aside from the trade was fixed (70,000 *ryō* from the *Nagasaki kaisho*) for the city only, the Osaka treasury received the increment.[105]

In the context of the new regulations, the shogunate aimed to improve the supply of export copper, since the revenues from the trade were worth the trouble to get actively involved. The shogunate began buying a proportion of copper directly from the mines, sending it to the refiners in Osaka.[106] Between 1716 and 1722 the copper guild administered its business from the *dōkaisho* in Osaka, as mentioned above, and since only two of its members had a branch office in Nagasaki the other fifteen members opened one common agency in Nagasaki, the *Nagasaki dōkaisho*, which was conveniently located next to the Izumi-ya branch store.[107] An edict of 1716/1 requested that 5,000,000 *kin* of unrefined copper were to be purchased from the mines and delivered between the first and eighth month to Osaka. From there 4,500,000 *kin* of staff copper had to be shipped to Nagasaki. The Osaka treasury advanced the money so that the domain mines could be paid by the time of the delivery of the raw copper, or in case of shogunal mines the deputies (*daikan* 代官) paid the mines, as soon as the refiners signed the receipts of the delivered copper. Moreover, in order to have the domains follow through with the desires of the shogunate, a fixed quota system (*gowariai goyōdō* 御割合御用銅) was established for twenty mines.

105 Innes 1980, 345–346.

106 In 1716 the deputies and agents of the lords were asked to buy more copper, which was then supposed to be delivered to the refiners. Yamawaki 1964, 606.

107 Imai 2006, 2. See also Iwasaki 2003, 7, about the factory which opened in 1712.

Table 8 Quota System for Mines (in *kin*)[108]

	1715	1716	1720	1721	1722
Akita	1,700,000	1,700,000	1,400,000	1,400,000	1,400,000
Mutsu[109]	650,000	750,000	450,000	450,000	400,000
Besshi*	1,000,000	1,000,000	850,000	850,000	850,000
Tatsukawa*	700,000	700,000	500,000	500,000	500,000
Ikuno*	400,000	–	–	–	–
Others	550,000	183,000	583,670	671,500	140,000
Total	**5,000,000**	**4,535,000**	**4,033,670**	**4,031,500**	**4,335,000**

* Shogunal mines

After the refiners received their copper shipments they presented the receipts to the magistrate's office, which would then pay the mines. The guild also stored the copper for export, and took care of the practical sides of the trade. The exchange was settled when the copper was sold in Nagasaki to the foreigners and the *Nagasaki kaisho* returned the money back to the treasury in Osaka. Again, however, the transactions did not always go smoothly. The shogunate was late in paying for the unrefined copper, and arrears amounted to 29,000 *ryō* in 1720 and 1721. For that reason, the distribution quota for the mines remained in force in name but its practice had been stopped.[110]

To improve the process, after 1722, the shogunate decided to transport the copper ore from the mines under shogunal jurisdiction directly to Nagasaki and to refine it there instead of in Osaka. For this end, the government opened in 1725 a refinery (*dōfukisho* 銅吹所) in Nagasaki, and soon another one in its outskirts.[111] Since the shogunal copper was not enough to

108 Nagazumi 1960, 411. Imai 1988, 52, gives the official quota as follows 5,000,000 *kin* for 1716; 4,000,000 *kin* for 1717; 1718: 5,000,000 *kin*; 1719: 4,410,000 *kin*; 1722: 4,335,000 *kin*. The table also shows the price of copper for each mine, which ranges from 117.137 *monme* (shogunal mine of Ikuno 生野) to 194.056 *monme* and 414.542 *monme* (domainal mine of Hida 飛騨, and Aizu 会津 respectively) in 1717.

109 Mutsu includes Osarizawa, Shirane, Kumazawa, Nambu, Oppu, and Morioka.

110 Kobata 1993, 34; Nagazumi 1960, 416.

111 See Iwasaki 1998, 19–42. The technical know-how necessary must have come from the Osaka refiners since it is claimed that only they knew how to efficiently separate copper ore. The refineries in Nagasaki were closed in 1736. Iwasaki 2003, 1.

supply the foreign trade, the Nagasaki magistrate was ordered to purchase copper from copper merchants. For instance, in the magistrate's name the Kyoto merchant house Echigo-ya 越後屋 bought two million *kin* in 1723.[112]

For the following decades the data of the sources are scantier, but the shogunate continued to strive for better solutions.[113] In 1732 the shogunate again ordered the copper guild to see to the provision of copper, but only until 1738, when a second *dōza* was opened, today commonly called *Genbun dōza* 元文銅座. From the setting up of this agency, the mines were prohibited from selling copper to anyone but the *dōza*.[114] In 1746 the quota for export copper was reduced to 3,100,000 *kin* (2,000,000 *kin* for the Chinese merchants and 1,100,000 *kin* for the VOC), but according to the available data this amount was hardly ever reached. It seems that this office, too, faced problems, which led to its closure in 1750. From this year, the *Nagasaki kaisho* purchased the export copper directly from the mines.[115]

Table 9 Agencies for Export Copper

1701–1712	*Genroku dōza*
1712–1722	Refiners Guild's trading office
1722–1732	Shogunal copper and Nagasaki refinery
1732–1738	Refiners Guild's trading office
1738–1750	*Genbun dōza*
1750–1768	*Nagasaki kaisho*
1766–1868	*Meiwa dōza*

112 Yamawaki 1964, 606–607.

113 For a discussion of the period after 1740, see Iwasaki 2000.

114 Iwasaki 2003, 1–42.

115 Besshi received previously 180 *monme* for 100 *kin*, which was in 1751 reduced to 139.48 *monme*. See Imai 2006, 2. It seems this office existed before the Genbun dōza and was closed with the latter's opening. After the dōza was closed, it was reinstalled. Imai 2006, 4.

7. Conclusion

In regard to foreign trade conducted through Nagasaki between 1670 and 1720, a distinct economic theory behind shogunal decisions is not obvious beyond the notion that excessive export of silver and gold had to be stopped for fear of domestic depletion. The negative mercantilism pursued certainly did not include copper. Copper, even though it was needed for domestic currency, was singled out as export commodity in particular due to the foreign traders' ready acceptance, as well as the revenues it brought to the shogunate. Throughout the decades investigated here, the shogunate did not prohibit the export of copper. Bullionism, if practiced, did not include the red metal. The problem was its procurement. Production, labor, and transport of the bulky commodity were costly, and the inflation caused by the debasement policies at the turn of the seventeenth century made mining even less profitable. The risk of opening new mines, in particular when under domainal jurisdiction, was therefore prohibitive.[116] The policies to limit the copper exports can therefore not be seen as being part of bullionist policies but as inevitable since supply was a continued obstacle.

The motivation for the shogunate's involvement in the copper trade was a decision not to take tighter control, but for want of a better solution. When its efforts bore no fruits, plans were changed. Thus the channeling of the export copper to Nagasaki came under the management of government officials to varying degrees. Shogunal policies were changed, readjusted, and institutions established and abolished along the way. Instead of one economic view, we see pragmatic approaches to changing demands and conditions; there was no static copper policy.

In regard to the official trade limitations and its reality some further consideration is necessary. Ōba Osamu argues that even though the trade volume for the Chinese merchants after 1717 (8,000 *kanme* or *kan*) never reached previous levels, it is necessary to consider that what "was initially the overall volume of trade, later became the portion of the total trade transacted in copper" only. Other trade was not included, as, for instance, in 1804 "there were eleven vessels and overall amount of trade was over 7,345 *kan*; in 1840 there were nine ships with a total trading volume of over 9,217

116 Kobata 1980, 171.

kan."[117] Self-sufficiency was a guiding aim in the minds of some thinkers, but the bureaucrats in the shogunate did not consider this path as desirable.

Copper would be transported to other parts of Asia for many more years to come, and the problem of cooperation would remain a key issue.[118] Without the support from mines, merchants, and refiners, the shogunate could decree copper quotas to no avail. The output of the mines was in decline, as has often been argued. For example, however, during the year 1764 the refinery's documents recorded about 5,000,000 *kin* of received copper shipments from only the three big mines. Although certainly a decline from the all-time high of 9,000,000 *kin* of total production around 1700, it may be less dramatic as sometimes suggested. The organization and transport of copper were not solved until the third *dōza*, *Meiwa dōza*, which lasted until the end of the shogunate in 1868, but what happened at the end of the production, at the mines, is something that needs our close attention as well.

While I considered only the side of the supplier, the Asian economies which depended on Japanese copper were not static either. For instance, despite trade restrictions by the Japanese (and we have to remember that these restrictions were revoked at times) and the rise in price, Japanese copper remained in great demand, in particular in South Asia. It was not until 1760–1790 that there was a gradual decrease in profit for the VOC caused by the new competition with the English East India Company; yet due to the lesser quality of European copper the decline in the market share for the VOC was not rapid.[119] Thus the Nagasaki copper trade cannot be understood only from the perspective of Japanese sources, but also needs to be analyzed by considering the trade as a whole, which offers a more complex view.

117 Ōba 1996, 53.

118 Shimada describes how from 1710 onwards about 1 million Dutch pounds of Japanese copper were annually sold in Asia, ninety per cent of it in South Asia, bringing the VOC throughout the eighteenth century about ten per cent of the total sales profits in whole Asia. Shimada 2006, 142–143.

119 Shimada 2006, Chapter 3.

Appendix:

Trade regulations by year (trade ceiling and number of vessels)[120]

Year	VOC ceiling (*kanme*)	VOC ships[121]	Chinese ceiling (*kanme*)	Chinese ships[122]
1672				(43)
1682				(26)
1683				(24)
1684				(24)
1685	**3,000**	(4)	**6,000** (ca.22,500 kg)	(73)[123]
1688				(117)[124]
1689	3,000	(4)	6,000	70 (61)
1698	**3,000 (additional copper and sea barter trade of 1,800)**	(6)	**6,000 (additional copper and sea barter trade of 5,200)**	80 (68)
1709	3,000 (add. copper barter trade 800)	(4)	6,000 (add. copper barter trade 4,200)	59 (54)

120 Yamawaki 1986, 604; Liu 1997, 298, and Yamawaki 1964, 163–165. Yamawaki 1964, 206 for 1804, and 208 for 1840. By the end of the Tokugawa period the Sino-Japanese trade was almost a free trade (Yamawaki 1964, 209). See for a list of the number of Chinese ships between 1650 until 1800 Shimada 2006, Appendix 2. For Dutch ships, see Shimada 2006, Appendix I.

121 (…) indicates the actual number of vessels trading in Nagasaki.

122 (…) indicates the actual number of vessels trading in Nagasaki. Either the Chinese junks were turned away or they had to wait until the next year for their merchandise (mostly copper) arrived.

123 12 junks had to be turned away.

124 75 junks had to be turned away.

1715	**3,000**	**2** (3)	**6,000** (with limit of 3,000,000 *kin* of copper)	**30**[125] (7)
1717		(2)	**8,000**	**40** (43)
1719		(0)	**4,000**	**30** (37)
1720	1,700	(2)		
1732		(2)	4,000	29 (36)
1733	**1,100**	(2)		
1736		(2)	4,000	25 (16)
1739		(2)	4,000	20 (20)
1742		(2)	2,000	20 (15)
1743	**550**	1 (2)	**2,000**	**10** (15)
1746	800 (+450)	2 (3)		
1749		(2)	4,110 (4,500)	15 (13)
1765		(1)	3,510	13 (12)
1791		0	2,740	10 (10)
1804			< 7,000	4
1840			9,000	

Units:

Weight Measures:

1 *kan* 貫 or *1 kanme* 貫目 = 1,000 *monme* 匁 = 3.75 kg

100 *kin* 斤 = 1 picul = 60 kg

Currency:

Official exchange rate (changed over time):

Gold 1 *ryō* = Silver 50 *monme* = Copper 4 *kan* (4,000 *mon*)

Silver plate (by weight): 1 *kanme* or *kan* = 1,000 *monme*

Copper coin (by tale): 1 *kanmon* = 1,000 *mon*

Dates:

Throughout I converted years to the Gregorian calendar, while days and months are left in the original numbering of the lunar calendar, unless otherwise indicated.

125 The *Deshima Diary* of January 6, 1715 (which is still in 1714 according to the Japanese calendar) mentions that "the number of junks that is allowed to trade has been fixed at forty."

8. References

Chang, Aloysius (1970). *The Chinese Community of Nagasaki in the First Century of the Tokugawa Period*. Ph.D. Diss., St. John's University, New York.

Deshima Diaries Marginalia I, 1700–1740 (1992). Leonard Blussé, Cynthia Viallé, et al. (eds.). Tokyo: The Japan-Netherlands Institute.

Glamann, Kristof (1953). "The Dutch East India Company's Trade in Japanese Copper, 1645–1736." *Scandinavian Economic History Review* 1-1 : 41–79.

Hall, John W. (1949). "Notes on the Early Ch'ing Copper Trade with Japan." *Harvard Journal of Asiatic Studies* 12 : 444–461.

Hellyer, Robert I. (2005). "Intra-Asian Trade and the Bakumatsu Crisis: Reconsidering Tokugawa Commercial Policies in Late Edo Period Japan." *International Journal of Asian Studies* 2-1 : 83–110.

Higuchi Hiroshi 樋口弘 (1956). *Nihon Tōgyōshi* 日本糖業史 (History of Sugar Production). Tokyo: Mitō Shooku.

Honchō Hōka Tsūyō Jiryaku 本朝宝貨通用事略 (Study of Japanese Coins). In *Arai Hakuseki Zenshū* 新井白石全集, vol. 3 (Collected Works by Arai Hakuseki). Tokyo: Kokusho Kankōkai, 1905–1907.

Imai Noriko 今井典子 (1999). "Kinsei Osaka no Dō Kanrengyōsha 近世大阪の銅関連業者 (Copper Merchants of Osaka in Early Modern Japan)." Osakashi Bunka Saikyōkai (ed.). *Kenkyū kiyō* 研究紀要. 1999–3 : 193–202.

______ (1989). "Kaidai 解題 (Introduction)." In Kobata Atsushi (ed.). *Dōza kōyōdome* 銅座公用留; *Dōza goyōkō* 銅座御用扣 (Official Records of the Copper Agency). Sumitomo Shiryōsōsho 住友史料叢書 4. Kyoto: Shibunkaku Shuppan, pp. 1–22.

______ (1988). "Kinsei chūki no chiuri dō ni tsuite 近世中期の地売銅について (Domestic Copper during the Mid-Tokugawa Period)." *Nihon Rekishi* 日本歴史 480 : 50–67.

Innes, Robert L. (1980). *The Door Ajar: Japan's Foreign Trade in the Seventeenth Century*. Ph. D. Dissertation, University of Michigan.

Iwasaki Yoshinori 岩崎義則 (2003). "Genbun dōza-ki no Nagasaki kaidō to Nagasaki bōeki 元文銅座期の長崎廻銅と長崎貿易 (Nagasaki Copper Transport and Nagasaki Trade of the Copper Agency during the Genbun Period)." *Sumitomo shiryōkan-pō* 34 : 1–42.

______ (2000). "*Kanpō—Kan'en-ki no bōeki kaikaku to dōtōseisaku* 寛保—寛延期の貿易改革と銅統政策 (Trade Reforms and Centralization Policies of Copper in the Kanpō and Kan'en Periods." *Sumitomo shiryōkan-pō* 31 : 39–68.

______ (1998). "Kinsei Nagasaki dōfukisho ni tsuite 近世長崎銅吹所について (Nagasaki Copper Refinery in the Tokugawa Period)." *Kyūshū daigaku bungakubu 'Shien'* 九州大学文学部「史淵」135–3 : 19–42.

______ (1997)."Nagasaki kaidō to sono kikō 長崎廻銅とその機構 (The Organization of Copper Transport)." In Nakamura Tadashi (ed.). *Sakoku to kokusai kankei* 鎖国と国際関係. Tokyo: Yoshikawa Kōbunkan, pp. 356–376.

Katsu Kaishu 勝海舟 (1970). *Suijinroku* 吹塵錄 (Records of Blowing Away Dust). In *Katsu Kaishū zenshū* 9. Tokyo: Keisō Shobō.

Kobata Atsushi 小葉田淳 (1999). *Kahei to kōzan* 貨幣と鉱山 (Currency and Mining). Kyōto-shi: Shibunkaku Shuppan.

______ (1993). *Nihon dōkōgyō shi no kenkyū* 日本銅鉱業史研究 (Study of the Japanese Copper Mining Industry). Kyoto: Shibunkaku Shuppan.

______ (1980). "*Daiichiji dōza to Sumitomo: dō bōeki to bakufu no dō seisaku* 第一次銅座と住友: 銅貿易と幕府の銅政策 (The First Copper Agency and Sumitomo: Copper Trade and Shogunal Copper Policies)." In *Sen'oku sōkō* 泉屋叢考 18. Kobe: Sumitomo Shūshishitsu 住友修史室, pp. 1–173.

______ (1968). *Nihon kōzanshi no kenkyū* 日本の鉱山史の研究 (Japanese History of Mining). Tokyo: Iwanami Shoten.

______ (1957). "Kinsei zenki ni okeru dōbōeki to Sumitomo 近世前期に於ける銅貿易と住友 (Copper Trade and Sumitomo in the Early Tokugawa Period)." In *Sen'oku sōkō* 泉屋叢考 9. Kobe: Sumitomo Shūshishitsu 住友修史室, pp. 1–144.

Liu Xufeng 劉序楓 (1999)."Qing Kangxi-Qianlong jiannian yangtong de jinkou yu liutong wenti 清康熙-乾隆年間洋銅的進口與流通問題 ([The Problem of] Import and Circulation of Japanese Copper from the Kangxi to the Qianlong reigns of the Qing Dynasty)." In: *Zhongguo haiyang fazhanshi lunwenji* 中國海洋發展史論文集 (Essays in Chinese Martime History). Vol. 7/ Part I, pp. 93–144.

______ (1997). "Kyōhō nenkan no tōsenbōeki to Nihondō 享保年間の唐船貿易と日本銅 (Chinese Foreign Trade and Japanese Copper during the Kyōhō era)." In Nakamura Tadashi (ed.). *Sakoku to Kokusai kankei* 鎖国と国際関係. Tokyo: Yoshikawa Kōbunkan, pp. 296–326.

Munro, Neil Gordon (1904). *Coins of Japan*. Yokohama: Printed by the Box of curios printing and Pub. Co.

Nagazumi Yoko 永積洋子 (2000). The Decline of Trade and Russian Expansion in East Asia." In Leonard Blussé, et al. (eds.). *Bridging the Divide*. Hotei Publishing, pp. 55–72.

______ (1960). "Ōsaka dōza 大阪銅座 (Osaka Copper Agency)." In Chihōshi kenkyū kyōgikai (ed.). *Nihon Sangyōshi Taikei* (Survey of the History of Japanese Industries), vol. 6. Tokyo: Tokyo University Press, pp. 408–419.

Nakai, Kate Wildman (1988). *Shogunal Politics: Arai Hakuseki and the Premises of Tokugawa Rule*. Harvard East Asian monographs, 134. Cambridge, Mass: Council on East Asian Studies, Harvard University.

Ōba Osamu 大庭脩 (1996). "Sino-Japanese Relations in the Edo Period, Part 2." *Sino-Japanese Studies* 8-2 (May 1996) : 50–61.

______ (1980). *Edo jidai no Nitchū hiwa* 江戸時代の日中秘話 (Unknown Stories about Sino-Japanese Relations during the Tokugawa Period). Tokyo: Tōhō sensho.

Ofuregaki Kampō shūsei 御触書寛保集成 (Ordinances [of the Tokugawa Government] Compiled in the Kampō Period). Takayanagi Shinzō and Ishii Ryōsuke (eds.). Tokyo: Iwanami shoten, 1958.

Ōta Katsuya 太田勝也 (1992). *Sakoku jidai Nagasaki Bōeki shi no kenkyū* 鎖国時代長崎貿易史の研究 (Study of the Nagasaki Trade in the Period of Seclusion). Kyoto: Shibunkaku Shuppan.

Sasaki Junnosuke 佐々木潤之介 (1983). "Dōzan no keiei to gijutsu 銅山の経営と技術 (Administration and Technology of Copper Mines)." In Nagahara Keiji and Yamaguchi Keichi (eds). *Kōza Nihon Gijutsu no shakaishi* 講座日本技術の社会史 (Social History of Japan's Technology) vol. 5. Tokyo: Nihon Hyōronsha, pp. 177–210.

Shimada Ryūto (2006). *The Intra-Asian Trade in Japanese Copper by the Dutch East India Company during the Eightenth Century*. TANAP monographs on the history of the Asian-European interaction, v. 4. Leiden: Brill.

Shokoku dōzan oboegaki 諸国銅山覚書 (Memorandum to Copper Mines in the Realm). In Kobata Atsushi (ed.). *Dōza kōyōdome*; *dōza goyōkō*. Sumitomo Shiryōsōsho 住友史料叢書 4. Kyoto: Shibunkaku Shuppan.

Sumitomo Shiryōsōsho 住友史料叢書 (Series of Sumitomo Sources) 21 (2006). Asao Naohiro (ed.). *Dōzakata yōyōhikae* 銅座方要用控. Kyoto: Shibunkaku Shuppan.

Suzuki Yasuko 鈴木康子 (2004). *Kinsei Nichi-Ran bōekishi no kenkyū* 近世日蘭貿易史の研究 (History of Dutch-Japanese Trade in the Early Modern Period). Kyoto: Shibunkaku Shuppan.

Taigaikankeishi sōgō nenpyō 対外関係史総合年表 (Comprehensive Chronological Table of Foreign Relations) (1999). Taigaikankeishi sōgō nenpyō henshū iinkai (ed.). Tokyo: Yoshikawa Kōbunkan.

Tashiro Kazui (1976). "Tsushima han's Korean Trade, 1684–1710." *Acta Asiatica* 30 : 85–105.

Tokugawa kinreikō 徳川禁令考 (Tokugawa Prohibitions), *Zenshū dai* 前集第 6. Kikuchi Shunsuke and Ishii Ryo suke (eds.). Tokyo: Sōbunsha, 1959–1961.

Tsūkō ichiran 通航一覧 4 (Japan's Foreign Relations). Hayashi Fukusai (ed.). Tokyo: Kokusho Kankōkai, 1912.

von Glahn, Richard (1996). "Myth and Reality of China's Seventeenth-Century Monetary Crisis." *The Journal of Economic History* 56-2 (June 1996) : 429–454.

Yamawaki Teijirō 山脇悌二郎 (1986). "Tōsei bōeki no tenkai 統制貿易の展開 (Development of Controlled Foreign Trade)." In *Nagasaki kenshi* 長崎県史 (History of Nagasaki Prefecture), Taigai kōshōshi hen (Volume of the Foreign Relations). Tokyo: Yoshikawa Kōbunkan, pp. 525–552.

______ (1964). *Nagasaki no Tōjin Bōeki* 長崎の唐人貿易 (Chinese Trade in Nagasaki.) Tokyo: Yoshikawa Kōbunkan.

Yao Keisuke 八百啓介 (2006). "18seiki no Deshima oranda shōkan no wakini bōeki to dōyūshutsu 十八世紀の出島オランダ商館の脇荷貿易と銅輸出 (Private Trade and Copper Export of the VOC on Deshima in the Eighteenth Century)." *Geppō*. Asao Naohiro (ed.). *Dōzakata yōyōhikae* 銅座方要用控. *Sumitomo Shiryōsōsho* 住友史料叢書 21. Kyoto: Shibunkaku Shuppan.

______ (2000). "Nagasaki Kaisho (The Geldkamer)." In Leonard Blussé, et al. (eds.). *Bridging the Divide.* Hotei Publishing, p. 60.

______ (1998). *Kinsei Oranda Bōeki to Sakoku* 近世オランダ貿易と鎖国 (The Dutch Trade and National Seclusion in Early Modern Japan.) Tokyo: Yoshikawa Kōbunkan.

Yoon, Byung Nam (1995). Domain and Bakufu in Tokugawa Japan: The Copper Trade and Development of Akita Domain Mines. Ph. D. Dissertation. Princeton University, New Jersey.

Money in the Kingdom of Ryukyu

Gregory Smits

Until the seventeenth century, most of the coins circulating in the Kingdom of Ryukyu were of Chinese or Japanese origin. The knowledge and technology for minting coins appeared in the kingdom during the middle of the fifteenth century, and several Ryukyuan kings issued coins. The quantity of these coins was small, however, and it is likely that their main function was symbolic. In other words, their minting was part of a package of symbols to bolster royal authority. During the seventeenth century, the royal government established mints to create *hatomesen,* a standardized form of cheap copper cash. From 1713, the royal government adopted *hatomesen* as the official unit for government accounting and otherwise promoted the use of *hatomesen* for domestic transactions. Lacking significant deposits of metal, Ryukyu relied on the Japanese domain of Satsuma for copper and for specially minted silver coins for use in tribute trade with China.

Introduction

At the height of its economic and military power in the early sixteenth century, the Kingdom of Ryukyu extended from the islands of the Amami-Ōshima group in the north, through the island of Yonaguni to the south and west. This kingdom was a small-scale empire. Starting in the early fifteenth century, the kings of Okinawa steadily expanded their control over other Ryukyu Islands through military conquest and periodic re-conquest. As the Ryukyu Empire expanded northward, it frequently clashed or competed with Japanese rulers based in the province of Satsuma, who sought to expand southward. In the opposite direction, the Ryukyu state developed strong ties of trade with Ming China and participated in formal tributary relations. The royal court at Shuri, on the island of Okinawa, prospered as Ryukyuan ships traded extensively throughout South, Southeast, and East Asia.

By the late sixteenth century, the kingdom's prosperity declined significantly owing to competition from Portuguese and Japanese traders. This decline set the stage for a disastrous military defeat in a war with the Japanese domain of Satsuma in 1609. Conquest by Satsuma meant that Ryukyu became a de facto part of Japan's *bakuhan* 幕藩 state, although the kingdom appeared to operate as an independent country. The rise of the Qing dynasty and bakufu anxieties over Chinese military power enabled Ryukyu to regain a substantial degree of autonomy. Satsuma guided Ryukyu's foreign policy indirectly, and Ryukyu became an important conduit of goods and information between China and Japan.[1] Maintaining tributary ties with China, however, was very expensive, and Ryukyu would have been unable to do so without substantial material support from Satsuma. Ryukyu had no copper or silver mines, for example, and Satsuma provided Ryukyu with specially minted silver coins for use in official trade with China.

This paper surveys the major forms of money in the Ryukyu kingdom between the time it rose to power as a small-scale empire in the fifteenth century and its annexation by Japan in the 1870s. In addition to intrinsic interest, an examination of Ryukyuan currency also sheds light on Ryukyuan economic, political, and social issues and its relations with China and Japan. The emphasis in this paper will be on the development of Ryukyuan *hatomesen* 鳩目銭 (pigeon-eye cash) in the context of broader economic and political developments.

Early Forms of Copper Cash

There is little direct documentation of Ryukyuan coins minted before the seventeenth century, and many of the details of their manufacture, use, and quantities remain uncertain. Particularly mysterious is the *chūzan tsūhō* 中山通寶 cash. Some sources have speculated that it is the oldest form of Ryukyuan money, but others say that these coins were manufactured during the reign of Shō Shin 尚真 (r. 1477–1526).[2] In any case, there is no extant evidence to date these coins, and there are very few surviving examples.

The three other varieties of early Ryukyuan copper cash can be dated with reasonable certainty based on indirect evidence. *Taisei tsūhō* 大世通寶 were minted during the reign of King Shō Taikyū 尚泰久 (r. 1454–1461), whose posthumous title was Ōyo no nushi 大世主. Likewise, *sedaka tsūhō* 世高通寶 coins were minted during the reign of Shō Toku 尚徳 (r. 1461–

1 For a detailed discussion of the status of early-modern Ryukyu vis-à-vis Japan and China, see Smits 1999, 15–49.

2 Higashionna 1955–1956, 31 and Yamauchi 2004, 64.

1469) and reflect his posthumous title. It seems likely that Ryukyu's connection with China was the main impetus for the minting of these coins, although the circumstances of their production are unclear.

Figure 1. The Ryukyu Islands
SOURCE: Gregory Smits 1999, 4.

One of the rulers of Okinawa established tributary relations with Ming China in 1372. It was not until the early fifteenth century, however, that Okinawan kings received a crown, robes, and the full array other accouterments of investtiture from the Ming court.[3] After the kings of the first Shō dynasty consolidated their control over Okinawa during the first decades of the fifteenth century, trade with China began to con-tribute prominently to the economic foun-dation of the kingdom. The increasing frequency of trade resulted in a shortage of cash. The Ryukyu court repeatedly asked Ming officials to supply it with Yongle coins 永楽銭 (copper cash first minted in 1408) and often had to resort to a type of money order called *chao* 鈔. Because Chinese merchants greatly preferred cash, *chao* traded at a substantial discount to their face value. This money shortage

3 There is an extensive literature on the early development of Ryukyu's relations with China. The best current summary can be found in Tomiyama 2004, 20–53.

was especially acute during the reigns of Shō Taikyū and Shō Toku and is the most likely proximate cause of Ryukyu's minting of coins at this time.[4]

We cannot be certain of the metalworking and minting technology that Ryukyu possessed during the reigns of Shō Taikyū and Shō Toku. Several sources speak vaguely of immigrant Chinese who brought minting techniques to Ryukyu. An analysis of monuments and other public inscriptions suggests that the reign of Shō Taikyū was a transitional period for metalwork. Prior to this reign, Japanese craftsmen inscribed monuments and performed other metalworking tasks, but after Shō Taikyū, Ryukyuans performed all metalwork. It is reasonable to assume that Ryukyuans came to possess the skills and tools needed for minting coins by the middle of the fifteenth century or shortly thereafter.[5] It appears that few if any of the *taisei* and *sedaka* coins were minted from scratch. Instead, they were Yongle coins (possibly damaged or worn) with two characters replaced. Whatever the exact circumstances of their minting may have been, the quality of these coins was poor and not on a par with those produced in China.[6]

Figure 2. Ryukyuan coins
SOURCE: Higashionna Kanjun (1955-1956), front matter.

The quantity of these early Ryukyuan coins was likely quite small for the simple reason that the kingdom lacked any known deposits of copper. Higashionna Kanjun has argued that the royal court produced its own coins to augment the cash shortage and thus facilitate trade with China.[7] Yamauchi Masanao, however, seems skeptical of this claim and suggests that these

4 Higashionna 1955–1956, 19–22.

5 Higashionna 1955–1956, 22–27.

6 Yamauchi Masanao 2004, 62, 64–65.

7 Higashionna 1955–1956, 19–22.

relatively inferior Ryukyuan coins may have been used for domestic purposes.[8] Another possibility is that the minting of these coins served no significant economic purpose. Doing so was an act of symbolic importance for enhancing the political legitimacy of the Ryukyuan kings. At this time, the kings were engaged in attempts to conquer the other Ryukyu Islands, but they also had to be wary of the power of local warlords in Okinawa. Ryukyuan kings sought to legitimize and enhance their power through a variety of symbolic moves, and it is likely that minting cash was part of this effort. It is probably significant that following Shō Shin's reign, when centralized royal authority had become nearly absolute, the minting of coins stopped for over a century. The fourth type of Ryukyuan coin is called *kanamaru sehō* or *kin'en sehō* 金圓世寶. All circumstantial evidence suggests these coins were minted during the reign of Shō En 尚圓 (r. 1470–1476), a former royal official who staged a coup against Shō Toku and founded the second Shō dynasty. The quality of existing coins is superior to that of *taisei* or *sedaka* cash, suggesting an improvement in Ryukyuan minting capabilities.[9] Otherwise, we know very little about these coins. It is likely that they, too, were produced as part of a package of symbolic actions that served to augment the king's authority. Prior to the seventeenth century, the vast majority of Ryukyu's coins came from China and Japan, not from the royal government mints.

The Creation and Official Promotion of Hatomesen

The coins of Japan's Ise Shrine (*gūsen* 宮銭) were called "*hatomesen,*" "*hato no me,*" or "*Ise no hatome.*" Terms such as these also occur in other Japanese contexts in reference to coins of inferior quality. In this broad sense, the term "*hatomesen*" is the rough equivalent of *bitasen* 鐚銭, a general term for unofficial coins. Although the Ryukyuan term "*hatomesen*" undoubtedly derives from Japanese usage, Ryukyuan minting of *hatomesen* was an effort to standardize and improve the currency urban Okinawans used for their ordinary, domestic transactions. It is important to distinguish, there-

8 Yamauchi 2004, 64.
9 Yamauchi Masanao 2004, 65.

fore, between *bitasen,* a variety of coins of different sizes and origins, and *hatomesen,* a standardized from of inexpensive cash produced by government mints. In general, various forms of *bitasen* that had accumulated in Ryukyu were re-minted into *hatomesen* during the middle of the seventeenth century. Early in the eighteenth century, Ryukyu's government sought to remove all other forms of copper cash from daily use, thereby requiring Ryukyuans to use only *hatomesen.* The *bitasen* that became the raw material for the *hatomesen* included several types of inferior cash that circulated in Japanese markets during the late Muromachi and very early Tokugawa periods. As higher quality coins drove inferior cash out of use in Japanese markets, merchants based in Hakata brought many of these undesirable coins to Ryukyu. Furthermore, large quantities of *kinsen* 京銭, mainly inferior coins produced by or for the Southern Ming court, circulated in Ryukyu. During the second half of the seventeenth century, Ryukyuan officials re-cast these coins into *hatomesen*.

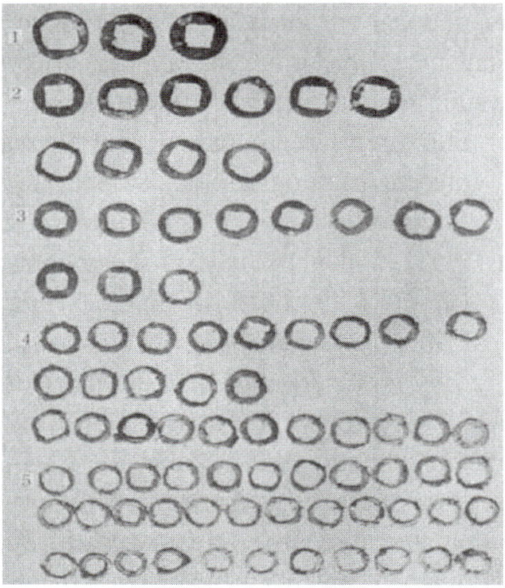

Figure 3. Types of *hatomesen*
SOURCE: Higashionna Kanjun (1955-1956), front matter.

The most important source of raw material for *hatomesen* was the large quantities of *kajikisen* 加治木銭 locked away in storage in Satsuma. *Kajikisen* were privately produced coins for use in Satsuma's territories. Their face resembled Chinese Hongwu cash 洪武通寶, but on the back of each coin was the character *ka, ji,* or *ki,* hence the name *kajikisen.* In 1643, the bakufu strictly prohibited the use of these coins, and Satsuma took them out of circulation and put them into storage. Ijichi Tarōemon Jūchin, later known as Tōma Jūchin 當間重陳 (1591–1676), gave new life to these prohibited coins.[10]

Tōma came to Ryukyu from Satsuma at a young age as a minor official. In a very unusual move, he stayed in Ryukyu, changed his hairstyle and dress to the local manner, and otherwise "went native." With his knowledge of Satsuma, Tōma was an asset to the royal government, and he enjoyed a successful bureaucratic career. In 1656, he visited Satsuma for the first time in forty-five years. There, he obtained permission to return to Ryukyu with large quantities of *kajikisen*. Domain officials also gave him copper Buddhist temple objects confiscated from the outlawed Ikkō sect. With these raw materials in hand, Tōma established mints at Ō-no-yama and Ikehara Village in the district of Goeku. The coins produced from that project were called "*tōmasen.*" The next large-scale minting of *hatomesen* took place in 1715, most likely in preparation for the investiture of King Shō Kei 尚敬 (r. 1713–1751), which took place in 1719. Prior to investiture, Ryukyuan mints produced approximately 110,000 *kan* (1 *kan* = 1000 coins) of *hatomesen*.[11] The various *bitasen* circulating in Ryukyu were gradually minted into *hatomesen* during the late sixteenth and early seventeenth centuries. Based on small variations in diameter and weight, Ryukyuan mints eventually produced five different types of *hatomesen.*[12]

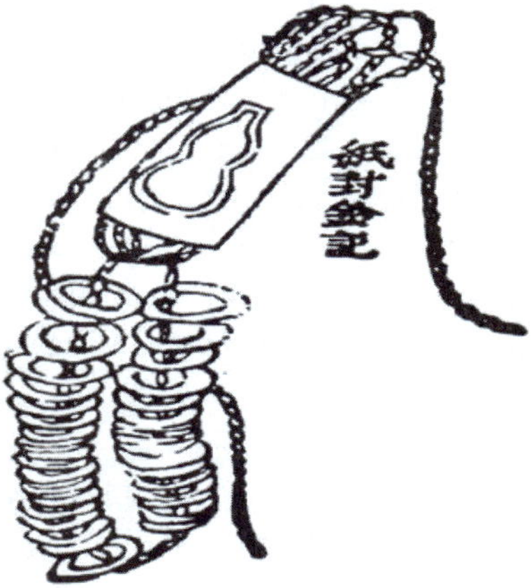

Figure 4. String of sealed *hatomesen* from the *Chūzan denshinroku*
SOURCE: Xu Baoguang 1982, 344.

Prior to the arrival of the Chinese investiture envoys and their entourage of merchants in 1719, the royal government withdrew all Japanese coins

10 The creation of *hatomesen* is discussed to some extent in nearly every general history of Ryukyu. For the most detailed account, see Higashionna 1955–1956, 32–55.

11 Higashionna 1955–1956, 53–54.

12 See Higashionna 1955–1956, last page of the front matter, for a photograph of these five types.

from circulation in the capital region, replacing them with *hatomesen.* The two apparent reasons were to prevent the loss of high-quality coins that might have found their way into the hands of the Chinese merchants via private trade. The other reason for this move was that it was part of a broader effort to hide from Chinese eyes Ryukyu's extensive ties with Japan. If indeed this second reason was behind the withdrawal of Japanese coins, it did not succeed. Investiture envoy Xu Baoguang 徐葆光 wrote an extensive account of conditions in Ryukyu, as was customary. In his account, he explained that previous envoys had reported the extensive use of Japanese coins in the Ryukyuan market places. However, "these coins were temporarily withdrawn and replaced by *hatomesen.* After the envoys went back to China, things returned to their previous condition."[13] Xu was also aware of the origins of *hatomesen:*

> In the marketplace, Ryukyuans conduct their business using cash. There are no silver coins. Among the copper cash are old coins or coins without a clearly-defined border. The square hole in the center is large, and the characters "Hongwu" appear on the face. Such coins have become fewer in number. The main coins in use now are thin iron discs, a string of which is hardly 9-12 centimeters in length, with a weight that amounts to less than a *tael*. The knot on a string of such cash is sealed, and if the seal is broken it cannot be used.[14]

The coins bearing the characters "Hongwu" would have been *kajikisen.* Xu was apparently relying in part on the writing of previous envoys, and his comment that few of these *kajikisen* were now in circulation fits the general trend of the Royal government re-minting all forms of inferior cash into *hatomesen.* The comment about *hatomesen* being "iron" refers to the fact that these coins, although theoretically copper, often contained noticeable admixtures of iron.

During the reign of Shō Kei, the royal government adopted *hatomesen* as the basis for official domestic business and government accounting. Therefore, all cash figures in "*mon*" 文 from 1713 and later refer to *hatomesen.* Prior to this time, "*mon*" might refer to its Japanese value or to *hatomesen* (in some contexts both figures were listed), which were valued at only 1/50th

13 Xu 1982, 345. See also Higashionna 1955–1956, 51–55.

14 Xu 1982, 345, sketch on p. 344. See Figure 4.

of a Japanese *mon*.[15] The government adoption of a *hatomesen*-based financial system was part of a broader effort to require Ryukyuans to use only *hatomesen.* All evidence indicates, however, that Ryukyuans preferred Japanese or Chinese cash whenever possible. By the end of the eighteenth century, Japanese cash began crowding out *hatomesen* in private transactions. *Hatomesen,* however, remained an important currency in Ryukyu until the end of the kingdom. During the eighteenth century, a total of approximately twenty-five varieties of Ryukyuan, Chinese, and Japanese cash circulated in Ryukyu.

Sai On's Theory of the Ryukyuan State

Sai On 蔡温 (1682–1761) was Ryukyu's most prominent politician and scholar. Broadly speaking, he sought, with mixed success, to transform Ryukyu into a Confucian society. Unlike the stereotype of Confucian idealists, Sai On's policies were often rooted in pragmatic considerations. He was well aware that Ryukyu would never become the ideal Confucian society he envisioned without a solid basis of material prosperity. Therefore, the bulk of his administrative effort went toward measures to advance the kingdom's economic wellbeing.

Sai On also adumbrated a theory of the Ryukyuan state. This theory acknowledged the essential role of Satsuma while also minimizing that role and arguing that Ryukyuans themselves bore the main responsibility for the future of their society. This theory can be found in the essay *Hitori monogatari* 獨物語 (One man's views). Briefly, Sai On claimed that Ryukyu had survived as a distinct country for hundreds of years only because of fortuitous accidents of geography, being located under an especially potent array of stars and being shaped like a dragon. Nevertheless, he argued, if the kingdom were to survive and prosper into the future, it must advance the "Way of Government," one of several terms that served as shorthand for his vision of an ideal Confucian society. This Way of Government rested on a material basis, which is the relevant part of his theory for our purposes.

15 Higashionna 1955–1956, 12.

Sai On defined a "country" (*kokudo* 國土) as any place possessing a sufficient material foundation and whose society is guided by proper ethical norms. He defined the material foundation simply as the presence of all five of the agents of *yin* and *yang* (Ch. *wuxing,* Jp. *gogyō* 五行). In this context, the *gogyō* are best regarded as concrete elements, not abstract phases or agents. Furthermore, water, fire, and earth are ubiquitous, so the key variables are wood and metal. Ryukyu possessed forests suitable for timber production and harvesting. Indeed, Sai On's most successful project was an ambitions program of forest cultivation, preservation, and management, implemented throughout the kingdom. In *Hitori monogatari,* Sai On argued that although Ryukyu lacked metal deposits, it could exist as a proper country by using its surplus of wood to import metal from Satsuma.[16] In this way, Sai On acknowledged Satsuma's essential role in supporting Ryukyu but at the same time, he relegated Satsuma to the relatively mundane role of supplier of metal.

We have seen that one example of Satsuma's metal was the *kajikisen* and other copper items that became the raw material for the kingdom's first minting of *hatomesen.* As important as this copper was, Sai On may have been thinking more of silver when he wrote *Hitori monogatari.* The debasements of bakufu silver coins were a severe problem for Ryukyu in conducting its official trade with China. In 1697 the Ryukyuan court sent an envoy to Satsuma, who explained that the newly-minted Genroku coins were not suitable for trade. A decline in the quality of imported Chinese goods in subsequent years and a series of petitions by the royal government starting in 1702 finally convinced Satsuma to approach the bakufu about this matter. Satsuma had been reluctant to do so owing to a desire not to reveal too much about the domain's dealings with Ryukyu and China. Satsuma asked the bakufu for permission to mint coins of pre-1695 silver content. At first, the bakufu was uncooperative, but Satsuma finally attained permission by arguing that if Ryukyu could not fulfill its obligations vis-à-vis the Qing court, then international unrest might result. Ever nervous about Qing military capabilities, the bakufu agreed to the Satsuma petition.[17]

16 Sai On 1984, 88. See also Smits 1999, 84–85. For the details of Sai On's forest policy, see pp. 103–110.

17 For more details, see Smits 1999, 33–34.

Ryukyu's ties to China constituted its political lifeline. Without its access to Chinese goods and information in the context of the lack of official Japanese relations with the Qing court, Ryukyu's quasi-autonomous existence would have ended with Satsuma's 1609 invasion. It was most likely these basic facts, about which Sai On could not directly speak, that he was attempting to remind his readers of in *Hitori monogatari*. Ryukyu's existence as a quasi-independent kingdom indeed depended in part on Satsuma's metal in the form of silver coins and copper for Ryukyuan mints.

References

Higashionna Kanjun 東恩納寛惇 (1955–1956). "Nantō tsūkashi no kenkyū" 南島通貨志の研究 (Research in the History of the Currency of the Southern Islands). In Ryūkyū shinpōsha (comp.) (1979), *Higashionna Kanjun zenshū* 東恩納寛惇全集 (Collected Works of Higashionna Kanjun). Tokyo: Dai'ichi shobō, pp. 3–147.

Sai On 蔡温 (1984). *Sai On zenshū* 蔡温全集. Edited by Sakihama Shūmei 崎濱秀明. Tokyo: Honpō shoseki.

Smits, Gregory (1999). *Visions of Ryukyu: Identity and Ideology in Early-Modern Thought and Politics*. Honolulu: University of Hawai'i Press.

Tomiyama Kazuyuki (2004). *Ryūkyū ōkoku no gaikō to ōken* 琉球王国の外交と王権 (Foreign Relations and Royal Authority in the Ryukyu Kingdom). Tokyo: Yoshikawa kōbunkan.

Xu Baoguang 徐葆光 (1982). *Chūzan denshinroku* 中山伝信録. Translated and edited by Harada Nobuo 原田禹雄. Tokyo: Gensōsha. Chinese version originally published in 1721.

Yamauchi Masanao 山内昌尚 (2004). *Sengo Okinawa tsūka hensenshi: beigun tōchi jidai o chūshin ni* 戦後沖縄通貨変遷史：米軍統治時代を中心に (The History of Postwar Okinawa Currency Changes Focusing on the Period of Untied States Military Occupation). Naha, Japan: Ryūkyū shinpōsha.

Copper Smelting and Fuel Consumption in Yunnan, Eighteenth to Nineteenth Centuries*

Hans Ulrich Vogel

This article provides a systematic introduction to the history of smelting technology and fuel consumption in eighteenth and nineteenth century Yunnan. In the first section, based on Chinese sources and Western and Japanese reports, types and categories of ores mined in Yunnan and the names given to them by miners or officials are identified. The second describes the different roasting, smelting, separation and cupellation processes used by Yunnanese metallurgists. Finally, data on the consumption of fuel for various metallurgical processes is analyzed. A detailed reconstruction of mining and smelting techniques in use in Yunnan during different periods is important not only for our knowledge on the history of the Chinese mining industry, but also for a better understanding of environmental problems caused by this industry, with effects that in some areas are still painfully felt today.

Introduction

This study attempts to reconstruct the historical copper roasting and smelting techniques in Yunnan province in the eighteenth and nineteenth centuries, with a focus on problems of fuel supply for the operations involved. The main source for the investigation is the *Diannan kuangchang tulüe* 滇南礦廠圖略 (An Illustrated Account of the Mines and Smelters of Yunnan; hereafter: DNKCTL), published in 1844 by Wu Qijun 吳其濬 (1789–1847), with illustrations by Xu Jinsheng 徐金生. The first chapter of this work contains a number of entries and essays concerning social, economic, technical and cultural dimensions of mining and smelting.[1] In addition to rela-

* I would like to thank Prof. Andreas Hauptmann of the Deutsche Bergbau-Museum in Bochum, Germany, and Dr. Nanny Kim for their critical remarks on the manuscript, which were helpful in improving it. For revising my English I am indebted to Mrs. Kim Fechner of the Institute of Chinese and Korean Studies at Tübingen University.

1 This main chapter was translated into English in 1999 and 2000 by Peter J. Golas (University of Denver), Michael Schön (Universität Tübingen), and Hans Ulrich Vogel (Universität Tübingen) within the framework of a project supported by the DAAD and the ACLS. The titel of the project was *Wu Qijun (1789–1847) and the Diannan kuangchang tulüe (Illustrated Account of the Mines and Smelters of Yunnan): Mining and Smelting*

tively general information on these aspects, the DNKCTL also contains material from the lost work [*Yunnan*] *tongzheng quanshu* [雲南]銅政全書 (Complete Writings on the Copper Administration of Yunnan), a compilation in 50 chapters commissioned by the Yunnan Financial Commissioner Wang Chang 王昶 (1724–1806) in 1787.[2] At some point of time before the compilation, investigations were carried out by collecting quite specific information on prospecting, mining, and smelting techniques from the responsible mining officials. It appears that mining officials, i.e. local officials who were at the same time responsible for the mines within their jurisdiction in different parts of the province, were confronted with a sort of questionnaire which they had to answer. The tenor of the information can be gathered from the following excerpt from an exchange concerning prospecting:

> Questions: "Earth is the mother of Metal. If the *qi* of Earth is not substantial, it cannot give rise to Metal. Yunnan produces the Five Metals, of which copper is essential for minting. We have heard that prospectors' inevitably examining the formation of mountains is equivalent to geomancers' divining the earth's physiognomy. This is because the form (*xing* 形) and the formation (*shi* 勢) of mountains not only constitute their surface appearance, but, in reality, also make up the embryo of ores (*kuang zhi peitai* 鑛之胚胎). How does one have to assess [the terrain] and initiate excavations in order to obtain hall ore (*tang-kuang* 堂鑛)?"
>
> …
>
> Wu Daya 吳大雅, the mining official (*changyuan* 廠員) of the Wanbao 萬寶 and Yidu 義都 mines and acting District Magistrate of Yimen 義門 District, reported to us: "It is a general rule that the *qi* of the Five Phases in movement flows and in concentration coagulates. …"[3]

This unique information contained in the DNKCTL is supplemented with accounts provided in other Chinese sources of the period and Western and

Technology in Late Imperial China.
Members of the research group have translated Wang Taiyue's 王太岳 lengthy essay 'Deliberations about the Copper Administration' (*Tongzheng yi* 銅政議) of 1775. This essay is part of the second main chapter of the DNKCTL. Presently, Chen Hailian and Gao Xuan of the Institute for History of Science and Technology & Ancient Texts, Tsinghua University, are undertaking a thorough analysis of the administrative parts in the second main chapter of the DNKCTL.

2 On this work see Vogel (1983), Appendix A.

3 DNKCTL, chap. A, 38a.

Japanese field reports of the late nineteenth and early twentieth centuries.[4] To date, the topic of smelting and fuel consumption in late imperial Yunnan has been little studied, both in Western and Chinese languages. Information on various types of copper ores and copper minerals, as well as on the specific names under which they were known in traditional China, can be found in the *Science and Civilisation in China* series; particular reference is being made in the volumes on practical alchemy[5] and mining.[6] The monograph on Chinese mining history published by Xia Xiangrong and his collaborators, which contains some paragraphs on the ores and smelting methods in late imperial Yunnan, is another contribution to the field.[7] Fuel consumption has to some extent been researched with regard to traditional forestry management[8] and environmental history.[9] Yang Yuda has recently published an innovative article on copper mining in north-eastern Yunnan in the period from 1726 to 1855, focusing on its horrendous impact on the environment, especially through deforestation.[10]

4 Rocher 1879, vol. 2, 195–260; Brown 1923, including summaries of the reports of Duclos 1896–1897, Leclère 1891, Lantenois 1903–1904, and Deprat & Mansuy 1909–1911.

5 Needham & Lu 1974, 162–187, Table 95, Nomenclature of chemical substances, ores and minerals.

6 See Golas 1999, 70, Table 6, Main copper ores exploited by the Chinese in traditional times.

7 Xia Xiangrong et al. 1980, especially 242–253, 258–260, 266–269.

8 Cf. Menzies 1996, 616–622, 654–667, who, however, is mainly concerned with forestry in an agricultural environment, so-called agroforestry. Menzies 1996, 629, states that China was much more characterized by intensive forestry than by extensive silviculture. Moreover, he mentions that the effects on the forests of cutting for fuel wood and charcoal are hard to gauge, because of the scarcity of relevant information (656), and that in China the technology for using coal in iron smelting was available much earlier than in Europe, may thus have relieved the pressure on charcoal, and offered little incentive to practice extensive forestry (666). As will be shown in this study, charcoal and fuel wood, and not coal, were by far the most important fuels for the Yunnan smelting industry from the eighteenth to the mid-nineteenth centuries.

9 Cf. with regard to mining Vermeer 1998, 247–252; Dunstan 1998, 603–610. On the patterns of deforestation in China see Elvin 2004, 19–85, 244–252.

10 See Yang Yuda 2004. I am grateful to Nanny Kim for pointing out this article to me.

Types of Copper Ores

The main copper ores of the Yunnan mines which could be processed with traditional techniques were—in modern geological terms—native copper (Cu, *zirantong* 自然銅 etc.), tenorite (CuO, oxide, *huoyaosu* 火藥酥), chalcocite (Cu_2S, sulphide, *lüxila* 綠錫蠟 etc.), bornite (Cu_5FeS_4, sulphide, *zijin xila* 紫金錫蠟 etc.), as well as malachite ($Cu_2(CO_3)(OH)_2$, carbonate, *molü* 墨綠 etc.). Belonging to the zone of secondary enrichment, they were of high tenor, and often located above the water table. Another ore was chalcopyrite ($CuFeS_2$, sulphide, *huangjinbo* 黃金箔), a mineral belonging to the category of primary ores.[11] The latter was of low tenor and mostly located deep down, usually below the water table. Its deposits, however, were much larger than those of the ores of the secondary zone.[12] "[This ore] is often accompanied by water, but can be exploited for a very long time."[13] *Baixila* 白錫蠟 seems to have been present, as well. If following the conventional reading, it corresponds either to enargite (Cu_3AsS_4, sulphosalt) or tetrahedrite ($Cu_{12}Sb_4S_{13}$, sulphosalt).[14] Covellite (CuS, sulphide) is a further mineral which is mentioned.[15]

The ores of the famous mines of Dongchuan were deposits that had formed in layers in marine sediments. They were composed mainly of malachite, chalcocite and bornite, being deposited in oxidation zones, as well as zones of secondary enrichment. Azurite ($Cu_3(CO_3)_2(OH)_2$) and chalcopyrite as primary ores are also mentioned. The geological conditions required for intense oxidation were actually not ideal in Dongchuan, due to the relatively low proportion of pyrite (iron disulfide, FeS_2, *huangtiekuang* 黃鐵礦). Moreover, carbonate, located in the surrounding carbonate rock, caused the copper sulphate solutions to produce malachite and azurite. Both hindered the process of secondary enrichment. Nevertheless, in the course of long geological periods very large deposits of secondary sulphides were successively formed. This process was facilitated by the presence of friable rock.

11 Xia Xiangrong et al. 1980, 253; see also Table 1.

12 Xia Xiangrong et al. 1980, 253.

13 DNKCTL, chap. A, 6b.

14 See Table 2.

15 See Table 1, Pe-si-la.

The latter had a positive influence on the formation of an oxidation zone, which reached a depth of more than 600 m.[16]

In the early twentieth century Japanese researchers reported the presence of native copper deposits. These formed either plates or flakes both at Houyan 猴岩 and Zhatang 札塘. Both mines were located at a distance of one and a half days' journey from Dongchuan city. The researchers also pointed out that the copper ore veins, which they had seen, varied considerably in thickness. This variation ranged between 2 to 5 *chi* (1 *chi* = ca. 0.32 m) at a length of several *li* (1 *li* = ca. 576 m). Several small veins could join to form a large vein, which was 20 to 30 *chi* thick. At Longweiba 龍尾巴 the vein measured 50 feet in thickness at a length of several *li*.[17]

Sources from the period of the Great Leap Forward, in which native methods of copper smelting (*tufa liantong* 土法练铜) were investigated, indicate that Dongchuan copper ore consisted mainly of carbonates, especially malachite and azurite. The composition of two individual samples which had been prepared and washed for smelting is stated to be as follows:

	copper Cu	iron oxide Fe_2O_3	aluminium oxide Al_2O_3	calcium oxide CaO	magnesium oxide MgO	silicon dioxide SiO_2	sulphur S
%	10.74	3.36	2.94	17.45	13.45	17.75	2.78
%	14.54	8.72	1.97	13.01	8.04	22.55	1.88

The tenor of the ore was over 10 percent. Its content of calcium and magnesium was high, whereas that of iron and sulphur was low.[18]

Lantenois observed in 1903 that secondary enrichment was strong and prevalent in Yunnan. He distinguished four types of copper ore deposits,

16 Xia Xiangrong et al. 1980, 259.

17 Cf. *Unnanshō jijō*, vol. 2, 124–125; *Shina shōbetsu zenshi*, vol. 3, 720–721. I am grateful to Prof. Kuroda Akinobu for having provided me with copies of the relevant sections of these work.

18 Cf. Dongchuan kuangwuju 1959, 1. On pp. 7 and 8, however, the percentages of Fe_2O_3 are different for the same samples, namely 2.69 and 6.98 percent respectively. I am indebted to Nanny Kim for having provided me with a copy of this report from the Yunnan University Library.

which were all more or less in direct association with eruptive rocks such as andesites and basalts:

- in contraction fissures and cracks of the eruptive rocks;
- pocket deposits in the contact zone of eruptive rocks and limestone;
- in irregular fissures in limestone in the vicinity of eruptive rocks;
- in more or less open fractures continuous across limestone and shale.[19]

Table 1 is a summary of the mineralogical observations made by French, English and Japanese explorers at the turn of the twentieth century.

Traditional Ways of Differentiating Types of Ores

In Qing period Yunnan, ores were differentiated by tenor as well as by colour, shape, pattern and appearance:

- The first type of ore was native copper (*shengtong* 生銅, *zilaitong* 自來銅 etc.). Its actual content of copper could be as high as 99 percent (Table 2). The sources indicate that adding an ore of such metallic substance in a smelting process (*gaijian* 改煎) could increase [the overall copper] tenor of the load. Large pieces of native copper were sometimes made [directly] into vessels.[20] This type of relatively pure copper ore was certainly rare.[21]
- The second type of high-quality ore was tenorite (*huoyaosu* 火藥酥). It was not easy to obtain either. Being black and brittle, it was occasionally mixed with native copper or cuprite (Cu_2O; oxide, modern term: *chitongkuang* 赤銅礦). The mixture obtained could then reach a tenor of 90 percent. It was thus rightly considered to be of extraordinary high quality.[22]

19 Lantenois 1907, 406, summarized by Brown 1923, 103.

20 DNKCTL, chap. A, 6b. The statement that large pieces of native copper were directly used for making vessels makes clear that the meaning of *zirantong* 自然銅 corresponds to 'native copper' at this point. Xia Xiangrong et al. 1980, 243, mention that *zirantong* usually refers to pyrites in ancient texts. See also Golas 1999, 58n2.

21 See Ni Shenshu 倪慎樹, 'Cai tong lian tong ji' 採銅煉銅記 (Account of the Mining and Smelting of Copper), in DNKCTL, chap. A, 34a. During their field trip in March/April 2007, lumps of *zirantong* were seen by Nanny Kim and Hans-Joachim Rosner at the house of an artisan who directly casts thin-walled objects from this copper, which are then polished and laquered.

22 DNKCTL, chap. A, 12b, and *Tongzheng quanshu*, in DNKCTL, chap. A, 39b.

- A third group comprised the so-called 'tin wax' (*xila* 錫蠟)[23] ores. In geological and chemical terms, this group comprised various types of ores, such as sulphides of "green" chalcocite (*lüxila* 綠錫蠟) and "red" bornite (*zijin xila* 紫金錫蠟 etc.). It might also have included the "white" sulphosalts enargite or tetrahedrite (*baixila* 白錫蠟). For the traditional miners, high tenor as well as glossiness and waxy appearance of these ores, which were of different colours, were the most common characteristics for distinguishing them. In ca. 1799 Tan Cui 檀萃 wrote that [among the ordinary ores, i.e. with the exception of native copper and tenorite] the *xila* 錫鑞 ores are best. These are followed by malachite types (*molü* 墨綠) and chalcopyrite (*huangjinbo* 黃金箔). Among the *xila* ores Tan Cui rates *lüxila* 綠錫蠟 (chalcosite) highest, followed by *baixila* 白錫蠟 (probably enargite or tetrahedrite?), *lantou xila* 爛頭錫蠟 (not identified), and, finally, *zhuhong xila* 硃硔錫蠟 (bornite).[24]
- The fourth group consisted of 'green ores', which apparently was malachite, such as *molü* 墨綠, *huangpanglü* 黃胖綠, *douqinglü* 豆青綠, and *heilü* 黑綠. These were all considered to be relatively rich ores. The *yazikuang* 亞子鑛 or *dayazi* 大亞子 and the *chuanhualü* 穿花綠 belonged to the category of green ores, as well. The former could form substantial deposits in the form of bricks, while the latter were rather poor ores, interspersed with large amounts of rock. Further types of 'green ores', *songlü* 鬆綠, *lüsong* 綠松, *lükuang* 綠礦 etc. were not used for smelting, but only as colouring agents. It is not entirely clear whether all these types can be identified as malachite. Moreover, there was one type of ore which, though greenish in colour, was not separately classified as *xila* ore: the 'green tin wax' (*lüxila* 綠錫蠟). It seems, however, that *xila* ores generally came in lumps with a shiny metallic gloss. This characteristic does not apply to the malachite ores, and therefore may have been the criterion for the differentiation between 'green ores' and green *xila* ores.[25]

23 Sometimes the second character is written with the 'stone' or 'metal' radical, i.e. 鑞 or [石+巤]. See, e.g. *Dianhai yuheng zhi*, chap. 2, 1b, and *Diannan xinyu*, chap. 4, 229b (6060), respectively.

24 *Dianhai yuheng zhi*, chap. 2, 1b, 2b.

25 Xia Xiangrong et al. 1980, 250.

- The fifth type of ore was chalcopyrite (*huangjinpo* 黄金箔). These ores were of rather low tenor. Being ore of the primary zone chalcopyrite occurred in large quantities and could be mined for a long period of time. It was associated with water, as the deposits were located deep down, actually below the water table. In Chinese natural thought metal and water were closely related.
- In addition to copper ores, the DNKCTL also mentions copper-silver ores, silver-copper ores, silver ores, and galena (PbS) mixed with copper and silver. Silver ores from Yunnan contained not only copper and lead, but often also gold. Such ores were extracted for example in the famous mines of Gejiu 箇舊, and the mining districts of Shiyangchang, Bainiu 白牛 and Malong 馬龍 in Lin'an 臨安.[26]

Interestingly, the copper ores of Yunnan were of relatively high tenor compared to other Chinese copper ores of whose copper content we have some conception. Xia Xiangrong et al. provide figures on copper ores from different historical periods. These examples—few as they may be—show that in other periods of Chinese history smelters often had to make do with ores of much lower quality, for example ores of 2.08–4.16 percent copper content in the Wei period (4th–6th centuries) and of 3.3 and 11–15 percent in the Ming period (1368–1644).[27] The tenors of the Yunnan ores could be nearly 100 percent for native copper, while ranging from 90 (tenorite) to 30–60 percent (*xila* ores) for the better qualities. Tan Cui explains that ores with a copper content as low as ca. 4–5 percent could not be profitably smelted if used in their pure form. These had to be mixed [to a certain extent] with good quality ores.[28] In the late nineteenth and early twentieth century western observers noted that smelting in Yunnan mostly used ores with a copper content above 20 percent. Ores of only 10 percent copper content were rarely processed (see Table 1). At the Lao-tchang (Laochang 老廠) mine in Dongchuan smelters accepted only ores with a copper tenor of 20 percent or more.[29] It seems that by the late nineteenth and early twentieth century, min-

26 Rocher 1879, 238–239.

27 Xia Xiangrong et al. 1980, 251–252.

28 *Dianhai yuheng zhi*, chap. 2, 2b.

29 Brown 1923, 106.

ers and smelters had to be content with ores of lower quality than only a century earlier.

Traditional Methods of Processing Ores

Ore that consisted of earth and stone had to be crushed, segregated, washed and sieved before smelting.[30] Since ores contained gangue, they first had to be broken up into pieces. These were then washed in a sieve [partially suspended] in water, which caused the light gangue to float on the surface, where it could then be washed away by water. The heavy ore settled down in the sieves. This was the sign for its readiness to be smelted.[31] Furthermore, we are being told here that ore was crushed and sifted if rocky, while washed if embedded in a clayish matrix.[32]

When Brown visited the Pao-p'ing-ch'ang mine west of Yongbei 永北 in 1909, he reported that the larger pieces were broken up and spread on sorting tables after having been carried to the surface in baskets by boys. Each sorting table was staffed with 8 to 10 women, who would skilfully pick the rich pieces and place them into baskets.[33] In the case of processing galena (PbS) in Western Yunnan, larger pieces of ore were not only broken apart using hammers, but also with the help of water-driven stamps. The latter worked in the same way as an ordinary Chinese overshot waterwheel used for the husking of rice:

> … Two heavy bars of wood are let in at right angels into the axle on both sides of the wheel. They are so arranged that as the wheel revolves they strike alternately heavy wooden beams which are poised as levers, by being supported at about two-thirds of their length. The blow delivered on one end of the beam depresses it and lifts up the other end. To the latter end a pestle is attached, made of wood as in the case of a rice mill, but fitted with a heavy iron shoe when stone is to be crushed. The pestle falls into a mortar in which the pieces

30 Ni Shenshu, in DNKCTL, chap. A, 34b.

31 *Tongzheng quanshu*, in DNKCTL, chap. A, 39b.

32 *Tongzheng quanshu*, in DNKCTL, chap. A, 41a.

33 Brown 1923, 115.

of ore are placed. A strong stream of water carried in a box to the wheel serves to drive this rough but none the less useful machine.[34]

Traditional Methods of Mixing Ores

All traditional Chinese authors stress the fact that ores needed to be balanced with regard to their density when subjected to smelting. If the melt of an ore was too "oily" or thick, a thin ore was to be added. Sometimes also white rock (*baishi* 白石) was used for this purpose. If the melt of the ore was clear and thin, one could add thick ore or yellow earth (*huangtu* 黄土) to balance.[35] Such admixtures with rock and earth as fluxing agents were referred to as 'stone additives' (*daishi* 帶石),[36] 'diluting rock' (*xishi* 稀石, Dabao mine)[37] or 'agent stone' (*daishi* 代石).[38] Rocher noted in 1873 that copper ore was placed in a furnace and then admixed with a siliceous stone called 'changing stone' (*gaishi* 改石), after the crushing and washing procedure. The amount of the latter corresponded to 1/5 of the ore's own weight. As for smelting at the Tangdan mines, this stone was obtained from nearby Xuanwei Department 宣威州. Half a pound cost 1 cash coin at the smelting site.[39]

Occasionally the ore melt did not segregate during smelting, but instead congealed and formed lumps. This could occur even if the ore filled into the furnace was of very good quality. An imbalance of either ore density or the firing process was held responsible for this phenomenon.[40] Another text passage attributes the congealing of ore and slag into one big chunk to an imbalance in the ore mixture. This unfortunate result was referred to as 'raising the monk's head' (*tai heshang tou* 擡和尚頭).[41]

34 Brown 1923, 133.

35 Ni Shenshu, in DNKCTL, chap. A, 34b.

36 Ni Shenshu, in DNKCTL, chap. A, 34b; *Tongzheng quanshu*, in DNKCTL, chap. A, 40a (Dabao mine), 42a, 45a.

37 *Tongzheng quanshu*, in DNKCTL, chap. A, 45a.

38 *Tongzheng quanshu*, in DNKCTL, chap. A, 41a.

39 Rocher 1879, vol. 2, 225.

40 Ni Shenshu, in DNKCTL, chap. A, 34b; *Tongzheng quanshu*, in DNKCTL, chap. A, 45a.

41 See DNKCTL, chap. A, 9a. A similar, though perhaps not the same problem, occurred during the oxidation phase of the Japanese *mabuki* 間吹 process, when a part of the sulphur oxidized to SO_3 and SO_2, while copper partly oxidised to Cu_2O and CuO. Because

Traditional Methods of Roasting and Smelting Ores and Separating Metals

The most systematic descriptions of the smelting processes of copper, silver-copper and copper-silver ores can be found in Ni Shenshu's 倪慎樹 'Account of the mining and smelting of copper' ('Cai tong lian tong ji' 採銅煉銅記, in DNKCTL), the *Tongzheng quanshu* (in DNKCTL), and in the summaries of mining and smelting in the DNKCTL. Basically, these treatises describe six different types of smelting operations related to the smelting of high quality copper ores: 'thorough' copper ores, poor copper ores, *mingkuang* 明鑛 ores (galena (PbS) mixed with copper and silver), copper-silver ores, and silver-copper ores:[42]

Type A. Smelting of high quality copper ores

Some ores did not require roasting, but had to be subjected to only one smelting process. This type of smelting, which was only applicable to ores of high quality, was called 'copper-produced-by-one-firing' (*yi huo cheng tong* 一火成銅).[43] It is stated that this type of ore could increase [the overall copper] tenor of a furnace load if added to another smelting process (*gaijian* 改煎).[44] Ni Shenshu points out that ore which contained a high percentage of copper could be loaded instantly (*ji* 即) into the great smelting furnace (*dalu* 大爐). There it would be fired for a whole day and a whole night. The ashes would be snagged and removed from the furnace's 'metal gate'. Eventually, the molten copper would sink to the bottom of the furnace, where it would flash and bubble. Water which had been used to wash rice[45] was poured on

the copper oxides are less fusible than Cu_2S, the melt shows the tendency to solidify and to stick to the walls of the hearth. See Okada 1911, 16.

42 This differentiation is much more the result of my own analysis than that of the DNKCTL itself.

43 DNKCTL, chap. A, 6a.

44 See DNKCTL, chap. A, 6b. As was mentioned above, large pieces of native copper were sometimes made [directly] into vessels.

45 In the *Tongzheng quanshu* (DNKCTL, chap. A, 45b) this was called "acid water in which rice had been washed" (*tao mi suanshui* 淘米酸水). Rocher 1879, vol. 2, 224–225, mentions the term 'rice soup' (*mitang* 米湯). He says that pouring this fluid on the copper

the melt, thus causing a layer of copper to congeal on the surface, which would be taken out with tongs. The outer surface of the copper would be polished using pine needles and chaff. Next, it would be immersed in water, causing it to directly turn into purple slabs (*ziban* 紫板).[46] 5 to 6 or even 7 cakes could be taken out in this manner. The first two discs to be extracted were not free of impurities and were referred to as 'coarse copper' (*maotong* 毛銅). Only re-smelting would turn it into pure [copper]. The discs extracted from the third, fourth and any further layer, though, were considered pure copper (*jingtong* 淨銅). Mines at which smelters could produce copper in one firing process were, however, very few.[47]

One such mine was the Xiangshupo 香樹坡 mine in Nan'an Department 南安州. The description of this mine in the *Tongzheng quanshu* resembles that by Ni Shenshu. The *Tongzheng quanshu* mentions the fact that for each firing 40 buckets [or: 4,000 *jin*][48] of superior ore were used. In addition, approximately 3,000 *jin* of charcoal were burnt. For ore of medium quality the figures are 70–80 buckets [7,000–8,000 *jin*] and ca. 3,500–3,600 *jin* respectively. For ore of inferior quality the corresponding figures are 110 buckets [11,000 *jin*] and slightly more than 4,000 *jin*. The refining of the coarse copper (*maotong*) is said to have been carried out in the smelting furnace (*lu* 鑪).[49] For the re-smelting of coarse copper 150–160 *jin* of charcoal were required. This resulted in a loss of 2–3 *jin* for every hundred *jin* of copper.[50] While in one instance it is clearly stated that the only process ap-

melt produces an acid effect, cleans the surface and creates a rose color which is appreciated by the buyers.

46 Rocher 1879, vol. 2, 225, who basically describes the same smelting process, gives a different sequence: First the copper cakes are spread on, and covered with, a layer of green pine twigs. After the twigs have been reduced to ashes, the cakes are cooled in water. The acid of the pine twigs cleans also the bottom of the copper cakes.

47 Ni Shenshu, in DNKCTL, chap. A, 34b–35a.

48 In selling ore, 'bucket' was used as the unit of volume. 1 bucket was roughly equivalent to one *hu* of granary *dou* (*cangdou* 倉斗). After soaking and washing, 2 or 3 *dou* of ore remained for further processing. See *Tongzheng quanshu*, in DNKCTL, chap. A, 42a. For an estimate of the weight of 1 bucket of ore see below, where I come to the conclusion that 1 bucket of ore was equivalent to about 100 *jin*.

49 It is not inconceivable that a crab shell furnace was used for this purpose, however.

50 *Tongzheng quanshu*, in DNKCTL, chap. A, 45a–b.

plied at the Xiangshupo mines is the smelting of copper in a great furnace,[51] another passage mentions the adoption of one or two roasting processes prior to smelting in the furnace (*lu*).[52] Thus, it appears that the processing in Xiangshupo was in between types A and B. At least for the cases of the more inferior ores mentioned above, this seems plausible.[53]

In 1898 Leclère visited the Tangdan mines of Dongchuan. He observed the smelting of carbonate ores in Japanese furnaces. The height of the furnaces was ca. 2m. They were equipped with a tuyere and typical Chinese piston bellows, exactly as for the common furnaces. The fusion generally lasted five days. After a preliminary filling of charcoal, small quantities of carbonate and charcoal were constantly added and from time to time also a little sulphide ore. Eventually, when the bottom was filled with crude copper, a hole was pierced into the door, through which the slag could escape. This type of furnace would produce ca. 300 kg of raw copper.[54]

Type B. Smelting of 'thorough' copper ores

With the exception of 'copper-produced-by-one-firing', all other smelting processes, by which ores were roasted or cupellated one to eight or nine times, were referred to as 'multiple-freezings-multiple-cupellations' (*ji bing ji zhao* 幾冰幾罩).[55] A distinction within the second type was made between ores that were easy to smelt and those that were difficult to process, the latter requiring several separate roastings. The available texts tell us that smelting of the so-called 'thorough ores' (*chekuang* 徹鑛) or 'pure ores' (*jingkuang* 淨鑛) was relatively easy.[56] The *Tongzheng quanshu* states that 'thorough ore' is very heavy and without any inclusion of earth, sand or other impuri-

51 *Tongzheng quanshu*, in DNKCTL, chap. A, 45a.

52 *Tongzheng quanshu*, in DNKCTL, chap. A, 45b.

53 Moreover, the Xiangshupo mines also seem to have adopted the smelting process of type C for poorer ores. Cf. *Tongzheng quanshu*, in DNKCTL, chap. A, 42a. Thus type A was not as exclusive there as it appears at first sight.

54 Leclère 1891, as paraphrased by Brown 1923, 107.

55 DNKCTL, chap. A, 6a.

56 Miners did not say 'good ores' (*haokuang* 好礦), because the character *hao* 好 (good) was homonymous with *hao* 耗 (waste), but preferred to talk of *chekuang* 徹礦 (thorough ore). See DNKCTL, chap. A, 22a.

ties.[57] According to Ni Shenshu's account the following ores belonged to the category of 'thorough ores': the tenorite *huoyaosu* 火藥酥; the malachite ores *huangpanglü* 黄胖綠, *douqinglü* 豆青綠, *heilü* 黑綠; the sulphosalt (?) *baixila* 白錫蠟; the sulphides *hongxila* 紅錫蠟 and *zijin xila* 紫金錫蠟; and last *youxila* 油錫蠟.[58] In a similar vein, the *Tongzheng quanshu* lists the following ores as ores of high tenor: the 'green ores' or malachite ores *molü* 墨綠 and *douqing* 豆青; the *xila* ores *baixila*, *youxila*, *zijin xila*, the tenorite *huoyaosu*.[59]

In most Yunnan mines it was necessary to roast the ore in kilns (*yao* 窰), before it could be processed further in the smelting furnace (*lu*). The ore was placed between layers of firewood and charcoal and sealed with mud on the outside. Something akin to a chimney hole (*huokou* 火口; lit. 'fire hole') was left on top. 'Thorough ores' and other ores which were easy to smelt were roasted twice in such kilns before being smelted once in a furnace (*lu*). The result was black copper (*heitong* 黑銅), that was then put into a crab shell furnace (*xiekelu* 蟹殼鑪) in order to further smelt it into crab shell copper (*xieketong* 蟹殼銅). We are being told here that the lifting out and the cooling [of crab shell copper] (by immersing it in water) were largely done in the same way as in type A smelting.[60]

In the Dagong mine 大功 in Yunlong Department 雲龍州 the ore was first placed in the roasting kiln (*weiyao* 煨窰) for two roastings. Next, it would be transferred to great smelting furnaces (*dalu* 大鑪), which could be loaded with ca. 20 buckets [2,000 *jin*] of ore and used up more than 2,000 *jin* of pine charcoal. The smelting continued day and night until the molten copper flowed into a cavity at the bottom of the furnace to form black slab copper (*heibantong* 黑板銅). This substance was then loaded into the crab shell furnace (*xiekelu*) and smelted therein until crab shell copper, the intended product, could be lifted out. For each crab shell furnace charge of ca. 400 *jin* of black copper (*heitong* 黑銅) ca. 500 *jin* of charcoal were required. After the molten copper had flown into the bottom cavity, it was be sprinkled with a ladle filled with [rice] water. Thereafter one disc of copper after the next

57 *Tongzheng quanshu*, in DNKCTL, chap. A, 42a.

58 Ni Shenshu, in DNKCTL, chap. A, 34a.

59 *Tongzheng quanshu*, in DNKCTL, chap. A, 40b–41a.

60 Ni Shenshu, in DNKCTL, chap. A, 35a–b.

was lifted out. The transformation of black copper into crab shell copper resulted in a loss of about 10 *jin* for every hundred *jin* of metal.[61]

This process as described by traditional Chinese sources is basically similar to that observed by Brown in 1909 at the Pao-p'ing-ch'ang mines west of Yongbei. As the latter is regarded one of the most detailed reports on Yunnan smelting operations, and as it contains information on different types of kilns and furnaces, as well as on operation periods, it deserves to be quoted in full length:

> The rich picked ores, consisting chiefly of erubescite [i.e. bornite, Cu_5FeS_4] and chalcopyrite [$CuFeS_2$] are carried down to the smelters which are situated in the village. They are first of all roasted in large quadrangular kilns for three days with ironstone, charcoal and wood. The caked masses from this operation go into the large blast furnaces; the smalls and dust are washed, the heavier portions kept, and smelted in a special furnace of smaller dimensions. The preliminary calcination appears to drive off volatile impurities, to reduce the ores to a certain extent and to prepare a hard porous cake in good condition for the final operation in the blast furnace. Three sizes of blast furnace are made use of generally in benches of six. The largest are 20 to 25 feet high with a covered-in chimney, but with a long opening in front, above the wall of the actual reaction chamber, which is of course smaller. The other furnaces are about 15 feet high, and there is also a still smaller type. The smelting operation takes three days to complete in the biggest furnaces, working day and night, and twelve hours in the smallest type. The blast is supplied from large cylindrical blowers worked by relays of coolies. The molten metal is not tapped, but when the reaction is completed the front of the furnace is broken in, leaving a bath of molten metal at the bottom in the hemispherical-based crucible. This is allowed to cool down, and the cooling process is hastened by spraying rice water on the hot surface, which as it solidifies is removed in plates.[62]

According to a Japanese report of the early twentieth century, roasting ore in Dongchuan took five days and required two to three men. As for the smelting process, a period of three to five days is indicated.[63]

Agricola wrote that ore was roasted for two reasons, firstly in order to make hard ore soft and friable, secondly to burn off 'fat substances' like sul-

61 *Tongzheng quanshu*, in DNKCTL, chap. A, 42b–43a.

62 Brown 1923, 115.

63 *Unnanshō jijō*, vol. 2, 129.

phur, bitumen, realgar, and orpiment.[64] In Pao-p'ing-ch'ang it was obviously for the second reason, i.e. the treatment of sulphide ores, that roasting was adopted. Sulphur had to be burnt off, because it would otherwise, in the words of Agricola, consume the metal in the intense heat of the furnace, turn it to ashes and transmit it to slag.[65] Brown noted in his report that the furnace was not tapped, but that typically the molten copper was lifted from the bottom of the furnace in the shape of round plates. These plates solidified when rice water was sprayed on the surface of the molten metal.[66]

Type C. Smelting of poor copper ores

At the Zhe'nang 者囊 mine in Wenshan District 文山縣 the ore was first loaded in great kilns (*dayao* 大窑) and then roasted once. One charge would correspond to 10,000 *jin* and require over 400 *jin* of charcoal. The loss of ore amounted to 300–400 *jin*. Next, a kind of agent stone of greenish- white colour (*qingbai daishi* 青白帶石) was added as fluxing agent. Then the mixture was fired in great smelting furnaces (*dalu* 大鑪). For 1,600–1,700 *jin* of frozen copper (*bingtong* 冰銅) obtained, 7,800–7,900 *jin* of metal would be lost. The frozen copper was then roasted seven or eight times in a small kiln (*xiaoyao* 小窑), resulting in an additional loss of ca. 200 *jin*. After a second charge of the great smelting furnace a second smelting would cause another loss of 700–800 *jin*. Eventually, 600–700 *jin* of pure copper (*jingtong* 淨銅) would be lifted out of the great smelting furnace,[67] cooled by immersing it in water as in the processes described above.[68]

The special feature of this process is the subjection of the ore to several roastings. Xia Xiangrong et al. have claimed with the help of a flow diagram that that the produce of the great smelting furnace was not pure copper (*jingtong*), but 'purple slab copper' (*zibantong* 紫板銅). This was then further refined to crab shell copper (*xieketong*) in the crab shell furnace.[69] The

64 Agricola 1556, 235.

65 Agricola 1556, 236.

66 This is the procedure decribed by an about sixty-year-old inhabitant of Maolu to Nanny Kim during her field trip in March/April 2007.

67 *Tongzheng quanshu*, in DNKCTL, chap. A, 43b–44a.

68 Ni Shenshu, in DNKCTL, chap. A, 35b.

69 Xia Xiangrong et al. 1980, 269.

sources available to me do not show this stage in type C smelting, but it is not inconceivable that such an additional refining process was adopted.

A Japanese report of the early twentieth century indicates that from 100 *jin* of ore as raw material 8 to 10 *jin* of raw copper were obtained in Dongchuan. The yield per furnace varied from 300 to 1,000 *jin* of raw copper. The copper tenor was 85 percent.[70] Both Japanese and Western reports provide detailed descriptions of the various methods for refining raw copper in special furnaces during the late nineteenth and early twentieth centuries.[71]

Type D. Smelting of *mingkuang* ores (galena mixed with copper and silver)

A description with specific detail of this smelting method can be found in the *Tongzheng quanshu*. Its subject is the Jiada 戛達 mine in Wenshan District 文山縣. Being a collection of investigative reports, it gives the information that 10,000 *jin* of ore were reduced by 300–400 *jin* during one roasting process in great kilns. When balanced with greenish-white agent stone and fired in great smelting furnaces (*dalu*), another 7,800–7,900 *jin* were lost. From this process, 1,600–1,700 *jin* of 'frozen copper' (*bingtong*) were obtained, which were again loaded into small kilns (*dayao*) and successively roasted 6 or 7 times, causing a loss of over 200 *jin*. Thereafter the copper was mixed with 'bottom mother' (*dimu* 底母) and fired in the separation furnace (*tuilu* 推鑪). This process led to a reduction by another 800–900 *jin*. Eventually, 500–600 *jin* of pure copper were obtained. A lead[-silver] mixture was obtained as a precious by-product that ran off during smelting. This was further processed in a cupellation furnace (*zhao* 罩),[72] yielding 10–20 *liang* of silver.[73] Ni Shenshu's description of the treatment of shiny ore (*mingkuang* 明鑛) is very similar.[74] Thus we may assume that this smelting method was closely related to the specific type of copper-silver-lead ore. We know from the *Tongzheng quanshu* that 'bottom mother' is lead (*qian* 鉛)[75] and was

70 See *Shina shōbetsu zenshi*, vol. 3, 730.

71 For details see *Shina shōbetsu zenshi*, vol. 3, 731–734; Rocher 1879, vol. 2, 226–230.

72 Rocher 1879, vol. 2, 242, renders this furnace with the expression *zhaozi* 照子.

73 *Tongzheng quanshu*, in DNKCTL, chap. A, 44b.

74 Ni Shenshu, in DNKCTL, chap. A, 36a.

75 Perhaps this was litharge (PbO).

used for smelting silver from copper-silver ores in cupellation furnaces.[76] The following descriptions make clear that 'bottom mother' was added to both copper-silver and silver-copper ores, although—apparently—less with cupellation furnaces than with smelting furnaces, especially separation furnaces. This kind of procedure used for the smelting of copper-silver ores explains how the saying "Nine freezings, nine cupellations, and the copper is made" (*jiubing jiuzhao er cheng tong* 九冰九罩而成銅)[77] originated.

The smelting methods E and F concern processes of separating copper and silver using lead. In Europe, the basic principles of this procedure were as follows: first, adding large amounts of lead to the copper-silver melt (*Kupferfrischen*); second, internally separating the copper from silver containing lead by means of dendritic crystallisation; third, externally separating copper and silver by means of selective melting (*Saigern*). After the copper cakes and the molten mix of lead-silver had been separated, the lead-silver mixture was then subjected to a process of cupellation, which would separate silver and lead.[78] Neither Chinese officials nor Western observers have passed down a detailed description of how Yunnanese smelters carried out the separation of copper and silver. The little information available seems to suggest that the Yunnanese *Saiger* process was roughly similar to the Japanese method.[79] It neither resembles the processes described by Agricola in the mid-sixteenth century, nor the process used in Tyrol from the mid-fifteenth century onwards, which was even more complex and efficient.[80] When blending copper and lead Yunnanese smelters most probably added much less lead than the European smelters (Japan: 8 parts of copper and 2 parts of lead; Europe: 3 parts of copper and 11 parts of lead). The result might have been comparable to those in Japan: Yunnanese smelters were able to produce lead, which was rich in silver, and copper with a low content of silver and lead.[81] Alternatively, as mentioned by Andreas Hauptmann in a

76 *Tongzheng quanshu*, in DNKCTL, chap. A, 39b.
77 *Tongzheng quanshu*, in DNKCTL, chap. A, 45a–b.
78 See Suhling 1980, 157–159.
79 Lewin & Hauptmann 1984, 111–114.
80 Cf. Suhling 1980, 160–170.
81 Lewin & Hauptmann 1984, 112–116.

private communication, it is also possible that a kind of copper with a relatively high content of silver was produced.

Furthermore, Yunnan smelters used a special cupellation hearth for the separation of silver and lead, which was quite different from both European and Japanese cupellation devices.[82] The Yunnan cupellation hearth was built in the shape of a baker's oven. Yet it had a special, striking feature which the European and Japanese hearths lacked: the metal was placed below the fire and heated by radiation from above. Brown composed a detailed description of the Yunnan cupellation process he observed in ca. 1909:

> The furnace, ... is generally of a hemispherical shape. (The Baldwin furnaces were more of a beehive pattern than any I have seen in Yunnan.) ... Two doors in the wall which forms the front of the furnace serve, in the case of the lower as a charging door [for the metal], and in the case of the upper as the door from which the firing is done. ... The section of the dome-shaped oven is semicircular and at about half the distance up, that is to say between the level of the hearth and the top of the dome, is placed the grating which supports the fire. ... After the fire is lighted and the furnace well warmed, the lead to be cupelled is placed on the hearth, where it soon melts. A bridge of sand is built across the charging door to form a side for the bath of molten metal and to prevent it flowing out. The fire is kept going by the introduction of more charcoal, which has to be placed very carefully across the somewhat flimsy grating [made from a mixture of sand and clay]. As the temperature rises litharge commences to form, and when sufficient has accumulated it is removed by the introduction of an iron rod to which layer after layer of the litharge sticks as it is skimmed away. Sticks of stratified litharge, hollow down the centre, are sometimes found on old Chinese slag heaps. I have come across them both in Baldwin and in Yunnan. Nothing now remains but to keep the operation going by regulating the fire and removing the litharge as fast as it is formed. The process is a very tedious one and is prolonged sometimes for two days and nights. The silver which remains is far from pure and has to go through the hands of a refiner before it can be used as bullion. I understand that the Government insisted on a purity of 98 percent. The litharge is either sold as such or is resmelted with charcoal in the ordinary way. Owing to the somewhat rough treatment which the furnace undergoes, there is nothing much left but the outside walls and it has to be practically rebuilt inside before another cupellation can be undertaken.[83]

82 Cf. Agricola 1556, 399–413; Lewin & Hauptmann 1984, 116–118.

83 Brown 1923, 135–136.

A somewhat different harvesting procedure was reported by Rocher in 1873. He writes that as soon as litharge would form in the furnace, additional packages of charcoal, each weighing 4 to 5 pounds, would be loaded onto the grating in order to have the oxide melt rapidly. If the litharge was sufficiently fluid, the smelter would make a trench in the bottom of the hearth, which he would continuously deepen further. Through this trench the litharge would be drained off at a high and constant temperature. The whole process took approximately three days. The final stage was marked by lowering the temperature. From the moment in which all the lead had been oxidised there was an intensive glimmering of the remaining material. The charge of such a furnace amounted to ca. 700 *jin* of lead-silver mixture, which is rather large in comparison to the figure of 50–60 *jin* to be mentioned next for the type E procedure. The silver obtained from type D contained between 15 and 20 percent of other substances and was therefore far from pure. It had to be subjected to a special refining process through which its purity would be raised to 98 percent, the percentage stipulated by the government.[84]

Type E. Smelting of copper-silver ores

Ni Shenshu states that some [ore], after having been roasted several times in a kiln, was loaded directly into the general's furnace (*jiangjunlu* 將軍鑪), a large type of smelting furnace, and smelted for one day. The molten copper would flow to the bottom cavity of the furnace, the molten silver[-lead mixture] to the outside. Next, the copper was loaded into the separation furnace (*tuilu*) and smelted to black copper (*heitong* 黑銅). This was then put into the crab shell furnace, out of which the final copper could be lifted. The [silver-]lead [mixture] was placed into the cupellation furnace and smelted to silver. Approximately 10,000 *jin* of ore required 8,000 or 9,000 *jin* of charcoal. This amount would result in an output of 500 or 600 *jin* of copper and 10 or 20 *liang* of mine cake silver (*changbingyin* 廠餅銀).[85]

The same procedure is described for the Baiyang 白羊 mine of Yunlong 雲龍 in the *Tongzheng quanshu,* along with the additional information that 'bottom mother' was added to the great smelting furnace. The figures of this

84 Rocher 1879, vol. 2, 241–242.

85 Ni Shenshu, in DNKCTL, chap. A, 36a.

source are in accordance with Ni Shenshu: we are told that a charge of a cupellation furnace amounted to 50–60 *jin* of molten silver[-lead] with a yield of 1–2 *liang* of mine cake silver.[86] According to the procedure described in both sources, 'bottom mother' was apparently added prior to or during the firing of ore in the smelting furnace.

In European smelting, black copper (*cuprum nigrum*, *cuprum durum*) was a rather brittle and inflexible product, which contained silver and other metals.[87] The Jinchai 金釵 mine, which was located in Lin'an 臨安府 Prefecture, produced a copper called 'dark [or: black] copper' (*wutong* 烏銅), which derived its colour probably from a small amount of gold and from lead.[88]

Type F. Smelting of silver-copper ores

'Silver-dominating-copper' (*yinchetong* 銀徹銅) ore was fired in a smelting furnace and would yield "two kinds of frozen copper (*bingtong*)", which would float on the surface. These were taken out and mixed with 'bottom mother'. A [separation] furnace was then used to separate the copper from the [silver-]lead [mixture]. The copper was returned to a smelting furnace and re-fired to crab shells. The lead[-silver mixture] was added to a cupellation furnace, by whose means pure silver was obtained.[89]

Fuels

The various texts compiled in the DNKCTL offer invaluable data on the origins, kinds, uses, prices and consumption of charcoal, coal and wood in the Yunnan mining industry. Three types of quantitative data on the use of fuel for roasting, smelting, separation and cupellation are available: a) overall estimates of fuel consumption per 100 *jin* of copper produced; b) charcoal

86 *Tongzheng quanshu*, in DNKCTL, chap. A, 43–b.

87 Stromer 1995, 192, cf. also Agricola 1556, 355.

88 Rocher 1879, vol. 2, 256: "....cette couleur, paraît-il, provient au cuivre d'une petite quantité d'or et de plomb qu'il contient."

89 *Tongzheng quanshu*, in DNKCTL, chap. A, 41a.

consumption for processing good and bad ores in the smelting furnace; c) fuel consumption for individual kilns and furnaces.

a) Overall estimates of fuel consumption per production of 100 *jin* of copper

- For type C, smelting of poor copper ores at the Zhe'nang mine, comprising 7–8 roastings and 2 smeltings, 1,400 to 1,500 *jin* of charcoal were necessary to produce 100 *jin* copper.[90]
- For type D, smelting of *mingkuang* ores (galena mixed with copper and silver) at the Jiada mine, 1,400 to 1,500 *jin* of charcoal and some 200 *jin* of firewood were used to produce 100 *jin* of copper by means of 7–8 roastings, smelting, separation and cupellation.[91]
- For type E, smelting of copper-silver ores, 10,000 *jin* of ore corresponded to 8,000 to 9,000 *jin* of charcoal, but this figure would yield only 500 to 600 *jin* of copper and 10 to 20 *liang* of 'mine cake silver'.[92] In other words, for obtaining 100 *jin* copper ca. 1,500 *jin* of charcoal were consumed.

These data enable as well an estimate to be made of the total fuel consumption of the Yunnan copper mines during those periods for which we have data on copper output.

b) Charcoal consumption for the processing of good and bad ores in the smelting furnace

- For each firing of a great smelting furnace at Xiangshupo 40 buckets (ca. 4,000 *jin*) of superior ore and approximately 3,000 *jin* of charcoal were needed; either 70–80 buckets (ca. 7,000–8,000 *jin*) of medium quality ore and approximately 3,500–3,600 *jin* of charcoal, or 110 buckets (ca. 11,000 *jin*) of inferior ore and a little over 4,000 *jin* of charcoal. If the firing was well controlled and steady, copper would have been obtained by the end of a double shift (*duishi* 對時; i.e., 24 hours[93]).[94] In other words, compared to

90 *Tongzheng quanshu*, in DNKCTL, chap. A, 44a; see also Ni Shenshu, in DNKCTL, chap. A, 35b.

91 *Tongzheng quanshu*, in DNKCTL, chap. A, 44b.

92 Ni Shenshu, in DNKCTL, chap. A, 36a.

93 Cf. DNKCTL, chap. A, 8b.

94 *Tongzheng quanshu*, in DNKCTL, chap. A, 45a.

high quality ores, for medium quality ore the quantity of ore had to be almost doubled and an extra 1/6 of charcoal added. For inferior ores the quantity of ore was almost tripled and the amount of charcoal increased by a third.[95] Thus, the use of more inferior ore did not necessarily lead to a proportional increase in the amount of charcoal used.

c) Fuel consumption of individual kilns and furnaces

- Each roasting of 10,000 *jin* of copper ore required 2,000 to 3,000 *jin* of charcoal.[96] The very different figure of only 400 *jin* of charcoal for 10,000 *jin* of ore is indicated for the great kilns of the Zhe'nang mine.[97] 400 *jin* is also the figure given for the great kilns of the Jiada mine.[98]
- For every 1,000 *jin* of copper ore which were processed in a smelting furnace ca. 1,000 *jin* of charcoal were required.[99]

A Japanese report of the early twentieth century states that roasting kilns in Dongchuan had a capacity to take in 12,000 to 18,000 *jin* of ore. Furthermore, it is mentioned that for 15,000 *jin* of ore, 5,000 *jin* of firewood and 200 *jin* of charcoal were needed.[100] Hence the figures given for the great kilns of Zhe'nang and Jiada are credible, provided that substantial amounts of firewood were used in addition to charcoal. Another passage states that the charge of a smelting furnace at the Dagong mine amounted to some 20 buckets of ore, for which 2,000 *jin* of pine charcoal were used.[101] From these indications we may infer that 1 bucket of ore corresponded to ca. 100 *jin*. At the Jiada mine a smelting furnace was filled with 400–500 *jin* of ore and ca. 330 *jin* of charcoal.[102]

In 1909 Brown reported the following charges for the largest sized furnaces of the Pao-p'ing-ch'ang smelters west of Yongbei:

95 Cf. the similar wording of Ni Shenshu, in DNKCTL, chap. A, 34b.
96 DNKCTL, chap. A, 12b.
97 *Tongzheng quanshu*, in DNKCTL, chap. A, 43b.
98 *Tongzheng quanshu*, in DNKCTL, chap. A, 44a.
99 DNKCTL, chap. A, 12a.
100 *Unnanshō jijō*, vol. 2, 129–130.
101 *Tongzheng quanshu*, in DNKCTL, chap. A, 43a.
102 *Tongzheng quanshu*, in DNKCTL, chap. A, 44a.

calcined ore	40 loads	say 3.0 tons
iron ore	20 loads	1.5 tons
charcoal	40 loads	3.0 tons
limestone	20 loads	1.5 tons

The amount of copper produced was said to range between 1/5 and 1/2 tons.[103]

- At the Jiada mine a <u>small kiln</u> accommodated ca. 500 *jin* of frozen copper (*bingtong*), which was roasted eight times in succession. The [whole] operation required 600 *jin* of charcoal.[104]
- A load of a <u>crab shell furnace</u> at the Dagong mine amounted to some 400 *jin* of black copper (*heitong*) and 500 *jin* of charcoal.[105] This corresponds roughly to the data provided by Rocher in 1873. He recorded a furnace filling of 350 to 400 pounds, producing ca. 55 to 70 percent pure copper, valued at 4.5 to 5.5 silver tael per 100 *jin*. The proportion of ore to charcoal was about 1 to 1.5.[106]
- For <u>[separation] furnaces</u> at silver mines, 600 to 700 *jin* of charcoal were consumed during a period of six times two hours.[107] The separation furnaces at the Jiada mine were filled with ca. 50 *jin* of frozen copper (*bingtong*) and 70–80 *jin* of firewood.[108]
- For <u>cupellation furnaces</u> 300 to 400 *jin* of charcoal were used for a period of a whole day and night.[109]

What kind of fuel was used for the different types of kilns and furnaces? The basic fuel of the Yunnan smelters was charcoal. In addition, wood was used for the firing of the kilns. Moreover, it seems that a limited number of smelters fed their furnaces with coal. Ni Shenshu summarizes the use of charcoal and wood at the Yunnan smelters in the following way:

> For the firing of <u>kilns</u> [emphasis here and thereafter by HUV], it is best to pile up the firewood in spiral fashion while placing small amounts of charcoal in

103 Brown 1923, 115.
104 *Tongzheng quanshu*, in DNKCTL, chap. A, 44a.
105 *Tongzheng quanshu*, in DNKCTL, chap. A, 43a.
106 Rocher 1879, vol. 2, 226.
107 DNKCTL, chap. A, 12b.
108 *Tongzheng quanshu*, in DNKCTL, chap. A, 44a.
109 DNKCTL, chap. A, 12b.

> the interstices. This produces a long lasting fire. In the smelting furnace[110] one can only use charcoal. Pine charcoal and miscellaneous wood charcoal are used for their fierce burning, while chestnut charcoal burns evenly and [penetrates] fully. There are also cases where they are mixed because of their price differentials. This then is [an example of applying] careful planning and comparison to human affairs. But in the smelting of crab shell copper one must use pine charcoal, taking advantage of its extremely fierce burning, which makes it easy to thoroughly run off the slag and scoria. One must under no circumstances mix other [kinds of] charcoal with it.[111]

Ni Shenshu's summary makes clear that for firing in kilns firewood was more important than charcoal. Another passage in the DNKCTL states that branches and tree roots were mixed with charcoal.[112] For this reason it is surprising that only charcoal is mentioned when figures of fuel consumption of kilns are indicated![113] Only in the case of type D, smelting of *mingkuang* ores (galena mixed with copper and silver) at the Jiada mine, does a figure regarding firewood happen to be included in the total figures of fuel consumption (see above). Moreover, this mine also reports the use of firewood for cupellation.

In smelting furnaces different kinds of charcoals were used, depending on the local conditions. "Generally one uses chestnut charcoal, because with its very few flames it transforms the ore relatively slowly. If one uses pine charcoal exclusively, you cannot have a long-lasting firing, because its nature is that it burns up quickly."[114] However, there were certainly many instances in which smelters simply relied on the charcoals available within a reasonable distance. In 1873 Rocher mentioned both chestnut and pine charcoal, the latter being probably more dominant than the former.[115]

A specific problem of fuel supply, however, had to be faced at the mines which had to produce crab shell copper for the capital mints. For crab shell furnaces only pine charcoal was suitable. Due to its burning in fierce flames,

110 The text mistakenly has *kuang* 礦 (ore) for *lu* 鑪.

111 Ni Shenshu, in DNKCTL, chap. A, 36b.

112 DNKCTL, chap. A, 12b.

113 See the examples given above.

114 *Tongzheng quanshu*, in DNKCTL, chap. A, 46b.

115 See Rocher 1879, vol. 2, 225. See also Brown 1923, 106, who speaks of charcoal made of resinous wood used at Lao-tchang in the Tangdan mining region of Dongchuan.

the smelters could separate the slags out very easily. As a result the extracted copper would be of constant thinness and would glitter with a bright glow.[116]

The accounts given in the *Tongzheng quanshu* make clear that problems of fuel supply, though not insurmountable, did exist. It is explicitly stated that the mines had been in operation for a long period, leading to the cutting down of all trees in the immediate vicinity of the mines. Furthermore, the transportation routes for the procurement of charcoal became ever longer.[117] For the Xiangshupo mine, for example, it is reported that a hundred *jin* of charcoal cost only 220 or 230 copper cash when its copper was assigned to the Yunnan mints for the first time. At the time of the report, however, this price had increased to more than 300 cash. Fortunately, in the view of the responsible mining official who was questioned by his superior, this specific mine did not have to produce crab shell copper. Since the production of crab shell copper required pine charcoal, it was thus spared the expense of procuring pine charcoal from distant forests. Due to this fact, in the words of the mining officials, the price of charcoal remained moderate, for it could be made from any kind of wood. During the slack season, such charcoal could be easily bought from, as well as transported by farmers.[118] For the Xiangshupo mine the price of charcoal fluctuated between 0.26 and 0.3 tael of silver per hundred *jin*, depending on weather conditions.[119] The mining official responsible for the Zhe'nang and Jiada mines did not appear to have been very worried about charcoal supply either. These mines, too, did not have to produce crab shell copper and thus did not have to procure pine charcoal at any cost. Yet because there was also no chestnut charcoal available nearby, both mines used charcoal made from miscellaneous woods. Moreover, the output of these mines was moderate. They thus had only a limited demand for fuel. Charcoal sources, so the words of the mining official, were not too distant: only some 80 or 90 *li* away.[120]

Certainly more intense were the conditions in the highly productive Dongchuan Prefecture, for which Leclère and Brown reported fuel costs of 7

116 *Tongzheng quanshu*, in DNKCTL, chap. A, 47a.
117 *Tongzheng quanshu*, in DNKCTL, chap. A, 46a.
118 *Tongzheng quanshu*, in DNKCTL, chap. A, 47a.
119 *Tongzheng quanshu*, in DNKCTL, chap. A, 45b.
120 *Tongzheng quanshu*, in DNKCTL, chap. A, 47a.

tael silver per 100 pounds of crude copper in 1898 and 1909 respectively. Charcoal had to be transported from forests which were located three to four day stages away.[121] Brown referred to the destruction of the forests and the consequent lack of large quantities of charcoal for reasonable prices as one of the four major reasons for the decline of the Yunnan copper mining industry.[122]

When asked about problems of fuel supply, mining officials frequently made proposals such as: "There should be an order to the people in that area to cut down the pine trees in the neighboring mountains [selectively] over a broad area, and not to destroy them by careless cutting. Only thus can we hope that the forest will continue to grow for a long time and that we may avoid coming to a point in the future where there are no longer any trees to be harvested."[123] They also suggested that people should be encouraged to plant trees, and that the slash-and-burn agriculture should be prohibited. Both regional and local officials were aware that mines not only consumed wood as fuel, but also required substantial amounts for the framing or their galleries.[124]

Parallel to the salt industry of Yunnan, coal was of little importance for the mining industry. It was, however, not totally ignored, as is made clear by an account given in the DNKCTL. This source tells us that in the smelting furnaces a type of 'processed coal' (*liantan* [煉炭) could be used.[125] There were two subcategories of coal (*mei* 煤), which were distinguished by the nature of their seams (*shuan* 閂).[126] The first was the so-called 'silver seams' (*yinshuan* 銀閂),[127] which were heavy and could only be used in silver furnaces (*lu*). The second, the 'copper seams' (*tongshuan* 銅閂), were lighter

121 Brown 1923, 106, 108.

122 Brown 1923, 123.

123 *Tongzheng quanshu*, in DNKCTL, chap. A, 46b.

124 *Tongzheng quanshu*, in DNKCTL, chap. A, 47b.

125 *Liantan* literally means 'processed charcoal'. This may well be possible, but in view of the following passages it seems more likely that this expression referred to coal.

126 For the complex form of this character, which could not reproduced here, see Luo Zhufeng et al. 1987–1995, vol. 4, 1369.

127 This appears to be a miner's term meaning 'seams of coal used in silver furnaces'. The same applies to the term 'copper seams'.

and were only applied in copper furnaces.[128] The combustive force of coal was double that of charcoal, but whether it was to be mixed with charcoal or used by itself was dependent on the nature of the ore (namely whether its density and dryness was considered appropriate or not). Knowledge of coal deposits was, however, limited. Our source only mentions Xuanwei 宣威 and Luquan 祿勸 in Yunnan, and Huili 會理 in Sichuan.[129] Use of coal or coke in the Huili valley is also attested by Davies in 1899.[130] Although Huili was located only ca. 100 km east of Dongchuan, topography and transport conditions were prohibitive for shipping coal from Huili to Yunnan's most productive copper mining region.

A Japanese report from the early twentieth century draws attention to coal deposits within a distance of several tens of *li* from Tiechang 鐵廠 in Dongchuan, and to coke produced in Malongying 馬隆營, Yazitang 鴨子塘 and Zhile 至樂 in Dongchuan.[131]

Concluding Remarks

The data provided by the DNKCTL are unusual in comparison with other reports that are available in traditional Chinese sources. The DNKCTL provides information not only on labour organisation, economic aspects, religious beliefs as well as mining administration and regulations, but also on the technical dimensions of mining and smelting. It is the only traditional Chinese text to provide detail on aspects such as mining and smelting equipment, types of ores, roasting and smelting processes. Moreover, it gives figures on fuel and ore consumption for individual smelting processes, roasting kilns and furnaces. Supplemented with reports of Western and Japanese authors, a relatively clear picture of the technological and economic aspects of Yunnan smelting traditions can be put together. A first attempt to collect, analyze and reconstruct relevant data on ores, their processing, smelting and

128 The method [of processing coal] is as follows: First one sorts and cleans the coal, which is then roasted in an earthen kiln where it forms lumps. Thereafter it is broken into [smaller] pieces for use [in the furnace].

129 DNKCTL, chap. A, 12b.

130 Brown 1923, 121; see also 79–81 on Yunnan coal deposits and their limitations.

131 *Shina shōbetsu zenshi*, vol. 3, 721.

refining, as well as on quantitative aspects of fuel consumption, has been undertaken in this article. It will be followed by a more in-depth investigation. The reconstruction of the history of the mining and smelting industry of Yunnan will establish a solid basis on which Yunnanese methods can be compared with Japanese and Western processes.

In the conventional PRC historiography the Yunnan mining industry was often mentioned with reference to the development of sprouts of capitalism within traditional Chinese economy and society. Yunnan copper mining, especially the copper mines of Dongchuan, were presented as a stock example for the production capacity and high degree of labour division which arose in the bosom of traditional Chinese society. It was also often stressed that copper mining and transportation were important activities which fostered the economic, social and political development of Yunnan province. While both Yunnan and the empire clearly profited in many respects from the rise of Yunnan copper mining, this was in no way free of charge. In particular the impact on the environment, a burning issue in our own times as well, is an aspect which has been neglected in research thus far. In a recent article Yang Yuda has pointed out that environmental costs for the supply of copper for the mints in the empire were indeed high, with repercussions even to today. Environmental damage caused by mining especially in north-eastern Yunnan was manifold. It includes not only the pollution of water[132] and air, but also the erosion and destruction of the surrounding landscapes by extensive mining for overburden ore (*caopikuang* 草皮矿), by the construction of roads and paths for transportation, and by population increase. Every year several ten thousand tons of debris and slag were produced and deposited in the landscape. Forests were exploited for frames and supporting pillars in shafts, adits and galleries, as well as for fire-setting in mines, but even more so for charcoal production. Yang Yuda estimates that from 1726 to 1855 ca. 6,450 km^2, or ca. 20 percent, of the forest[133]—and along with it the

132 Brown 1923, 115: At Pao-p'ing-ch'ang the rich ore pieces were picked out and placed in baskets. The remainder went to the dumps, which consisted of the gangue and also of the low-grade ores, disseminated sulphides and carbonates. "The water percolating through the dumps was of a bright blue colour and appeared to bear an appreciable quantity of copper salts in solution."

133 Yang Yuda is basing his calculations on the following estimates, equations and assumptions:

thin and delicate vegetation stratum—were destroyed in north-eastern Yunnan. In spite of reforestation since the mid-nineteenth century, the region of Dongchuan is notorious for the occurrence of mud slides (*nishiliu* 泥石流). They, too, have a big impact on the sediment charge and ultimately on the quality of the water of the Changjiang.[134] Indeed, in order to feed the hunger of the mints of the empire for metal, the Qing government had to exert its organizational capacities. It needed to invest heavily in mining and transportation routes in Yunnan and Guizhou. On the one hand, this dependency on mint metals, and especially the dependency on copper, enhanced the political position of Yunnan province vis-à-vis the capital and other provinces. It spurred economic and social development to a certain degree, and, furthermore, generated additional fiscal income. On the other hand, there are the negative consequences of mining: social disruption, ethnic tensions, and long-lasting environmental damage. The last point holds true especially for the thriving mining regions of the eighteenth and nineteenth century.

100 *jin* copper = 1,000 *jin* charcoal
100 *jin* charcoal = 300 *jin* wood
1 *jin* = ca. 660 g
100 m3 of forest = 90 tons of wood
forest exploitation rate = 30 %

134 Cf. Yang Yuda 2004.

Appendix

Table 1: Copper Ores in Yunnan as identified by Western and Japanese Explorers in the Late Nineteenth and Early Twentieth Centuries

Name of mine Lat./Long.	administrative unit	ores	tenor of exploited ores	source, date of observation
Wei-teou-chan 23°36'/102°52'	Lin'anfu	bornite, copper and iron pyrites	20–25 %	Brown, 1905
Tien-pao 24°40'/102°55'	Chengjiangfu	balls rich in copper carbonate	20 % after washing	Lantenois, 1903/04 Deprat, 1910
Po-hsi 24°6'/102°8'	Tonghaixian	copper carbonate		Deprat, 1910
Lao-tchou-chan	Chengjiangfu	copper pyrites		Lantenois, 1903/04
Lou-pou	Dongchuanfu	horizontal band of barytes ($BaSO_4$) carrying native copper and its oxides	20–40 %; waste material contains 15 % copper	Leclère, 1898 Deprat, 1910
Lao-tchang (Tang-tan) (Laochang 老廠)	Dongchuanfu	originally copper pyrites, now carbonate associated with concretions of banded barytes	20 %	Leclère, 1898 Deprat, 1910
Lao-sin-tchang (Tang-tan)	Dongchuanfu	copper pyrite		Leclère, 1898 Deprat, 1910
Pe-si-la (Tangtan 湯丹)	Dongchuanfu	mainly bornite with some covellite (CuS) found in veinlets in a compact form		Leclère, 1898 Deprat, 1910
Kouen-in-sa	Dongchuanfu	prospecting copper carbonate		Leclère, 1898 Deprat, 1910
Sin-tien-fong	Dongchuanfu	traces of copper carbonate		Leclère, 1898 Deprat, 1910
Lo-suy	Dongchuanfu	thin lode of copper carbonates with phillipsite		Leclère, 1898 Deprat, 1910
Mo-lou-tchang	Dongchuanfu	copper carbonates and copper pyrites		Leclère, 1898 Deprat, 1910

Tangdan 湯丹, Luoxue 落雪 etc. Houyan 猴岩 and Zhatang 札塘	Dongchuan	bornite, chalcopyrite, malachite native copper	10-20 %	*Unnanshō jijō* and *Shina shōbetsu zenshi*, early twentieth century
Pao-p'ing-ch'ang	Yongbeiting	mainly erubescite [bornite], but also chalcopyrite; smaller quantities of chalcocite, malachite and azurite		Brown, 1909
San-chia-ch'ang (Sanjiachang 三家廠)	Yimenxian	chalcopyrite with small amounts of enriched sulphides		Brown, 1908
Ta-tsang-kuan-miao	Menghuating	prospecting for bornite, in the size of pidgeons' eggs, coated with thin crusts of decomposed matter containing blue and green copper carbonates; traces of malachite		Brown, 1910
Sha-ho-ch'ang	Yongchangfu	quartz vein 5-9 inches thick containing abundant chalcopyrite		Brown, 1909
Tung-shan mines	Tengyueting	oxidised copper with galena and zinc		Brown, 1909
Hung-tu-hai	Tengyueting	chalcopyrite with pyrite and galena		Brown, 1909
T'ang-t'ang (i.e. Tangtang 倘塘)	Weiningfu	ore of purple colour	10 %	Davies, 1899

SOURCE: Brown 1923, 102–123; *Unnanshō jijō*, vol. 2, 124–125; *Shina shōbetsu zenshi*, vol. 3, 720–721.

Notes on the location of the mines:

Lao-tchou-chan, village in the valley of the Ta-chaing Ho, east of the city of Chengjiangfu.

Kouen-in-sa, three hours from Lao-tchang.

Sin-tien-fong, four hours north-west of Lao-tchang.

Lo-suy, one stage west of Lao-tchang, at an altitude of 2,520 m.

Mo-lou-tchang, 200 m above the Yangtze river, 3.5 stages from Dongchuanfu.

Pao-p'ing-ch'ang, west of Yongbeiting.

San-chia-ch'ang, 5 stages south-west of Yunnanfu.

Ta-tsang-kuan-miao, 2 miles east-south-east of Ta-tsang-kai, a village about 10 miles north of Menghuating.
Sha-ho-ch'ang, about 15 miles north-north-west of Yongchangfu.
Tung-shan mines, in the Ming-kuang valley, north of Tengyueting.
Hung-tu-hai, in the Ming-kuang valley, north of Tengyueting.
T'ang-t'ang, in the border region of Yunnan, belonging to Weiningfu in Guizhou.

Table 2. Copper Ores and Some Silver and Lead Ores in Yunnan as Mainly Identified by Chinese Authors in the Late Eighteenth and Early Nineteenth Centuries

Copper Ores

Native Copper

mineral (modern term)[a]		max. Cu (%)[b]	traditional name	spatial specification	remarks (sources)
native copper Cu	*zirantong* 自然铜	99+	*shengtong* 生銅 'raw copper'	general	sometimes admixed to other ores in order to increase their tenor; sometimes made directly into vessels (DNKCTL, chap. A, 6b)
			zirantong 自然銅 'spontaneous copper'	general, Dongchuan	sometimes admixed to other ores in order to increase their tenor; sometimes made directly into vessels (DNKCTL, chap. A, 6b) in Dongchuan found at Houyan 猴岩 and Zhatang 札塘 (*Unnanshō jijō*, vol. 2, 125; *Shina shōbetsu zenshi*, vol. 3, 721)
			zilaitong 自來銅 'copper-coming-about-by-itself'	general	needs no smelting (*Dianhai yuheng zhi*, chap. 2, 1b)
			tianshengtong 天生銅 'heavenly born copper'	general	copper enclosed in the mountain, the 'copper mother' (*tongmu* 銅母) which cannot be mined (*Dianhai yuheng zhi*, chap. 2, 1b)

Carbonates

mineral (modern term)		max. Cu (%)	traditional name	spatial specification	remarks (sources)
malachite **$Cu_2(CO_3)(OH)_2$**	*kongque-shi* 孔雀石	57.5	*huangpang*[*lü*] 黄胖[綠] 'yellow fatty [green]'	general, Wanbao mine	belongs to the very best ores, 'thorough ore' (Ni Shenshu, in DNKCTL, chap. A, 34a (*huang-panglü*); *Tongzheng quanshu*, in DNKCTL, chap. A, 41b (*huangpang*, Wanbao))
			douqing[*lü*] 豆青[綠] 'light-green [green]'	general, Wanbao mine	belongs to the very best ores, 'thorough ore' (Ni Shenshu, in DNKCTL, chap. A, 34a (*dou-qinglü*); *Tongzheng quanshu*, in DNKCTL, chap. A, pp. 40b, 41b (*douqing*, Wanbao))
			heilü 黑綠 'blackish green'[c]	general	belongs to the very best ores, 'thorough ore' (Ni Shenshu, in DNKCTL, chap. A, 34a)
			molü 墨綠 'blackish green'	general, Dongchuan	high tenor ore (DNKCTL); second best group of ores (*Diannan yuheng zhi*) (*Tongzheng quanshu*, in DNKCTL, chap. A, 41a, 41b; *Dianhai yuheng zhi*, chap. 2, 1b; Xia Xiangrong et al. (1980), 260 (Dongchuan))
			mailü 脈綠 'green vein'[d]	Xiangshupo mine	(*Tongzheng quanshu*, in DNKCTL, chap. A, 42a)
			songlü 鬆綠 'loose green'	general	lowest quality copper ore, green inside and outside, only used as colouring agent (Ni Shenshu, in DNKCTL, chap. A, 34a)
			lüsong 綠松 'green pine'	general	lowest quality copper ore, green inside and outside, only used as colouring agent (*Tongzheng quanshu*, in DNKCTL, chap. A, 38b)
			songlü 松綠 'pine green'	general	green inside and outside, low tenor, only used as colouring agent, submerged in water it is of deep kingfisher blue (*Tongzheng quanshu*, in DNKCTL, chap. A, 39b)

			tonglü 銅綠 'copper green' *lükuang* 綠礦 'green ore' *dalü* 大綠 'big green'	Luoci 羅次, Wuding 武定 and Lufeng 錄豐	*tonglü* (or *lükuang*) is used for making vessels; when grinded for colouring it is called *dalü*; produced in the mines of Luoci, Wuding and Lufeng; much less suitable than *xila* for copper smelting (*Dianhai yuheng zhi*, chap. 2, 3a; Xia Xiangrong et al. 1980, 245)
azurite $\mathbf{Cu_3(CO_3)_2(OH)_2}$	*lantong-kuang* 蓝铜矿	55.3	*shiqing* 石青 'stony blue'	Dongchuan	(Xia Xiangrong et al. 1980, 259)

Oxides

mineral (modern term)		max. Cu (%)	traditional name	spatial specification	remarks (sources)
tenorite **CuO**	*heitong-kuang* 黑铜矿	79.8	*huoyaosu* 火藥酥 'gunpowder crisp'[e]	general	ore of especially high quality, "thorough ore", of deep black colour, brittle, resembles gunpowder (Ni Shenshu, in DNKCTL, chap. A, 34a; see also *Tongzheng quanshu*, in DNKCTL, chap. A, 38b ("... ore with the highest tenor ..."))

Sulphosalts

mineral (modern term)		max. Cu (%)	traditional name	spatial specification	remarks (sources)
enargite?[f] $\mathbf{Cu_3AsS_4}$ or **tetrahedrite**?[f] $\mathbf{Cu_{12}Sb_4S_{13}}$	*liushen-tong-kuang* 硫砷铜矿 *youtong-kuang* 黝铜矿	48.4 23-45	*baixila* 白錫蠟 'white tin wax'	general	high quality ore, 'thorough ore', white and heavy, broken faces show pattern like pointed arrowheads; second best ore with a yield of 30–40 percent (Ni Shenshu, in DNKCTL, chap. A, 34a; see also *Tongzheng quanshu*, in DNKCTL, chap. A, 41a; *Dianhai yuheng zhi*, chap. 2, 2b (30–40 percent))
			[*bai*]*xila* [白]錫蠟 '[white] tin wax'	general, Dabao mine	of a colour like white wax; fractures look like pointed arrowheads (*Tongzheng quanshu*, in DNKCTL, chap. A, 39b)

Sulphides

mineral (modern term)		max. Cu (%)	traditional name	spatial specification	remarks (sources)
chalcopyrite **$CuFeS_2$**	*huang-tong-kuang* 黄铜矿	34.7	*huangjinbo* 黃金箔 'gold leaf'[g]	general, Dongchuan	often accompanied by water, can be exploited for a long time (DNKCTL); third best group of ores (*Dianhai yuheng zhi*); one of the main ores in Dongchuan next to *lüxila* and *zijin xila* (DNKCTL, chap. A, 6b; *Dianhai yuheng zhi*, chap. 2, 1b; Xia Xiangrong et al. 1980, 259 (Dong-chuan))
			madouzi 馬豆子 'horsebeans'[h]	general, Dongchuan	[high quality copper ore], tenor of 7–8 *liu*, never forms 'halls' (DNKCTL, chap. A, 6b) pyrite, chalcopyrite and bornite in the form of small lumps (*Shina shōbetsu zenshi*, vol. 3, 721 (Dongchuan))
covellite **CuS**		66.5		Pe-si-la, Dongchuanfu	mainly bornite with some covellite found in vein-lets in a compact state (Brown 1923, 107)
chalcocite **Cu_2S**	*huitong-kuang* 辉铜矿	79.9	*lüxila* 綠錫蠟 'green tin wax'	general, Dongchuan	best ore with a yield of 50 to 60 percent; main ores in Dongchuan together with *zijin xila* and *huang-jinbo* (*Dianhai yuheng zhi*, chap. 2, 2b (general); Xia Xiangrong et al. 1980, 259 (Dongchuan))
			honglü xila 紅綠錫蠟 'red green tin wax'	Xiangshupo mine	a mixture of *hongxila* (bornite) and *lüxila* (chal-cocite)? (*Tongzheng quanshu*, in DNKCTL, chap. A, 42a)
bornite **Cu_5FeS_4**	*bantong-kuang* 斑铜矿	63.4	*zijin* 紫金 'purple gold'	general, Yidu mine	highest quality ore; over 5 *liu* in tenor; (DNKCTL, chap. A, 6a (general); *Tongzheng quanshu*, in DNKCTL, chap. A, 41a (Yidu))

			huoliyan 火裹餤 'flaring fire'	general	*zijin* with a red halo during smelting; over 5 *liu* in tenor (DNKCTL, chap. A, 6a)
			laoyaling 老鴉翎 'crow feather'	general	*zijin* with a red and blue halo during smelting; over 5 *liu* of tenor (DNKCTL, chap. A, 6b)
			zijin xila 紫金錫蠟 'purple gold tin wax'	general, Xiangshupo mine, Wanbao mine, Dongchuan	high quality ore, 'thorough ore', deep purple; only few of it at the Wanbao mine; main ores in Dong-chuan together with *lüxila* and *huangjinbo* (Ni Shenshu, in DNKCTL, chap. A, 34a; *Tongzheng quanshu*, in DNKCTL, chap. A, 41a, 41b (Wanbao), 42a (Xiangshupo); Xia Xiangrong et al. 1980, 259 (Dongchuan))
			hongxila 紅錫蠟 'red tin wax'	general	high quality ore, 'thorough ore', red (Ni Shenshu, in DNKCTL, chap. A, 34a)
			zhuhong xila 硃硔蠟 'cinnabar-ore tin wax'	general	third best ore with a yield of 30–40 percent copper (*Dianhai yuheng zhi*, chap. 2, 2b)
			zhusha xila 硃砂錫[石+巤] 'cinnabar-gravel tin wax'	general	third best ore with a yield of 30–40 percent copper (*Diannan xinyu*, chap. 4, 230a (p. 6060))
			honglü xila 紅綠錫蠟 'red-green tin wax'	Xiangshupo mine	a mixture of *hongxila* (bornite) and *lüxila* (chal-cocite)? (*Tongzheng quanshu*, see DNKCTL, chap. A, 42a)

Copper-silver Ores

mineral (modern term)		max. Cu (%)	traditional name	spatial specification	remarks (sources)
			tonggaiyin heikuang 銅蓋銀黑鑛 'black-ore-where-copper-disguises-silver'	general	second quality glittering ore which is related to *yansha* (salt sand) (DNKCTL, chap. A, 6b)
			tongcheyin 銅徹銀 'copper dominating silver'	general	(*Tongzheng quanshu*, in DNKCTL, chap. A, 38b)
			yanshakuang 鹽沙鑛 'salt sand ore'	general	[lower quality ore], green-black; ore with yellow-green tint is of lesser quality; tenor ranges from 1 *liang* to 7–8 *liang peizi* (Ni Shenshu, in DNKCTL, chap. A, 34a; DNKCTL, chap. A, 6b)

Silver-copper Ores

mineral (modern term)		max. Cu (%)	traditional name	spatial specification	remarks (sources)
			yin'gaitongkuang 銀蓋銅鑛 'ore-where- silver-disguises- copper'	general	greenish, contains horse tooth [crystals] (DNKCTL, chap. A, 7a)
			yinchetong 銀徹銅 'silver dominating copper'	general	(*Tongzheng quanshu*, in DNKCTL, chap. A, 38b, 41a)

Silver Ores

mineral (modern term)		max. Cu (%)[h]	traditional name	spatial specification	remarks (sources)
			molu 墨碌 'black jasper'[i]	general	best silver ore, tenor ranges from 1 *liang* to 7–8 *liang peizi* (DNKCTL, chap. A, 6b)
			qiaomianhuang 蕎麵黃 'buckwheat flour yellow'	general	silver ore of second quality, scalding ore (DNKCTL, chap. A, 6b)
			huoyaosu 火藥酥 'gunpowder crisp'[j]	general	silver ore of second quality, scalding ore (DNKCTL, chap. A, 6b)

Galena mixed with Silver and Copper

mineral (modern term)		max. Cu (%)	traditional name	spatial specification	remarks (sources)
galena (**PbS**) mixed with copper and silver			*mingkuang* 明鑛 'shiny ore'	general	contains no more than a few *fen peizi* of silver; hard and black like fine iron; contains 'lead mother' (*qianmu* 鎌母) (DNKCTL, chap. A, 6b; see also Ni Shenshu in DNKCTL, chap. A, 36a; *Tongzheng quanshu*, in DNKCTL, chap. A, 41a)
galena mixed with silver (and copper)			*dahua* 大花 'large efflorecences'	general	variety of *mingkuang*, contains no more than a few *fen peizi* of silver (DNKCTL, chap. A, 6b) argentiferous galena, abundant in the south and south-east of Yunnan, rich in lead, poor in silver (Rocher 1879, 238)
galena mixed with silver			*zhonghua* 中花 'middle-sized efflorescences'	general	argentiferous galena (Rocher 1879, 238)

galena mixed with silver			*xiaohua* 小花 'small efflorescences'	general	argentiferous galena, relatively rich in silver (Rocher 1879, 239)
galena mixed with copper and silver			*xihua* 細花 'delicate efflorescences'	general	variety of *mingkuang*, contains no more than a few *fen peizi* of silver (DNKCTL, chap. A, 6b)
galena mixed with copper and silver			*dahua mingkuang* 大花明鑛 'shiny ore with large efflorescences'	general	one variety with patches of green, the other with patches of black, both contain silver (*Tongzheng quanshu*, in DNKCTL, chap. A, 41a)
galena mixed with copper and silver			*pichai* 劈柴 'split firewood'	general	variety of *mingkuang*, contains no more than a few *fen peizi* of silver (DNKCTL, chap. A, 6b)

Unidentified Ores

mineral (modern term)		max. Cu (%)	traditional name	spatial specification	remarks (sources)
			yazikuang 亞子鑛 'secondary ore'	general	high quality copper ore, piled up in layers of bricks (Ni Shenshu, in DNKCTL, chap. A, 34a)
			dayazi 大亞子 'big secondary'	general	green [copper ore], contains a great deal of rocks, piled up like bricks (*Tongzheng quanshu*, in DNKCTL, chap. A, 40b)
			chuanhua[*lü*] 穿花[綠] 'threaded efflorescence [green]'	general, Wanbao mine	low quality ore, contains a large amount of rock; green; perhaps lead ore containing copper? (Ni Shenshu, in DNKCTL, chap. A, 34a (*chuanhualü*); *Tongzheng quanshu*, in DNKCTL, chap. A, pp. 40b, 41b (*chuanhua*, Wanbao))

			xila 錫蠟 'tin wax'	general	*xila* is often used as a generic term comprising ores such as *baixila*, *lüxila*, *zijin xila* etc., referred to as best group of ores in *Dianhai yuheng zhi* (*Tongzheng quanshu*, in DNKCTL, chap. A, 38b; *Dianhai yuheng zhi*, chap. 2, 1b)
			youxila 油錫蠟 'oily tin wax'	general	high quality copper ore, 'thorough ore', with shiny bright colour (Ni Shenshu, in DNKCTL, chap. A, 34a; see also *Tongzheng quanshu*, in DNKCTL, chap. A, 41a)
			lantou xila 爛頭錫蠟 'rotten-head tin wax'	general	second best ore with a yield of 30-40 percent copper (*Dianhai yuheng zhi*, chap. 2, 2b)
			huangshabao 黃沙包 'yellow sand cake'[k]	Dabao mine	mentioned together with [*bai*]*xila* as the then only ores of the Dabao mine (*Tongzheng quanshu*, see DNKCTL, chap. A, 40a)
			niubanjin 牛版筋 'ox board sinews'	general	lowest degree of workable ore covering only the costs of charcoal (*Dianhai yuheng zhi*, chap. 2, 2b)

NOTES:

[a] The chemical formulas indicate the average composition.

[b] These are theoretical percentages, and not necessarily representative for the actual Yunnan ores.

[c] Is *heilü* 黑綠 (blackish green) the same as, or related to, the silver ore *heilu* 黑碌 (black jasper)?

[d] Is *mailü* 脈綠 (green vein) an error for *molü* 墨綠 (blackish green)?

[e] This is listed as a silver ore in DNKCTL, chap. A, 6b, but clearly as a copper ore in *Tongzheng quanshu* in DNKCTL, chap. A, 39b and other places.

[f] According to the *Dianhai yuheng zhi*, chap. 2, 2b, this ore had a copper tenor of 30–40 percent. Thus enargite and tetrahedrite would be suitable ores for the Yunnanese smelters, while the maximum amount of copper (13.0 percent) of bournonite (*chelunkuang* 車輪礦) or $CuPbSbS_3$ is perhaps too low. Cf. Golas 1999, 70.

[g] An alternative name for *huangjinbo* that was used in the copper mine of Yingjing 荥经 in Sichuan was *huangjinbao* 黄金宝 (gold treasure). The 'old' (*lao* 老) type of this ore contained 20 percent copper, the tender (*nen* 嫩) one contained 10 percent. See Xia Xiangrong 1980, 249, referring to the *Tufa liantong* 土法炼铜 (Smelting of Copper by Native Methods), Yejin gongye chubanshe, 1958, vol. 1, 79–80.

[h] In the Yingjing copper mine of Sichuan *madouzi* is ore in the form of gravel, while *gen'genkuang* 根根礦 ('root ore') takes the shape of large interrelated pieces. See Xia Xiangrong 1980, 251, referring to the *Tufa liantong* 土法炼铜 (Smelting of Copper by Native Methods), Yejin gongye chubanshe, 1958, vol. 1, 79.

[i] Perhaps the correct name rather is *molü* 墨綠 or 'blackish green'.

[j] *Huoyaosu* is mentioned as a copper ore by Ni Shenshu in DNKCTL, chap. A, 34a, and by the *Tongzheng quanshu* in DNKCTL, chap. A, 39b.

[k] The same as *huangjinbo* 黄金箔 (gold leaf)?

Type A: Smelting of high quality copper ores, Yunnan, 18th–19th centuries

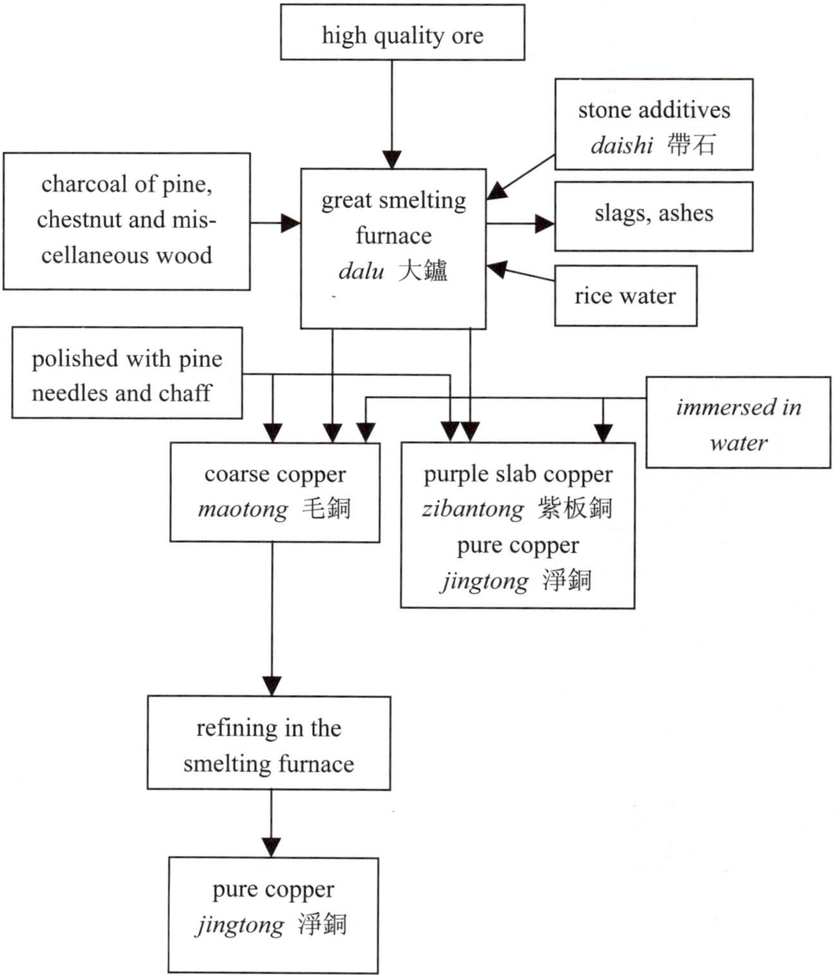

Type B: Smelting of 'thorough' copper ores, Yunnan, 18th–19th centuries

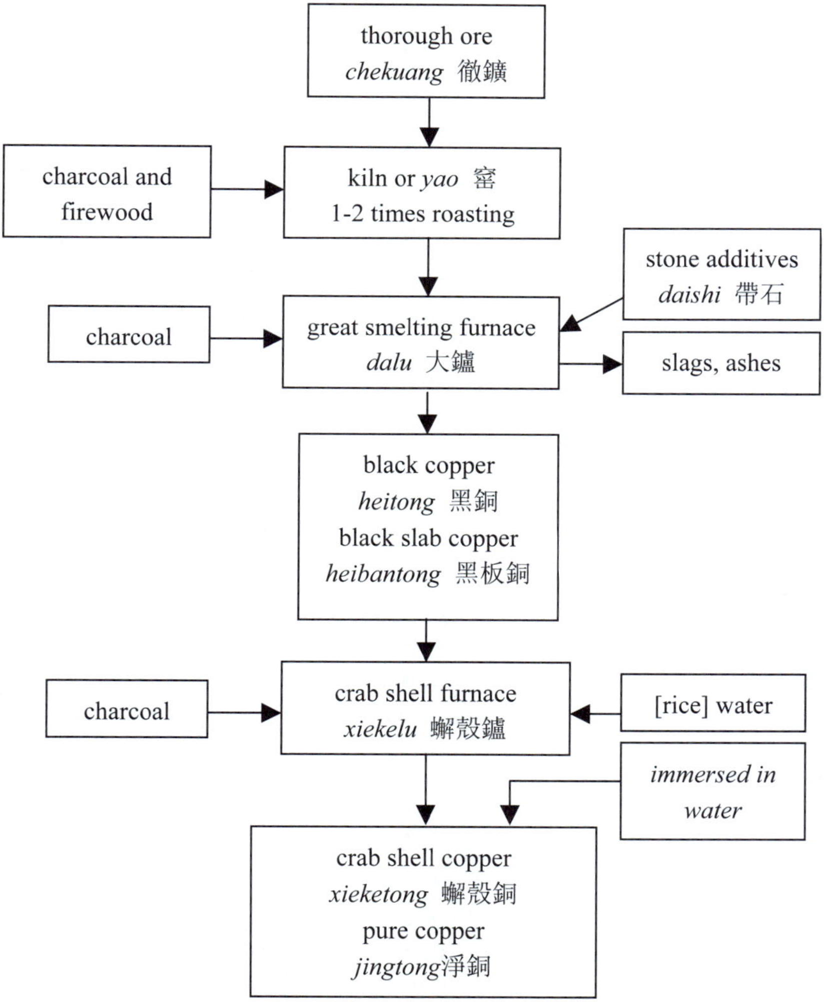

Note: It is not clear whether 'black copper' was also lifted out of the furnace by pouring [rice] water on the molten metal and whether the black copper lumps were also immersed in water for cooling.

Type C: Smelting of poor copper ores, Yunnan, 18th–19th centuries

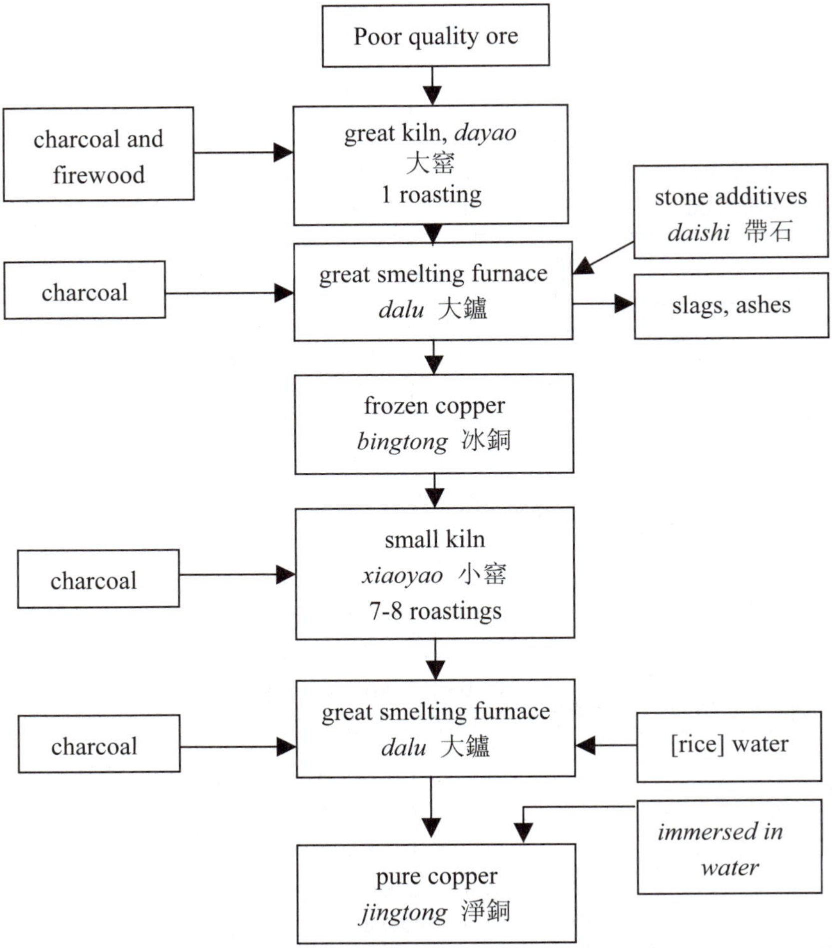

Note: It is not clear whether 'frozen copper' was also lifted out of the furnace by pouring [rice] water on the molten metal and whether these copper lumps were immersed in water for cooling.
This flow diagram differs from Xia Xiangrong et al. 1980, 269, who give 'purple slab copper' (*zibantong*) instead of 'pure copper' and state that it was further refined in crab shell furnaces to produce 'crab shell copper'. I have not been able find a confirmation for such a procedure in the sources, but it is not inconceivable that such an additional refining process was adopted.

Type D: Smelting of *mingkuang* ores (galena mixed with copper and silver, Yunnan, 18th–19th centuries)

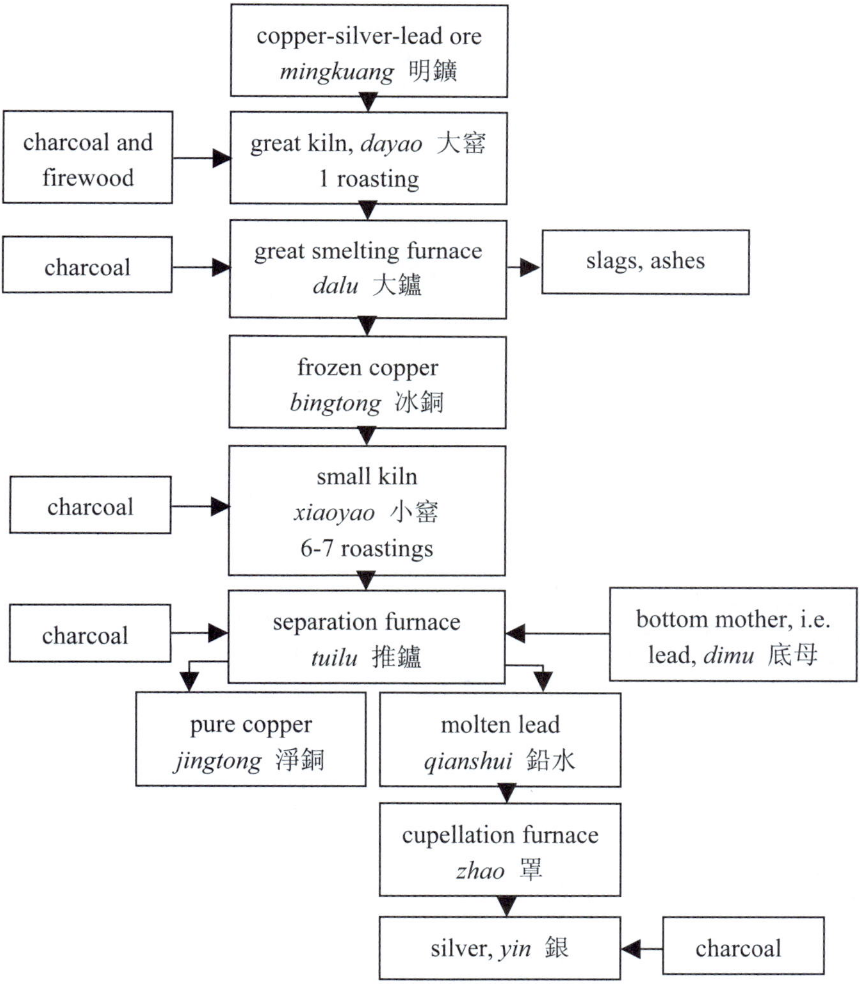

Note: It is not clear whether 'frozen copper' was also lifted out of the furnace by pouring [rice] water on the molten metal and whether the copper lumps were immersed in water for cooling.
This flow diagram differs from Xia Xiangrong et al. (1980), p. 269, who give 'purple slab copper' (*zibantong*) instead of 'pure copper'. They also indicate that 'purple slab copper' was further subjected to a treatment in the crab shell furnace to produce crab shell copper. I have not been able find a confirmation for such a procedure in the sources.

Type E: Smelting of copper-silver ores, Yunnan, 18th–19th centuries

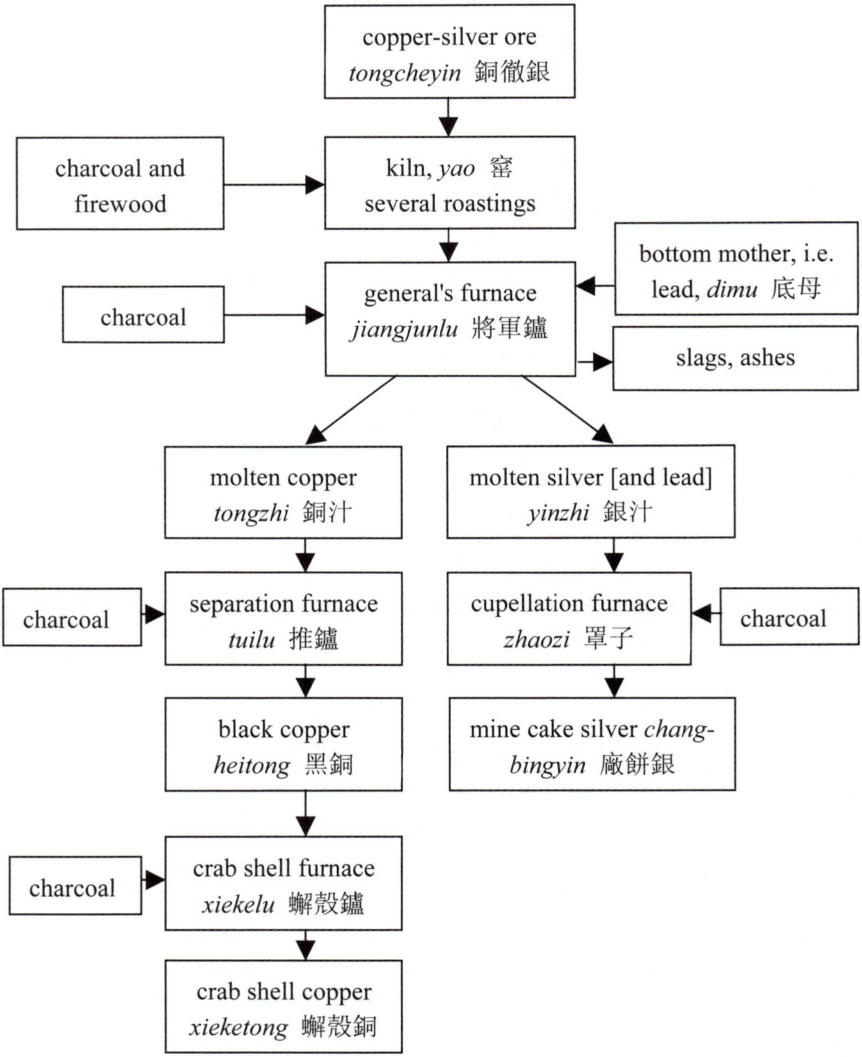

Type F: Smelting of silver-copper ores, Yunnan, 18th–19th centuries

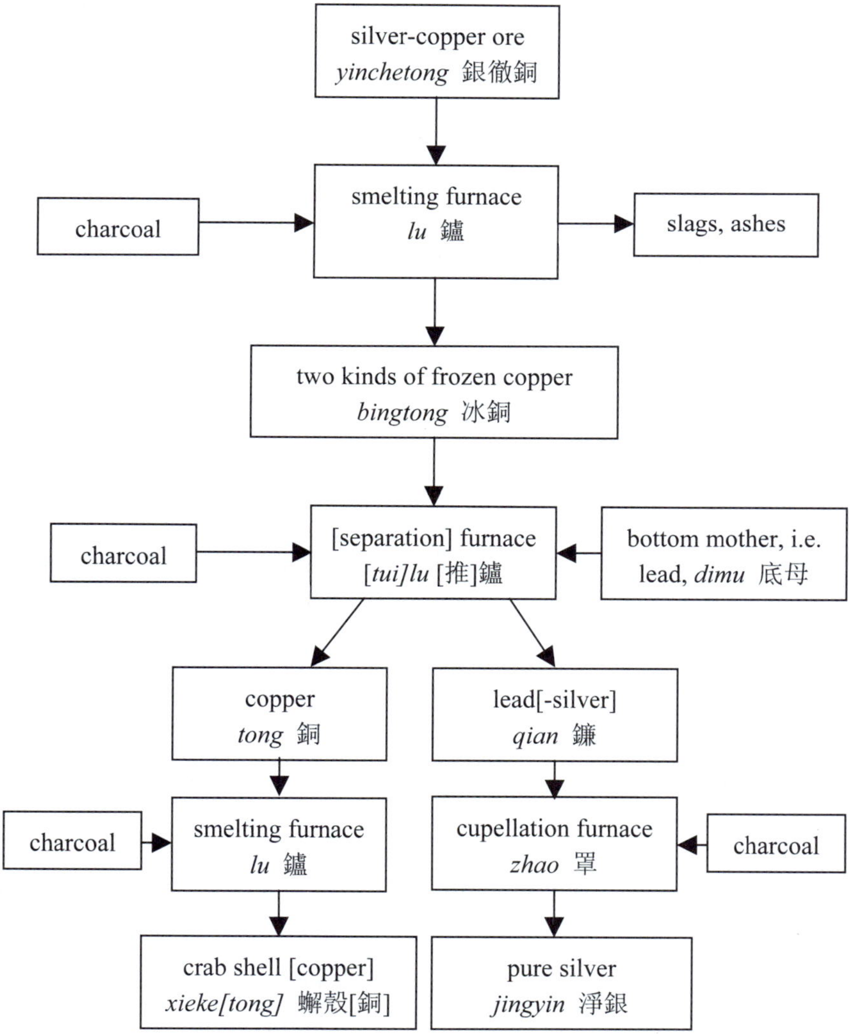

Bibliography

Agricola, Georg. (1556). *Zwölf Bücher vom Berg- und Hüttenwesen in denen die Ämter, Instrumente, Maschinen und alle Dinge, die zum Berg- und Hüttenwesen gehören, nicht nur aufs deutlichste beschrieben, sondern auch durch Abbildungen, die am gehörigen Ort eingefügt sind, unter Angabe der lateinischen und deutschen Bezeichnungen aufs klarste vor Augen gestellt werden sowie das Buch von den Lebewesen unter Tage.* German translation of 1928. Repr. München: Deutscher Taschenbuch Verlag, 1977.

Brown, J. Coggin (1923). "The Mines and Mineral Resources of Yunnan, with Short Accounts of its Agricultural Products and Trade." *Memoirs of the Geological Survey of India* 47: 1–201.

Davies, Henry R. (1909). *Yün-nan, the Link between India and the Yang-tze*. Cambridge.

Deprat, Jacques, and Mansuy, H. (1912). *Mémoires du Service géologique de l'Indo-Chine*.

Dianhai yuheng zhi 滇海虞衡志 (A Guide to the Region of the Dianchi and Erhai Lakes), by Tan Cui 檀萃, rev. by Shi Fan 師範. Prefaces dated 1799 and 1804. Ed. in *Wenyinglou yudi congshu* 問影樓輿地叢書.

Diannan kuangchang tulüe 滇南礦廠圖略 (An Illustrated Account of the Mines and Smelters of Yunnan), comp. by Wu Qijun 吳其濬, illustrations by Xu Jinsheng 徐金生. 1844. The second chap. also printed under the title *Diannan kuangchang yucheng tulüe* 滇南礦廠輿程圖略 (An Illustrated Account of the Location and Transportation Routes of the Mines and Smelters in Yunnan).

Diannan xinyu 滇南新語 (A New Account of Yunnan), by Zhang Hong 張泓. N.d. Ed. in *Xiaofanghuzhai yudi congshu* 小方壺齋輿地叢書, vol. 11, 6055–6075.

Dongchuan kuangwuju 东川矿务局 (Dongchuan Mining Office) (comp.) (1959). *Dongchuan tufa liantong jingyan* 东川土法炼铜经验 (Experiences with Smelting Copper by Native Methods in Dongchuan). Dongchuan.

Duclos, P. (1898). [Report on the mines and metallurgical industry of Yunnan, Guizhou and Sichuan]. In *La Mission Lyonnaise d'exploration commerciale en Chine, 1895–1897*. Lyon: Rey, pp. 283–314.

Dunstan, Helen (1998). "Official Thinking on Environmental Issues and the State's Environmental Roles in Eighteenth-Century China." In Mark Elvin and Liu Ts'ui-jung (eds.), pp. 585–616.

Elvin, Mark, and Liu Ts'ui-jung (eds.) (1998). *Sediments of Time: Environment and Society in Chinese History*. Cambridge: Cambridge University Press.

Elvin, Mark (2004): *The Retreat of the Elephants: An Environmental History of China*. New Haven [u.a.]: Yale University Press.

Golas, Peter J. (1999). *Science and Civilisation in China*. Vol. 5: *Chemistry and Chemical Technology*. Part 13: *Mining*. Ed. by Joseph Needham et al. Cambridge: Cambridge University Press.

Lantenois, Honoré (1907). "Résultats de la Mission géologique et minière du Yunnan méridional." *Annales des mines* 11: 298–503.

Leclère, André (1901). "Étude géologique et minière des provinces Chinoises voisines du Tonkin." *Annales des mines* 20: 287–492.

Lewin, Bruno, and Andreas Hauptmann (1984). *Kodō-zuroku "Illustrierte Abhandlung über die Verhüttung des Kupfers", 1801*. Bochum: Deutsches Bergbau-Museum.

Luo Zhufeng 罗竹凤 et al. (1987–1995). *Hanyu da cidian* 汉语大辞典 (Great Dictionary of the Chinese Language). Xianggang: Sanlian shudian.

Menzies, Nicholas K. (1996). *Science and Civilisation in China.* Vol. 6: *Biology and Biological Technology.* Part 3: *Agro-industries and Forestry.* Ed. by Joseph Needham et al. Cambridge: Cambridge University Press.

Needham, Joseph, and Lu Gwei-Djen (1974). *Science and Civilisation in China.* Vol. 5: *Chemistry and Chemical Technology.* Part 2: *Spagyrical Discovery and Invention; Magisteries of Gold and Immortality*. Cambridge: Cambridge University Press.

Okada, Yoichi (1911). *Der 'Mabuki'-Prozess: Die japanische Gewinnungsmethode des metallischen Kupfers aus Kupferstein*. Freiberg in Sachsen: Verlag von Craz & Gerlach (Joh. Stettner).

Rocher, Emile (1879). *La province du Yunnan*. Paris: Leroux.

Shina shōbetsu zenshi 支那省別全誌 (Comprehensive Gazetteer of the Individual Provinces of China), comp. by Tōa dōbunkai 東亞同文會 (East Asian Common Language Society). Tōa dōbun sho'in, 1918.

Stromer, Wolfgang von (1995). "Die Saigerhütten-Industrie des Spätmittelalters. Entwicklung der Kupfer-Silber-Scheidekünste zur «ars conflatoria separantia argentum a cupro cum plumbo»." *Technikgeschichte* 62.3: 187–219.

Suhling, Lothar (1980). "Bergbau, Territorialherrschaft und technologischer Wandel. Prozessinnovationen im Montanwesen der Renaissance am Beispiel der mitteleuropäischen Silberproduktion." In Ulrich Troitzsch and Gabriele Wohlauf (eds.) (1980), *Technikgeschichte: Historische Beiträge und neuere Ansätze.* Frankfurt am Main: Suhrkamp, pp. 150–170.

Unnanshō jijō 雲南省事情 (Conditions in Yunnan Province), comp. by Taiwan sōtoku kambō chōsaka 臺灣總督官方調查課 (Research Division of the Secretariat of the Taiwan Governor-general). 1924.

Vermeer, Eduard B. (1998). "Population and Ecology along the Frontier in Qing China." In Mark Elvin and Liu Ts'ui-jung (eds.), pp. 235–282.

Vogel, Hans Ulrich (1983). *Chinese Central Monetary Policy and the Yunnan Copper Mining Industry in the Early Qing (1644–1800)*. Zürich: Ph.D. Dissertation.

Xia Xiangrong 夏湘蓉 et al. (1980). *Zhongguo gudai kuangye kaifashi* 中国古代矿业开发史 (The History of the Development of the Ancient Chinese Mining Industry). Beijing: Dizhi chubanshe.

Yang Yuda 杨煜达 (2004). "Qingdai qianqi (1724–1855 nian) Diandongbei de tongye kaifa yu huanjing bianqian" 清代前期（1724–1855 年）滇东北的铜业开发与环境变迁 (The Development of Copper Mining and Environmental Change in North-eastern Yunnan during the Early Qing Period (1726–1855)). *Zhongguoshi yanjiu* 中国史研究 (Chinese Historical Research), 3: 157–174.

Coin Production during the Qianlong and Jiaqing Reigns (1736–1820): Issues in Cash and Silver Supply

Werner Burger

This paper discusses issues in the monetary supply of Qing China from the Qianlong era onwards. It argues that a monetary crisis in both copper cash and silver monies was imminent by the end of the Jiaqing reign. The supply of cash coins was less than plentiful, even during the most productive period of the mints in the Qianlong reign, while the deteriorating efficiency of traditional state policies from the late eighteenth century onwards caused both production and minting quality to deteriorate. Almost contemporaneously, from the early years of the nineteenth century China was affected by the global silver shortage following the American revolutions and the re-shaping of global trade patterns. Faced with massive problems in monetary supply, the inadequacy of traditional monetary policies became starkly obvious.

The monetised economy

China during the reigns of the sixth and seventh Qing emperors (1736–1820) knew money in the form of a physical commodity only, namely un-minted silver by weight and minted copper coins of a single value: one cash. Since the beginning of the dynasty in 1644, the monetary system had remained unchanged. This paper examines roots of the disastrous events that devastated China in the middle of the nineteenth century in the light of evidence of developments in the supply of the two monies that clearly show signs of crisis by 1820.

One can regard China as a completely monetised economy, i.e. all economic transactions were based on one of the two forms of money. Therefore the economic law stating how money supply influences the economy applies to that period, whether the government of the time was aware of it or not. The value of money, i.e. the purchasing power of money, is defined by the formula: **M**oney x the **V**elocity of circulation = **P**rice x **T**rade (number of transactions). Everybody depended on their savings. Everybody spent only what they absolutely had to, and everybody kept as much money for emergencies as they could afford. To buy on credit was frowned upon and government deficit financing is a very modern invention. The imperial treasury as well as every yamen was ordered to keep as much silver in store as possible for emergencies, and ordinary people kept their cash coins for a rainy day. This means that the V, P, and T of the formula were very small, therefore M relied very heavily on newly-minted coins, i.e. government expenditure. Newly-minted coins were primarily used to pay the salaries of soldiers, mint workers, yamen runners, and all kinds of public works. Newly cast cash was essential for a functioning government, because only very few cash coins were collected as taxes or revenues. Falling cash production meant that a great many public work tasks simply were not done anymore, people were not employed anymore, and the general quality of life deteriorated.

This problem was clear to those responsible for monetary affairs, and they tried to manage the flow of cash coins in a number of ways. In Qianlong 9 (1744) and again in Qianlong 25 (1760), very detailed imperial edicts were issued, determining when officials were to use cash coins in paying out public monies and when silver. This policy to influence the amount of cash in circulation was continued in the Jiaqing period. In Jiaqing 4 (1799) an edict gave the following explanation:

> "Because in the past the people's cash became cheaper daily, all mints were ordered to decrease their quotas and then to stop casting altogether. Later, the provincial mints restored their quotas but the capital mints did not. The Board of Revenue shall cast again 17 of the 35 *mao* 卯[1] they had to reduced before, and the Board of Works shall cast again 15 of the 30 reduced *mao*."[2]

A year later—the Qianlong emperor had passed away at the advanced age of 87 and He Shen (Hošen), the powerful eunuch and 'Minister of Finance' had been forced to commit suicide—the two mints in the capital resumed production, now at their full quotas.

1 *Qingchao wenxian tongkao*, 4966 states: "The period of time in which a mint is working is called mao."

2 *Qingchao xu wenxian tongkao*, 7688.

The quality of money

But there are a lot of other factors which influenced the cash coin circulation, notably the problem of counterfeit coins. As a rule these were smaller, lighter and of inferior quality. In times of a strong government these inferior cash, when collected for sundry payments by a yamen, were sold as scrap metal to the mints, and there are many such instances mentioned in official documents, e.g. in Shanxi, Jiangsu, Zhejiang, and Fujian. In Guangdong in the years Qianlong 27, 29, 32, 42, 43 (1762, 1764, 1767, 1777, 1778), and from Qianlong 35 to 39 (1770–1774), Guangdong only re-cast 'small cash', a euphemism for counterfeit coins. At the beginning of Jiaqing this very important practice continued. Most of this re-melting was done in Yunnan, which is not that surprising given that most of the forgeries came across the border from Vietnam.[3] The minting and mining rights in Vietnam were leased to resident Chinese who paid with their counterfeits for the import of Chinese goods. J.R. Morrison writes in his "A Chinese Commercial Guide"[4]:

> "Although of no greater value than about the twelfth part of a cent, this money is nevertheless much adulterated by forgers, and depreciated by the government: inferior descriptions of it are also imported in considerable quantities, particularly from Cochin China, were tutenage is almost the only ingredient used in its composition."

During the Jiaqing reign (1796–1820), mints were re-opened and new ones built just to convert these underweight counterfeits into standard cash. In Yunnan province, Lin'an 臨安 and the new mint of Guangnan 廣南 only produced cash from 'small cash', while the Old Mint of Dongchuan 東川舊局 and the new mints of Xiaguan 下關, Chuxiong 楚雄, and Yongchang 永昌 used only counterfeit coins as raw material in their first year of operation, Jiaqing 4 (1799). For Yunnan province alone, the total amount of cash produced from counterfeit coins that had been withdrawn from circulation amounted to over 1 million strings of cash. However, the practise is mentioned the last time for Sichuan in Jiaqing 7 (1802), whereas the amount of counterfeit money, mainly from south of the border region, continued to increase.

3 Morrison 1848, 233.
4 Ibid.

The graph below shows the annual production of coins by all mints throughout the empire in relation to official population figures, providing an indication of available cash per person.[5]

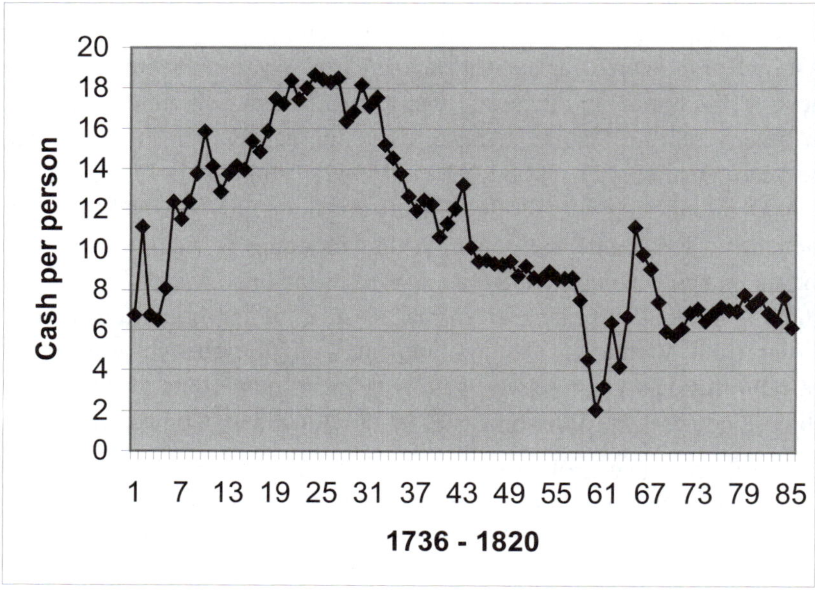

The total average for the Qianlong period (1736–1795) was 12.5 cash per person per year, and for the Jiaqing period (1796–1820) only about half of that, namely 6.9 cash. Let's compare that to some earlier production figures: In the Hongwu reign (1368–1399), the total output was only around 190 million cash per year. For a population of around 60 million that was only 3 cash per person. Naturally, that was not enough, which was the reason for the use of paper notes in the Ming.[6] In Yongzheng 2 (1724), cash production was around a billion cash, so with a population of around 125 million that is 8 cash per person per year (the cash were 16% heavier too, namely 1.4 *mace*, or 5,22 g, while the Qianlong and Jiaqing cash weighed only 1.2

5 For the figures on which the graph is based, see the Tables "Cash coin production figures in the Qianlong period" and "Cash coin production figures in the Jiaqing period" in the appendix.

6 Peng Xinwei 1965, 668.

mace, or 4.48 g).[7] However, during the Yuanfeng Period (1078–1085) of the North Song Dynasty, the 17 mints cast 5.06 million strings annually, plus over a million iron cash at 9 mints. Since at that time a string contained 770 coins, the total was around 4,773,410,180 cash per year. Many of the iron cash had a value of 2 coins. The population was around 50–55 million, which makes for close to 100 cash per person per year![8]

However, from the Jiaqing era onwards the exchange rate of cash to silver fell constantly, i.e. one needed more and more cash to get one tael of silver. A shop in Hebei province kept continuous silver/cash exchange records from 1798–1850. The figures up to 1820, the end of the Jiaqing period, are given below:[9]

Year	Silver/cash exchange rate	Year	Silver/cash exchange rate	Year	Silver/cash exchange rate
JQ 3 1798	1,090	JQ 11 1806	963	JQ 19 1814	1,102
JQ 4 1799	1,033	JQ 12 1807	970	JQ 20 1815	
JQ 5 1800	1,070	JQ 13 1808	1,040	JQ 21 1816	1,177
JQ 6 1801	1,041	JQ 14 1809	1,065	JQ 22 1817	1,217
JQ 7 1802	997	JQ 15 1810	1,133	JQ 23 1818	1,246
JQ 8 1803	967	JQ 16 1811	1,085	JQ 24 1819	
JQ 9 1804	920	JQ 17 1812	1,094	JQ 25 1820	1,224
JQ 10 1805	936	JQ 18 1813	1,090		

This trend is corroborated by many other sources from throughout the empire. These figures show clearly the process described above: after the massive withdrawal action during the early years of the Jiaqing period the exchange rate stabilised around the 'ideal' figure of 1000 cash per tael of silver. But then, some time after 1802, the policy was discontinued, and more and

7 Burger 1976, 103.

8 Peng Xinwei 1965, 401, 416, 457.

9 Yan Zhongping 1955, 37.

more cash was needed to get 1 tael of silver, simply because the quality of the cash deteriorated unchecked.

A number of provinces reported this fall of the value of cash to the throne, and mostly they also proposed a remedy, namely a reduction in coin production. This was not logical. A decrease in coin production does not bring the exchange rate back to 1000 : 1. Only by taking bad coins out of circulation could the situation be remedied. The strange logic does however explain certain abrupt changes, such as the closure of five Yunnan mints in Qianlong 35 (1770) and again in Qianlong 44/45 (1779/1780). Then in Qianlong 58/59 (1793/1794) every mint in the rest of the empire was closed and the output of the two capital mints halved. Jiaqing restored coin production, but he did not keep it up, that is, look after the welfare of the coins of his realm, because he was preoccupied with fighting several rebellions, like the White Lotus Sect. This was a quasi-religious movement which had started in the Yuan Dynasty and flared up again towards the end of the Qianlong reign (1736–1795). Many used the opportunity to enrich themselves from the military campaigns, foremost among them the infamous He Shen (Hošen). The official reason for Jiaqing's making him commit suicide was his failure to subdue the movement. Bands of disgruntled farmers terrorized Henan, Sichuan, Shaanxi, and Hubei until their main forces were defeated around 1804.[10]

Government responses

At the end of the Jiaqing reign (1796–1820), there was not yet any real problem, but the trend was obvious and administrative measures would have been needed to counter the development before it got out of hand. But no action was taken, and even the traditional Chinese remedies (like taking counterfeits out of circulation) were not implemented anymore. That would have really improved the silver/cash exchange rate, not the counterproductive measure of reducing coin output.

The situation only became serious, however, in the succeeding Daoguang reign (1821–1850), which brought the Opium war (1839–1842) and the dev-

10 Jiang Weiming 1985; Gu Haideng 1976.

astating Taiping Rebellion (1851–1864). To illustrate the problem caused by debased cash, let me quote a paragraph from the *North China Herald* by Joseph Edkins[11] (although this quotation is from a few years later it describes the market situation very well from the 1830s onward):

> "The subject of Chinese currency demands not a brief paragraph, but a comprehensive essay, or rather a volume. Its chaotic eccentricities would drive any occidental nation to madness in a single generation, or more probably such gigantic evils would speedily work their own cure. In speaking of the disregard of accuracy we have mentioned a few of the more prominent annoyances. One hundred cash are not 100, and 1,000 cash are not 1,000, but some other and totally uncertain number, to be ascertained only by experience. In wide regions of the Empire 1 cash counts for 2.[12] that is, it does so in numbers above 20, so that when one hears that he is to be paid 500 cash he understands that he will receive 250 pieces, less the local abatement, which perpetually shifts in different places. There is a constant inter-mixture of small or spurious cash, leading to inevitable disputes between dealers in any commodity. At irregular intervals the local magistrates become impressed with the evil of this debasement of the currency and issue stern proclamations against it. This gives the swarm of underlings in the magistrate's yamen an opportunity to levy squeezes on all the cash shops in the district and to make the transaction of all business more or less difficult. Prices at once rise to meet the temporary necessity for pure cash. As soon as the paying ore in this vein is exhausted, and it is not worked to any extent, the bad cash returns, but prices do not fall. Thus the irrepressible law by which the worse currency drives out the better is never for an instant suspended. The condition of the cash becomes worse and worse until, as in some parts of the Province of Honan, everyone goes to market with two entirely distinct sets of cash, one of which is the ordinary mixture of good with bad, and the other is composed exclusively of counterfeit pieces. Certain articles are paid for with the spurious cash only. But in regard to other commodities this is a matter of special bargain, and accordingly there is for these articles a double market price. That enormous losses must result from such a state of things is, to any westerner, obvious at a glance, although the Chinese are so accustomed to inconveniences of this sort that they seem almost unconscious of their existence, and the evils are felt only as the pressure of the atmosphere is felt. Chinese cash is emphatically 'filthy lucre'. It cannot be handled without contami-

11 North China Herald, 1889, 411.

12 A result of the two-tier cash system which was (unofficially) introduced in Kangxi 41 (1702) and remained in force until Kangxi 61 (1722). See: Burger 1976, 69–78 and Kangxi Year Table III.

> nation. The strings of 500 or 1,000 (nominal) pieces are exceedingly liable to break, which involves great trouble in recounting and retying. There is no uniformity of weight in the current copper cash, but all is both bulky and heavy. Cash to the value of a Mexican dollar weigh not less than 8 pounds avoirdupois. A few hundred cash are all that anyone can carry about in the little bags which are suspended for this purpose from the girdle. If it is desired to use a larger sum than a few strings the transportation becomes a serious matter. The losses on transactions in ingots of sycee are always great, and the person who uses them is inevitably cheated, both in buying and in selling. If he employs the bills of cash shops the difficulty is not greatly relieved, since those of one region are either wholly uncurrent in another region not far away, or will be taken only at a heavy discount, while the person who at last takes them to be redeemed has in prospect a certain battle with the harpies of the shop by which the bills were issued as to the quality of the cash which is to be paid for them. Under these grave disabilities the wonder is that the Chinese are able to do any business at all, and yet, as we daily perceive, they are so accustomed to these annoyances that their burden appears scarcely felt, and the only serious complaint on this score comes from foreigners."

A German traveller at the end of the nineteenth century made a photo of the cash in circulation in Shandong. I consider this picture representative of the cash situation: only 2 out of 10 coins are of the correct size and weight, the others are privately made cash or debased 'mint counterfeits'.[13] That an ever-increasing number of such coins were needed to get one tael of silver is not surprising.

13 Kürschner 1901, 395–396.

A photograph of late nineteenth century cash coins shows the wild mixture of coins in use.

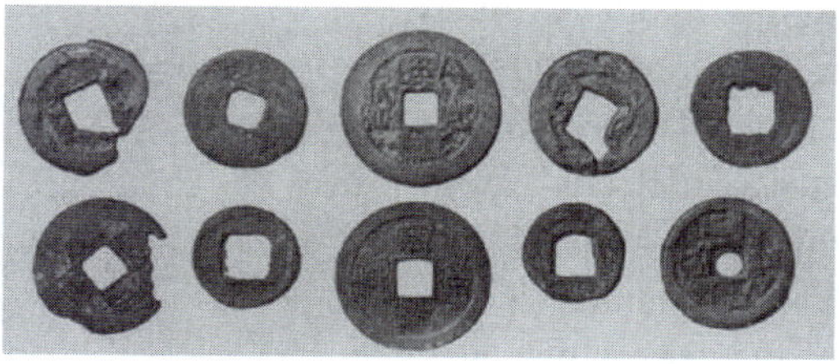

To remedy the situation, the government would have had to increase the quality of the coins in circulation. For any transaction above 1,000 cash silver was used. Government salaries as well as taxes were quoted in silver. In the eighteenth and early nineteenth centuries silver was not minted and primarily a commodity, traded by weight only. 'Money' was *qian* 錢 and *qian* was a cash coin. Coined silver in the form of Spanish pillar dollars or pieces of eight was chopped for authenticity and during Qianlong mostly melted down into silver ingots of maximum 50 tael, which is around 1.86 kg. An East Indiaman had to pay duty on the silver coins in her cargo, like on any other cargo she carried. Everybody naturally did their best to conceal the amount of silver they brought in.

> "In a line of reasoning in which the value of the imports is the concern, there is no difference between a cargo of silver and a cargo of cotton; both are used to procure a return cargo based on their value. Why then, should import duties suffer just because foreigners bring silver instead of cotton?"[14]

Throughout the Canton trade all foreigners always protested about being taxed for their import silver. Often the foreigners threatened to cease trading with China and so managed often to pay only relatively small fees for a chop (and another fee for procuring the chop), because that would seriously affect the income of the Hoppos, but the idea that silver is a commodity and must be taxed survived throughout the Canton era. Silver was finally officially recognised as *huobi* 貨幣, currency, towards the end of the Tongzhi period (1862–1875).

14 Van Dyke 2005, 117–120.

The global silver shortage

The Pillar Dollar:

Silver entered China on two routes: via Manila and via Canton. Spain occupied the Philippines in 1565 and from that year onward until 1815 they sent on average two 'Manila galleons' from Acapulco to Manila each year. These ships brought silver to Manila to pay for silk, porcelain and tea, which was brought to Manila primarily by traders from Zhejiang and Fujian. The amount of silver was around 2 million Spanish dollars annually, i.e. about 1.5 million tael (over 54 t silver) every year. After Napoleon occupied Spain in 1808 and triggered the independence movements in Spanish America, that trade stopped.

The Carolus III Dollar:

Initially, silver came in the form of irregularly hammered pieces, but from 1732 onward they were properly struck coins, the famous pillar dollars, or pieces of eight (or *columnaria* or *mundos y mare* as they were known in Spanish). From 1772 to 1808 the coins bore the portrait of Charles III and then Charles IIII, with the Chinese nicknaming these 'head dollars' (*fanmian* 梵面). The two busts were known as the *sangong* 三工 ("three 'gong' characters") and the *sigong* 四工 ("four 'gong' characters") coins, because of the way the III and the IIII were written on the coins. The coins of Ferdinand VII (1808–1821), called the *ergong pitou xiao yigui* 二工披頭小衣鬼 ("two 'gong' characters and a foreign devil with open hair and robe") were simply not accepted by the Chinese, or only at a very great discount of 14%, 18% or even 30% against the *si gong zhatou dayi gui* 四工札頭大衣鬼 ("four 'gong' characters and a foreign devil with queue and armour")

The Carolus IIII Dollar:

(Carolus IIII), very much to the annoyance of the Honourable East India Company. That naturally did not reflect the real silver value of those new pesos, but it shows very, very clearly what was wrong with the Chinese

The Carolus IIII Dollar in a Chinese illustrated Manual:

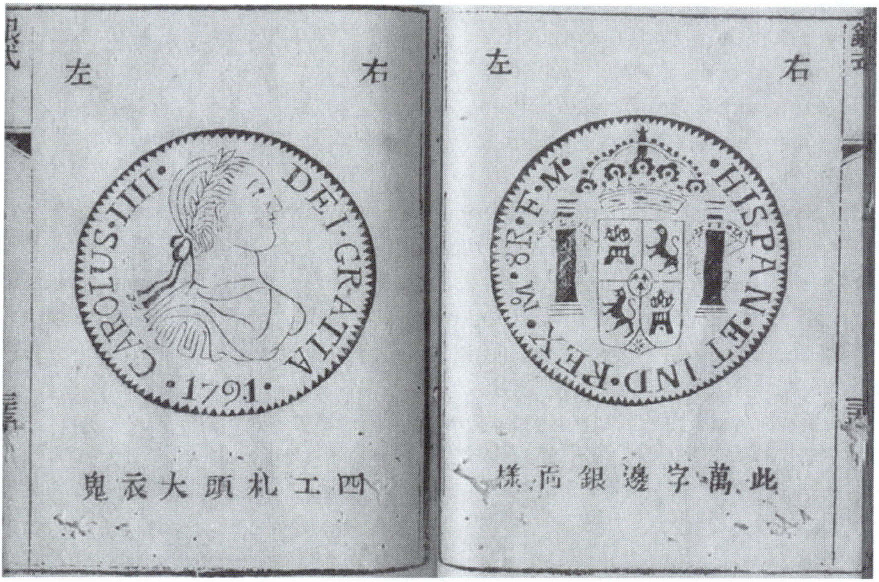

economy: the lack of a reliable, secure means of payment. This was true for the 'lowly' cash just as much as for the new silver coming to China. When the East India Company brought two chests of Dutch and French silver coins to Canton in 1798, the Chinese accepted them only after they had negotiated a discount of nearly 20%,[15] while at the same time Spanish head dollars were just counted and not weighed anymore.

The Ferdinand VII Dollar:

The revolutions in Spanish America had worldwide repercussions. They affected world trade, which was then conducted in silver, because of the drastic silver supply shortages they caused. In the 1790s Spanish America had an average output of 38 million pieces of eight. In the two decades after 1808 the whole of Spanish-speaking America produced not even one-tenth

The Ferdinand VII Dollar: in a Chinese illustrated Manual:

of that figure. In addition, the *pesos* struck by the new republican mints were no longer uniform. For example, the Chilean *peso* weighed 26.59 g and the Mexican 27.06 g. Only from the 1830s onward did the Mexican silver dollar penetrate the market again, but by then the disruption of trade due to the severe silver shortage had become quite serious. This was a grave problem for the British. The relative price of silver in British controlled territories rose considerably, so the British started to extract silver from Canton. In 1813 a British guide to Oriental Commerce still reported that between 1792 and 1809 the balance of payment was "in favour of Canton by £13,021,692; being on an average £765,892 per annum"[16], equivalent to 39 million tael or 1,455 t silver. (The Chinese Imperial household only had a budget of 10 million tael a year.)

> "Previous to the Commutation Act, which took place in 1784[17] the imports from England were small, and (what is extraordinary) were difficult to sell. The Chinese received them with reluctance, and upon some occasion, as the only mode of payment the Company had to offer. Subsequent to that period, means have been found to impress upon the minds of the Chinese, that Great Britain could not continue to receive teas to such an immense value, unless the Chinese would encourage her manufactures and produce in return, and that commercial profits to the Chinese would attach equally to the import as well as to the export trade."[18]

But starting in the second decade of the nineteenth century the British, on balance, took silver out of China. Because of the Americans bringing in large amounts of silver, the overall Canton balance of payment became slightly negative for the first time only in 1826/1827. Between 1785 and 1833 a total of 157,866,830 silver pesos entered Canton, which is on average 3.29 million pesos per year, or 2.37 million tael.

The American Revolution started in Boston with a dispute over tax on tea, which the British brought from Canton. After independence the founding fathers advised their fellow Americans that it was their patriotic duty to

15 Morse 1926, II, 301.

16 Milburn 1813, II, 478.

17 This Act reduced the tax on tea from 119% to 12.5% ad valorem and returned the tea trade to the EIC from the hands of smugglers.

18 Milburn 1813, II, 475.

switch to coffee, which came from the Americas, rather than continue drinking "British" tea. In the first decade of the nineteenth century American merchants had a great advantage in the China trade and they made full use of it. They became the major supplier of silver pesos to China, because they earned Spanish American silver coins in their trade with Central and South America whereas Spain was occupied by Napoleon and so the East India Company had great problems in obtaining quality Spanish silver coins. The Americans bought "things Chinese" not only for their new country but for all the new states in the Americas.

When increasing trade needs more capital, a modern state simply prints more money. But there was no mechanism in the Chinese traditional economy to increase the money supply. The Chinese mandarins certainly knew about the scarcity of silver, but instead of trying to increase the supply, they only knew one time-honoured traditional way: to forbid the export of silver. The first restrictions were already issued in Jiaqing 14 (1809) and again in Jiaqing 19 (1814). During the Daoguang reign (1821–1850) they were repeated again and again.

Looking a little closer, the situation is not too difficult to understand: The new activities in Canton needed a lot of silver. Calculating the trade with the British alone between 1793 and 1810, the trade needed a minimum of 5 million tael of silver a year. Because merchants had to buy the goods and wait until the next season to sell them, a minimum of 20 million tael were absorbed by these activities. But the amount of silver in circulation in Canton remained constant, so silver became scarce, and to buy a tael of silver one needed more and more cash coins. In addition the coins became increasingly of lower quality. And this was only the trade with the British. Another 25 percent was carried out at that time by (mostly Chinese) junk export, (mainly to Siam and the Dutch East Indies), another 10 percent by the Macau trade, and smaller East India companies (many of them native Indian, Armenians, Parsees, Muslim, etc.) added another 34 percent of the trade.[19] That brings the total to 35 million tael (1,300 t of silver). 35 million tael does not sound like a lot, but let us not forget that was **real** money, not the modern fiat variety.

19 Van Dyke 2005, 160.

The scarcity of silver caused another great innovation in the China trade: the introduction of bills of exchange. These bills had been common in Europe already since the sixteenth century, but came to China only when silver became scarce. Because of the great demand for silver in Canton, and to the East India Company's great "embarrassment", the reluctant Hong merchants finally had to accept bills.[20] The bills were drawn on London, without a drawer and drawee. That practice started during the temporary acute shortage of silver in 1797–1798, and was resumed only in the 1820s, after silver became scarce worldwide. American traders used bills (drawn on London) only a few times before 1833 to circumvent the trade embargo by President Jefferson, which was in response to British and French interference with neutral US merchant ships during the Napoleonic Wars, but as an act of Congress the embargo also applied to the trade with China. The embargo was lifted in 1809, but continued British interference with US shipping led America to declare war on England in 1812.

It took a number of decades for the Chinese merchants to get to trust the pillar and head dollars. But when they then found out that the new Spanish coins were of inferior quality the trust was gone, never to return. When after the 1830s the Mexican silver pesos assumed again a steady quality, Hong Kong and the international settlements in Shanghai accepted the new coin as legal tender, but not so the rest of China. In the 1920s H.B. Morse was quite surprised that

> "A hundred years later Spanish dollars with the imprint of Charles IV, deposed in 1808 and succeeded by Ferdinand VII, were found to command a premium of 40 per cent for use in buying tea in Anhwei"[21]

Just how sensitive the Chinese market was can be clearly seen from the fact that the head dollar traded at a slight premium over the pillar dollar and sycee silver, [22] with 100 head dollars equal to 98 pillar dollars. That shows that the Chinese merchants were aware of the difference between the two coins. Both weighed 27.07 g, but the pillar dollar was .917 fine and the head dollar .903, a difference of only 1.55%. In spite of all that, there was no coordinated response to the devalued silver coins. This shows once again that

20 Morse 1926, II, 301.
21 Morse 1926, III, 162.
22 Ibid., II, 324.

Qing China at the beginning of the nineteenth century had no proper administrative institution to deal with monetary problems, such as the deterioration in the quality of the silver supply.

References

Burger, Werner (1976). *Ch'ing Cash until 1735*. Taipei: Mei Ya.

Gu Haideng 辜海澄 (1976). *Chuan-Chu-Shan bailian jiaoluan shimo* 川陝楚白蓮教亂始末 (A Chronology of the White Lotus Upheaval in Sichuan, Hubei and Shaanxi). Taizhong.

Jiang Weiming 蒋维明 (1985). *Chuan-Chu-Shan bailianjiao qiyi* 川楚陕白莲教起义 (The White Lotus Uprising in Sichuan, Hubei and Shaanxi). Chengdu.

Kürschner, Joseph (1901). *China. Schilderungen aus Leben und Geschichte, Krieg und Sieg*. Berlin.

Milburn, William (1813). *Oriental Commerce*. London.

Morrison, John R. (1848). *A Chinese Commercial Guide*. Canton.

Morse, Hosea Ballou (1926). *Chronicles of the East India Company Trading to China, 1635–1834*. Cambridge.

North China Herald.

Peng Xinwei 彭信威 (1965). *Zhongguo huobi shi* 中国货币史 (A History of Chinese Currency). Shanghai: Shanghai renmin chubanshe.

Qingchao wenxian tongkao 清朝文獻通考 (Encyclopedia of the Historical Records of the Qing Dynasty). Compilation ordered in 1767. Taibei, Xinxing shuju, 1963 reprint.

Qingchao xu wenxian tongkao 清朝續文獻通考 (Encylopedia of the Historical Records of the Qing Dynasty Continued). Taibei, Xinxing shuju, 1965 reprint.

Van Dyke, Paul A. (2005). *The Canton Trade*. Hong Kong.

Yan Zhongping 嚴中平 (ed.) (1955). *Zhongguo jindai jingjishi tongji ziliao xuanji* 中國近代經濟史統計資料選集 (Selected Statistical Material for Modern Chinese Economic History). Beijing.

Appendix

The two tables below detail the total annual coin production from Qianlong 1 (1736) until Jiaqing 25 (1820):

Year of the Qianlong reign period	Total coin production	Total population	Coins per person
1	968,237,800	143,411,559	6.751
2	1,596,986,284	143,411,559	11.136
3	969,199,846	143,411,559	6.758
4	930,616,008	143,411,559	6.489
5	1,222,202,029	143,411,559	8.522
6	1,774,388,647	143,411,559	12.370
7	1,840,874,941	159,801,551	11.520
8	2,036,881,163	164,454,416	12.386
9	2,296,253,309	166,808,604	13.766
10	2,694,253,794	169,922,127	15.856
11	2,448,471,039	171,896,773	14.244
12	2,290,799,154	171,896,773	13.327
13	2,405,988,589	177,495,039	13.555
14	2,489,013,878	177,495,039	14.023
15	2,526,789,395	179,533,540	14.074
16	2,919,741,049	181,811,359	16.059
17	2,637,373,364	182,957,277	14.415
18	2,917,843,863	183,678,259	15.886
19	3,223,028,219	184,504,493	17.469
20	3,194,969,902	185,612,881	17.213
21	3,428,435,611	186,615,514	18.372
22	3,320,502,529	190,348,328	17.444
23	3,449,721,129	191,672,808	17.998
24	3,631,426,011	194,791,859	18.643
25	3,618,916,553	196,337,977	18.432
26	3,665,930,005	198,214,555	18.286
27	3,704,855,603	200,472,461	18.481
28	3,344,478,432	204,299,828	16.370
29	3,460,718,054	205,591,017	16.833

30	3,758,871,083	206,993,224	18.159
31	3,559,126,512	208,095,796	17.103
32	3,680,597,483	209,839,540	17.540
33	3,205,795,124	210,837,502	15.205
34	3,085,018,445	212,023,042	14.550
35	2,942,348,994	213,613,163	13.774
36	2,716,654,103	214,600,356	12.659
37	2,588,748,329	216,467,258	11.959
38	2,728,960,688	218,743,315	12.476
39	2,711,144,247	221,027,224	12.266
40	2,821,247,914	264,561,355	10.664
41	3,038,148,120	268,238,181	11.326
42	3,262,925,167	270,863,760	12.046
43	3,216,776,756	242,965,618	13.240
44	2,790,071,816	275,042,916	10.144
45	2,621,882,928	277,554,431	9.446
46	2,661,162,491	279,816,070	9.510
47	2,630,404,272	281,822,675	9.334
48	2,639,065,310	284,033,785	9.291
49	2,704,751,251	286,331,307	9.446
50	2,522,127,133	288,863,974	8.731
51	2,683,405,543	291,102,486	9.218
52	2,530,127,383	292,429,018	8.652
53	2,532,932,233	294,852,089	8.591
54	2,666,516,638	297,717,496	8.957
55	2,595,010,653	301,487,115	8.607
56	2,620,181,221	304,354,110	8.609
57	2,658,707,154	307,467,279	8.647
58	2,341,638,004	310,497,210	7.542
59	1,440,649,871	318,281,795	4.526
60	619,307,146	296,968,968	2.085
Total	**159,583,200,212**		**12.516**

Year of the Jiaqing reign period	Total coin production	Total population	Coins per person
1	878,445,924	275,662,044	3.187
2	1,740,150,878	271,333,544	6.413
3	1,216,167,083	290,982,980	4.180
4	1,837,923,469	293,283,179	6.267
5	3,134,952,132	295,237,311	10.618
6	2,667,244,200	297,501,548	8.965
7	2,721,711,334	299,749,770	9.080
8	2,251,625,084	302,250,673	7.450
9	1,822,350,890	304,461,284	5.985
10	1,919,888,331	332,181,403	5.780
11	2,055,699,498	335,369,469	6.130
12	2,338,318,415	338,262,439	6.913
13	2,496,581,579	350,291,724	7.127
14	2,295,141,009	352,900,024	6.504
15	2,377,867,499	345,717,214	6.878
16	2,588,309,423	358,610,039	7.218
17	2,353,678,494	333,700,560	7.053
18	2,357,092,671	336,451,672	7.006
19	2,472,234,886	316,574,895	7.809
20	2,381,691,390	326,574,895	7.293
21	2,510,835,070	328,814,957	7.636
22	2,290,552,182	331,330,433	6.913
23	2,279,943,481	348,820,037	6.536
24	2,271,098,512	301,260,545	7.539
25	2,165,105,224	353,377,694	6.127
Total	**55,424,608,658**		**6.913**

Copper Transports out of Yunnan, ca. 1750–1850: Transport Technologies, Natural Difficulties and Environmental Change in a Southwestern Highland Area

Nanny Kim

This investigation of copper transports out of northern Yunnan into Sichuan places transport technologies within the context of difficult natural conditions, social transformation, and ecological change. Two results emerge that change the picture of transport systems in the period: First, communication infrastructure, consisting of roads, bridges, mountain rivers made navigable, and safety provided by military and postal relay stations, was crucial to control, in-migration and development. It required and received massive investment, mainly motivated by the desire to enhance the procurement of copper for minting. Second, infrastructure projects, especially efforts to improve shipping, were decisive in maintaining massive volumes of transport despite grave environmental degradation. Nevertheless, deforestation also led to a fragility of the system, with maintenance requiring ever rising investments of labour and resources.

Copper cash and the southwestern frontier region

The Qing state faced an uncomfortable situation with regard to the minting of Cash coins: On the one hand, defining itself in the orthodox imperial tradition, the dynastic state regarded the minting of bronze coins as one of its important responsibilities. Statecraft traditions held that cash coins provided the practical means for the exchange of goods in order to "exchange what is abundant for what is lacking," thus playing their role in ensuring the well-being of all imperial subjects.[1] At the same time, the coins themselves symbolized dynastic authority. For durability, safety against re-use for the coins' intrinsic metal value, and on account of the venerability of the material, the coins had to be made of bronze, an alloy of copper and zinc with small quantities of lead and tin added.[2] On the other hand, however, in fact as a conse-

1 The *locus classicus* for this both moralist and positive ideal of a controlled market in a well-ordered state is *Mengzi: Gongsun Chou, part 2* 孟子：公孫丑下.

2 The large-scale, well-regulated production of bronze coins in the Tang period set the pattern for Cash minting, its shape and composition for all subsequent dynasties. From

quence of the exploitation over three millennia, resources of metal ore had become scarce. In particular, exploitable copper deposits in China proper had become all but exhausted. Therefore, when Tokugawa Japan cut down its copper exports in the early eighteenth century, the Qing state had no choice but to develop a system of supplying its mints with copper mined in distant Yunnan province. The decision in itself demonstrates considerable determination, for the far Southwest, while known to be rich in copper and other ores, was but a thinly settled frontier territory, rugged and inhabited by fiercely independent-minded aboriginal peoples.

Military occupation and administrative re-organization as a result of the wars first between the Qing forces under Wu Sangui 吳三桂 (1673–1681) against Ming loyalists and later against Wu Sangui's rebellion of the Three Feudatories lasted into the early eighteenth century, displacing tribal peoples and strengthening the presence of the state. The dynastic state was initially mainly represented by stationed troops and powerful provincial governors, later increasingly by Han-Chinese settlers. While control over the mining areas was thus established, the difficulties of transport with its high risks and costs remained the crux of Qing mint metal procurement.

For political reasons, the metropolitan mints in the city of Beijing were retained as the most important. To supply these mints approximately 4,000 t of copper, and almost the same amount of zinc, as well as relatively minor amounts of lead from Guizhou province and tin from Guangdong province had to be shipped over distances of over 4,000 km to Beijing. These shipments, as they were directly relevant to money minting, received considerable government attention. From the point of view of the historian, this attention is fortuitous, as it means extensive documentation. Copper procurement was most closely supervised, and for this reason transports of this monetary metal are the focus of this paper.

the perspective of the late imperial period, any variation, such as in metal composition and the paper money introduced in the Song had become discredited as they were associated with the weakness attributed to the Song on account of the dynasty's eventual subjugation by the Mongols. Paper money in particular was thoroughly abhorred as a sign of despotic exploitation, because it had been the standard form of currency during the Mongol Yuan dynasty and eventually led to catastrophic inflation. See von Glahn 1996, ch. 2, esp. 60–71.

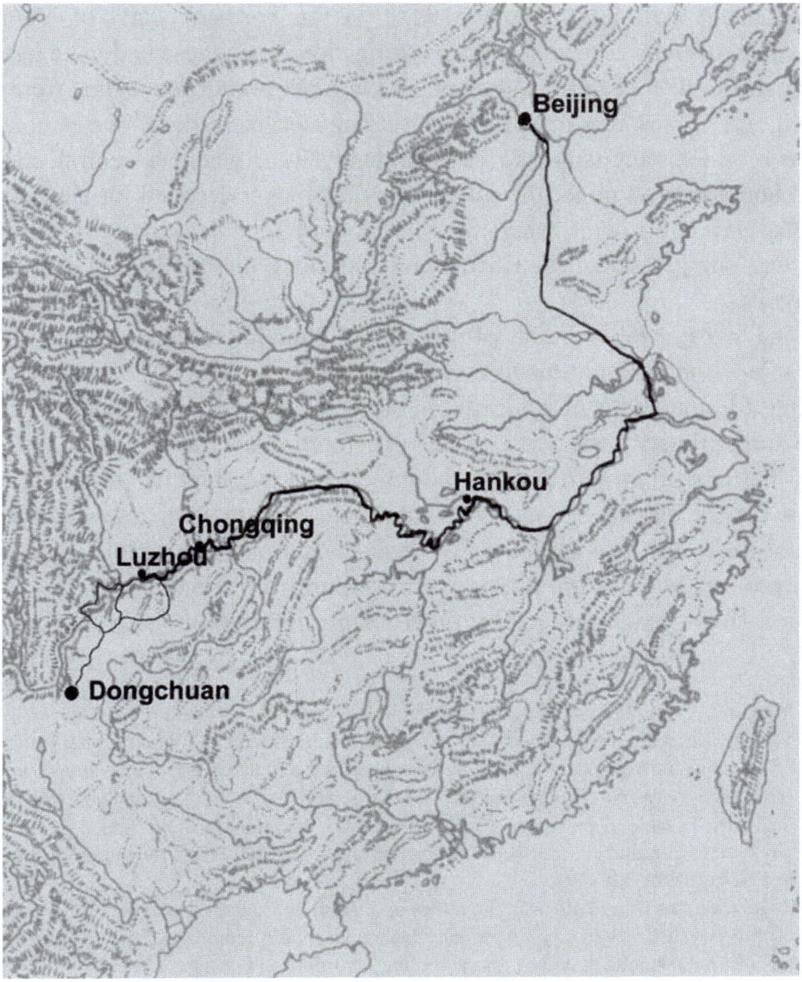

The route of copper transports from Dongchuan in Northeastern Yunnan to the metropolitan mints in Beijing. Map by the author.

The findings discussed here mainly concern the challenges of water transport out of northern Yunnan into southwestern Sichuan. The two prefectures Dongchuan 東川 and Zhaotong 昭通 in the northern "tail" of Yunnan province form the core area of the investigation, since these had to be passed through by all transports and some of the most productive mines were located here. Transports out of Yunnan terminated in Luzhou, on the confluence of the Changjiang and the Tuojiang 沱江, where a central copper storehouse was set up for the collection of all copper destined for the Beijing mints.[3] From this point, where the routes out of Yunnan converged, the copper was shipped down the Changjiang and along the Grand Canal in large convoys.[4]

The investigation consists of two parts. Following a sketch of the region, the mines and the mint metal transports, the discussion will concentrate on changes in the transport systems and projects for the improvement of infrastructure, primarily waterways. The concentration on waterways despite the fact that most transport through the region was overland has technical reasons. On the one hand, sources on road transport are comparatively scarce. On the other, the exploration of historical changes in shipping and infrastructure projects undertaken with the aim to improve navigation conditions on natural rivers bears particularly far-reaching implications both for rates of

3 Luzhou became the central collecting point for all copper destined for Beijing in 1759. Prior to this date, both Luzhou and Yongning functioned as end-points of the routes out of Yunnan. Between 1759 and 1806, the regulations stipulated that four regular convoys (*zhengyun* 正運) carrying about 440 t and two additional convoys (*jiayun* 加運) carrying ca. 610 t were dispatched per year. From 1807, the amounts to be carried by the convoys were reorganized, but the overall quota of almost 3000 tons remained unchanged. See Vogel 1989, 348–395.

4 Regulations on shipments from the mines of Yunnan to Luzhou demanded that transports used between 15 to 40 day stages and reached Luzhou 6 months to 2 years after departure from the smelters, laid to for each mine according to distance. The 3500 km on major waterways from Luzhou to Beijing were to be covered on a tighter schedule within 9 months. The difference in the time-frames strongly suggests different organizational structures. While the convoys that departed from Luzhou were tightly organized and well-documented, we know little about the transports out of Yunnan beyond the fact that the local governments were responsible for them. The regulations explicitly permitted delays during the busy agricultural seasons, thus to avoid harming the farming population by recruiting labouring animals when they were needed in the fields. It would appear that extremely difficult conditions during the monsoon season and snowfall.

environmental change and for the scope and limitations of human effort set against natural adversity.

The region

In the early eighteenth century, when the Qing central government turned its attention to the copper mines of Yunnan, the province was a recently occupied frontier region. Much of the Southwest, including Sichuan, Guizhou and Yunnan had been only sparsely inhabited since the thirteenth-century Mongol wars. Only in the later Ming, from the mid-fifteenth century onwards, had Sichuan recovered its former population density and economic importance. Meanwhile, the bordering areas to the South, now northern Yunnan and Guizhou, remained secluded minority lands throughout the Ming. At the end of the Ming period in the mid-seventeenth century, the Zhang Xianzhong 張獻忠 rebellion (1630–1646) utterly destroyed and depopulated Sichuan. Subsequently, the wars of the Qing against Ming loyalist forces (1657–59) and against the powerful general and fief-holder Wu Sangui left Yunnan and Guizhou destabilized, twice conquered territories. From the late seventeenth century onwards, resettlement of Sichuan set in swiftly, due mainly to in-migration from Hubei and Hunan, and soon spread to bordering areas. The formerly semi-independent border areas were brought under standard imperial administration by the early eighteenth century.[5] As governor-general of Yunnan and Guizhou, Ortai (E'ertai 鄂爾泰，1677–1745), one of the most powerful officials of his time, waged two ruthless colonial campaigns against Yi aboriginal leaders (Yi 彝, also referred to as Lolo in Western literature), creating the three new prefectures of Dongchuan, Zhaotong and Zhenxiong 鎮雄 as integrated parts of Yunnan province and firmly controlled by military colonists.[6] Shortly after the redrawing of the provincial borders, the responsibility of copper mining and procurement was placed in the hands of the Yunnan provincial government,

5 The formerly semi autonomous frontier areas under formally invested local rulers were made prefectures of Yunnan province in 1726. This political change meant the loss of authority and control of the aboriginal people and was fought against for several years in small-scale frontier wars which ended with the exhaustion of the aboriginal population.

6 For biographical information on Ortai, see Hummel 1943, 601f.

and copper mining for the supply of the imperial mints was developed swiftly from the 1730s onwards.

Mining and the transports of mint metals became the motor of a marked development in population density, agricultural and industrial productivity as well as the integration into Chinese trade systems.[7] Population developments, though hard to estimate, provide an idea of the change. According to James Lee's reconstruction of agricultural and population development in the Southwest, by the 1760s at least 300,000 people lived in Dongchuan and Zhaotong prefectures.[8] Whereas these figures seem moderate, with most of the area of both prefectures covered by rugged mountains, the population was in fact concentrated in small plains and narrow valleys, reaching considerable densities. Qin Shucai has pointed out that Green Standard troops, mostly consisting of men who originally came from the inner provinces of China, played an important role in the colonization of Yunnan. When Zhaotong and Dongchuan were set up as prefectures of Yunnan province, 6,800 troops, usually bringing along their families, were stationed here, probably fulfilling many pioneering functions.[9] During the mining boom in the 1750s, numbers of miners and smelterers were estimated at "several hundred-thousands."[10] If, as sources suggest, the majority of these workers were 'drifting people' (*liumin* 流民), unregistered people who went where they could find work, most of these would have been single males.[11] Even if this

7 Zhang Lihong 1994, Lan Yong 2006a.

8 Lee 1982, 730: table 7, footnote b. According to Lee, population increase was high throughout the one-and-a-half centuries of the high Qing. He states that by 1700 the Southwest had recovered its sixteenth-century population of 4 to 5 million. This figure at least doubled by 1775 and reached approximately 20 million by 1850. See ibid. p. 720, 732, and 736. For a more conservative estimate, see Cao Shuji 2001, 238–40. According to Cao, the total population of the two prefectures peaked about 1820 at just under 100,000.

9 Qin Shucai and Tian Zhiyong 2004, 35 and 37.

10 *Dongchuan fuzhi*, 104f.

11 This remains conjecture, as we have next to no information on the living and working conditions of miners and smelteres before the late period of traditional mining from the late nineteenth century onwards. The in-migration of Muslims, often from the northwestern regions of mining and metallurgy, as well as the substantial financial and technological requirements for the setting up of mines and smelters would suggest that at least lessees of mines and smelting headmen could not have been poverty stricken single males. According to the research of Li Tianhu, in the twentieth century whole communities

assumption is true and even if it was an over-estimation, the presence of large numbers of miners indicates an according expansion of the farming population, a relatively high agricultural productivity, and a lively trade of salt, grain, textiles and a multitude of other goods.[12] For the second half of the eighteenth and the first third of the nineteenth centuries, James Lee's estimate appears conservative rather than over-enthusiastic.

The expansion of Han-Chinese agriculture, characterized by irrigation and, in Mark Elvin's words, a "hostility to forests," pushed back or assimilated aboriginal peoples with their economic system of husbandry and slash-and-burn agriculture.[13] The intensive agricultural regime certainly contributed much to supporting large numbers of miners and transporters. At the same time, it led to massive, and on fragile slopes irreversible deforestation.[14]

With regard to transport conditions, effects of environmental degradation on waterways may be expected to have been especially pronounced. Erosion and accelerated run-off caused greater and more sudden rises and falls in water levels, while more debris was carried down and built up into shoals and rapids. Road transport can be expected to have been affected more indirectly: As intensive agriculture expanded at the expense of husbandry mixed with mobile slash and burn agriculture, winter pastures became scarce and it

were engaged in mining, with the men working as miners and the women and children breaking up the ore outside the mining galleries. (Communication with Li Tianhu 2007.03.29).

12 Many sources link the mining boom with a great intensification of trade. A particularly high density of guild halls in Huize and Zhaotong bear testimony to the influx of well organized and often wealthy merchants and specialists from many regions of China.
The volume of the trade in salt was considerable, as almost all salt was imported into the area. Prior to 1751, the Zhaotong and Dongchuan prefectures belonged to the Yunnan salt zone. Distance from the Yunnan salt producing areas drove up prices and encouraged illicit trade. From 1751 onwards, they were added to the Sichuan salt zone, which improved the situation (*Dongchuan fuzhi*, 92). By 1763, 4 million *jin* (2400 tons) of salt were recorded to be annually imported into the two prefectures Zhaotong and Dongchuan (*Yunnan tongzhi* 1894:72.66b, quoted from Lee 1982, 730). Nevertheless, salt remained dear and the salt consumption is said to have been much lower than in other parts of the empire.

13 Mark Elvin 2004, ch. 4, esp. p. 78.

14 Yang Yuda 2004.

appears probable that a shortage of labouring animals available for transport would have resulted.

Before we turn to the investigation of copper transport, however, it seems useful to conclude this brief survey of the region by noting that the situation described above fundamentally changed again in the early nineteenth century. In the years 1815–1817, Yunnan was hit by a devastating famine, which is thought to have been caused by the eruption of the Tambora Volcano in Indonesia.[15] Reconstruction after this natural disaster appears to have been relatively successful. Nevertheless, copper procurement is thought to have become increasingly beset by problems through the Jiaqing (1795–1820) and Daoguang (1821–1850) periods, probably due to various factors, including the exhaustion of mines, rising costs for timber and charcoal needed for smelting and mining, climatic cooling, and social conflicts over mining rights. When the Taiping armies reached the Changjiang in 1852, copper transports were brought to an end. During the civil wars of the mid-nineteenth century, the area investigated in this paper was wrecked by the Muslim rebellion (1855–1875) throughout the mining areas of Yunnan and affected by the uprising of transport and salt workers in Zhaotong prefecture and Southwestern Sichuan (1858–1860).[16] When reconstruction began in the last two decades of the century, it was hampered by the loss of know-how, capital and organizational structures of the mining industry.[17] Besides, the transport system had shifted to maritime transport. Shipments of monetary metals, when they were revived on a much reduced scale, partly took an eastward route down the Xijiang to be taken over by ocean steamers in Guangzhou.[18] For the purpose of this exploration, it is therefore important to keep in mind that the social and economic conditions of the Daoguang period differed considerably from those prior to 1815 and that the situation

15 Yang Yuda, Man Zhimin and Zheng Jingyun 2005.

16 The extent of the destruction may be glimpsed from the fact that in the late nineteenth century many villages were abandoned or renamed, as new in-migrants arrived to take over largely empty land. This process is recorded in the local gazetteers of the late Qing and Republican periods.

17 Reports of Western travelers state that mines were known to exist in many places, but that the means to exploit them were no longer available (Hosie 1890, 49, Mission Lyonnaise 1897, part 2, 291, Davies 1909, 164–167).

18 Hosie 1890, 49.

known from the late nineteenth and early twentieth centuries belongs to a different age.

The mint metal transports

The organization of the copper transports out of northern Yunnan for onward shipping to Beijing is known in its general outlines.[19] The copper ore was refined, cast into lumpy plates or bars and collected at copper storage facilities along the highways of Yunnan.[20] Copper agency officials and local magistrates were responsible for the transport out of Yunnan. They received a budget and regulations for this task, but left hardly any documentation on how they implemented it. Available sources directly relevant to copper transports are the regulations, i.e. normative guidelines that had to be followed in reporting procedures, a number of memorials in the context of major changes in the system, and isolated shreds of information recorded in local gazetteers.[21] As a result, an attempt at reconstructing copper transport systems frequently has to take recourse to context materials and conjecture.

Maps 2 and 3 showing the changes in the transport routes out of Yunnan present an attempt at reconstructing routes and amounts of copper from information provided in the regulations. They therefore represent the situation desired by the provincial authorities, not necessarily the actual conditions.

Nevertheless, a reconstruction based on the regulations of the mid-eighteenth century for copper transported along the Xundian 尋甸 and Dongchuan routes destined for the metropolitan mints provides an overall idea of what was involved. Assuming the full regular annual quota of 3,800 t

19 The shipments from Luzhou onwards, by contrast, provide the densest documentation in Qing transport systems, mainly thanks to a system that required memorial reports on each transport. For explorations of this part of the metropolitan copper transports, see Sun E-tu Zen 1971, Zhang Yonghai 1986, Lan Yong 2006, also Nanny Kim (forthcoming).

20 For the best reconstruction of the geography of the transports, with routes and storage facilities, see Lan Yong 2006a.

21 In the scope of this paper, it has not been possible to use further, less readily accessible sources, such as material remains, inscriptions, documents locally held, and unpublished memorials. It should be noted that zinc and lead transports from Yunnan and Guizhou were organized along similar lines, but less intensively supervised, so that we have even less sources on them.

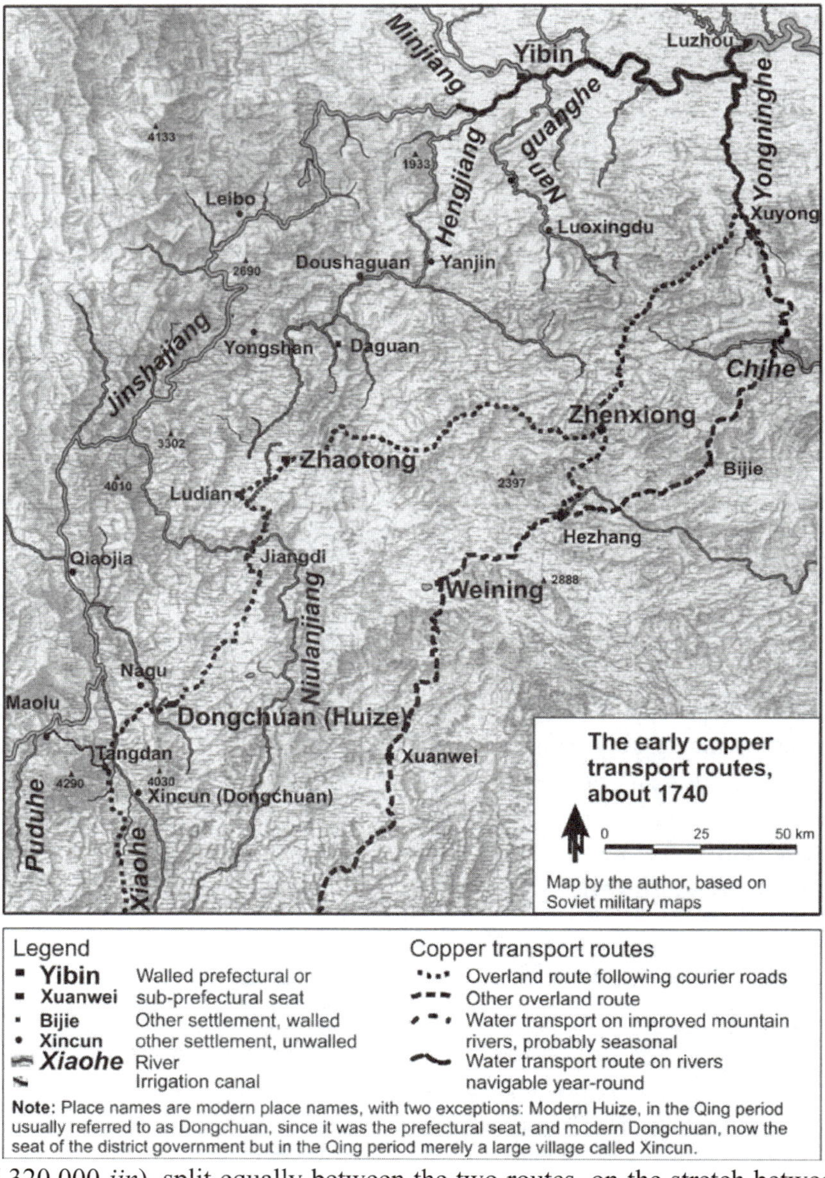

(6,320,000 *jin*), split equally between the two routes, on the stretch between Dongchuan and Zhaotong, we would be reckoning with at least 19,000 loads of pack mules or –horses, about 400 boatloads from Huangcaoping 黄草坪

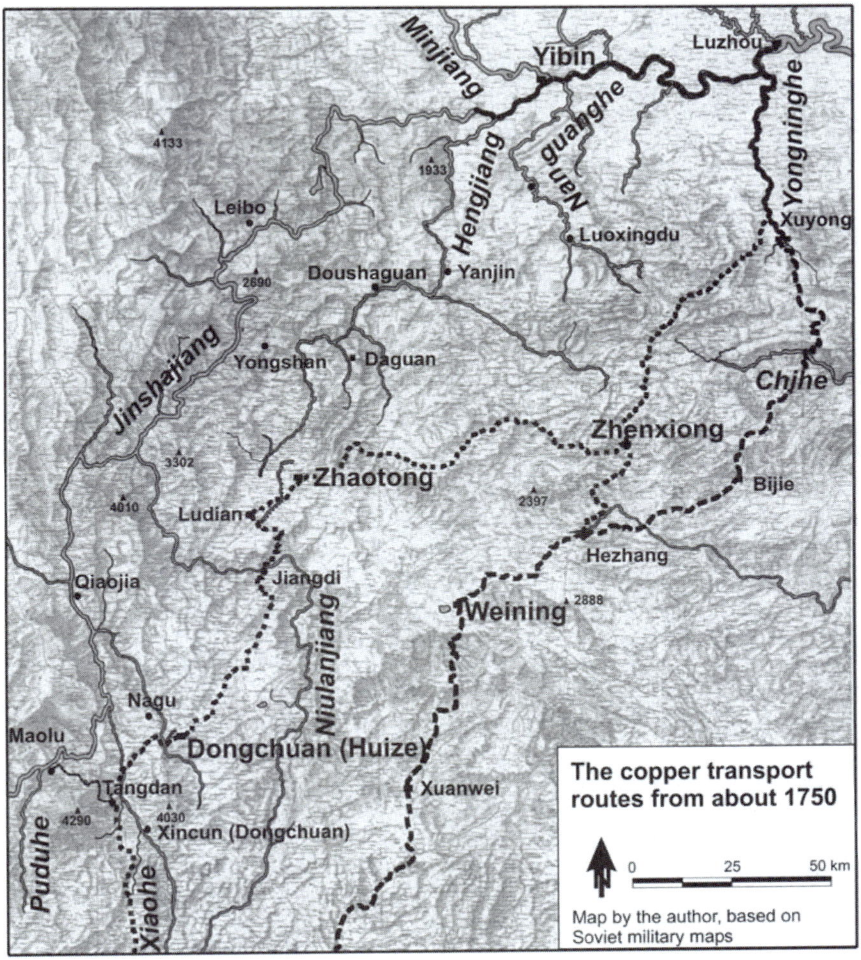

Legend

- **Yibin** Walled prefectural or
- **Xuanwei** sub-prefectural seat
- **Bijie** Other settlement, walled
- **Xincun** other settlement, unwalled
- ***Xiaohe*** River
- Irrigation canal

Copper transport routes

- Overland route following courier roads
- Other overland route
- Water transport on improved mountain rivers, probably seasonal
- Water transport route on rivers navigable year-round

Note: Place names are modern place names, with two exceptions: Modern Huize, in the Qing period usually referred to as Dongchuan, since it was the prefectural seat, and modern Dongchuan, now the seat of the district government but in the Qing period merely a large village called Xincun.

down the Jinshajiang 金沙江, and the same number down the Hengjiang 横江 from Yanjin 鹽津.[22] On the Xundian route, we would expect some 11,000 cartloads between Xundian and Weining 威寧,[23] 19,000 loads of pack horses or over 30,000 loads of porters between Weining and Luoxingdu 羅星渡 and Xuyong 敘永 respectively,[24] and between 200 and 400 boat-loads down the Nanguanghe 南廣河 from Luoxingdu and the Yongninghe 永寧河 from Xuyong 敘永 respectively.[25]

More specific aspects become visible when the information of maps and local gazetteer is added. For example, it becomes apparent that the reorganization of transports after the early years involved the redirecting of copper transports to more westerly routes. This meant the shortening of overland distances to be covered, but at the expense of carrying the copper over more rugged terrain. Pack horses were required on most of the western overland routes, while ox-drawn carts could be employed on the more level stretches

22 The numbers of loads of pack animals are calculated on the basis of 168 *jin* (101 kg) per pair of baskets for pack animals (*Tongzheng bianlan* a, 281 and 286f.), those for boats on the assumption that boats with capacities of 5 tons in use on the small southern tributaries of the Upper Changjiang in the Republican period carried about the same as their eighteenth-century predecessors.

23 This figure is calculated on the basis of the prescribed cartloads for copper transports on the stretch through Xuanwei district along the eastern route in the context of events of around 1780. Here, one cartload is given as one ma 碼 weighing 350 *jin* (210 kg) (*Xuanwei xianzhi gao* 336).

24 According to *Tongzheng bianlan* the copper transports from Zhenxiong to Luoxingdu were carried on the backs of men, although the original regulations stated pack horses as carriers (*Tongzheng bianlan* A, 285f.). Porters in northern Yunnan and Western Sichuan are recorded to have been carrying incredible loads of some 100 kg by observers of the late nineteenth and early twentieth centuries, sometimes exceeding the loads carried by mules and horses (e.g. Mission Lyonnaise 1897, part 1, 80). As we cannot confirm this practice for the eighteenth century, I have used the standard heavy porter load about 60 kg for this calculation.

25 I have not been able to trace specific information on boat transport in the Yunnan-Sichuan border region. Hosie records about 15 m long boats on the Yongninhe in 1882–83 (1897, 156), boat transport in winter 1896 appeared hazardous to the members of the Mission Lyonnaise on the Hengjiang above Pu'erdu (Mission Lyonnaise 1897, 81), Davies records sectional navigation by small craft even on the upper Niulanjiang and Yilihe (1909, 170 and 172). Further information may be deducted from boats in the painting 'Jinshajiang jiangshantu' (Vogel 1991) and information available for small mountain rivers in the Three Gorges region (Worcester 1971, 503f. on the Shenbozi of the Daninghe). I work with the assumption of 5 tons, and about 10 tons on the Yongninghe.

of the easterly routes. Contrary to expectation, however, this redirection may have been advantageous for two reasons. First, the western route ran through horse-breeding lands. As this was Yi country, we may assume that pack horses and drivers were relatively available, though safety remained an issue so close to the un-subjugated Yi of Western Sichuan. Second, reducing the volume carried along the eastern routes, which ran through Miao 苗 territories, might have eased the burden already placed on the area, since Western Guizhou was the main zinc mining region and northward transports would have used much the same routes.[26]

Moreover, the redrawing of the salt zones clearly was linked to the copper transports. Rough calculation shows that it arranged for an approximately equal transport volume out of and into Yunnan. This issue was raised in the Sichuan border counties as soon as the Nanguanghe 南廣河 was improved for copper transports. According to a proposal of about 1746 printed in the Gaoxian gazetteer, shifting salt transport to the counties along the Nanguanghe and to Zhenxiong from roads to the river would alleviate the problem of copper boats set up at relay stages having to return empty.[27] In response to the proposal, the prefectures Zhaotong, Dongchuan and Qujing 曲靖 were added to the Sichuan salt zone in 1751. Although illicit trade may be assumed to have been widespread, with the massive increase in the northward transport of copper, under-employment on the southward journey would have been a problem for recruiting transporters, even if we assume that the trade volume in grain was considerable in the early decades of agricultural expansion. By shifting the salt zone, this problem was alleviated. An annual transport volume in salt of perhaps 2,400 tons, together with sizeable trade volumes in grains, cotton cloth and other goods might have just about balanced the 4,000 tons of copper, to which relatively minor amounts of tea, copperware and white wax insects have to be added.[28] It

26 The reconstruction of the routes of zinc transports is difficult due to the scarcity of sources and to my knowledge has not been attempted.

27 *Gaoxian zhi*, 497–298. The proposal suggests shifting all transports to the waterway as well as slightly increasing the number salt tickets for the Sichuan border area, arguing that [legally] available salt was insufficient for the growing population of the area.

28 The figure for the transport volume of salt into the prefectures Zhaotong and Dongchuan is quoted for 1763 in Lee 1982, 370 from *Yunnan tongzhi*. To this amount, the salt trans-

appears however probable that transport volumes were less balanced on the eastern routes, as these overlapped with the zinc transport routes out of Guizhou from the Weining area onwards.[29]

Deforestation, erosion and increasing difficulties of water transport

The link between developments in water transport on the Jinshajiang and the small southern tributaries of the Upper Changjiang is obvious. In the early years of large-scale procurement for minting, copper transports used roads, probably the lines of communication and transport previously used for military purposes and perhaps improved during the war years. Soon, however, efforts were undertaken to shift the transports to waterways for the only part of the route where water transport was possible at all: the descent from the northernmost end of the Yunnan ranges into the Sichuan basin. In order to enable copper shipments to use these rivers, massive improvement projects were undertaken.

These projects provide the explanation to a perplexing conundrum: On the one hand, research indicates that deforestation and the expansion of agricultural land caused shipping conditions on the Upper Changjiang and its tributaries to deteriorate since at least the sixteenth century. At the same time, however, water transport apparently significantly intensified in the same period.

The historical geographer Lan Yong has shown that rivers, used by courier boats apparently without problems in the Song and Yuan periods, had become difficult by the Qing.[30] The most obvious sign of increasing

ported through the area for sale in Qujing prefecture should probably be added. The figure for the transport volume of copper is the maximum amount required for the metropolitan mints. The actual amount of copper transported through or out of the region was probably considerably greater, as private trade in copper and other metals flourished until mining productivity waned towards the end of the eighteenth century.

29 This is substantiated only by the fact that Xuyong was the collecting point of zinc transports. Since a reconstruction of zinc transport is still lacking, the routes and amounts remain unknown.

30 Lan Yong 1999.

The deeply cut valley of the Jinshjiang in the Dongchuan area. in modern Dongchuan district, spring 2007. View northwards from the confluence of the Puduhe 普渡河 with the Jinshajiang, near the Maolu 茂麓 mines on the eastern bank of the river in the Tangdan 湯丹 mining area. Photo by the author, April 2007.

erosion is the colour of the Changjiang. While the river in Sichuan is consistently described as jade-clear up to the Ming period, from the high Ming onwards it is recorded to have been turbid.[31] Deforestation, in particular throughout central Sichuan had greatly increased the sediment charge. The erosion along the Upper Changjiang and its tributaries affected water transport, as sediment would build up as shoals, sometimes very swiftly, and currents changed with rising and falling water levels. These were all the more dangerous for navigation, when muddy waters made submerged obstacles hard to spot. A photo of the Jinshajiang valley today gives an idea of the extreme gradients and the changeability of the river cut into quickly eroding mountains. It should be noted, however, that although deforestation was fairly advanced in throughout the mining and smelting area, the present situation of total lack of forest cover is probably at least partly the result of relatively recent degradation.

Despite deforestation and its consequence of increasingly difficult navigation conditions, the picture of Upper Changjiang shipping through the period in question is one of marked intensification. This development is particularly striking for the lower parts of the Upper Changjiang, which were affected by changes in the southwestern frontier region as well as by similar but even more pronounced destruction of forest and plant cover along the river valleys in Sichuan.[32]

This exploration suggests that while shipping conditions indeed worsened, water transport was maintained and even expanded through improvement works on natural rivers. Both developments were linked to the great increase in the procurement of mint metals from Yunnan.

Infrastructure improvement projects

Technologies of improving navigation conditions in difficult passages of natural rivers have a long tradition in China. The key technique applied was making solid rock brittle by heat. For this purpose, brushwood was piled up

31 For the colour of the Upper Changjiang through historic times, see Lan Yong 2003, 78–83.

32 Lan Yong 2001, 393–9; Kim (forthcoming b).

against the rock, burnt off and the heated stone then suddenly cooled by pouring on water, sometimes with added vinegar. As seasonal changes in water levels were so marked, much of the river-beds fell dry in winter. During these periods, the technique was used to remove rocks that formed dangerous reefs during the high water season, and tracking paths were cut into the rock face or constructed from debris. Debris hewn off the rocks and rock removed from the river bed was removed above the high water line or sunk in deep pools in the river bed, as whirlpools formed in these that could be so powerful as to swirl around large boats.[33]

When the copper transport system for the supply of the metropolitan mints was installed in 1739, all transport to Xuyong (also called Yongning 永寧) was overland. These transports must have been extraordinarily difficult. Copper lumps had to be carried on the backs of pack animals or men over some 400 km of rugged mountains with passes nearly 3000 m high and gorges at below 1,000 m in northern Yunnan, or across the infertile karst highlands of northern Guizhou. In addition, the route ran through recently occupied minority territories that were inhabited by a mix of badly decimated and uprooted aboriginal peoples and recent in-migrants from central Yunnan as well as other parts of China.

From the early 1740s, during the mining boom and only a few years after the metropolitan copper transports had been regularized, extensive improvement projects were undertaken on both roads and waterways. Three projects on rivers can be identified.[34] As a result, copper transport routes were reorganized and—as circumstantial evidence suggests—considerably eased. Budget regulations of Yunnan province state that out of the total yearly expenditures for metropolitan copper transports of some 1 million tael between 22,000 and 23,000 could be saved by about 1760.[35] These figures,

33 The best-known, because most ancient example, is the worst obstacle to shipping on the Huanghe, the entrance to the Sanmen Gorge. For an analysis of the projects to improve conditions at this danger spot by constructing tracking galleries, removing rocks in the river, and cutting a channel through massive rock, carried out in the Qin, Han and Tang periods, see Needham, *Science and civilisation in China*, vol. 4, part 3: 273–5.

34 In addition to these projects clearly connected to metropolitan copper transports, it seems probable that improvement efforts on the Chishuihe 赤水河 were linked to zinc transports out of northern Guizhou.

35 *Tongzheng bianlan* A, 297–302.

being fiscal regulations, cannot be taken to directly reflect corresponding rises in efficiency. They defined the framework within which the local administration operated, while the actual handling was their own affair, including the organization, payments, forms of recruitment, and means of transport. Moreover, costs for the maintenance of infrastructure were not included here. Nevertheless, the reduction both in overall expenditure and the number of day stages laid down in the regulations indicate considerable improvements. Besides, the system of perhaps semi-military relay stations was abandoned in 1759. The following reason is given for this change:

硐老山空出銅稀少，兼四路馬多足供運力	The mining galleries had become old and the mountain exhausted, while horses and human labour were plentiful along the four routes and sufficient for transport requirements.

It would seem that transporters could now be recruited on the market, presumably because sustained transport volumes in copper and other goods had led to the formation of a professional transport trade.[36] The improvement of transport infrastructure in and out of the area obviously contributed to furthering the swift economic development and the integration into Chinese trade networks.[37]

Yet our knowledge of these improvement projects, concerning both the concrete conditions under which they were undertaken and the consequences they had, remains far too sketchy for a substantial assessment. It therefore appears useful to take a closer look at the available details and to link them with general trends. About the construction of roads and bridges we know least, for these measures usually fell under the responsibility of the localities and were recorded only when they entailed fiscal consequences, namely the reduction of transport expenditures. Only one road improvement project is regularly mentioned in the sources, for precisely this reason: In 1751, the road between Xundian and Weining was "levelled and straightened," thus becoming suitable for cart transport and allowing for a reduction of the

36 The probability that for a period of time copper transports were organized relatively smoothly on the market is corroborated by a terse note in the Zhatong gazetteer, mentioning that in the heyday of copper transports these were organized by three locally "big names" (郡中大姓), which were also referred to as "copper transport households" 銅行戶, a situation that would not have been possible to impose if it had hurt these locally powerful families economically (*Zhaotong xianzhi*, 238).

37 See esp. Zhang Lihong 1994.

number of stages from 15 to 14.[38] We may safely assume that many more smaller scale projects were undertaken, and remains of old roads in the area, such as a road with a tunnel section and a chain-bridge in the gorge of the Yanshuihe 鹽水河, bear testimony to this.[39] Only towards the end of the era of copper transports in the early nineteenth century, shreds of information become available at the local level. Construction projects of individual bridges, more rarely of roads funded by private philanthropists now were sometimes recorded in local gazetteers or commemorated in stele inscriptions.

Sources on waterways are richer. Three river improvement projects directly connected to the metropolitan copper transports can be identified. In 1745 the Nanguanghe was made navigable for copper boats downriver of Luoxingdu (now Shangluo 上羅), providing a waterway of ca. 130 km length. In 1742 improvement works were carried out on the Hengjiang, enabling copper boats to use this river downriver of Yanjingdu 鹽井渡 (now Yanjin 鹽津), ca. 90 km from the river's mouth, with a later project extending navigation for another 35 km to Doushaguan 豆沙關.[40]

The most ambitious project was carried out from 1741 to 1748 on the Jinshajiang, the Changjiang upriver of Yibin 宜賓. Through eight winters, hundreds of danger spots were worked upon over a length of some 500 km, involving hundreds of workers and with total expenses reaching over 200,000 tael.[41] Whereas the other projects only receive brief mention, leaving us in the dark about all details, the Jinshajiang project was funded by the imperial treasury and left behind a record of numerous memorials as well as several scrolls of painting.[42] The memorials exchanged between provincial

38 *Tongzheng bianlan* A, 285 and 302 is the only source that specifies the location of the road construction as between "Xuanwei and Weining." Mention of the project and the reduction of stages is also recorded in *Tongzheng bianlan* B, unpag.

39 A section of this road southwest of Huize 會澤 near Nagu 那姑 is still extant. A stele commemorates the construction of the road and a chain bridge by member of the Qiaojia 巧家 gentry in 1791.

40 *Tongzheng bianlan* A, 297–302. The dates refer to the year in which the reorganized transport system was ordered to be installed. No information on the improvement projects themselves is provided.

41 Schön 1996, 83–87.

42 Two different collections of memorials on the Jinshajiang project have been transmitted. Hans Ulrich Vogel obtained a collection (Schön 2996, appendix), another has been

governors and other high officials and the emperor are most detailed on the planning and preparatory stage, but also contain reports of works completed. They are, however, silent on the effects of the project.

By 1749, according to matter-of-fact statements in the gazetteers, after only one year of trial shipments, the transport arrangements were changed again: The whole upper section of about 220 km length from the mouth of the Xiaojiang to Huangcaoping 黄草坪 (now Huangping 黄坪) was abandoned. Transports were redirected to overland roads, with river transport only beginning from Huangping.[43] In other words, the great project of opening up the Jinshajiang for regular navigation was at least a partial failure. Navigation conditions were presumably improved, but two danger spots below Huangping continued to require transshipping and considerable stretches of road transport remained. Although commercial boat traffic above Huangping probably increased, making Qiaojia 巧家, some 160 km upriver of Huangping, a busy town, the river was deemed too dangerous for copper transports.

Zhang Yunsui 張允隨 (1692–1751), who had been in office in Yunnan since 1718 and directed the opening of the Jinshajiang from beginning to end first as provincial governor and later as governor-general, played a key role in the project.[44] Zhang Yunsui is thought to have been thoroughly familiar with Yunnan, a resourceful administrator adept at finding and keeping capable men for the management and supervision of the project.[45] Why, however, he stuck to reporting the success of the project for the upper section to the point of submitting dubious figures and inconsistent reports, remains a

printed in *Lishi dang'an* (Liu Ruofang, Kong Weiming 2001). The edition of a complete set of memorials by Zhang Yunsui, published in Fang Guoyu (ed.) (1998). *Yunnan shiliao congkan* 雲南史料叢刊 (Series of Historical Documents on Yunnan), Kunming: Yunnan daxue chubanshe, was not yet available for this paper. The scrolls probably were executed as visual material to illustrate the situation to the emperor and his ministers in Beijing. For the analysis of a scroll held by a private collector in Germany, see Vogel 1991, the other two scrolls have been located at the Diyi Dang'anguan and the Shoudu bowuguan in Beijing by Lan Yong but were not available for research.

43 *Zhaotong xianzhi*, 236, *Dongchuan fuzhi*, 100.

44 For biographical information on Zhang Yunsui, see Schön 1996, 10f. and Ren Junshang and Wan Shifen 2003, 79.

45 See biography in *Qingshi gao*, vol. 35, 10555–8.

mystery.[46] He might have felt obliged to stick to a project that went back to Ortai, the powerful governor-general who left the province the year Zhang Yunsui became governor.[47] Besides, he might have had his own ambitions, or he might simply have been over-optimistic in actually believing that the project would open up a transport avenue into Yunnan. Whichever the case, the project obviously lost the emperor's support after the report of an investigation tour by officials dispatched for the purpose in 1749. While falling short of expectations, it appears nevertheless probable that navigation conditions were indeed improved and that sectional shipping contributed to developing trade in the area.

Environmental change and river navigation

A look at the morphology or at the rivers in their present state suffices to convince anyone that using them for water transport cannot have been easy at any time. The numerous water power plants along all rivers and streams in the area with the only exception of the Chishuihe 赤水河, however, rule out any conjecture of earlier conditions based on their present state.

While the documents on the Jinshajiang project provide useful insights in the administrative issues and structures, they do not allow a reconstruction of the works undertaken at any specific spot, the effects on navigation, or any conjecture as to how long the achieved improvements lasted.

Similarly, the available information on all practical issues of water transport is desperately thin. We know virtually nothing about seasonal restrictions of shipping, about the types and sizes of boats, navigation techniques

46 For an analysis of the project's financial reports, see Schön 1996, 83–87.

47 In his early memorials of December 1731 (Yongzheng 9) and November 1737 (Qianlong 2), Zhang Yunsui reports that Ortai advised him on the opening up of waterways that would link Yunnan with Guangxi, Guizhou and Sichuan, as well as that Ortai "had opened up [the Jinshajiang] at Huangcaoping as a port for merchant boats." This would imply that Ortai had already used the lower Jinshajiang as a waterway, most probably for military supplies. The Yongzheng emperor's rescript on the first memorial further tells us that it was "Ortai's wisdom" that made the emperor consider the project (Schön 1996, vol. 2, 2 and 5).

or organizational structures prior to the mid twentieth-century.[48] We may extrapolate that boat sizes between 12 and 5 tons in use around 1900 may have been fairly similar in the eighteenth century. The only means of comparing Qing period conditions of water transport with those of earlier ages are the terminal points of navigation and the regulations on the numbers of day stages.

A comparison using these rough indicators for the Jinshajiang and the Hengjiang suggests significant environmental change between Song and Yuan period courier routes and the conditions of eighteenth-century copper transports. On the Jinshajiang upriver of Yibin, Song water courier stations were set up to Leibo 雷波, with the journey of ca. 190 km to Shuifu 水富 expected to take ten days.[49] During the preparatory phase of the Jinshajiang project it was stated that shipping on the river had long ceased.[50] Some caution with this statement appears advisable, since the early memorials also suggest that military provisions had been shipped as far as Huangping prior to 1731 and that merchant boats had been using the river.[51] Nevertheless, it would appear that regular boat traffic on the lower Jinshajiang in existence during the Song and Yuan periods was no longer practical since at least the late Ming.[52] After the improvement project, shipping from Huangping, almost 80 km upriver of Leibo, to Luzhou, about 170 km or probably one-and-a-half to two stages downriver of Shuifu, was expected to be completed within just eight days.[53] Thus, Song courier boats were expected to take up to 10 days for 190 km through the gorges, while Qing period copper boats travelled 270 in six days, inclusive of two road stages to avoid unnavigable rapids.[54]

48 For Ming-Qing periods, Lan Yong records boats with capacities of up to 12 t for the high water season and of 5 t for the gorges above Jiangmen (Lan Yong 1999, 379).

49 Lan Yong 1999, 376–397.

50 This is stated in several memorials by Zhang Yunsui and recorded in the Veritable Records, e.g. *Qingshilu: Gaozong* part 1, 1269.

51 Memorial by Zhang Yunsui of December 1731, in Schön 1995, vol. 2, 2.

52 For the Ming period, Lan Yong records only timber rafting and the early seventeenth-century explorations. See 1999, 376–397.

53 *Tongzheng bianlan* A, 298f. gives eight stages, *Tongzheng bianlan* B, unpaginated, gives only seven.

54 *Tongzheng bianlan* B, unpaginated, mentions two day stages from the rapids Guoquanyan 鍋圈岩灘 to Dahancao 大漢槽灘. Although road transport is not specified, the

The shortening of the day stages between Song courier regulations and those for Qing copper transports suggest an improvement in shipping conditions. Yet insecurities remain. The Song regulations may refer either to upriver or downriver voyages or cover both, therefore allowing for a rather generous time-frame. Besides, the transportation of persons in the courier system, though running on a strict schedule, usually required no more than a maximum of 70 Li (ca. 40 km) for downriver journeys, while the copper shipments were expected to cover day stages of up to 140 Li (ca. 80 km) on the Upper and Middle Changjiang.

The comparison of Yuan and Qing regulation concerning boat transport on the Hengjiang is similarly puzzling. On this river, shipping as far upriver as Doushaguan some 125 km from the river's mouth at Anbian 安邊, is recorded for the Song period, and regular water courier stations for a service in six stages were installed during the Yuan dynasty. During the Ming period, shipping apparently became increasingly problematic.[55] After the improvement projects copper was required to be transported downriver in eight day stages from Yanjin to Luzhou.[56]

If we again assume between one-and-a-half and two stages from Anbian to Luzhou, the regulations would allow for six to six-and-a-half days on the Hengjiang; much the same as the Yuan courier system had required. As the distance was only 90 km, we may safely assume that navigation was problematic. For the late period of traditional shipping, we know of a dangerous section which required transshipment of the whole cargo.[57] While it seems probable that eighteenth century navigation was roughly similar, the avail-

fact that both above and below these danger spots transport defined as by boat, this seems to be the stretch on which the copper was taken by road. I have not yet been able to localize the rapids and the routes mentioned here.

55 Lan Yong 1999, 376–397.

56 *Tongzheng bianlan* A, 283 gives eight day stages from Yanjin to Luzhou and one from Doushaguan to Yanjin. *Tongzheng bianlan* B, unpaginated, however, gives 20 [!] stages from Yanjin, a probably erroneous figure.

57 Lan Yong 1999, 378, Hosie 1911, 39 and 41 confirms sectional navigation during springtime, with an interruption from above Zhangwo 張窩 (now Zhangwochang 張窩場), about 15 km from the river's mouth, to and the Jiulong rapids 九龍灘 near Tantou 灘頭. On the dangers of navigation on the Hengjiang, see also Mission Lyonnaise 1897, part 1, 79–81.

able data allow no conjecture concerning earlier conditions or on the effect of improvement measures undertaken in the mid-eighteenth century.

Conclusion

If it was the case that shipping conditions deteriorated already during the Ming period, the general trend of climatic cooling, which had set in around the year 1000, could have been the main factor.[58] If, however, the problems were felt only in the mid-eighteenth century and if they recurred or even increased after the improvement projects through the late eighteenth and nineteenth centuries, we would have sufficient grounds to directly link the effects of mining and agricultural development, namely together with the deforestation they brought about, to the increasingly difficult navigation conditions. At the present stage of this research, however, neither possibility can be convincingly substantiated.

Although further work is required, some conclusions can be drawn from the preliminary findings:

1. When considering transport infrastructure, we need to be aware that in addition to roads and bridges, rivers were developed and improved as maintained, albeit never actually tamable, waterways.
2. Rivers were kept open or opened up as navigable waterways despite environmental degradation. This was achieved with pre-modern technology, requiring much labour and logistic organization.
3. Costs for river improvements and maintenance appear to have been well above investments for road transport, while increases in efficiency were also significantly higher.
4. Costs of infrastructure projects and their maintenance need to be taken into consideration to assess the efficiency and burden of transports systems.

We can tentatively conclude that river works did make a difference but required considerable investment and maintenance. To come back to the earlier question of how an increase in water transport was possible at a time when shipping conditions are thought to have deteriorated, the preliminary

58 For the history of climatic change in China, see Liu Zhaomin 1992, 25 and 116ff.

conclusion would be that the detrimental effects of deforestation on river transport were indeed to some degree compensated by improvement works. At the present stage, the exploration of links between regional development, mint metal mining and transport systems appears to pose more questions than answers in gaining a better understanding of the role of the Qing state, available pre-industrial technologies and organizational capacities, economic systems and environmental change.

References

Antony, Robert J. and Jane Kate Leonard (eds.) (2002). *Dragons,Tigers and Dogs: Qing Crisis Management and the Boundaries of State Power in Late Imperial China*. Ithaca: Cornell University Press, 2002. (Cornell East Asia series 114)

Cao Chunlin 曹春林 and Shu Qiao 樹翹 (preface dated 1810). *Diannan zazhi* 滇南雜誌 (Miscellanea on Yunnan). In *Xiaofanghu zhai yudi congchao*, vol. 9, pp. 185a–221b.

Castell, Wulf Diether Graf zu. (1938). *Chinaflug*. Berlin: Atlantis.

Chen Ding 陳鼎 (late 17th cent.). *Dianyou ji* 滇遊記 (Record of a Journey to Yunnan). In *Xiaofanghu zhai yudi congchao*, vol. 9, pp. 255a–259a.

Dai, Yingcong (2005). "Yingyung Shengxi: Military Entrepreneurship in the High Qing Period, 1700–1800." *Late Imperial China* 26.2: 1–67.

Davies, Henry R. (1909). *Yün-nan: The Link between India and the Yangtze*. Cambridge: Cambridge University Press.

Dianhai yuhengzhi 滇海虞衡志 (Gazetteer of Dianhai). Tan Cui 檀萃 (comp.) (late 18th cent.). Reprint in Ren Jiyu 任继愈 and Tang Xiren 唐锡仁 (eds.) (1995). *Zhongguo kexue jishu dianji tonghui* 中國科學技術典籍通彙: 地学卷 (Source Collection on Chinese Science and Technology: Geography), vol. 5. Zhengzhou: Henan jiaoyu chubanshe.

Dongchuan fuzhi 東川府志 (Gazetteer of Dongchuan prefecture). Fang Guixiu 方桂修 (commissioned) (1761). Reprint in Lin Chaomin et al., vol. 26.

Dunstan, Helen (1992). "Safely Supping with the Devil: The Qing State and its Merchant Suppliers of Copper." *Late Imperial China*, 13.2: 42–81.

Elvin, Mark (2004). *The Retreat of the Elephants: An Environmental History of China*. New Haven: Yale University Press.

________ (1993). "3000 Years of Unsustainable Development: China's Environment from Archaic Times to the Present." *East Asian History* 6 (Dezember): 7–46.

Feuerwerker, Albert (1976). *State and Society in Eighteenth-Century China: The Ch'ing Empire in its Glory*. Ann Arbor, University of Michigan.

Franck, Harry A. *Roving through Southern China*. New York, London: The Century Co., 1925.

Gaoxian zhi 高縣志 (Gazetteer of Gao District). Commissioned by Ao Libang 敖立榜 (commissioned) (1866). Reprint in Lin Chaomin et al., vol. 14.

Gill, William (1883). *The River of Golden Sand: Being the Narrative of a Journey Through China and Eastern Tibet to Burmah*. London: Murray.

Guo Songyi 郭松义 and Zhang Zexian 张泽咸 (1997). *Zhongguo hangyunshi* 中国航运史 (A History of Chinese Shipping). Taibei: Wenjin chubanshe. (Zhongguo wenhua lishi congshu 61)

Hosie, Alexander (1890). *Three Years in Western China; a Narrative of Three Journeys in Ssu-ch'uan, Kuei-chow, and Yün-nan*. London: George Philip & Son.

________ (1911). *Report of a Journey in the Provinces of Szechuan, Yunnan and Kueichow*. Calcutta: Superint. Government Print, India.

Hummel, Arthur W. (ed.) (1943). *Eminent Chinese of the Ch'ing Period (1644–1912)*. 2 vols. Washington: U. S. Government Print.

Kim, Nanny (2007a). "'Traue nicht den Nachwächtern, halte dich bei Tempelfeiern zu Ehren des Stroms zurück:' Zu praktischen Bedenken von Kupfertransportbeamten auf der Fahrt durch die Drei Schluchten des Changjiang und ihrem Verhältnis zu angeheuerten Schiffern und Mannschaften." In Martina Eglauer and Clemens Treter (eds.). *Reisen in China*. Wiesbaden: Harrassowitz. (Jahrbuch der Deutschen Vereinigung für Chinastudien 2)

________ (forthcoming), "'With Each Summer Downpour, Rocks Start Rolling Down:' Shipping through the Three Gorges of the Yangzi, Environmental Change and River Improvement Projects." *Journal of the Economic and Social History of the Orient* (accepted for publication).

Lan Yong 蓝勇 (1999). "Lishi shiqi Changjiang shangyou hangdao weisuo yu duice yanjiu" 历史时期长江上游航道萎缩与对策研究 (The Shrinking Possibilities of Navigation on the Upper Changjiang and its Tributaries through Historic Times and Counter Measures Against this Trend). In ibid. *Gudai jiaotong shengtai yanjiu yu shidi kaocha* 古代交通生态研究与实地考察 (Fieldwork Research on Pre-modern Transport and Ecology). Chengdu: Sichuan renmin chubanshe, pp. 376–397.

________ (2006a). "Qingdai Diantong jingyun luxian kaoshi" 清代滇铜京运路线考释 (An Investigation of the Route of the Copper Transports from Yunnan to Beijing). *Lishi yianjiu* 历史研究 3: 86–97.

________ (2006b). "Qingdai Diantong jingyun dui yantu de yingxiang yanjiu - jianlun Min-Qing shiqi Zhongguo xinan ziyuan dongyun gongcheng" 清代滇铜京运对沿途的影响研究 - 兼论明清时期中国西南资源东运工程

(The Influence of Yunnan Copper Transports to the Capital on the Regions along the Route in the Qing Period: Also a Discussion of the Shipping of Resources from Southwestern to Eastern China in the Late Imperial Period). *Qinghua daxue xuebao* 清华大学学报 21 (August): 95–103.

________ (ed.) (2003). *Changjiang Sanxia lishi dili* 長江三峽歷史地理 (A Historical Geography of the Three Gorges of the Changgjiang). Chengdu: Sichuan renmin chubanshe.

Li, Lillian M. and Thomas G. Rawski (eds.) (1992a). *Chinese History in Economic Perspective*. Berkeley, CA: University of California Press.

Lin Chaomin 林超民, Zhang Xuejun 張學君, Wang Yongqiao 王水喬 (eds.) (2003). *Zhongguo xinan wenxian congshu, diyi ji: Xinan xijian fangzhi wenxian* 中國西南文獻叢書 第一輯：西南稀見方志文獻 (Collection of Sources on Southwestern China. First Series: Rare Local Gazetteers). Lanzhou: Lanzhou daxue chubanshe.

Little, Archibald John (1888). *Through the Yang-Tse Gorges, or Trade and Travel in Western China*. London: Sampson Low, Marston, Searle & Rivington.

________ (1910). *Across Yunnan: A Journey of Surprises, Including an Account of the Remarkable French Railway Line Now Completed to Yunnan-fu*. Edited by Mrs. Archibald Little. London: Sampson Low, Marston & Co.

Liu De'ou 刘德隅 (1995). "Yunnan senlin lishi bianqian chutan" 云南森林历史变迁初探 (A Preliminary Study on the Changes of Forest Cover in Yunnan through Historic Times). *Nongye kaogu* 农业考古 3: 191–4.

Liu Ruofang, Kong Weiming (eds.) (2001). "Qianlong nianjian shutong Jinshajiang shiliao" 乾隆年间疏通金沙江史料 (Materials on the Opening up of the Jinshajiang for Navigation in the Qianlong Era). *Lishi dang'an* 历史档案 no. 2: 47–61 and no. 3: 43–8.

Liu Wenwei 劉文蔚 (early 19th century). *Leibo suoji* 雷波瑣記 (Scattered Notes on Leibo). Reprint in *Zhonghua wenshi congshu,* disan ji; 22–24 中華文史叢書. 第 3 輯. Taibei: 台灣華文書局, 1968.

Liu Zhaomin 劉昭民 (1992). *Zhongguo lidai shang qihou zhi bianqian* 中國歷史上氣候之變遷 (Climatic Change through Chinese History). Taibei: Shangwu yinshuguan. (Xin renren wenku 20)

Luo Chuandong 罗传栋 (ed.) (1991). *Changjiang hangyunshi* 长江航运史 (The History of Shipping on the Changjiang). Beijing: Renmin jiaotong chubanshe.

Ma Weiliang 马维良 (1994). "Qingdai chuzhongqi Yunnan huizu de kuangyeye" 清代初中期云南回族的矿冶业 (The Muslim Mining and Smelting Industry in Yunnan during the Early and Mid-Qing). *Huizu yanjiu* 回族研究 no. 1: 31–9.

Mann, Susan (1987). *Local Merchants and the Chinese Bureaucracy: 1750–1950.* Stanford: Stanford University Press.

Ming-Qing shilu 明清實錄 (Veritable Records of the Ming and Qing Dynasties) (n.d.). Jeonnam University Library, Erudition digital publication.

Naquin, Susan and Evelyn Rawski (1987). *Chinese Society in the Eighteenth Century*. New Haven: Yale University Press.

Qin Shucai 秦树才 (2004). "Lun Yongzheng, Qianlong shiqi xuntang zhidu zai Yunnan de fazhan ji bianhua" 论雍正、乾隆时期汛塘制度在云南的发展及变化 (The Development and Transformation of the *xuntang* System in Yunnan during the Yongzheng and Qianlong Periods). *Yunnan minzu daxue xuebao* 云南民族大学学报 no. 4: 112–6.

Qin Shucai 秦树才 and Tian Zhiyuan 田志勇 (2004). "Lüyingbing yu Qingdai Yunnan yimin yanjiu" 绿营兵与清代云南移民研究 (Green Standard Soldiers and In-migration into Yunnan during the Qing Period). *Qingshi yanjiu* 清史研究 no. 3: 32–40.

Qingshi gao 清史稿 (Draft History of the Qing Dynasty). Zhao Erxun 趙爾尋 et al. (comp.) (1976–77) Beijing: Zhonghua shuju.

Schön, Michael (1996). "Der Versuch der Schiffbarmachung des Goldsandflusses, Yunnan 1740–1749." MA thesis, Heidelberg University.

Shi Fan 師範 (1808). *Dian xi* 滇繫 (Bits on Yunnan). Repr. In *Fangzhi congshu* 中國方志叢書 139. Taibei: Chengwen 1968.

Sun E-tu Zen (1971). "The Transportation of Yunnan Copper to Peking in the Ch'ing Period," *Journal of Oriental Studies*, 9:132–148.

Tongzheng bianlan 銅政便覽 A (The Handy Compendium on Copper Administration). Anonymous (n.d.). Repr. Taibei: Taiwan xuesheng shuju, 1986.

Tongzheng bianlan 銅政便覽 B (The Handy Compendium on Copper Administration). Anonymous manuscript (n.d.).

Vogel, Hans Ulrich (1991). *The Complete Map of the Jinshajiang (Jinshajiang quantu): An Extraordinary Document Relating to a River Dredging Project in the Chinese Province of Yunnan, 1741–1749*. München: Bruckmann Verlag (Sonderdruck).

________ (1989). "Chinese Central Monetary Policy and the Yunnan Copper Mining Industry in the Early Qing (1644–1800)." Zürich: Ph.D. Dissertation.

Wang Shigang 王轼刚 (ed.) (1993). *Changjiang hangdaoshi* 长江航道史 (The History of the Yangzi as a Waterway). Beijing: Renmin jiaotong chubanshe.

Watt, John R. (1972). *The District Magistrate in Late Imperial China*. New York: Columbia University Press.

Worcester, G. R. G. (1971). *Changjiang zhi fanchuan yu shanban* 長江之帆船與舢板 (The Junks and Sampans of the Yangtse). Repr. Annapolis: Naval Institute Press.

Xiaofanghuzhai yudi congchao 小方壺齋輿地叢鈔 (Geographic Writings Collected by Wang Xiqi). Wang Xiqi 王錫祺 (ed.) (1877–92). Reprint. Taibei: Guang wen shu ju, 1962.

Xu Zuanzeng 許纘曾 (Kangxi era). *Dianxing jicheng xuchao* 滇行紀程續鈔 (More Notes on a Journey to Yunnan). In *Xiaofanghu zhai yudi congchao*, vol. 9, pp. 264a–266a.

Xuanwei zhouzhi 宣威州志 (Gazetteer of Xuanwei Sub-prefecture). Liu Shilin 劉沛霖 (commissioned) (1844). Reprint in *Zhongguo fangzhi congshu* 中國方志叢書, vol. 33. Taibei: Chengwen 1967.

Yang Yuda 杨煜达 (2004). "Qingdai zhongqi Dian dongbei de tongye kaifa yu huanjing bianqian" 清代中期（公元 1726–1855 年）滇东北的铜业开发与环境变迁 (The Development of Copper Mining in Northeastern Yunnan in the Middle Qing Period and Environmental Change). *Zhongguo lishi yanjiu* 中国历史研究 no. 3: 158–74.

Yang Yuda 杨煜达; Man Zhimin 满志敏 and Zheng Jingyun 郑景云 (2005). "Jiaqing Yunnan da jihuang (1815–1817) yu Tanbola huoshan penfa" 嘉庆云南大饥荒 (1815–1817) 与坦博拉火山喷发 (The Great Yunnan Famine 1815–1817 and the Tambora Eruption). *Fudan xuebao* 复旦学报 2005 no. 1: 79–84.

Zelin, Madeleine (1984). *The Magistrate's Tael: Rationalizing Fiscal Reform in Eighteenth-Century Ch'ing China*. Berkeley, Los Angeles, London: University of California Press.

Zhang Lihong 张莉红 (1994). "Changjiang shangyou hangdao de kaituo yu Qingdai Sichuan yanjiang maoyi de fazhan" 长江上游航道的开拓与清代四川沿江贸易的发展 (The Opening of the Upper Changjiang for Navigation and the Development of Trade in Sichuan along the River). In *Tianfu xinlun* (December): 78–86.

Zhang Yonghai 張永海 (1986). "Qingdai jingtong jingqian churu Chuanjiang luxian yu zhuanyun zuzhi zhidu" 清代京銅京鉛出入川江路綫與轉運組織制度 (Transport Organization System and the Transport of the Peking Mints' Copper and Zinc on the Yangtzekiang in Sichuan), in Sichuansheng Zhongguo jingjishi xuehui 四川省中國經濟史學會, ed., *Zhongguo jingjishi yanjiu luncong* 中國經濟研究論叢 (Collected Articles on Research on Chinese Economic History), pp. 203–212.

Zhanyi zhouzhi 霑益州志 (Gazetteer of Zhanyi Sub-prefecture). Chen Yan 陳燕 and Li Jingxian 李景賢 (commissioned) (1875). Reprint in *Zhongguo fangzhi congshu* 35. Taibei: Chengwen 1967.

Zhaotong xianzhi gao 昭通縣志稿 (Draft Gazetteer of Zhaotong District). Lu Jinxi 盧金錫 (commissioned) (1936). Reprint in *Zhongguo fangzhi congshu* 37. Taibei: Chengwen 1967.

Zhaotong xianzhi gao 昭通縣志稿 (Draft Gazetteer of Zhaotong District). Yang Lüqian 楊履乾 (commissioned) (1924). Reprint in *Zhongguo fangzhi congshu* 36. Taibei: Chengwen 1967.

Zhenxiong zhouzhi 鎮雄州志 (Gazetteer of Zhenxiong Sub-prefecture) (1887). Commissioned by Wu Guanghan 吳光漢. No date: no place.

Zhenxiong zhouzhi 鎮雄州志 (Gazetteer of Zhenxiong Sub-prefecture). Commissioned by Tu Shuliang 屠述濂 (1784). No place.

Zhili Xuyong tingzhi 直隸敘永廳志 (Gazetteer of Xuyong Sub-prefecture). Zhou Weiye 周偉業 et al. (commissioned) (1809). Reprint in Lin Chaomin et al., vol. 12.

Zhou Jiong 周琼 (2001). "Gaitu guiliu hou de Zhaotong tunken" 改土归流后的昭通屯垦 (Colonial Settlements in Zhatong after the Replacement of Aboriginal Lords with Qing Officials). *Minzu yanjiu* 民族研究 6: 92–99.

Mint Metal Procurement for Jiangsu and Zhejiang during the Qianlong Period (1736–1795): An Inquiry into the Central Government's Expectations and the Provinces' Strategies of Implementation*

Thomas Hirzel

This paper examines mint metal procurement for the provincial mints of Jiangsu and Zhejiang during the Qianlong reign (1736–1795), with a focus on state capabilities in implementing a closely regulated system. To this end, stipulations for copper transports with regard to transport routes, time limits and annual quotas laid down in the regulatory code are compared with reports in archival documents that relate the actual performance of individual transports from Yunnan to the mints. The preliminary investigation demonstrates that archival records are of crucial importance for the reconstruction of the mint metal procurement system, for in some respects striking gaps can be identified between the central government's expectations formulated in the regulations and their and actual implementation by the provincial governments.

Introduction

Traditional statecraft held that the welfare and prosperity of the common people depended directly on the stability of the monetary system. Consequently, the Qing felt in duty bound to produce and circulate a sufficient amount of copper cash. In order to achieve these goals, a constant supply of the mint metals copper, tin, lead and zinc was of vital importance. Therefore the Qing bureaucracy expended considerable energies on assuring a reliable supply of metals for minting copper cash.

The central government, primarily the Ministry of Revenue (戶部 Hubu), subjected mint metal procurement for the metropolitan and provincial mints to detailed regulations. On the basis of these official guidelines, provincial officials were assigned to procure copper, and proceeded to organize complex collaborative arrangements with transporters for the ship-

* I would like to thank Prof. Jane Kate Leonard and Dr. Nanny Kim for their critical remarks on the manuscript, which were helpful in improving it. For polishing my English I am indebted to Tony Howes, Dr. Nanny Kim, and Prof. Jane Kate Leonard.

ping of mint metals from the mines, mostly located in southwestern Yunnan and Guizhou, to the metropolitan and provincial mints. Here, copper cash was cast, providing the medium of exchange for small-scale transactions in the expanding market economy of Qing China. The officials charged with the procurement of mint metals had to submit reports on the progress of their convoys to each district and department seat, and received documentation from all military and civil authorities enroute. On the basis of this documentation, which was passed on by local governments to the provincial level, provincial governments submitted memorials to the throne reporting on all mint metal convoys passing through their jurisdiction. Thousands of such memorials survive in the imperial archives, constituting one of the central source materials of the research group 'Monies, Markets and Finance in China and East Asia.'

An adequate supply of mint metals was of particular importance for the two provinces Jiangsu and Zhejiang, as they constituted the leading economic core of the Qing empire. This paper examines Qing organization and management of mint metal procurement for the provincial mints of these provinces during the Qianlong reign (1736–1795), by inquiring into the central government's expectations and the provinces' strategies of implementation. For this purpose, the archival documents are subjected to the following investigations:

To assess the reliability and specificity of information contained in the selected archival documents, the data extracted from these are contrasted with the information on mint metal procurement for Jiangsu and Zhejiang province found in the regulations. More specifically, several steps are involved. First, data on individual convoys is put together from memorials submitted by the various provinces through which the shipments passed. These reassembled data sets are then compared to regulations on aspects such as transport routes, time limits, and amounts of mint metal transported. In the assessment of the two types of sources, points of divergence are naturally of special interest.

The examination concentrates on copper transports. The reason for this restriction is the fact that regulatory texts and archival documents for this metal are particularly rich and detailed. For the investigation of time limits and amounts of mint metal, we will focus on archival documents on copper transports from Yunnan to the provincial mint of Zhejiang during the four years 1774 to 1776 and 1784 (Qianlong 39 to 41, and 49), because the transports of these years are especially apt to show the gap between stipulations and actual performance.

The copper for the provincial mints of Jiangsu and Zhejiang was mainly procured and transported from mines located in Yunnan in southwestern China. In addition, relatively minor amounts were imported from Japan.[1] Officials in charge of transports faced manifold difficulties of overland and riverine transport from Yunnan to Suzhou and Hangzhou, the cities in which the provincial mints were located, as well as being burdened my much paperwork and bureaucratic procedures.

As outlined above, the investigation draws on two types of sources. The first consists of officially endorsed and semi-official compilations of regulations on mint metal transports that provided the administrative framework to these tasks. Such compilations include the official Hubu codes[2] and semi-official compilations, composed to guide the officials in charge of the procurement, such as the *Tongzheng bianlan* 銅政便覽 (A Manual on Copper Administration) and the *Yunnan tongzhi* (雲南銅志) (On the Copper of Yunnan).[3] In these texts the established procedures for the procurement of mint metals are recorded, covering in considerable detail all steps of the transports from Yunnan to Jiangsu and Zhejiang as well as the overall Hubu regulations and precedents concerning provincial mint metal transports. These regulations can be regarded as an ideal norm on how the transports should be carried out.

1 Vogel 1989; Hirzel, unpublished paper presented at the AAS conference Boston 2007.

2 *Qinding Da Qing huidian shili* 欽定大清會典事例 (Imperially Endorsed Precedents of the Collected Statutes of the Great Qing Dynasty). Guangxu edition; *Qinding Hubu guzhu zeli* 欽定戶部鼓鑄則例 (Imperially Endorsed Regulations and Precedents for Minting of the Ministry of Revenue); *Qinding Hubu zeli* 欽定戶部則例 (Imperially Endorsed Regulations and Precedents of the Board of Revenue)

3 Both the *Yunnan tongzhi* and the *Tongzheng bianlan* provide detailed information on copper mining, transportation, minting, and their administrative regulations. The *Tongzheng bianlan* is more concise and represents the regulations in force at the date of compilation. The *Yunnan tongzhi*, in addition, also informs on former regulations and conditions and indicates the names of officials responsible for the introduction of new administrative regulations. These sources are based on the official compilations of regulations.

The second type of source are palace memorials that describe the actual and sometimes chaotic experiences. The archival record is rich from 1762 (Qianlong 27) onwards, when the Qianlong Emperor decreed that governors-general and provincial governors were to submit regular palace memorials on all mint metal transports that passed through their areas of jurisdiction.[4] In the event of unusual occurrences, such as shipwrecks, theft or the illness or death of the official directing the transport, the governors were required to immediately report on them. Each memorial recorded the total amount of metal and the dates of entry into and exit from the respective areas under jurisdiction, with further information added as required. Even the basic information is, however, not always complete. In some documents governors reported the passage through their province, giving the names of the transport officials, but omitted the amounts transported and the entry and exit dates.[5] In others, much more detail is provided, especially when reporting accidents and incidents that were suspected to have involved fraud.

An analysis of the two types of sources provides insights into how Qing officials approached the tasks associated with the procurement of mint metals and how they coped with problems arising during their implementation. In this respect, it provides insights into the organizational capacity of the Qing state in this critically important area of fiscal management.

The procurement of mint metals for Jiangsu and Zhejiang

When a provincial government intended to purchase copper from Yunnan, it had to memorialize to the throne indicating why a particular purchase was necessary and how much copper it intended to buy.[6] Once permission was obtained, the provincial authorities[7] appointed an official at the assistant

4 *Qinding Da Qing huidian shili* 欽定大清會典事例 (Imperially Endorsed Precedents of the Collected Statutes of the Great Qing Dynasty). Guangxu edition. 1899. (GX-HDSL) 218:10a; *Qianlong chao shangyu dang* 乾隆朝上諭檔 (Archives of the Imperial Edicts of the Qianlong Reign) (QCSYD) vol. 3, p. 812 [Edict number 2270].

5 For example: *Gongzhongdang Qianlongchao zouzhe* 宮中檔乾隆朝奏摺 (Palace Memorials of the Qianlong Reign) (GZDQL) 30:34. See also: GZDQL 36: 446.

6 Shulman 1989: 128.

7 The provincial authorities responsible for the designation of transport officials were the governor-general, the governor and the treasurer of the respective province. If they failed

magisterial level[8] to proceed to Yunnan with a small entourage to buy the metal on behalf of the provincial mint. In the case of Jiangsu and Zhejiang, the designated transport officials had to direct the mint metal convoy along the overland and riverine route from the mines in Yunnan to the mints of Suzhou and Hangzhou respectively. During the journey these officials supervised the transport, recruiting transport workers, draught animals and riverine craft over a distance of approximately 3650 km passing six provinces in the case of Jiangsu, and about 3800 and seven provinces in the case of Zhejiang.[9]

The transport route

Copper shipments out of Yunnan followed two main routes. While copper for the metropolitan mints was transported through northeastern Yunnan to Luzhou and onwards to Beijing, copper for the provincial mints took a different route. These shipments followed an overland route from the mines to Bo'ai (剝隘) in southeastern Yunnan near the Guangxi border. From Bo'ai onwards, the convoys used waterways via the Xiyangjiang (西洋江), the Youjiang (右江) and the Xijiang (西江) to the Guijiang (桂江) and the Lijiang (灕江). The watershed between the Lijiang and the Xiangjiang (湘江) was crossed via the Lingqu (靈渠), the Magic Canal. From here, the

in appointing a capable official and irregularities such as deficits on account of misappropriation or any others had occurred, these provincial authorities were held responsible. GX-HDSL 218:12b.

8 The Qianlong emperor decreed in his 40th year that local officials, such as district magistrates or prefectural assistants, like *tongzhi* (同知) und *tongpan* (通判), should be appointed to perform and supervise copper transports from Yunnan to the provincial mints. Even if there were sub-bureaucratic Yamen personnel or low rank military officials who would be capable and trustworthy of performing such a task, they should not be allowed to do so, because this would cause transport delays. They should only be allowed as additional transport personnel. The emperor furthermore noted that the appointed local officials had to be wealthy, probably to make sure that in case of deficits due to embezzlement or other reasons they could compensate for the loss. Later in the same year the Ministry of Revenue also stipulated that for copper transports exceeding the amount of 10,000 *jin* reliable assistant department or district magistrates should be appointed. GX-HDSL 218:12b

9 The convoy started in Yunnan and proceeded through Guangxi, Hunan, Hubei, Jiangxi, and Anhui to end in Suzhou (Jiangsu province) or in Hangzhou (Zhejiang province).

boats followed the Xiangjiang downriver to Lake Dongting (洞庭湖) and the Middle Yangzi. They then travelled down the great river to the Grand Canal at Zhenjiang, where they turned south into the canal to Suzhou or further on to Hangzhou. Through Yunnan province, the copper was transported overland by pack animals, but from the Guangxi border by boat.

Morse indicates that the Xijiang and his tributaries constituted the most important east-west connection in southern China:

> The West River [Xijiang] route from Canton commands the whole of the trade of Kwangsi, and penetrates into Yunnan and Kweichow. At Wuchow the Cassia River [Guijiang] provides a water-way, interrupted by rapids but navigable by small boats, to the provincial capital, Kweilin. Farther up [the West River], at Tamchow, the route again divides […]. The southern of the two branches at Tamchow continues the name of the West River until, some 30 miles above Nanning, it divides into the Left Branch […], and the Right Branch [Youjiang] leading north-west to Poseh [Baise]: to this point boats of 25 tons deadweight capacity can safely pass the rapids. From Poseh runs the main trade route for traffic by pack-animal into western and central Yunnan.[10]

As there are no palace memorials on transports within Yunnan, this paper concentrates on the route from Bo'ai to Suzhou and Hangzhou. For this part of the journey the administrative regulations provide no specific information on how boats were hired, on work conditions of the crews, on navigation technologies or on anchoring places. As can be seen from the map below, these sources only tell us that from Bo'ai onwards the shipments proceeded via Guilin and Hankou to Suzhou or Hangzhou.

However, we can obtain more specific detail from memorials that report the stages of the transport route and describe problems, crises or difficulties. On the basis of the memorials we have identified and mapped 35 stages of the transport route in addition to the four mentioned in the regulatory code. Thus, while the scanty information on the riverine route of the copper transports from Bo'ai in Yunnan to the provincial mints of Jiangsu and Zhejiang in the regulatory texts would not allow a meaningful reconstruction, additional information from the memorials allows the route to be defined with some security. The map below shows the reconstructed route to Suzhou and Hangzhou. So far, no deviations from this route have been found.

10 Morse 1975: 304.

Graph 1:

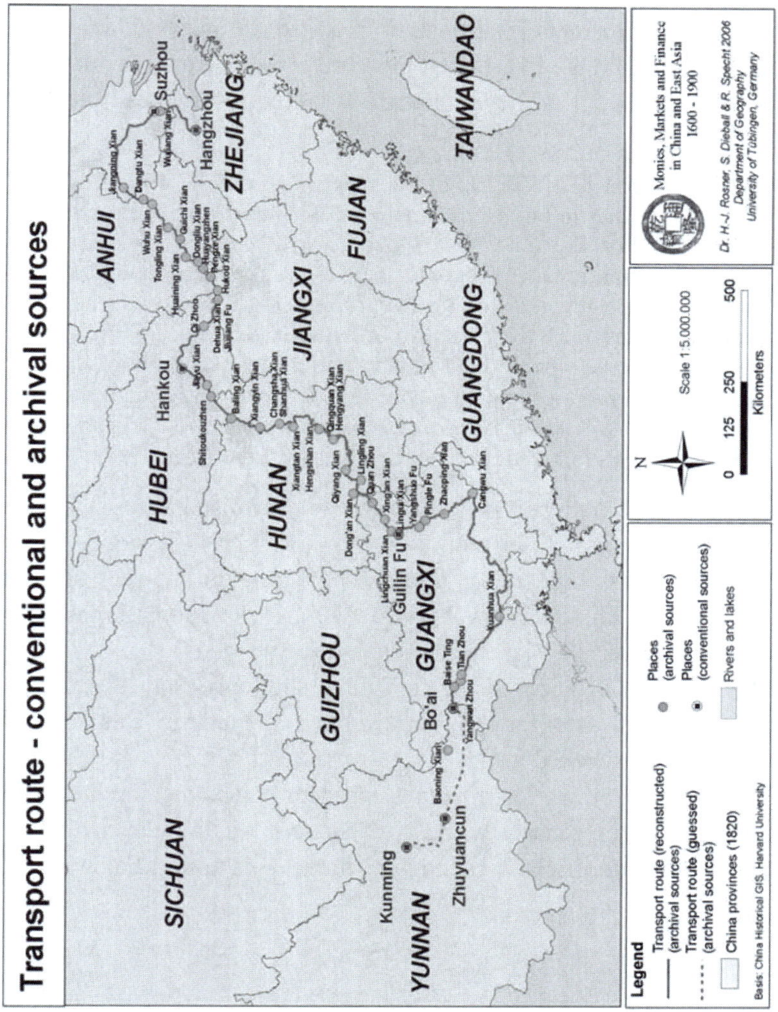
Transport route - conventional and archival sources
SICHUAN
HUBEI
HUNAN
ANHUI
JIANGXI
FUJIAN
ZHEJIANG
GUIZHOU
GUANGXI
GUANGDONG
YUNNAN
TAIWANDAO
Kunming
Zhuyuancun
Bo'ai
Guilin Fu
Hankou
Suzhou
Hangzhou
Legend
Transport route (reconstructed) (archival sources)
Transport route (guessed) (archival sources)
China provinces (1820)
Places (archival sources)
Places (conventional sources)
Rivers and lakes
Basis: China Historical GIS, Harvard University
Scale 1:5.000.000
0 125 250 500
Kilometers
Monies, Markets and Finance in China and East Asia 1600 - 1900
Dr. H.-J. Rosner, S. Dieball & R. Specht 2006
Department of Geography
University of Tübingen, Germany

Time limits

Time limits are an aspect covered in both regulations and memorials. Divergencies provide insights into tensions between the demands on the part of the government and the interests of those involved in carrying out the tasks.

In the year 1770 (in late Qianlong 34) the emperor issued the following edict:

> Whenever transport officials of the [copper procuring] provinces proceed to Yunnan in order to buy copper there are stipulated time limits for the way to Yunnan and back to Zhejiang. But as many of those officials use pretexts to delay these transports and do not adhere to the stipulated time limits, we order the provincials governor [of Yunnan] to report in a memorial [the date of] the arrival and departure from Yunnan of the officials. Concerning the date of arrival in the home province and whether there were delays or not, I order the respective governors-general and governors to verify and submit a memorial. If there were delays without reason, the names [of the officials] and an impeachment are to be submitted and investigations are to be carried out.[11]

The edict accuses transport officials of commonly disregarding the stipulated time limits, ordering closer monitoring to stop such malpractice. How long were the transports supposed to take and how long did they actually take? In order to answer this question, we will take a look at four shipments which took place between 1774 and 1784 (Qianlong 39 and 49):

The transport officials of the first three shipments stayed within the set time limit of 120 days for the journey from Zhejiang to Yunnan, only the 1784 shipment exceeded it.[12]

As to the fourth, we learn from a pertinent palace memorial that adverse weather conditions caused the delay.[13] Since it was a delay by a few days only, the transport official escaped punishment (see table 1 below).

11 GZDQL 38: 151.

12 We have no information on the route along which the officials proceeded to Yunnan. But considering the stipulated time limits – the time limit for Zhejiang (120 days) was shorter than that for Jiangsu (182 days) – we can be sure that the transport officials of Zhejiang did not travel on the same route as they returned from Yunnan but probably followed the main courier routes.

13 GZDQL 69: 49–50.

In the case of the first transport of 1774 (Qianlong 39), the time limit for the overland part of the transport from the mine Wanbao (萬寶) to Bo'ai was 283 days. The transport official, however, exceeded the time limit by 72 days. He reported that because his transport coincided with the harvest time he had not been able to meet the stipulated limit.[14] As oxen and horses presumably were employed in farmwork, the official had enormous problems to find enough pack animals, the convoy having to wait until they became available. According to the regulations, the time limit could be extended for 60 days in such a case:

> If a transport is conducted during the fifth or sixth month, when the transport labourers (*jiaohu* 腳戶) return home in order to cultivate their fields, or during the eighth or ninth month, when it is time for the harvest, the transport must not be pushed forwards. In compliance with the regulations, the local officials have to investigate and to confirm the matter and submit a report. The time limit will then be extended for two months.[15]

It was on account of his late reporting on this time transgression that the transport official was impeached by the provincial governor of Yunnan. The governor thereupon received a communication from the Ministry of Revenue to wait in this matter until the transport had reached its final destination, the Zhejiang mint.

The time limit from Bo'ai to Hangzhou was 211 days. Because of delays caused by the changing of boats, adverse weather, the paying of duty at customs-posts and other reasons, the time limit was extended by 101 days.

When the transport official finally arrived at Hangzhou, he had exceeded the time limit by altogether 28 days. In accordance with the regulations (see table 1), he was exempted from punishment.

14 GZDQL 38: 152.

15 TZBL 7: 5a–b. Translation by the author.

Table 1:

Period of time in exceedance of the time limits	Punitive Measures
Up to one month	Exemption from punishment
One month and more	Forfeit of salary for one year
Two months and more	Demotion by one rank but retention in office
Three months and more	Demotion by one rank and transfer
Four months and more	Demotion by two ranks and transfer
Five months and more	Demotion by three ranks and transfer
Six months and more	Dismissal

Sources: GX-HDSL 219:3a; TZBL 7:6a.

In the case of the second transport of 1775 (Qianlong 40), the transport official received copper from the Jinchai (金釵) mine as well as from the storehouses at the prefectural seat Yunnanfu (modern Kunming). His transport also coincided with the gathering of the harvest, but he was granted an additional 60 days according to the regulations. The time limit for the transport from the Yunnan mines to Hangzhou would have been 537 days. In the event, the convoy reached Hongzhou 43 days early. We will come back to this transport later, because in this case the period of time which the transport official needed to procure the copper was surprisingly short compared with other transports.

The transport official of the transport in 1776 (Qianlong 41) needed only 416 days for his journey from the Jinchai mine in Yunnan to Hangzhou, i.e. 78 days less than the his colleague in the preceeding year, while transporting the same amount of copper.

The transport official of the transport of 1784 (Qianlong 49) was less fortunate. In Yunnan, he fell sick for 90 days, and, in accordance with the regulations, the transport was halted until his recovery:

> If a transport official falls ill en route, the local officials have to investigate and to confirm the matter and to send in a report. The time from his sickness to his recovery has to be entered in the final report of Yunnan province on this transport and be deducted from the time limit.[16]

On the return voyage, not far from his destination, one of his boats sank in Anhui province and all the copper with it. In this case as in other memorials reporting irregularities, we find revealing information. We learn from the Anhui provincial governor's report that the transport had been split up into two convoys, the first of which consisted of six boats. Furthermore, it is reported that the sunken boat was loaded with 23,800 *jin* of copper, approximately thirteen tons. In spite of the shipwreck, the transport official finally arrived at Hangzhou before the expiration of the time limit.[17]

Table 2:

Source	Year of transport	Duration in days Zhejiang to Yunnanfu	Duration in days stay in Yunnan	Duration in days Yunnan to Zhejiang
GZDQL* 38/151–153	1774	115	234	622
GZDQL* 39/863	1775	113	159	494
GZDQL* 48/183	1776	115	363	416
GZDQL* 69/49–50	1784	139	534	791

16 TZBL 7: 5b. Translation by the author.

17 GZDQL 68, 250.

The differences in the length of time within which different transport officials finished all bureaucratic procedures in Yunnanfu, set out to the mine, obtained the allocated copper, and departed from the mine, are remarkable. We have not yet been able to find any information in the palace memorials as to why it sometimes took so long for a transport official to set out on his return voyage to his home province. There were, of course, time limits for all procedures in Kunming, the journey to the mines, and the handing over of the copper at the mines, but since we have hardly any information on how these steps were actually handled in individual cases, we are not able to reconstruct them. From the regulations we know that the main problem was the handing over of the copper at the mines, for which there were no time limits before 1770 (Qianlong 35), when the Ministry of Revenue eventually set fixed time limits.[18] Nevertheless, the problems continued.

As can be seen from the table above, the transport official of the transport of 1784 (Qianlong 49) was made to wait almost one and a half years before being granted the full copper quota. According to my calculations, the time limit would have been between 150 and 200 days. The available documents do not tell us whether this massive transgression of time stipulations had any unpleasant consequences for the officials involved. The transport of 1775 (Qianlong 40) stayed within the time limit, but in this special case copper was handed over at the storehouses in Yunnanfu as well as at the mines.

As a result of the continuing problems at the mines, the emperor issued an edict in 1789 (Qianlong 54) in which he expressed fears that corruption among the Yunnan mine officials caused these delays. It seems that at times these officials provided preferential treatment to transport officials who had arrived later than others, presumably due to bribes. In order to eradicate these practices the emperor ordered strict measures to be taken.[19]

By comparing the stipulated time limits with the times reported for individual transports, we conclude that shipments rarely met the regular time limits. Due to delays on account of adverse weather, the changing of boats, the paying of customs duties, illness of the transport official, shortage of pack animals because of agricultural demands, trans-shipment at shoals or rapids, repair of boats, shipwreck and other reasons the time limit had to be

18 GX-HDSL 219: 3a.
19 GX-HDSL 219:4b.

officially extended time and again. These complicated rules and exemptions in themselves demonstrate how challenging the tranport official's task was, and how much ingenuity he needed to direct his convoy from Yunnan to his destination. More research is needed to explore the reasons that led to the gap between expected time limits and the actual duration of mint metal transports.

At the present point of research, data is insufficient for statistical analysis. The preliminary investigations leave us with the impression that transport officials usually managed to escape punishment, although one of the four transports took two years and another even twice as long (four years), greatly exceeding the stipulated duration.

Quantitative reconstruction of copper transports

In the official regulatory code no stipulations on annual copper quotas are to be found. As mentioned above, each time a provincial government needed to purchase copper from Yunnan, it had to memorialize the throne.

However, in the compilations *Tongzheng bianlan* and the *Yunnan tongzhi* we find quantitative figures on copper allocations to Zhejiang from 1740 to 1802[20] and to Jiangsu from 1740 to 1808[21]. Although each of these entries concern a specific year, we have no indication whether this is the year when the copper allocation was received and the transport convoys started from Yunnan, or the year when Yunnan sent a report to Zhejiang on the amount of copper allocated, or any other date. Furthermore, we only find figures on the 'regular' copper allocation in the *Tongzheng bianlan* as well as in the *Yunnan tongzhi*. But whenever a transport official received the quota amount of copper at the mine, he obtained in addition a certain amount of copper which served to compensate for quality and transport losses. Thus, the amounts actually transported was considerably more than those mentioned in these compilations.

This means that on the basis of the regulatory sources we can reconstruct neither the year of a transport nor the actual amount of copper transported. By contrast, the palace memorials reporting on individual copper transports provide dates as well as the amounts of transported copper.

20 TZBL 7: 16a–17b; YNTZ 7: 15a–16a.

21 TZBL 7: 12a–12b; YNTZ 7: 12a–12b.

Table 3:

Source	Year of transport	Regular copper quota in *jin*[22]	Total amount in *jin*	Difference in tons
GZDQL 37: 527f	1774	180,000 (about 107 tons)	204,575 (about 122 tons)	15 tons
GZDQL 38: 42	1775	200,000 (about 119 tons)	229,375 (about 137 tons)	18 tons
GZDQL 46: 490f.	1776	200,000 (about 119 tons)	229,375 (about 137 tons)	18 tons
GZDQL 65: 427	1784	280,000 (about 167 tons)	321,125 (about 192 tons)	25 tons

Table 3 shows the regular copper quota without the additional amounts, and the total amount of copper which the transport officials directing the transports discussed above actually transported. The difference between the regular quota and the actual transported amounts to some 15 to 25 tons or 14-15%.

Information on amounts transported recorded in the memorials will allow us to construct reliable statistics.

Conclusion

This preliminary investigation contrasted the central government's expectations concerning transport routes and time limits as formulated in the regulatory with recorded performances of actual shipments, obtained from archival materials. The results of this comparison are: We find no deviations from the stipulations on transport routes, but a striking discrepancy between expected time limits and the actual duration of actual transports. Furthermore, the

22 1 *jin* is equal to 0.597g.

normative sources contain no stipulated quotas for annual mint metal procurement of the Jiangsu and Zhejiang mints, data from archival materials enables us to fill this gap.

In order to reconstruct the mint metal procurement system of Jiangsu and Zhejiang, archival materials such as memorials and edicts are of crucial importance. These provide information concerning the concrete performance of transports and supply data on the transport route, the duration of the transports, and the amounts of mint metal transported. Based on this method, with a sufficiently large set of data harvested from the archival record, this project aims at a systematic analysis of quantitative and qualitative data, leading to anassessment of functional and dysfunctional factors at work in the mint metal procurement for Jiangsu and Zhejiang.

References

Gongzhong dang Qianlong chao zouzhe. 宮中檔乾隆朝奏摺 (Secret Palace Memorials of the Ch'ien-lung Period). Guoli gugong bowuyuan 國立故宮博物院 (National Palace Museum) (ed.). Taibei, 1982–88. 75 vols.

Morse, Hosea Ballou (1975). *The trade and administration of the Chinese empire*. Taibei.

Qianlong chao shangyu dang 乾隆朝上諭檔 (Archives of the Imprial Edicts of the Qianlong Reign). Zhongguo diyi lishi dang'anguan 中國第一歷史檔案館 (First Historical Archives of China) (comp.). Beijing, Zhongguo dang'an chubanshe, 1991, 1998 reprint. 18 vols.

Qinding Da Qing huidian shili 欽定大清會典事例 (Imperially Endorsed Precedents of the Collected Statutes of the Great Qing Dynasty). Jiaqing edition. 1818.

Qinding Hubu guzhu zeli 欽定戶部鼓鑄則例 (Imperially Endorsed Regulations and Precedents for Minting of the Ministry of Revenue). Fu Heng 傅恒 et al. (comp.). 1769. Haikou: Hainan chubanshe, 2000 reprint (*Gugong zhenben congkan*, 287).

Qinding Hubu zeli 欽定戶部則例 (Imperially Endorsed Regulations of the Board of Revenue), 1782 ed.

Shulman, Anna (1989). "Copper, Copper Cash, and Government Controls in Ch'ing China (1644–1795)." Ph.D. Diss., University of Maryland, College Park.

Tongzheng bianlan 銅政便覽 (A Manual on Copper Administration), 1820s or 1830s, as quoted in *Zhongguo jindai shougongye shi ziliao* 中國近代手工

業史資料 (Materials on Modern Chinese Handicraft History), vol. 1, pp. 117–119. Now also available as reprint of Taiwan xuesheng shuju (Student Book Co., Taiwan).

Vogel, Hans Ulrich (1989). "Chinese Central Monetary Policy and the Yunnan Copper Mining Industry in the Early Qing (1644–1800)." Ph.D. Diss., University of Zürich, 1983. Revised version of 1989.

Yunnan tongzhi 雲南銅治 (On the Copper of Yunnan). Dai Ruizheng 戴瑞徵 (comp.). Manuscript, (n.pl.), 1819.

Reconstruction of Copper Transportation Routes in Qing China —A Multi-Source Approach

Hans-Joachim Rosner, Stefan Dieball, Rüdiger Specht

The project group no. 4 'Cartography and GIS-based analysis' at the Geography Department at Tübingen University is reconstructing copper transport routes in the Qing period on the basis of Chinese original sources. A central field of activity is working with Geographical Information Systems. This report gives a first review of the approach and the data that is used, as well as presenting first results.

1. Introduction

The project group no. 4 'Cartography and GIS-based analysis' at the Geography Department at Tübingen University is part of the project 'Monies, Markets, and Finance in China and East Asia, 1600–1900: Local, Regional, National and International Dimensions' (MMF), funded by the German Research Foundation (DFG).

In this project, Qing archival documents concerning mining and transportation of monetary metals are analysed. The huge quantity of data calls for cartographic and statistical analysis to be carried out. The information on mining, refining, and transportation of the metals yields sufficient data for electronic analysis by means of Geographic Information Systems (GIS). These are used to analyse and to visualise the transportation process in general, and to make component maps for individual provinces, transportation routes, and river segments both in spatial and temporal terms. On the basis of digitised analogous maps, thematic maps are set up, covering such themes as terrain models, hydrography, settlement, and administrative units. Detailed maps are designed in scales of 1:500,000 to 1:5,000,000 reflecting the situation at several temporal and regional segments for:

- the locations of mines and mints,
- the course of transportation routes,
- the representation of transportation volumes,
- the calculation of transportation costs from the mines to the mints,

- the infrastructural settings,
- monetary exchange rates and prices.

2. Geographic Information Systems (GIS)

Geographic Information Systems (GIS) play a central role in this project. They can be defined as a system consisting of hardware, software, and data for the capture, storage, retrieval, analysis, and display of objects that can be related to space. In other words, GIS is a tool that allows users to create interactive queries, analyse and visualise spatial information, and edit data. GIS are used in this project because spatial data is used and produced here. "Spatial data means related to the space around us, in which we live and function."[1] Spatial data can be linked to maps, therefore the reference to geographic coordinates is important, as the coordinates link the data with the map. The data represents two categories of real world objects: discrete objects like houses, or continuous fields like rain fall. Furthermore, the data in a GIS can be distinguished into spatial data with topologic attributes and data with thematic attributes. For each object in the GIS there exists a corresponding table where thematic attributes can be added.

GIS can also be defined as an information system that delivers answers to questions. In short, it can answer the questions "where is what?" and "what is where?" With the right data, GIS can answer questions like "on which river passages have there been the biggest losses of copper during the transport?" or "how many stage points are in a given province?" One can also add abstract objects and information, for example about population. The range of applications of GIS is almost unlimited, as long as spatial data is used.

GIS can also be seen as a new approach to science. It has changed the way data can be managed or analysed. Now it is possible to gather new information by (re-)combining data in a way that before was impossible. It has to be emphasized that GIS are not only useful for geo-scientists, but for everyone dealing with spatial data.

1 See Clarke 1997, 3.

3. Data

Essential for a GIS is the data. The benefit increases with the quality and the quantity of the data that can be used. In the project "Monies, Markets, and Finance in China and East Asia 1600–1900: Local, Regional, National and International Dimensions – Cartography and GIS-based Analyses" different kinds of data are used for reconstructing the transportation routes. When used in a GIS, rectifying all the following data is essential for overlaying information and matching different themes to the same place.

3.1 The transportation data base

The transportation data base contains information about the transportation of mint metals from Luzhou (Sichuan Province) to Tongzhou/Beijing. The data is being added to the data base by various colleagues in Germany and China. The data base can be accessed via the Internet. It contains e.g. information about the places that were passed, the material and the amount that was transported, and the transportation time.

3.2 Geo data base

This data base is being set up by the Geography project group. The information given in Chinese historical documents is stored here to reconstruct transportation routes from the Yunnanese mines to the collecting points in Yunnan and Sichuan. The core of the data base is tables with information on locations and the routes. The tables contain information about e.g. the name, opening date or quota of mines, or about the different stage points of the transportation routes. The content of the tables and the links between them can be taken from figure 1.

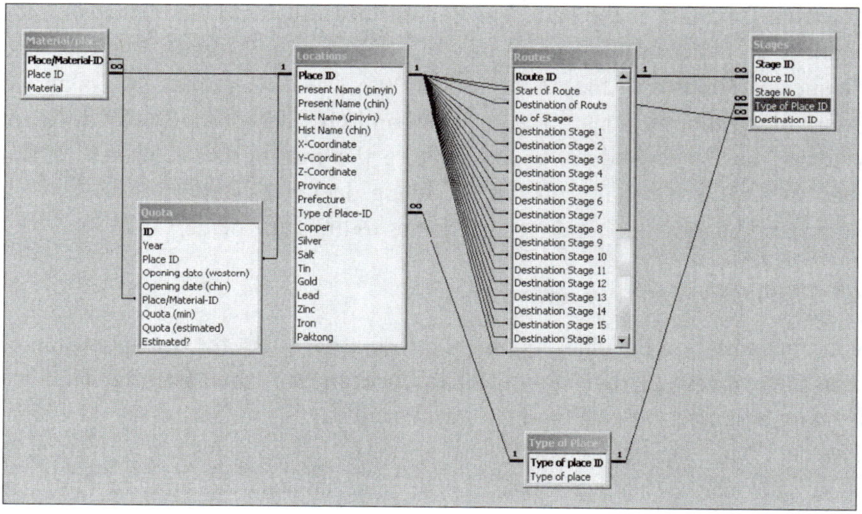

Figure 5. Structure of the geo data base in MS Access

SOURCE: *MMF project group no. 4*

When added to the data base, mines and stage points are located if possible, and then added to the project GIS.

Figure 6. Resources in Yunnan

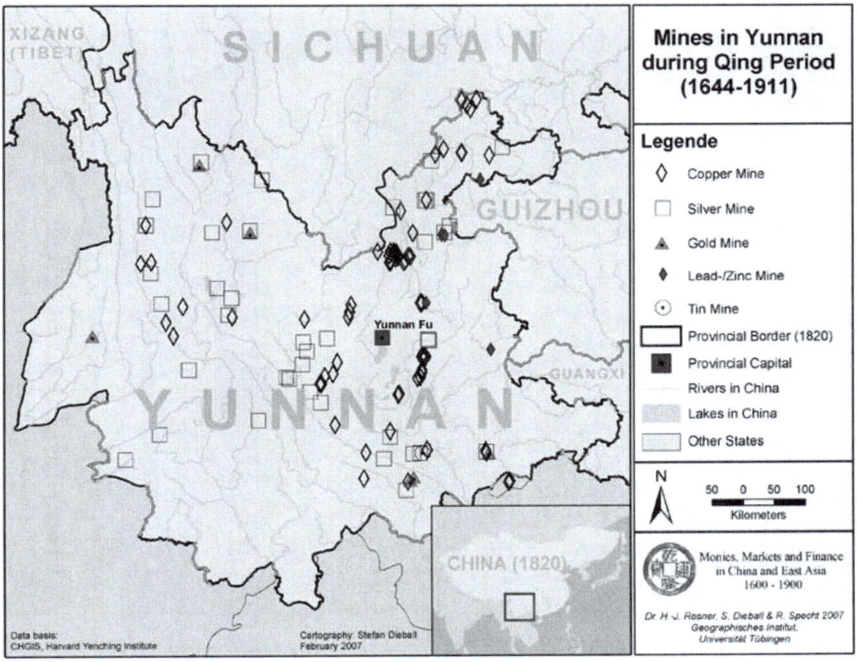

SOURCE*: MMF project group no. 4, base data: CHGIS*

3.3 Rectified digital maps

To get detailed information about different regions in China, maps with relevant information for the reconstruction task are essential. In this project, various maps are used, especially military maps.

3.3.1 Soviet military maps

These maps for the Soviet army derive from aerial stereo-photographs and were produced in the 1960s to 1980s. The age of the maps can be seen as an advantage, as most recent changes in China are not mapped. Maps in the scale of 1:500,000 and 1:200,000 are used for the reconstruction. Being topographic maps, they show information e.g. on morphology and streets or waterways. The legend is in Cyrillic.

Figure 7. Kunming and surroundings on the Soviet military map NG48B

SOURCE: *ROSKARTOGRAFIJA, Soviet military map NG48B*

3.3.2 U.S. military maps

These maps were produced for the U.S. army from the 1930s to the 1950s. Maps in the scale of 1:250,000 for the South and the East of China are used. In contrast to the Soviet maps, Chinese characters are used here in addition to Wade-Giles transcription.

Figure 8. Kunming and surroundings on a US military map NG48-9

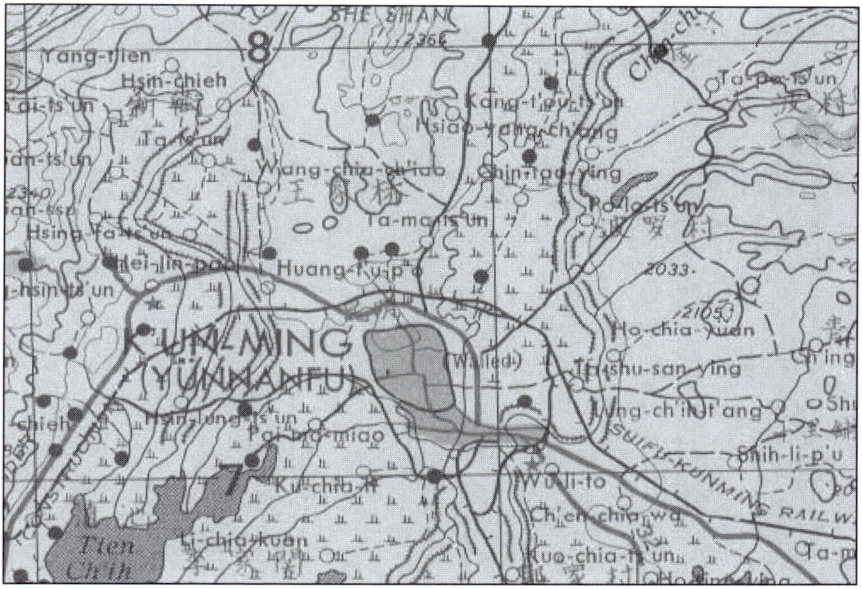

SOURCE: *U.S. Army maps – Series L500, sheet NG48-9*

3.3.3 Others

Other maps, such as modern Chinese maps (see chap. 4.1), French geological maps from very early 20th century, and a copy of the Yunnan sheet taken from the Jesuit Atlas in Kangxi reign-period, are available too.

3.4 The China Historical GIS (CHGIS)

A team from Harvard Yenching Institute has already produced several very useful GIS data sets of the years 1820, 1911, and 1990 for China called 'China Historical GIS' (CHGIS)[2]. They are used as a basis for the project GIS (MMF-GIS). In this project, the GIS data for the year 1820 is used in par-

2 The data is available on http://www.fas.harvard.edu/~chgis/

ticular. It contains layers with administrative borders, rivers and lakes and settlements.

Figure 9. Yunnan province with rivers, lakes, and settlements on the basis of the CHGIS data set for 1820

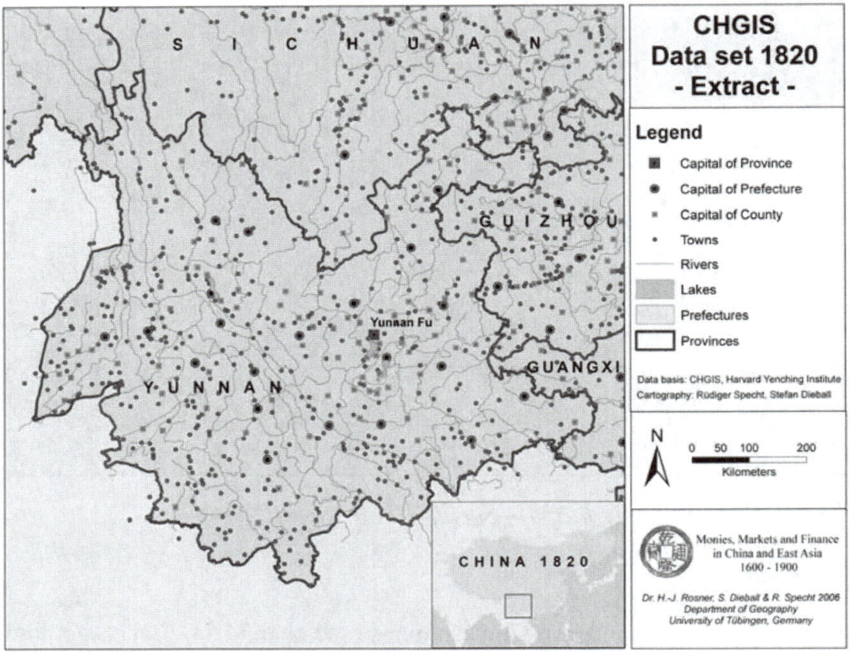

SOURCE: *MMF project group no. 4, base data: CHGIS*

3.5 Satellite images and digital elevation models (DEM)

With the help of satellite images, 3-dimensional models of the transportation regions are created. For this, SRTM-3 version 2 images from the Shuttle Radar Topography Mission in February 2000 are used. For China, the images have a resolution of three arc seconds. At the equator three arc seconds correspond to roughly 90 meters horizontal extent, towards the poles it is less.

In addition, Landsat ETM+ satellite images with three spectral bands (mid-infrared light, near-infrared light, and visible green light) are available. The resolution is 15m.

4. From mines to branch offices in Yunnan Province – reconstructing transportation routes over land

An important task in this project group is the reconstruction of transportation routes within Yunnan Province. Analyzing this data helps in understanding traffic routes and infrastructure, methods and daily transportation performances in Qing China.

Qing copper transportation was performed in different segments. The first segment was the transportation of mint metal from the copper mines to collecting points (*dian* 店), where copper from different mines was stored for further transportation. This was in most cases accomplished by transportation over land in daily distances from one stage point (*chengzhan* 程站) to the next. Qing regulative sources, e.g. the "Manual on Copper Administration" (*Tongzheng bianlan* 銅政便覽), lists in all 11 collecting points, all but two in Yunnan (see Figure 6).

Figure 10. Mines and collection points in Southwest China

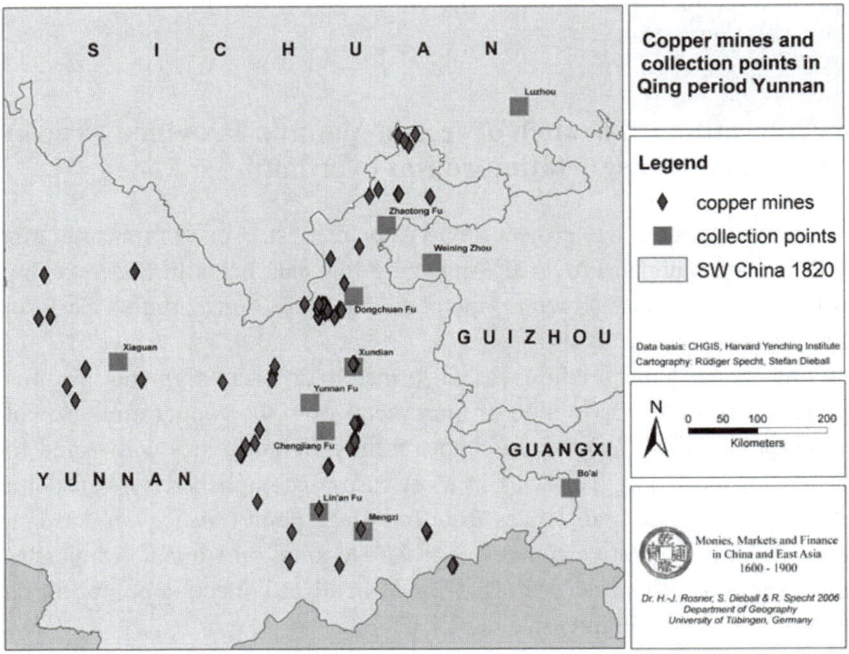

SOURCE: *MMF project group no. 4, base data: CHGIS*

4.1 Data sources

In order to reconstruct historic transportation routes in Yunnan and Sichuan, a variety of digital and non-digital sources have been drawn upon:

- Qing regulative sources, in the first place the "Manual on Copper Administration" (*Tongzheng bianlan* 銅政便覽)
- Modern Chinese maps, mainly the "Atlas of Yunnan" (*Yunnan sheng dituce* 云南省地图册) and the "Atlas of cultural relics of China – part Yunnan" (*Zhongguo Wenwu Dituji / Yunnan Fence* 中国文物地图集 / 云南份册) for identifying the places and settlements given in the historic documents
- CHGIS Harvard University data set (see chap. 3.4)

- Topographic maps in the scales 1: 500,000 and 1: 250,000 for identifying places and reconstructing transportation routes (see chap. 3.3.1 and chap. 3.3.2).

4.2 Transportation routes

Based on the data given in the "Manual on Copper Administration", 59 transportation routes were examined. If possible, the stage points were localized digitally in the GIS with the help of the rectified topographic maps. To localize them as precisely as possible, the places or settlements were first sought for in the Chinese maps and the atlases listed above which depict Yunnan territory on the basis of counties (*xian* 县). The scales of these maps range from 1: 250,000 to about 1: 900,000. So far, 133 out of 311 place names rendered in the "Manual" have been identified in maps. 10 out of the 38 mines have been localized precisely. Four transportation routes could be reconstructed completely, including the exact localization of the mine. The other transportation routes given in the "Manual" have so far only been able to be reconstructed in parts. This data is entered into the geo-data base, making inquiries on transportation routes, transportation time and amounts of transported metal possible in future.

4.2.1 Example Qinglong – Kunming, Yunnan Province

Figure 11. Copper transportation route from Qinglong mine to Kunming

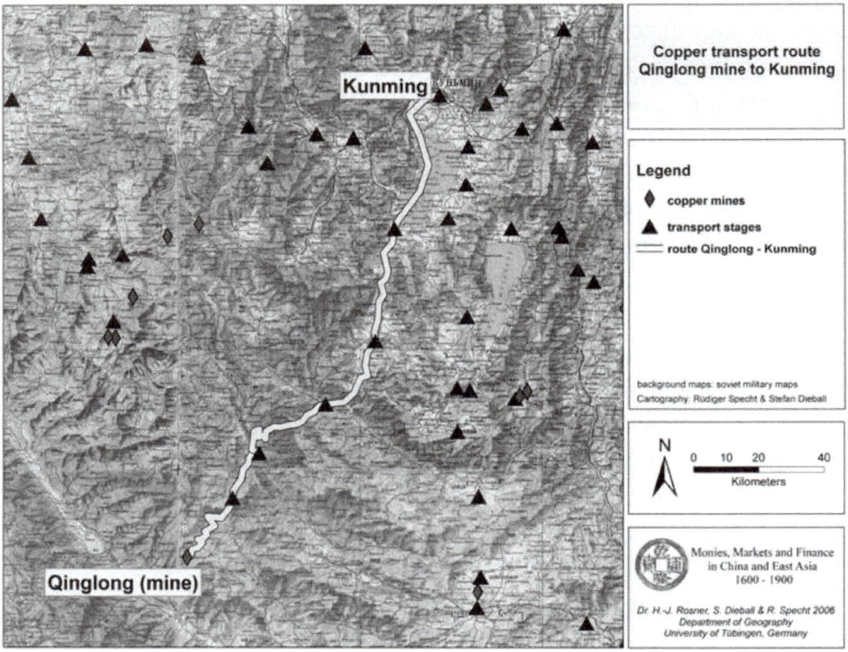

SOURCE: *MMF project group no. 4, base data: CHGIS*

The copper transportation route from Qinglong mine to Kunming is shown as an example for several reasons:

1. The Qinglong mine can be easily identified with modern Qinglong-chang Zhen 青龙厂镇.
2. All stage points have been identified.
3. The transportation route with six stages is rather short and can be displayed as a whole.

4.3 Challenges

Comparison of the names given in the historic document with those in modern maps reveals some difficulties. Some challenges to cope with in reconstruction are:

Modern traffic routes versus historic transportation routes

In reconstructing transportation routes, we follow the main traffic routes shown in the Russian maps, assuming that for most parts of the route they trace historic pathways. This should be seen as the closest guess we have been able to make so far. Nevertheless, if it comes down to the detail, we will have to refer to other sources such as historic descriptions for confirmation. In some cases, historic pathways may not coincide with post-war roads in China.

Difficulties in the identification of place names

Often, names are written differently today, sometimes due to their origin in indigenous languages, which may be transliterated in another way in modern China. Moreover, changes of place names have actually occurred. Some names (e.g. Hongshiyan 紅石岩, Huangcaoping 黄草坪) are common and have been given to several places, making exact localizing difficult. Some settlements may be too small to be shown in maps, while others may have been abandoned since Qing times and are not likely to be identified nowadays. And last, some place names have been transferred to other settlements, as is the case with old Dongchuan 東川, today Huize 会泽.

Transcription problems

If relying on the Soviet military maps, the transcription of Chinese names in Russian might be another source of mistakes. To minimize the risk, identification was done mainly with the help of the given Chinese maps, as the rendering of place names in Chinese characters seemed to be more reliable.

Distances given in historic documents

If examined closely, the distances between stage points sometimes do not seem to be realistic in terms of physical transportation performances, but may rather correspond to administrative units. This applies even more to distances given in Chinese miles (*li* 里). Further investigations have to be done in this aspect in order to be able to judge the historic data correctly.

Location of mines

It has not been possible to confirm the location of most of the mines as of yet, so in most cases the crucial starting point is still missing. It should be kept in mind that the basis of the data is the "Manual on Copper Administration" where the location of the mines is only very roughly described. In many cases even the locations given by the CHGIS are likely not to be reliable. In two cases where the location could be checked by detailed maps, the CHGIS points were not sufficiently precise and failed the locations by 13 and 38 km respectively.

5. First results

At the moment, the creation of the MMF-GIS and the task of reconstruction is far from being completed. The following will show the first examples of reconstructing transportation routes.

5.1 Reconstructions of transportation routes from the mines in Yunnan to the collecting points in Yunnan and Sichuan

The first kind of transportation routes that will be reconstructed are those from the mines in Yunnan to the collecting points in Yunnan and Sichuan. Once the mines and the stage points have been added to the geo-data base, they will be located on maps and added into the GIS. The procedure of the reconstruction is described in chapter 4.

In figure 8, the route from the mine Xiangshupo to the collecting point Xundian is shown. The mine has not yet been located exactly, but all stage points have. To provide the background, the Soviet military topographic maps are used here.

Figure 12. Transportation route Xiangshupo-Xundian

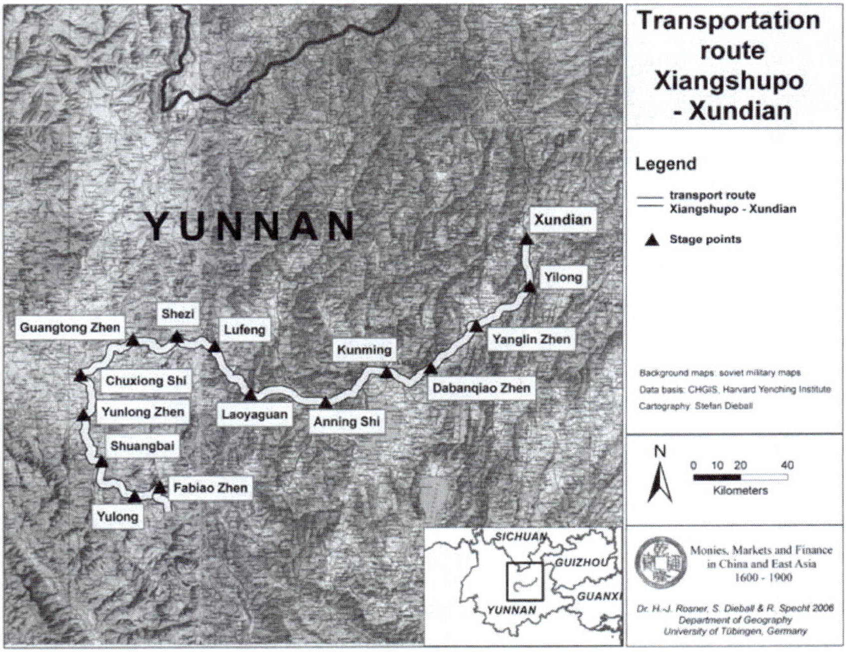

SOURCE: *MMF project group no. 4, base data: CHGIS*

With the help of satellite images 3-dimensional models (see chap. 3.5) of the transportation route and the regions that were passed were created. This has several advantages:

- a better impression of the region than from a 'flat' 2-dimensional map can be gained,
- the course of the route can be checked,
- a profile can be created and new information, such as the highest altitude that had to be passed, can be derived.

Figure 13. A part of the transportation route Xiangshupo-Xundian in a 3-dimensional model

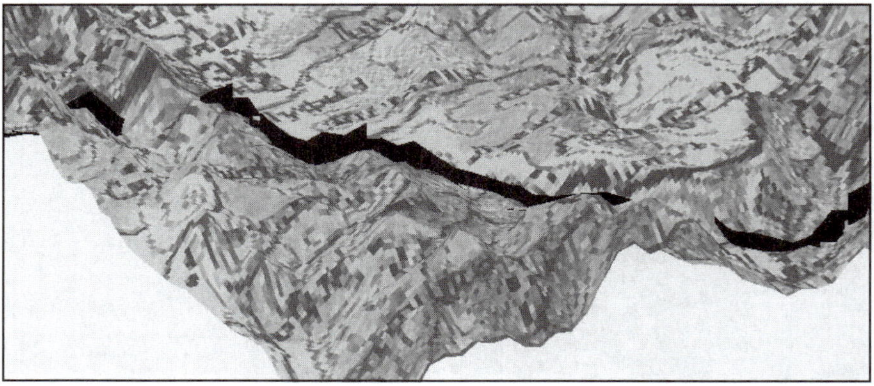

SOURCE: *MMF project group no. 4, base data: SRTM-3 version 2*

5.2 The reconstructions of transportation routes from the transportation data base

The routes from the transportation data base will also be taken into the project GIS. As this data base is far from being completed, it is not possible at the moment to reconstruct complete routes.

As an example, route 296 was chosen. For this route many documents have already been evaluated and many stage points are known. The reconstruction procedure is the same as mentioned in chapter 4. Nevertheless, new problems arise: On the one hand, the reconstruction turns out to be easier, as the transportation is done on waterways all the way from Luzhou to Tongzhou near Beijing. On the other hand, the documents unfortunately do not tell in detail which places are passed. Only the prefecture that is entered is named in the documents. An example can be seen on figure 10. As place names Peixian and Yicheng are given, but the corresponding cities were probably not passed along the waterway.

The benefit of using the GIS will clearly be enhanced when the attribute information from the data base is included in the GIS, thus making analysis possible. A possible query might be: "Show me all passages where there were shipwrecks". A lot more queries can be made, depending on the data that will be included.

Once the routes are in the GIS, distances can be measured as well.

Figure 14. Extract of the transportation route 296 from the transportation data base

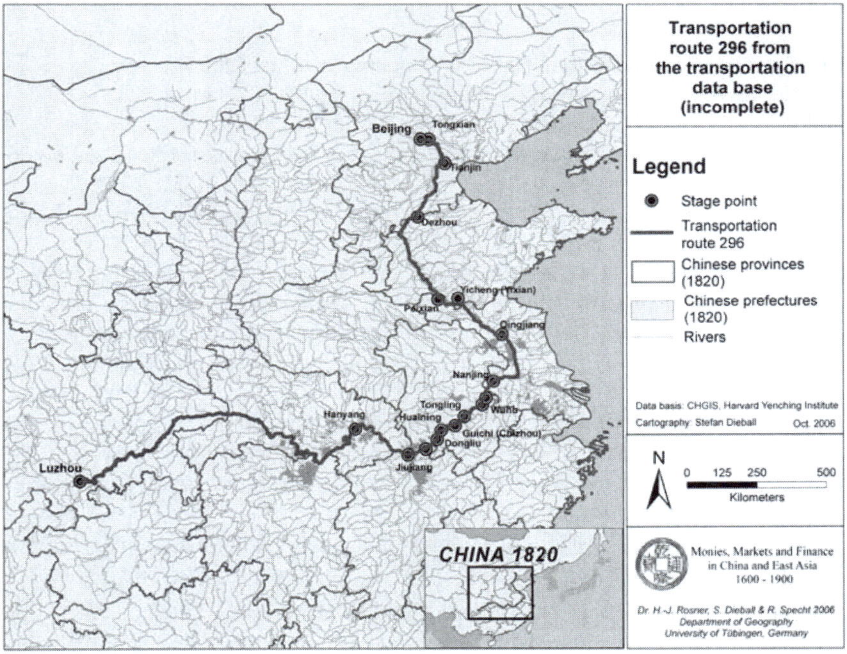

SOURCE: *MMF project group no. 4, base data: CHGIS*

6. Further objectives

The following tasks remain to be done: The geo data base has to be completed; with more entries, further reconstructions of transportation routes can be made. The transported amount has to be added into the GIS and visualised. Various visualisations need to be made. As a further step, animations of the transportation will be created. Beyond this, investigations of infrastructure effects will be undertaken.

Some problems remain:

- the precise localisation of places and routes,
- the determination of the amounts that were actually transported: only the quotas are given for the mines.

7. References

CHGIS, Version 3, Cambridge: Harvard Yenching Institute (2006). http://www.fas.harvard.edu/~chgis/ (Accessed 06-10-31).

CGIAR, SRTM 90m Digital Elevation Data (2006). ftp://e0srp01u.ecs.nasa.gov/srtm/version2/SRTM3/Eurasia/ (Accessed on 06-10-31)

Clarke, K.C. (1997). *Getting Started with Geographic Information Systems*. - Upper Saddle River, NJ: Prentice Hall.

Fuchs, Walter (1943). *Der Jesuiten-Atlas der Kanghsi-Zeit: seine Entstehungsgeschichte nebst Namensindices für die Karten der Mandjurei, Mongolei, Ostturkestan und Tibet mit Wiedergabe der Jesuiten-Karten in Originalgrösse; [China und die Aussenlaender]*. Peking: Catholic Univ. Press.

NASA, Applied Research & Technology Project Office (2006). https://zulu.ssc.nasa.gov/mrsid/ (Accessed 06-08-22).

ROSKARTOGRAFIJA. *Russian Federal Service of Geodesy and Cartography. Soviet military maps*. Moskow.

Tongzheng bianlan 銅政便覽 (A Manual on Copper Administration), 1820s or 1830s, as quoted in *Zhongguo jindai shougongye shi ziliao* 中國近代手工業史資料 (Materials on Modern Chinese Handicraft History), vol. 1, pp. 117–119. Now also available as reprint of Taiwan xuesheng shuju (Student Book Co., Taiwan).

U.S Army Map Service. *U.S. Army maps – Series L500*. Washington, D.C.

Yunnan sheng dituce 云南省地图册 (Atlas of Yunnan Province). Zhao Dinghan 赵 鼎 汉 et al. Beijing: Zhongguo ditu chubanshe, 1999.

Zhongguo Wenwu Dituji / Yunnan Fence 中国文物地图集 / 云南份册 (Atlas of Cultural Relics of China – Part Yunnan). Edited by Guojia wenwu ju (Department for National cultural heritage). Kunming: Yunnan kezhi chubanshe, 1999.

Stretching the Bureaucracy: Ad Hoc Agencies and Recruitment in the 1826 Sea Transport Experiment

Jane Kate Leonard

The paper examines the steps taken by the Qing leadership to resolve the grain transport crisis in 1825 after the destruction of the Grand Canal near the confluence of the Grand Canal and Yellow River. It analyzes how the Qing leadership mobilized bureaucratic resources (personnel and organizations) to carry out the innovation of sea transport in spite of an extremely spare governing structure that hardly penetrated the sub-county arena in the canal zone where the principal tasks of grain transport were performed. The study argues that two governing tools—ad hoc organizations (*ju* 局) and the recruitment (*zhaolai* 招來) of extra-bureaucratic personnel—were used in tandem to temporarily expand the Qing bureaucracy in Shanghai to craft and implement sea transport. The decision to "stretch" the bureaucracy in this case flowed from the inner court's determination to adopt a new dual strategy for capital grain supply that used both the Grand Canal and the sea route, and their appointment of a skilled cadre of Banner elite and Han Chinese officials to organize a unique collaboration of local Shanghai officials, irregular expectant officials, and Shanghai merchant shippers to implement the project.

Introduction

Since the 1980s, scholarly studies of Qing administration have begun to highlight the flexibility of the Qing governing style and state collaboration with private commercial organizations in creating economic prosperity and social stability—goals that the Qing leadership considered fundamental to successful dynastic rule and its Confucian moral mission.[1] The Qing leadership drew a distinction between the state's strategic sphere of responsibilities

1 One of the few early scholars who recognized the Qing state's administrative flexibility and its role in the economy was Thomas Metzger. He drew attention to the significance of the periodic revision of the administrative codes of the various central ministries (1966, 4–10; 1970, 23–46; 1972, 9–45; 1973; 1977).

and the fiscal resources (*guoji* 國計) that were directly related to the political security of the realm, on the one hand, and the people's productive sphere and the economic work they performed in the pursuit of their livelihoods (*minsheng* 民生) on the other. The former sought to fund and feed the essential, but limited, functions of the state "under the six boards", while the latter hummed along at the sub-county level, seemingly independent and apart, protected by the thinly spread fabric of the imperial state.

While the state's strategic sphere and the people's productive sphere were separated conceptually, there was a great deal of overlap between the two that was affirmed by custom, administrative statute, and by the very practical needs of the government to work alongside ordinary people at the sub-county level in the performance of some of its key functions. Thus, the state and private economic organizations in China's many diverse regional locales were "joined at the hip," so to speak. Nowhere is this more clear than in the operation of the territorially vast and logistically complex networks of grain and monetary copper supply.[2]

The performance of well-defined tasks carried out at the county and sub-county levels, far from the Qing imperial and provincial capitals, was, of course, dependent on a diverse array of local conditions and a mix of sub-bureaucratic and extra-bureaucratic individuals and organizations.[3] So too was the performance of other less well-defined tasks that emerged slowly from long-term change, and dealing with short-term contingent crises that posed new challenges to the Qing administration that were neither "covered" in the administrative code nor could be managed with the slender bureaucratic resources that were spread paper-thin across the empire. Having no solution in the established administrative codes or customary practice, these challenges required creative problem-solving and the resort to a range of institutional tools that included, to name a few, the periodic revision and adjustment of the administrative code, the assignment of new responsibilities to pre-existing official posts, the creation of temporary managerial organizations/bureaus (*ju* 局), and the temporary recruitment (*zhaolai* 招來,

2 Hirzel 2006; Kim 2006; Leonard 1996, 79–108; Perdue 1992, 100–125; Sun 1971, 132–148; Will 1990, 311–318; Will and Wong 1991.

3 Antony and Leonard 2002, 1–26.

zhaoshang 招商) of non-state, or extra-bureaucratic, organizations and groups.

The latter two—ad hoc bureaucratic organizations and recruitment—were particularly useful because they were plastic and adaptable, capable of being stretched and molded to fit the needs of changing times, as was the case for sea transport in 1826, when the state had no administrative blueprint or the time and resources to develop one. Ad hoc bureaus had great advantages from the point of view of the central government.[4] They could be organized quickly to respond to challenging events and crises, and staffed with a variety of bureaucratic, sub-bureaucratic, and extra-bureaucratic personnel. Most importantly, these organizations did not extend the permanent structures and, thus, the costs of government. Although scholars have studied these organizations in the post-Opium War period,[5] their use prior to the Opium War is not as well understood.[6]

Often used in tandem with ad hoc bureaucratic organizations, recruitment was a tool that the state used "to call" or "beckon" private, extra-bureaucratic resources to aid the government in the performance of its key functions. It had a long history in Chinese statecraft and had been used to good effect earlier in the Qing period to facilitate the performance of such tasks as military grain transfers, lumbering, famine relief, and copper mining,[7] and during the early nineteenth century the dynasty used recruitment to adjust to a host of new problems that flowed from demographic change, from the maturing of the dynasty itself, and from the changed circumstances that it faced.[8]

The Grand Canal crisis in the mid-1820s required the use of all these various Qing governing tools—long-established practices and temporary expedients. All were part and parcel of the late imperial game of juggling scarce bureaucratic resources to overcome basic systemic weaknesses in the Qing governing system.[9] This paper analyzes that juggling game in 1825 at

4 *Ibid.*

5 Chan 1980, 416–462; Liu 1990; Leung 2002, 61–79; Lai 1991, 139–156.

6 See Kaske 2006, 1–12 for a discussion of the use of irregular 'expectant' officials.

7 Perdue 1992, 100–125; Sun 1968, 835–845; 1971, 132–48; 1992, 9–20; Will 1990.

8 Antony and Leonard 2002, 1–26; Kwan 2001.

9 *Ibid.* 2002, 2–7.

the height of the grain transport crisis, which enabled the Qing leadership to complete the successful innovation of sea transport in 1826 and to revive canal transport by 1827. It will examine the leadership role of high-ranking officials in Jiangsu, their approach to the reallocation of bureaucratic resources to meet the crisis, the adaptation of the administrative code governing grain transport (*Qinding Hubu caoyun quanshu* 欽定戶部漕運全書), and finally their creation of a temporary management organization and a recruitment plan in Shanghai to carry out sea transport.

The Crisis Setting

One of the most daunting problems facing the Qing in the early nineteenth century was the breakdown of the Grand Canal in northern Jiangsu in 1824–1825, which led to the collapse of capital grain transport and the urgent need to devise quickly a plan for sea transport by the early spring of 1826. Ecological degradation leading to the breakdown of the section of the canal in northern Jiangsu province from the Huanghe-Huaihe and the Yangzi had been intensifying since the late eighteenth century.[10] It had come to a head in 1825 when floods destroyed the complex of Grand Canal hydraulic facilities at its junction with the Yellow River at Qingjiangpu (清江浦) near Huai'an (淮安), crippling capital grain transport to Beijing.[11]

The Qing leadership responded in late 1825 with a series of important innovations designed to reconfigure the canal facilities at the Grand Canal–Yellow River junction, and, to set up an emergency plan to hire merchant shippers in Shanghai for the 1826 grain transport cycle.[12] The Daoguang Emperor (1772–1850; r. 1821–1850) raised the sea transport idea in the second month of 1825, within weeks of the disaster.[13] By the late fifth month,

10 In the late Ming and Qing periods, the main arm of the Huanghe (Yellow River) followed a southerly course around the Shandong massif, taking over the bed of the Huaihe in its lower course. During this period, the river was stabilized in this course by the construction of a narrow diking system. From 1853 to 1855, the river shifted to its present course.

11 Leonard 1996.

12 Leonard 2005, 451–458.

13 Shangyudang fangben 上諭檔方本 (Record Books of Ordinary Grand Council Affairs). S 5.2.5.; Jiaobu tingjidang 剿捕廷寄檔 (Record Books of Court Letter Drafts). TJ 5.2.5. Hereafter the letters S, TJ, and P indicate secret edict, court letter draft, and public

he had appointed new officials to the top bureaucratic posts in Liangjiang 兩江, the provinces of Jiangsu and Jiangxi,[14] and by the early eighth month, these Qing officials had mapped out a plan to recruit over a thousand sand junks (*shachuan* 沙船) from the Shanghai Merchant Shipping Guild in Shanghai to carry 1.5 to 1.6 million *shi* of tax grain, or grain "tribute," from the Jiangsu grain districts of Suzhou, Songjiang, Changzhou, Zhenjiang and Taicang (Susongchangzhentai 蘇松常鎮太) to Tianjin by sea.[15] The regulations and the recruitment agreement were finalized early in the ninth month,[16] and by the eleventh month, private lighters were shuttling tax grain from the canal anchorages to Shanghai for loading onto sand junks lined up along the docks on the Huangpu (黃浦) River between Shanghai and Wusong (吳淞).[17] The last of the sand junks had set sail by the middle of the sixth month of 1826, and the experiment was concluded successfully by the middle of the eighth month of that year, completing the transport of 1,633,000 *shi* of tax grain in 1,562 sand junks, with only one ship lost at sea and three others damaged and incurring grain losses.[18] It was, by all accounts, an impressive organizational feat.

The feat was achieved by smart leadership and organizational decisions made from the fifth to the eighth months of 1825. High-level regional officials in Jiangsu in charge of resolving the crisis played a decisive role in creating workable innovations that could be implemented even with the imperium's slender bureaucratic resources. To do so they set up an ad hoc management organization based in Shanghai that created the regulatory framework for sea transport, supervised and implemented the plan, all the while collaborating closely with Shanghai merchant shippers to achieve a fair and streamlined sea transport operation that protected merchants from the extortion of grain brokers, officials, and clerks and runners.

edict respectively. Public edicts are contained in the Shangyudang fangben as well as the secret edicts. The numbers indicate the reign period year, month, and day.

14 P5.5.22.

15 S5.8.9; JSHY 5.9.2, 1:62–70b.

16 P5.9.8.

17 JSHY 5.11.17, 2:13–16b.

18 P6.6.17; P6.8.13.

By the fifth day of the second month of 1825, a month after the destruction of the canal in northern Jiangsu, and amid reports of chaos at the canal–Yellow River junction, the Daoguang Emperor ordered a review of the state of the grain transport system and asked for proposals that would insure its long-term operation, thus guaranteeing capital grain supply for the future.[19] He ordered officials to look particularly at the feasibility of sea transport to serve, not just as a temporary expedient to help get through the grain shipping crisis of 1825–1826, but as a permanent part of a new dual approach to capital grain supply. This dual strategy kept canal transport as the centerpiece of capital grain supply, but institutionalized the use of sea transport during times of canal crisis, thus "taking the burden off the canal." Although sea transport had been discussed since the early Jiaqing period (1796–1820; r. 1796–1820), the crisis in 1825 was so profound that the emperor and his allies felt impelled to act boldly "to alter the old regulations".[20]

From the second month to the middle of the fifth month, the canal crisis deepened. Canal officials in northern Jiangsu grasped desperately at one tactic after another to keep the canal junction open for the crossing of grain fleets, starting with the established "accumulation of clear water" (*xuqingshui shuahung jiyun* 蓄清水刷黃濟) from Hongze Lake (洪澤) to float the fleets through the canal head at Yuhuang Dam (禦黃). When that did not work because of the depletion of clear water in the Hongze reservoir, they turned to the use of Yellow River backspills into the canal head so that junks could be pulled through Yuhuang Dam on the inflow of highly silted river water—a tactic called "leading in the Yellow to aid transport" (*yinhuang jiyun* 引黃濟運).[21] When back-spills turned the canal head into a quagmire of muddy silt, officials turned to yet another temporary expedient called relay shipping, or "crossing the embankments to connect the transport" (*panba jieyun* 盤壩接運). In this last tactic, grain cargoes were transferred from government grain junks to smaller craft called lighters, as well as carts, for transport along smaller, secondary canals and roadways over the dike embankment to the south bank of the Yellow River and so to waiting craft

19 S/TJ5.2.5.
20 JSHY 5.6.15, 1:29b.
21 5.2.7/5.3.29.

drawn from Henan, Shandong, and Jiangsu north of the Yellow River.[22] This began a series of relays northward along the canal until the grain finally reached the capital granaries.

Begun early in the fourth month, relay shipping required the mobilization of thousands of craft from four provinces (Jiangsu, Henan, Shandong, and Zhili) and was enormously expensive and time consuming. By the middle of the fifth month, it too had broken down, much to the chagrin of the emperor and his inner court advisor, Yinghe (英和 1771–1839).[23] Besides the catalogue of failures, none of the high-level officials in charge of grain transport in northern Jiangsu had made the slightest effort to figure out a way to fix the grain transport system for the long-term, nor had a single one of them lifted a finger to assess the possibilities of sea transport. Instead, they brushed the issue aside, observing that it was "too difficult."[24] And with that, they turned their attention back to the canal and relay shipping. The Daoguang emperor was outraged, and he singled out the acting grain transport director, Wei Yuanyu (魏元煜), as the worst case of an official shirking his responsibility to provide the emperor and the inner court with policy ideas and assessments. The emperor was hamstrung without these assessments because, as he complained, he could not "control from afar" (*yaozhi* 遙制) by himself, far from the scene of the canal disaster.[25]

The only official to offer a comprehensive plan and to outline an approach to sea transport was Yinghe, President of the Board of Revenue, and the Daoguang Emperor's special financial adviser on the Grand Council.[26] Early in the fourth month, at the point when relay shipping began, Yinghe wrote a memorial arguing for the use of sea transport during 1825 and 1826—the presumed period of time needed to "harness the river" and repair the canal.[27] The Jiaqing Emperor (1796–1820) and his inner court advisers had discussed sea transport earlier, as had the Daoguang Emperor's advisory circle, but they had not arrived at a consensus because many "were unaltera-

22 Leonard 1996, 41–49, 151–172.

23 Hummel 1967, 931–933.

24 S5.4.2.

25 S/TJ5.6.6; JSHY 5.6.23, 1:32b.

26 Sun 1962–1963, 175–227.

27 JSHY5.4.10, 1:4–14b.

bly opposed to sea transport."[28] The 1825 crisis provided an opportunity to experiment with sea transport, and then if successful, the Qing leadership could incorporate this innovation into the grain transport code, thus institutionalizing it for the future. Yinghe's memorial should be seen as a product of inner court deliberations ongoing since the Jiaqing reign.

Yinghe laid out a framework for the recruitment of Shanghai merchant shippers to carry 1.5 to 1.6 million *shi* from Jiangnan, the economic core area south of the Lower Yangzi, to the port of Tianjin by sea for transfer back into government hands and final shipment to the Beijing. He also argued for closing the canal in 1825 so that fundamental repairs could be made to the hydraulic facilities that linked the Hongze Lake reservoir with the canal and the Yellow River. To pay for this audacious plan, he advocated commuting the remainder of southern tax grain from the Yangtze provinces and Zhejiang to silver to pay for reconstruction.

A second memorial by Yinghe was written in the late fifth month when relay shipping had began to falter and three days after the emperor made sweeping changes in the leadership in Jiangsu province,[29] sacking the incumbents and setting up a new cadre of officials headed by Qishan (琦善 , d. 1854),[30] a skilled and trusted member of the Banner elite.[31] He was posted to Qingjiangpu at the canal-river junction to revive relay shipping, renovate the hydraulic facilities in northern Jiangsu, and galvanize the planning for sea transport from Shanghai. By this point in the canal crisis, the main features of the comprehensive plan had been drawn up, the basic objections raised, and the new leadership was in place and poised for action. Yinghe's second memorial "elaborated in greater detail" the most controversial parts of the comprehensive plan (sea transport and the commutation of tax grain), but it also contained a stinging rebuke of Jiangsu officials for their failure to engage in serious discussion about the comprehensive plan, especially sea transport. It is precisely this discussion of official failures that sheds important light on the Qing leadership's view of how the governing process was supposed to work. It highlighted the creative role that officials

28 S/TJ5.2.5.

29 S/TJ5.5.19; JSHY5.5.22, 1:16–22.

30 Hummel 1967, 126–129.

31 Hummel 1967, 126–129; Wei Xiumei 1993, 463–503; 1994, 135–160.

were supposed to play in adapting and altering the administrative code to meet the needs of changing times, and it demonstrates how high-ranking regional officials approached the question of reallocating bureaucratic resources to make the barebones structure of imperial government work.

Official Problem-solving

In his first memorial, Yinghe had articulated the need for innovation and the adjustment of existing administrative practice. He quoted the great Song scholar Cheng Hao's (程顥) assertion that one had to embrace "great change in order to reap great benefits." To do just that, Yinghe urged the Qing leadership "to strike down the precedents" to accord with the times and reap the benefits. In his second memorial, however, he became more aggressive and weighed in against officials for slacking and failing to come up with solutions to the problems raised by his comprehensive plan, especially sea transport. From his point of view, the grain transport crisis, as with each and every other governmental problem, could be managed successfully with a blend of imaginative leadership and creative adaptation of the existing regulatory guidelines enshrined in the code. When searching for solutions to pressing problems facing imperial government, he argued, officials would never find the perfect answer because all solutions "had both advantages and disadvantages." It was the job of officials not to whine about difficulties but "to build on the advantages and eliminate the disadvantages." Without exception, in his view, the critical element that determined success or failure was "the judgment and authority of the officials" in charge.[32] In other words, everything rested on an official's problem-solving abilities.

Yet, how, he pointedly asked, had leading officials in Jiangsu responded to the canal disaster? A "full six months" had elapsed since the emperor's call for discussions of long-term approaches to grain transport, and not a single memorial had arrived with "real substantive words" to address these issues. Instead, official reports were "muddled and ambiguous." "They only discussed the on-going plan for relay shipping"—a plan that intensified labor

32 JSHY 1:16b.

shortages in northern Jiangsu and did nothing to solve the long-term grain transport crisis.[33]

In Yinghe's view, the guide to problem solving was the administrative code. Most of the issues raised by the comprehensive plan, he asserted, could be solved by "adapting and expanding the code," and he reminded officials that he had done just that in his first memorial. In the case of grain transport personnel who were fearful of losing their income and jobs, he reiterated that the salaries, the honesty stipends, the salaries for reduced work periods, special fees, and travel stipends for civilian boatmen were "all detailed in the code."[34] Moreover, he pointedly noted that if Jiangsu officials had been thinking creatively, they would have seen that the present crisis in northern Jiangsu offered an additional source of income for these very people. Low-level grain transport officers and their Banner crews could be sent to the reconstruction sites in northern Jiangsu where there were severe labor shortages. If they were to do so, then "Banner officers and workers will have work, and the work sites more workers." This, in his words, "would kill two birds with one stone."[35]

Similarly, if officials were worried about the safety of grain cargoes at sea, then they should simply order naval officials to adjust their coastal patrolling schedule to coincide with the departure of the grain fleets from Shanghai. At that time, Zhejiang marine units should intensify their patrols near the Zhaobao (招寶) and Chenqian (陳錢) Islands that lay off the northeast coast of Hangzhou Bay, and those in Jiangnan should converge on the Yangshan (洋山) and Majishan (馬跡山) Islands on the eastern edge of the Yangzi estuary. As the grain fleets sailed northward, Shandong marine units should then sail out from bases on the Chengshan Promontory (成山) and Stone Island (Shidao石島) on the eastern end of the peninsula and proceed to Yingyoumen (鷹游門) on the Jiangsu-Shandong border to wait for the grain fleets[36] and escort them through Shandong coastal waters. All of these difficulties seemed completely manageable to Yinghe, if only officials would think creatively.

33 JSHY 1:17.
34 JSHY 1:19.
35 JSHY 1:18b–19.
36 JSHY 1:19b–20.

Finally, with respect to objections raised about the commutation of tax grain, which officials in the field had opposed from the start, he explained that the code spelled out a variety of procedures for commuting tax grain to currency that dated from the Shunzhi reign (1638–1661; r. 1644–1661), and the code also outlined measures to curtail the corrupt manipulation of the conversion process.[37] He pointed out in exasperation that these issues were not, in any sense, new. Their solution could be found in the code and *then adapted to new conditions* [emphasis added]. And, moreover, "the provinces know this full well!" Creative adaptation of the code would solve the commutation difficulties if only officials kept a central principle in mind—that solutions must be workable, "suiting the needs of officials implementing the plan as well as the needs of the people commuting their tax grain," a view reiterated by Qishan.[38] If, as officials complained, the plan required more time than the normal tax collection process, then, by all means, "extend the time limit for payment from the tenth month of 1825 to the fourth month of 1826!" Finally, if local county and department officials could no longer be trusted to fix the conversion price of grain to silver, then they should assign the task of doing so to the provincial treasurers in the southern canal zone provinces, to circumvent the "the private interests of yamen clerks."[39] It all seemed doable to Yinghe from his lofty position in Beijing. But what if, after tinkering with the code even with imagination, there were too few bureaucratic officials and agencies to manage the work at hand?

The Reallocation of Bureaucratic Resources

By the nineteenth day of the fifth month of 1825, the emperor's new appointees had arrived at their posts in Jiangsu; they had completed some fact-finding missions and discussions in the region; and they had submitted preliminary conclusions about the prospects for fixing the grain transport system.[40] These initial investigations had made clear that the central difficulty in resolving the grain transport crisis was finding experienced mid-level

37 JSHY 1:20–22b.

38 JSHY5.6.22, 1:34.

39 JSHY 1:22.

40 JSHY5.6.22, 1:32–37b; 5.7.22, 1:42–43; 5.7.23, 1:44–47.

officials who were capable of managing complex and innovative grain transport tasks. These tasks were both supervisory and operational, thus extremely personnel-intensive, reaching down vertically to the sub-county arena in Jiangnan. They placed heavy demands on officials, and they required the leadership of officials who were "incorrupt, experienced, and highly skilled," with enough imagination to create new workable regulations that "would not place undue burdens on either officials or the people."[41] But how could "undue burdens on government officials" be avoided when the government structure was so thinly spread across the empire and lacked vertical depth to carry out tasks at the sub-county level? And how could officials avoid these burdens when the performance of these complex grain supply tasks, indeed tasks and responsibilities relating to the entire empire-wide grain supply network, were so central to the Qing imperial mission?

Depending on the task at hand, the Qing practice was to find those needed bureaucratic resources in several ways. They either appointed imperial commissioners as trouble-shooters for emergencies of limited duration, or, alternatively, they assigned new tasks and responsibilities to already existing posts, to be managed concurrently with an official's regular, routine responsibilities.[42] If neither of these approaches was adequate for the task at hand, they created temporary ad hoc organizations to manage discrete problems, and they staffed them with specially appointed mid-level officials, assisted by a mix of regular local officials and expectant officials, as well as sub-bureaucratic and extra-bureaucratic personnel, the latter of whom, in this case, were merchant shippers. An important function of ad hoc agencies, often used in tandem with recruitment, was the negotiation of collaborative agreements that defined the responsibilities of extra-bureaucratic parties and their relationship to the government in what might be termed "quasi-joint enterprises." Therefore, they played a very important role in defining the boundaries of state power and the divide between the state's and the people's spheres of action.

One can see all these alternative methods of mobilizing and extending bureaucratic resources at play in the grain transport crisis. At the beginning of the crisis before Qishan arrived in northern Jiangsu, the Qing leadership had

41 JSHY5.6.22, 1:34.

42 Antony 2002, 27–59; Antony and Leonard 2002, 2–10.

begun to propose the reassignment of officials to carry out the grain transport reforms. For example, as soon as word of the floods and destruction of the canal arrived in Beijing in the first month of 1825, the emperor had dispatched two imperial commissioners to travel to northern Jiangsu for a limited period of time to assess the causes and scope of the damage to the hydraulic facilities at the canal head. In the fourth month, Yinghe had also proposed that the senior officials from the Board of Revenue take responsibility for supervising the examination and transfer of grain from the sand junks to canal boats in Tianjin, and he also suggested that the Liangjiang governor-general order the Shanghai intendant to summon and negotiate the recruitment agreement with merchant shippers and then have the court appoint a special commissioner to implement it. In both cases, high-ranking bureaucratic officials were deemed essential to insure the integrity of the administrative process, guard against grain loss, and protect merchant shippers from extortion by local officials and licensed grain brokers.[43]

Perhaps the best example of loading additional tasks onto pre-existing offices was the appointment of Qishan to the post of Liangjiang governor-general.[44] His assignment carried all the burdens of the governor-generalship, arguably the single most important regional post in the empire,[45] but on top of that load, the emperor gave him the added tasks of expediting relay shipping and managing the reconstruction of hydraulic projects in northern Jiangsu, plus the important responsibility of creating a wholly new administrative structure for sea transport, for which there was no blueprint in the Qing code. Thus, his responsibilities were expanded to include those of an imperial commissioner.

Once Qishan arrived in northern Jiangsu in the fifth month, he bore the lion's share of responsibility for decisions about the allocation of scarce bureaucratic resources to the solution of myriad problems of grain transport restoration. He was assisted in these tasks by a small circle of top-level Jiangsu officials: Governor Tao Zhu (陶澍 1779–1839); Treasurer He Changling (賀長齡 1785–1848); and both the Grand Canal and Grain

43 JSHY 5.4.10, 1:10b, 13b.

44 S/TJ5.5.19; S5.5.25.

45 Chu and Saywell 1984, 1–25, 71–85.

Transport directors.[46] But Qishan had his limits, and he made those limits clear. He stated explicitly that he was constrained by being confined geographically to Qingjiangpu until relay shipping and canal reconstruction were completed.[47] After touring the construction sites and consulting with the officials in charge, he affirmed hesitantly that he could probably manage the stalled relay shipping process and canal reconstruction, although he was not completely sure; but he could not repeatedly travel to Jiangnan and Shanghai to carry out similar oversight functions for sea transport.[48] For these tasks, he initially turned to Tao Zhu and He Changling.

Three crucial tasks had to be carried out immediately: fact-finding about the feasibility of the plan, the creation of a workable regulatory framework for sea transport, and then its implementation—to begin by the end of 1825. Early in the sixth month, soon after Tao Zhu had taken up his post, he had travelled to Qingjiang to consult with Qishan, in order to discuss the preliminary information gathered by He Changling, the Jiangsu treasurer, during the latter's two earlier fact-finding trips to Shanghai. During those trips, He had made contact with the Merchant Shipping Guild, assessed harbor facilities for loading grain from canal lighters to sand junks, and estimated the number of sand junks that might be available for grain transport to begin in late autumn. But at the end of the sixth month, reports suggested that there might be too few sand junks to carry 1.5 million *shi* of tax grain.[49] To clarify this issue, Qishan sent He on a third mission, but he recognized that He could not dwell in Shanghai indefinitely working on sea transport arrangements because of the press of his regular administrative duties as provincial treasurer based in Suzhou (蘇州).[50]

There were also limits to what Tao Zhu could do. After returning from Qingjiang to Suzhou later in the sixth month, he then travelled to Shanghai to iron out some problems with the merchant shippers and negotiate a tentative deal with them.[51] On this trip, he took the time to tour the docking areas

46 P5.5.22, *Da Qing lizhao shilu*, Daoguang, vol. 3, p. 1500; Hummel 1967, 281–282, 710–711; Zhou and Xu 1992.

47 JSHY5.6.22, 1:33b–34.

48 JSHY5.6.22, 1:32–37.

49 JSHY5.6.22, 1:32–37; JSHY5.7.23, 1:40–47.

50 JSHY5.6.22, 1:39–b.

51 JSHY5.7.23, 1:44–47.

on the waterfront near Shanghai's East Gate, guided by a licensed shipping broker associated with the Merchant Shipping Guild, and he actually boarded and inspected a sand junk. He used the opportunity to "interview sailors about the geography and navigational conditions on the northeast coast," the results of which he subsequently included in his memorial reports and then incorporated in the sea transport compilation published in 1826.[52] But he still had to contend with the press of his regular gubernatorial responsibilities, as he noted in the late seventh month when turned over responsibility for sea transport to He Changling while he, Tao, travelled to Jiangning (modern Nanjing) to serve as the chief examiner in the provincial examination. "With regard to all the other [sea transport] regulations, I will, as is customary, order the treasurer, He Changling, to go to Shanghai to take care of the various arrangements for merchant boats, porterage labor, and wastage rice, and also to deliberate about sending military officers to escort the transport and civil officials to witness the transfer of grain [in Tianjin]."[53] Both Qishan and Tao Zhu seemed to recognize that the top three officials in Jiangsu could not manage the fact-finding, organizational, and supervisory tasks required to plan and carry out sea transport by themselves and with their limited staff.

Negotiating the recruitment of merchant shippers also had its own special difficulties and required more official involvement in the negotiations. This became clear as imperial officials sought to work out an agreement with the merchant shippers and overcome their reluctance to participate in sea transport. The central issue was ostensibly to clarify the number of ships available for the project, but the real issues were corruption, extortion, and merchant demands that both of these problems be eliminated from the sea transport operation. If they weren't, merchants believed that sub-bureaucratic personnel—clerks, runners, and grain brokers—would take a cut out of the shipping fees at both the Shanghai and Tianjin ends of the sea transport process, when tax grain was transferred to and from merchant hands.[54] They feared that sub-bureaucratic personnel would "cause trouble and delays" that would cost them the opportunity to sail to Fengtian for trade before returning to

52 JSHY 12:1–2b.

53 JSHY5.7.23, 1:45b–46.

54 JSHY5.4.10, 1:10b; JSHY5.7.23, 1:45–b.

Shanghai. There are numerous official and imperial references to the importance of streamlining the shipping process to avoid causing economic harm to merchants: "We should not cause harm for merchants and must design regulations that expedite the work."[55] One might realistically view this issue as a conflict between sub-bureaucratic and extra-bureaucratic interests, and one in which private interests ultimately prevailed because of the Qing state's overriding need for the sand junk fleets. It also draws attention to the fact the Qing leadership understood clearly that sub-bureaucratic corruption took a toll on administrative efficiency.

Yinghe had had an inkling of this problem earlier in the spring when he addressed the need for special arrangements to protect merchants from extortion in Tianjin. He was aware that merchant shippers had serious misgivings about collaborating on sea transport because of fears of extortion, especially in Tianjin.[56] They feared that they would be "treated just like the Banner officers on the canal grain fleets who were constantly pressured to pay special fees." They worried that if they agreed to ship the grain and then faced extortion and delays in Tianjin, they would be "afraid to protest to officials," in which case, they would lose their shipping fees and the opportunity to trade in the Manchurian ports before returning to Shanghai to pick up the second load of grain. In a word, merchant shippers wanted 'protection' from official extortion if they were going to participate in sea transport. And this would require the creation of a special bureaucratic framework through which mid- and high-ranking officials could exercise greater scrutiny and oversight.

By the late fifth month, Yinghe apparently realized that merchants were equally concerned about corruption in Shanghai. Merchants, he said, "are not accustomed to dealing with officials and clerks." Their subordinate position relative to that of officials left them "timid and cringing" in their presence.[57] Even with the prospect of lucrative shipping fees, they remained "fearful" of collaboration. To overcome merchant reluctance "to aid the state," Yinghe outlined some practical procedural protections for the loading of grain in

55 JSHY5.6.22, 1:34.
56 JSHY5.5.22, 1:17b.
57 JSHY5.5.22, 1:17b.

Shanghai.[58] In particular, he proposed more elaborate official participation in the planning and implementation of sea transport than he had in his first memorial, urging that the Liangjiang governor-general and Jiangsu governor "appoint one or two incorruptible and skilled officials to go to Shanghai to summon and discuss the project with the ship owners and to work out more carefully how much the government would pay them for shipping and for labor costs for the loading at Shanghai and unloading in Tianjin, with both categories of expenses calculated per *shi* of grain, using the established government measuring tool (*hu* 斛).[59]

After working out an agreement with the merchant shippers and creating the regulations with the help of local Shanghai officials, these two special officials would then supervise the loading of grain at the docks on the Huangpu River and issue a document to each ship-owner specifying the amount loaded on each and every sand junk, with a copy kept "in official hands." Yinghe explicitly excluded the use of yamen clerks (*xuli* 胥吏) from the process.[60] After the loading was completed, these officials would accompany the boats to Tianjin, carrying the documents with them for reference when the fleets arrived and Tianjin officials examined the quantity and quality of the grain and took possession of it. In a sense, these special officials would serve as advocates for merchant shippers and Jiangsu grain authorities in Tianjin.

To assure the honesty of the process in Tianjin, Yinghe proposed that a Granary Vice President and a high-ranking official from the Board of Revenue be sent to Tianjin in advance of the fleet's arrival to supervise the examination and receipt of the grain. They, and only they, should be empowered to pay the merchants directly, based on the documents issued in Shanghai that spelled out the "actual amount of grain" measured and loaded in Shanghai. At no time would yamen underlings or grain brokers be allowed to deal with or interact with the merchants in either Shanghai or Tianjin. He insisted that "all aspects of loading, unloading, and paying must be controlled by bureaucratic officials with no interference from grain brokers."[61]

58 JSHY5.5.22, 1:17b–18b.

59 JSHY5.5.22, 1:17b–18b.

60 *Ibid*, 1:18.

61 JSHY 5.5.22, 1:18.

No one was to be allowed to extort even the smallest part of the payments to the merchants. This process would protect the economic interests of the merchants while they "served the public good." Yinghe, at this stage, clearly indicated that the needs of the merchants had to be met because the state could not implement sea transport on its own. The state needed the merchants more than the reverse.

After Qishan arrived in Jiangsu and assumed responsibility for organizing sea transport, he began to focus on the bureaucratic resources needed to plan and implement the plan. Recognizing that the top three Jiangsu officials were limited in their ability to micro-manage events on the ground, his gaze first turned to Shanghai local officials who would normally be expected to play an important role in crafting the sea transport plan because of their grasp of local conditions.[62] Yet Qishan was not impressed with these particular officials and questioned whether they were up to the job, observing that they seemed "completely unable to manage the affairs of state." He immediately sacked the Shanghai county magistrate for incompetence, and he observed that the magistrate's replacement as well as the recently appointed intendant were mediocre in ability and not terribly knowledgeable about local conditions.[63] He was in a quandary about how to proceed because the new sea transport plan was "experimental and the planning had to be perfect"—planning that would depend on local officials' knowledge of local conditions. He needed officials who could "push action forward" (*zhenzuo* 振作).[64]

These worries came to a head in the fifth month when it was revealed, probably by Tao Zhu during his visit to Qingjiang, that sand junks were fleeing from the port of Shanghai and, consequently, there might be too few for hire in early 1826 to ship grain. The alleged shortage of sand junks had apparently been caused by the arbitrary actions of Tao Zhu's predecessor, Zhang Shicheng (張師誠), who earlier in the year when the possibility of sea transport for 1825 tax grain was still under consideration, had "commandeered" (*fengliu* 封留) all the sand junks then in the harbor in the event that they were needed, much to the consternation of the sand junk owners, who,

62 JSHY5.6.22, 1:32–37.
63 JSHY5.6.22, 1:39–b.
64 *Ibid.*,1:39b.

as a consequence, lost the chance to sail to the northeast ports to trade.[65] In retaliation, the sand junk owners had slipped out of the harbor on their ships and "disappeared at sea," and it was unclear if they would return to do the state's bidding at the end of the year. Playing the messenger with bad news, Qishan reported late in sixth month that until the question of ship availability was resolved, he "could not make any promises" about the number of private ships available for sea transport nor the amount of Jiangnan grain that might be shipped.[66]

The crisis of the "disappearing ships" highlighted the critical need, indeed, the imperative, for private sand junks if the Qing were to move ahead with sea transport. And this, in turn, focused attention on the dearth of bureaucratic personnel on the ground in Shanghai to spearhead its planning and implementation. To clarify the issue, Qishan immediately sent He Changling on a third trip to Shanghai, as noted above, to find out exactly how many ships were available. Without the ships, they would have to abandon sea transport. This was followed by Tao Zhu's elaborate trip, described above, to meet with the merchant shippers and finalize the recruitment agreement, which provided for a well-defined procedure for inspecting, loading, and verifying the loads in Shanghai as well as a parallel procedure for Tianjin that protected the shippers from official corruption and expedited the transfer of grain to Tianjin authorities so that shippers could proceed quickly to the southern Manchurian trading ports.

But after the deal was struck, the arduous follow-up work of devising the regulations and procedures still remained to be done. And it was at this crucial juncture that Qishan, drawing on ideas from Yinghe's second memorial, made the decision to establish a temporary management organization in Shanghai. He proposed sending two mid-ranking officials "who are impartial and skilled" (*gongzheng minggan* 公正明幹) to Shanghai to collaborate with local officials and merchant shippers in order to draw up the sea transport plan and supervise its implementation.[67] He chose two officials who had impressed him in Qingjiangpu—the former provincial judge Lin Zexu (林則徐), and Zou Xichun (鄒錫淳), a former Henan canal intendant. Both

65 JSHY5.6.28, 1:32–37.

66 JSHY5.6.22, 1:32–37.

67 JSHY5.6.22, 1:39–40.

had been sent to the canal junction to examine and verify the adequacy of the stonework repairs on the Nianyu dike (埝盱), and on the completion of this task, Qishan decided to send them to Shanghai to mastermind sea transport planning.[68] Due to illness and the death of a parent, Lin did not continue in the project, although he may have travelled to Shanghai once. Zou and Shanghai local officials constituted the core of the new sea transport management group.

Qishan repeatedly described the work of the new management group as "collaborative." While Zou, the outside appointee, would provide the leadership energy, or dynamism (*dutong* 督同), local officials, from intendant to county magistrate, would provide the Shanghai "local knowledge." Working together, they could craft a "perfect plan." Even though he was skeptical of the abilities of Shanghai local officials, Qishan apparently thought that their mediocrity could be offset by the dynamic leadership of Zou. After the Shanghai group produced a plan, Qishan and Tao Zhu would review it and revise it if necessary. Then, with the new regulations in place, "local officials will have no difficulty implementing the plan."[69]

Operating within the framework of the ad hoc management agency in Shanghai, Zou Xicheng served as the principal organizer and manager of sea transport. He bore the brunt of drafting the sea transport regulations in collaboration with both Shanghai local officials and members of the Merchant Shipping Guild, and after their adoption, he supervised the implementation of the plan with the aid of Shanghai local officials and an army of "assistant" and "expectant" officials. He took direct responsibility for the loading of sand junks and the payment of merchant shippers in Shanghai, after which he and a small coterie of deputies carried grain samples by land to Tianjin where he served as an advocate for Jiangsu interests in the final examination and transfer of grain cargoes to Zhili officials.

68 JSHY5.6.28, 1:40b–41.
69 JSHY5.6.22, 1:39b.

Conclusions

An examination of the unfolding events of the grain transport in 1825 shows that the early investigation and planning for sea transport centered on practical questions about the allocation of scarce bureaucratic resources. When it became clear that the scale of the canal disaster would require multiple complex responses and that administrative innovation (sea transport) was central among them, the Daoguang Emperor and his key inner court adviser, Yinghe, appointed a new leadership group for Jiangsu that was headed by the Banner elite, Qishan, and included two energetic and ambitious Chinese officials: Tao Zhu and He Changling, who shared responsibility for sea transport and who created a special ad hoc organization to implement it, thus extending temporarily the Qing bureaucracy.

These leadership changes and operational decisions were made because the need for creative planning was at a premium and the existing bureaucratic structures of the Qing "field" and "functional" administrations and their official appointees had neither the resources nor political will to do it. The leadership of Banner elites, Yinghe and Qishan, was critical to the sea transport experiment in the early stages because innovations in the canal-grain transport system were too strategically and politically dangerous for Chinese officials to initiate and undertake on their own. But once the concrete planning was underway, the role of high-level provincial officials in Jiangsu proved to be crucial. They were able to assess quickly the number and functions of officials needed on the Shanghai docks to carry out sea transport, and then they designed a streamlined and workable plan to achieve it.

The success of the sea transport experiment lay fundamentally with the creation of a temporary management organization in Shanghai that managed the recruitment of and collaboration with merchant shippers. It provided a regulatory framework and a disciplined core of officials on the ground, who succeeded in carrying out the plan and shielding merchant shippers from official extortion at both Shanghai and Tianjin. They did so by relying primarily on "assistant" and "expectant" officials, rather than sub-bureaucratic clerks and runners. The interests of extra-bureaucratic merchant shippers, in this case, seem to have trumped those of the sub-bureaucracy.

We can see, in retrospect, that the most difficult aspect of administrative innovation in this case was not conceptualizing concrete policy changes to the capital grain supply system or embracing the sea transport option. Ideas for such reforms abounded. It was, instead, figuring out how to instrument change with a paper-thin administrative superstructure. That was the rub. There was no "fat" in the Qing administrative system and no existing administrative guidelines, agencies, or personnel to carry out needed changes. The Qing leadership overcame these handicaps by stretching the bureaucracy temporarily with the use of long-established ad hoc governing tools—temporary agencies and recruitment—that enabled the dynasty to adjust to changing circumstances. How these tools were used in Qing requires much more investigation, especially in key strategic areas of government that were vitally important to the perpetuation of Qing rule, but for the innovation of sea transport in the 1820s, these tools and the officials who applied them carried the day.

References

Antony, Robert J. (2000). "Subcounty Officials, the State, and Local Communities in Guangdong Province, 1644–1860." In Antony and Leonard, pp. 27–59.

Antony, Robert J. and Jane Kate Leonard (eds.) (2002). *Dragons, Tigers, and Dogs. Qing Crisis Management and the Boundaries of State Power in Late Imperial China*. Cornell East Asia Series, No. 114. Ithaca, New York: East Asia Program, Cornell University.

Chan, Wellington K. K. (1980). "Government, Merchants and Industry to 1911." In John K. Fairbank and Kwang-ching Liu (eds.), *Cambridge History of China*, Vol. 11. Cambridge: Cambridge University Press, pp. 416–462.

Chu, Raymond W. and William G. Saywell (1984). *Career Patterns in the Ch'ing Dynasty. The Office of the Governor-General*. Ann Arbor: Center for Chinese Studies, The University of Michigan.

Da Qing lizhao shilu 大清歷朝實錄 (Veritable Records of the Successive Reigns of the Qing Dynasty). [1937] 1964. Daoguang: 4 vols. 4,485 *juan*. Reprint. Taibei.

Dodgen, Randall A. (2001). *Controlling the Dragon. Confucian Engineers and the Yellow River in Late Imperial China*. Honolulu: University of Hawaii Press.

Hirzel, Thomas (2006). Mint Metal Procurement for Jiangsu and Zhejiang during the Qianlong Period. An Inquiry into the Central Government's Expectations and the Provinces' Expectations and the Provinces" Strategies of Implementation. MMF, pp. 1–8.

Hummel, Arthur W. (ed.) (1967). *Eminent Chinese of the Ch'ing Period, 1644–1912*. 2 vols. in 1. Washington, D. C.: U. S. Government Printing Office, 1943–1944.

Jiangsu haiyun quan'an 江蘇海運全案 (The Complete Records on Jiangsu Sea Transport). He Changling 賀長齡, Tao Zhu (陶澍), Wei Yuan (魏源) (eds.) (1826). N.p. 12 *juan*.

Jiaobu tingjidang 剿捕廷寄檔 (Record Books of Court Letter Drafts). Qing Archives, National Palace Museum, Taibei, ROC.

Kaske, Elisabeth (2006). The Question of Money and Social Status in the Qing Contribution System. MMF, pp. 1–12.

Kim, Nanny (2006). Mint Metal Transports Out of Southwest China from the Eighteenth to the Early Nineteenth Centuries. MMF, pp. 1–15.

Kwan Manbun (2001). *The Salt Merchants of Tianjin. State-Making and Civil Society in Late Imperial China*. Honolulu: University of Hawaii Press.

Lai Chi-kong (1992). "The Qing State and Merchant Enterprise: The China Merchants' Company, 1872–1902." In Leonard and Watt 1992, pp. 139–155.

Leonard, Jane Kate (1996). *Controlling from Afar: The Daoguang Emperor's Management of the Grand Canal Crisis, 1824–1826*. Ann Arbor, MI: Center for Chinese Studies Publications, University of Michigan.

________ (2005). "Introduction: General Reflections on Regulations and Precedents (*zeli*)." In Vogel, Hans Ulrich et al. (eds.), pp. 27–31.

________ (2005). "Timeliness and Innovation: The 1845 Revision of the Complete Book on Grain Transport (*Caoyun quanshu*). In Vogel, Hans Ulrich et al. (eds.), pp. 449–464.

Leonard, Jane Kate and John R. Watt (eds.) (1992). *To Achieve Security and Wealth. The Qing Imperial State and the Economy, 1644–1911*. Cornell East Asia Series, No. 56.

Leung, Philip Y. S. (1990). *The Shanghai Taotai. Linkage Man in a Changing Society, 1843–90*. Asian Studies at Hawaii, No. 39. Honolulu: University of Hawaii Press.

________ (1996). "Qingmou de Tianjin dao yu Jin Haiguan dao 清末的天津道與津海關道 (The Two Intendants in Late Qing Tianjin. The Tianjin *dao* and Jin Haiguan *dao*), 25: 119–141 (June).

________ (2002). "Crisis Management and Institutional Reform. The Expectant Officials in the Late Qing." In Antony and Leonard, pp. 61–77.

Liu, Kwang-ching (1991). *Jingshi sixiang yu xinxing zhiye* 經世思想與新興企業 (Statecraft Thought and New Business Enterprise). Taibei: Lianjing.

Metzger, Thomas A. (1966). "Ch'ing Commercial Policy." *Ch'ing-shi wen-t'i* 1, 3:4–10 (February).

________ (1970). "The State and Commerce in Imperial China." *Asian and African Studies* 6:23–46.

________ (1972). "The Organizational Capabilities of the Ch'ing State in the Field of Commerce. The Liang-Huai Salt Monopoly, 1740–1840. In W. E. Willmott (ed.), *Economic Organization in Chinese Society*. Stanford, CA: Stanford University Press.

________ (1973). *The Internal Organization of Ch'ing Bureaucracy. Legal, Normative, and Commercialization Aspects*. Harvard Studies in East Asian Law, No. 7. Cambridge MA: Harvard University Press.

MMF: First International Workshop on Monies, Markets, and Finance in China and East Asia, 1600–1900. Institute of Chinese Studies. University of Heidelberg, 12–16 October 2006.

Perdue, Peter C. (1992). "The Qing State and the Gansu Grain Market, 1739–1864." In Rawski and Li (eds.), pp. 100–125.

Qinding Hubu caoyun quanshu 欽定戶部漕運全書 (The Board of Revenue's Complete Book on Grain Transport). Editions: 1766, 1845, 1875–76.

Rawski, Thomas G. and Lillian M. Li (eds.) (1992). *Chinese History in Economic Perspective*. Berkeley CA: University of California Press.

Shangyudang fangben 上諭檔方本 (Record Books of Ordinary Grand Council Affairs). Qing Archives, National Palace Museum, Taibei, ROC.

Sun E-tu Zen (1962–1963). "The Board of Revenue in 19th Century China." *Harvard Journal of Asiatic Studies* 24: 175–227.

________ (1968). "Ch'ing Government and the Mineral Industries before 1800." *Journal of Asian Studies* 27, 4: 835–845.

________ (1971). "The Transportation of Yunnan Copper to Peking in the Ch'ing Period." *Journal of Oriental Studies* 9:132–148.

________ (1992). "The Finance Ministry (Hubu) and Its Relationship to the Private Economy in Qing Times." In Leonard and Watt, pp. 9–20.

Vogel, Hans Ulrich, Christine Moll-Murata, and Song Jianze (eds.) (2005). *Chinese Handicraft Regulations of the Qing Dynasty. Theory and Application*. München: Iudicium.

Wei Xiumei 魏秀梅 (1993). "Qishan zai YuLu de zhengji, 1814–1829" 琦善在豫魯的政績，1814–1829 (Qishan's Political-administrative Achievements in Henan and Shandong, 1814–1829). Bulletin of the Institute of Modern History, Academia Sinica (Taibei) 22, 1:463–503.

________ (1994). "Qishan zai Liangjiang de zhengji, 1825–1827" 琦善在兩江的政績， 1825–1827 (Qishan's Political-administrative Achievements in Liangjiang, 1825–1827). *Bulletin of the Institute of Modern History*, Academia Sinica (Taibei) 23:135–160.

Will, Pierre-Etienne (1990). *Bureaucracy and Famine in Eighteenth-Century China*. Trans. By Elborg Forster. Rev. ed. Stanford: Stanford University Press.

Will, Pierre-Etienne and R. Bin Wong with James Lee (1991). *Nourish the People. The State Civilian Granary System in China, 1650–1850*. Ann Arbor: Center for Chinese Studies, University of Michigan.

Zhou Wu 周斌 and Xu Kangming 許康銘 (1992). *Tao Zhu lun* 陶澍論 (A Discussion of Tao Zhu). Changsha: Foulu.

The Price of an Office: Venality, the Individual and the State in 19th Century China

Elisabeth Kaske

This paper examines the sale of public offices in 19th century China, its ideological and institutional background and its functions for the state as supplier and the individual as purchaser. For the state, the sale of offices mainly functioned as an anti-deficit measure, whereas for the individual, it supplemented but did not replace the examinations system as a means by which to attain an appointment as a regular official. However, during the 19th century the role of venality changed, when the sale of office patents became divorced from actual appointments and expectancy by itself offered alternative modes of employment.

Venality of Office in Comparative Perspective

The sale of offices in Late Imperial China was not just another form of corruption, but part and parcel of the political and legal institutions of the empire. As early as in 1849, the *Chinese Repository* remarked that it was "one of the worst features in the present policy of the Chinese government."[1] In 1925, Pao Chao Hsieh expressed his surprise that "the purchase of office, popularly understood as a corrupt practice in the old Manchu Government, strangely enough had full legal sanction there."[2] However, what seemed strange and despicable to American missionaries and US educated Chinese students had in fact been a common phenomenon in Europe and its dependencies during a historical era identified with absolutism. Though most advanced in France under the Ancien Régime and long regarded as a "French addiction," it was also to be found in the Papal States, England, the Habsburg Empire, Württemberg, Brandenburg-Preußen, and other early modern states.[3]

1 *The Chinese Repository* XIII (1849), 207.

2 Hsieh 1925, 105.

3 Swart 1949; Parry 1953; Mousnier 1971; Malettke 1980; Bruce 1980. For the expression "French addiction" see: Doyle 1996, chap. 1.

In his 1949 dissertation, Koenraad Swart was the first European scholar to point out that "the universality of sale of offices indicates that this phenomenon was caused by factors which had a more general character than is usually assumed."[4] Wolfgang Reinhard, in a seminal paper published in 1974, emphasized that venality was a truly "universal historical phenomenon," especially if various related and transitional forms were taken into account.[5] European historians usually distinguish between venality of offices (*Ämterkäuflichkeit*, *venalité des offices*) in the narrow sense of the word, i.e. the legal and institutionalized sale of offices by the state, the semi-legal or illegal commerce of offices between private individuals (*Ämterhandel*, *commerce des offices*), transitional forms between the former and the latter, and, finally, related forms such as the sale of peerage, brevet titles and academic degrees. The fact that a private commerce of offices could develop into the public and legalized sale of offices was seen by Reinhard as due to a "phase shift of various historical processes." It was a coincidence of: (1) a medieval notion of office inherited from Canon law, which saw an official function (*officium*) as inseparably linked to a benefice (*beneficium*) and in fact made the office into a private property of the office-holder that could be resold (per "*resignatio in favorem tertii*") or even bequeathed to a son; (2) the monetarization of the economy and increased financial needs of the state, especially due to the extension of wars and the use of mercenary troops; and (3) an underdeveloped money and capital market, in which state loans were in fact private loans to the ruler whose credit rating was rather questionable. In such circumstances, the sale of offices was a convenient means for the ruler to obtain money by taking out loans from his subjects which were secured by conferring the benefice of an office to the lender. In most cases, such a loan was highly advantageous for the state because it was the populace who returned the interest by paying to the office-holder fees he was entitled to demand by virtue of the authority conferred to him by the state.[6]

Only venality of offices in the narrow sense is dealt with in this essay. Starting from Reinhard's comparative method three aspects of venality are

4 Swart 1949, 2.

5 Reinhard 1974, 289–292 (this paper was brought to my attention by Dr. Nicole Reinhardt).

6 Ibid., 294–313, 319.

investigated: first, the ideological and institutional background; second, the function of venality for the supplier of offices, i.e. the state; and third, the demand for offices on the purchasers' side.[7]

Venality as Contribution to the Public

Charles de Montesquieu (1689 - 1755), an apologist of venality in monarchic France, wrote in *The Spirit of the Law* that in despotic states (he considered China to be such) public employment should not be sold, because the "subjects must be instantaneously placed or displaced by the prince."[8] Montesquieu thought that one of the advantages of the sale of offices was that it gave permanency to a family's aspiration for employment. This, of course, would not be the case in a society where office was not considered a property right of its holder. Moreover, from a French point of view, the incentive to purchase an office with no security of life-time employment would seem rather weak.

The Chinese reality disproved Montesquieu's assumptions. In fact, China had not only created a remarkable meritocracy based on highly competitive civil service examinations, which strongly influenced enlightenment ideas in Europe,[9] but it also had the most impressive and most systematic system of venality of offices, titles and degrees. Chinese and European venality of office occurred almost at the same time. Although first reports regarding the sale of public offices can be traced back to antiquity in both cases,[10] systematic and institutionalized venality was a phenomenon of the early modern period. In France, it began in 1522, when the French king launched a military campaign into Italy and established the parts casual (*bureau des parties casuelles*) as a special office for the generation and collection of occasional and non-recurrent income.[11] For China, scholars agree that venality of office was a product of the Jingtai 景泰 era (1450–1456) of the Ming dynasty

7 Ibid., 293–294.

8 Montesquieu 1949, 69.

9 In contrast to Montesquieu, Voltaire, who was a staunch opponent of venality, was also known as a "sinophile," see: Guy 1963.

10 Leban 1990; Schuller 1994, 197–202.

11 Doyle 1996, 4.

when, following the infamous Tumu incident, the new emperor was in urgent need for provisions for his army in order to strengthen his defenses at the northern border.[12]

In both cases the financial needs caused by war played an important role in the state seeking additional revenues. However, the basis of legitimacy given to the sale of office differed. In a system in which officials were principally chosen by merit, Chinese rulers solved the problem of legitimacy by defining the bestowal of an office as an Imperial favor granted in return for a contribution to the public. Pao Chao Hsieh remarked:

> Clever employment of the artistic Chinese language designated the purchase as a "contribution for appointment to public office." Whatever terms might have been given to this detestable institution, a process of paying money or grains for the acquisition of an appointment was too evident to rid it of its commercial character.[13]

The designation of purchase as "contribution" was more than just "clever employment of the artistic Chinese language." The idea can be traced back to Chinese antiquity. The *Shangjunshu* 商君書 of Shang Yang 商鞅 (ca. 390–338 BC) held that:

> If the people have a surplus of grain, cause them to obtain office and rank by means of their cereals; if through their own efforts they can count upon obtaining office and rank, farmers will not be lazy. If a tube of no more than four inches has no bottom, it can certainly not be filled; to confer office, to give rank and to grant salaries, without regard to merit, is like having no bottom.[14]

Chao Cuo's 晁錯 (d. 154 BC) memorial to emperor Jingdi on the promotion of grain production, in which he argued that the bestowal of titles on wealthy men as a means to gain contributions of grain would lighten the tax burden of the populace, became a classical piece of literature and was included in widely-read anthologies such as the *Anthology of Classical Prose* (*Guwen Guanzhi* 古文觀止) published in 1695.[15]

12 Watari 1986, 20–35; Wu 2006, 55–80. For the abduction of the emperor in the Tumu incident of 1449 see: Mote 1974, 243–272.

13 Hsieh 1925, 105.

14 Shang 1928, 253.

15 Chao Cuo 晁錯, "Lun guisu shu 論貴粟疏," in Qian 1990, 177–184.

The definition (or disguising if you prefer) of the sale of offices as a reward for a contribution resulted in three characteristics of Chinese venality that were markedly different from the European example. First, there was a close relationship between the sale of office patents (i.e. substantive offices) to commoners, advancement in office for officials in active service, and academic degrees, honorary titles, brevet titles (i.e. official titles without actual office-holding), and other rewards. Therefore, venality of office in the narrow sense cannot be separated from the so-called "related forms" differentiated in European historical analysis. They formed a continuum of rewards granted on the basis of the actual status of the contributor, the amount contributed and the circumstances of the contribution. This continuum is known in Chinese scholarship as the "contribution system" (*juanna zhidu* 捐納制度, sometimes also called "subscription system").[16] In 19th century Qing China, the system of rewarding contributions in money or kind included the following rewards and honors:

> Rewards given to officials, ex-officials, expectant officials and (partly) bearers of official titles:
>
> - Promotion in sub-rank and recorded merits (*jiaji jilu* 加級紀錄) [purchased in advance in order to cancel out punishments for minor "public offences" (*gongzui* 公罪) if necessary]
> - Promotion in office and title (*shengzhi shengxian* 陞職陞銜)
> - Reinstatement and atonement (*juanfu* 捐復, *shuzui* 贖罪)
> - Honorary titles (*fengdian* 封典, bestowed on relatives of officials and title holders)
> - Plume Decorations (*lingzhi* 翎支, new after 1850s).

16 The term "contribution system" seems to have been coined by Xu Daling's pioneering work (Xu 1968).

Rewards given to commoners:

- Academic degree of a Student of the Imperial Academy (*jiansheng* 監生, *gongsheng* 貢生)
- Office diplomas (*shizhi* 實職, *shiren* 實任)
- Brevet titles (*zhixian* 職銜, *xuxian* 虛銜)
- Decorations and inscriptions (*gongpai* 功牌, *bian'e* 匾額, for small sums).

Rewards given to provinces and counties:

- Increase in the quota of provincial examinations and district school admission quota (only Xianfeng and Tongzhi eras, ca. 1853–1874).

Except for the decorations and inscriptions, all other rewards were somehow related to office-holding. The academic degree of a Student of the Imperial Academy (*jiansheng* 監生) conferred to *shengyuan* contributors since 1453 and to commoners since 1537[17] was the key to all further advancement. During the Qing dynasty, a *jiansheng* degree allowed the purchaser to compete for the *juren* degree in the Shuntian prefectural examinations instead of those of his home province.[18] The other option was the purchase of either a brevet title or an office diploma, for which a *jiansheng* degree was the necessary precondition. Even the brevet title, although sometimes called "empty title" (*xuxian* 虛銜) in Chinese, could serve as a stepping-stone to later purchase of a "substantive office" (*shizhi* 實職).[19] Given the huge investments in time and money people made in order to compete in the civil service examinations,[20] the incentive to shortcut or circumvent this torturous process through the payment of money was strong enough to make voluntary contributions attractive.

In Western scholarly literature, the *jiansheng* degree has received most attention as the stepping-stone from commoner status to gentry or official

17 Watari 1986.

18 Kondō 1963, 46.2, 89.

19 Chen 1968, 39–40.

20 Miyazaki 1976; Elman 1999.

status.[21] However, it should be kept in mind that the contribution system during the Qing dynasty penetrated the whole Imperial bureaucracy including appointment, advancement, commendation and reinstatement (after dismissal due to punishment) of officials. Moreover, the insecurity of office-holding allowed the state to exact even more contributions from the officials who strove to uphold their status. Thus, the state was able continually to secure its share of the irregular extra income officials were able to obtain from their positions (see below).[22]

The second characteristic, and already noted with some abhorrence by Pao Chao Hsieh in 1925, was that the sale of offices had full legal sanction in China. Moreover, it was highly codified. In France, the center of venality in Europe, the most important reference work used by both potential purchasers up to 1798 and today's scholars studying the sale of offices did not come from the laws of the state but from a description published in 1610 by an opponent of the system.[23] In China, the sale was legally codified in the *Precedents* (*shili* 事例), which have survived in full since the Qianlong era, but existed in only rudimentary form from the Ming dynasty.[24] The process of codification reached its peak in the Qianlong era (1735–1796) when in 1745 all rewards which did not involve the bestowal of substantive offices to commoners were codified as *Routine Precedents* (*Changli* 常例 or *Xianxing Shili* 現行事例). Only in times of financial emergencies (see below) were the *Routine Precedents* greatly expanded into *Temporary Precedents* (*Zanxing Shili* 暫行事例), which were limited in time and the revenue collected was earmarked for a specific purpose. These short-term contribution campaigns were also called "grand contributions" (*dajun* 大捐).[25]

The third characteristic of the Chinese sale of offices and even more of titles was its employment in the finance of famine relief and river conservancy measures. In Europe, most of the income obtained from the sale of offices was used to cover the "rising costs of sovereignty" of which war expendi-

21 Chang 1955, 103–109; Ho 1962, 49–52; Ch'ü 1962, 18–22. The most important study on the purchase of *jiansheng* degrees is still: Tang 1931, 432–444.

22 See: Chang 1962, 7–42.

23 Charles Loyseau, *Cinq livres du droit des offices* (Châteaudun, 1610), cited from: Doyle 1996, 7 ff.

24 See: Wu 2006, 70ff.

25 Xu Daling 1968, 77.

tures were the most important.[26] In China too, only matters of national interest were deemed sufficient to justify the sale of substantive offices. However, aside from contributions for military supplies, these included river conservancy and the needs of the capital Beijing in times of emergencies.[27] Famine relief in most cases was rewarded only according to the *Regular Precedents*, as were other local donations to public buildings, academies, etc.[28] The particular attitude towards war contributions is shown by an edict of November 5th, 1841, by the Daoguang emperor on the occasion of issuing *Regulations for Maritime Border Defense Contribution* to recover the costs of the First Opium War:

> If in the coastal provinces the gentry and merchants contribute silver to support military supplies, repair defense works, hire militias, build ships or cast cannons, these are all things advantageous for military supplies. These are all public-spirited people, and [their merits] are not less than those of warriors excelling themselves [in battle]. If we still reward them only according to the regular contribution statutes, this would not suffice to show encouragement. It is ordered that [contributors] have to be commended in a memorial, so that We can show our grace in an exceptional way. Moreover, the officials and commoners of other provinces who proceed to the maritime provinces to contribute capital for the support of the military supplies, shall also be listed for reward in the same manner. Their wish for advancement should not be obstructed.[29]

Contributions in kind, mentioned in the edict, played a more important role than in Europe (in the available literature on European venality I have not yet found any references to payment in kind for the purchase of an office). In times of war, contributions became a direct part of the military logistics with civilians supplying the troops with grain, building materials and even weapons being rewarded with titles and offices.

26 Reinhard 1974, 302.

27 Apart from large deficits in the treasury of the Board of Revenue (see below) this might at times include the supply of the capital stores with grain, or the delivery of copper.

28 "Qinding Libu Quanxuan Hanguan Zeli 欽定吏部銓選漢官則例," juan 8, "zali 雜例," ited from: Chen 1968, 38–39.

29 Zhongguo diyi lishi danganguan 1992, vol. 4, 310.

The Sale of Offices and Government Finance in Qing China

Which role did contributions in silver then play for government finance? The national economy of Late Imperial China, as Tanii Toshihito has shown, was built upon the belief that deficits (*kuikong* 虧空) in metropolitan or provincial treasuries should not be allowed to occur. Deficits were seen as an administrative problem, and punishments were meted out to the officials responsible.[30] However, because state revenue was dependent on fixed tax quota (*zheng'e* 正額) which did not allow for much flexibility, maintaining a positive balance of income over expenditures proved increasingly difficult. Thus, aside from the regular tax-based state revenue, a wide range of partly legalized irregular revenue developed with which the bureaucracy maintained itself and made up deficits within the treasuries. The sale of offices and titles was part of the government's legal anti-deficit policy.[31]

Revenue shortages mounted during the Jiaqing and Daoguang eras (1796 - 1850).[32] At the same time, according to a source published by Luo Yudong, income from contributions (i.e. the sale of offices and titles) began to make up a substantial part of the income of the treasury of the Board of Revenue.[33] To take the Daoguang era (1821–1850) as an example, Tang Xianglong in his study of the sale of licentiate (*jiansheng* 監生) degrees has calculated that during these 30 years the nationwide (excluding Zhili province) sale of 315,825 degrees yielded 33,886,530 *liang*. Of this revenue, 52% was delivered to the Board of Revenue, 24% went to the provincial treasuries, and the remainder was spent on public building measures, famine relief, military expenditure and other purposes.[34] Alongside with the regular contributions, of which the sale of *jiansheng* degrees formed a part, there were five "grand contributions" (selling office patents), of which three – in 1827, 1834, and 1842 – had a direct impact on the finances of the Board of Revenue treasury.

30 Tanii 2004.

31 Zhou 2000, 68–74; Iwai 2004, chap. 1, 3.

32 Zhou 2000, 64–119; Iwai 2004, chap. 3; Lin 2006.

33 See: "Linian Hubu yinku dajin ce 歷年戶部銀庫大進冊" (1724–1853), in: Luo 1979, 6–7. This source has been used by: Zhou 2000, 72 (only for the years 1840–1950); Iwai 2004, 89.

34 Tang 1931, 439–441.

Precedents of the Daoguang era	Begin	End	Contribution delivered to
Zhuozeng Changli 酌增常例 (Extended Regular Precedents)	Jan. 1827	Mar. 1828	Board of Revenue, Gansu province
Choubei Jingfei Shili 籌備經費事例 (Budget Supplementation Contribution)	Oct. 1833	Jul. 1834	Board of Revenue and provinces
Yugong Shili 豫工事例 (Henan Yellow River Conservancy Contribution)	June 1841 March 1843	Sept. 1842 Apr. 1844	Board of Revenue and provinces
Donghe Zankai Juanli 東河暫開捐例 (Temporary Contribution for Eastern Yellow River Conservancy)	Aug. 1844	1845?	Henan
Chouzhen Shili 籌賑事例 (Relief Contribution)	Aug. 1849	1850?	Shuntian prefecture

The *Extended Regular Precedents* were promulgated in 1827 to recover the deficit in the Board of Revenue treasury caused by the Grand Canal crisis.[35] The *Budget Supplementation Contribution* of 1833 and the *Henan Yellow River Conservancy Contribution* of 1841 were conducted under the pretext of famine relief and rebuilding measures at the Southern Grand Canal and the Yellow River dikes. In both cases the income was divided between the Board and the provincial treasuries. Moreover, these contributions were also used for war finance. In early 1828, part of the income from the *Extended Regular Precedents* was channeled to Gansu to finance the campaign against the Khoja revolts in Xinjiang. Part of the following *Budget Supplementation Contribution* of 1833 still went to fund the Xinjiang wars.[36] Finally, under the *Henan Yellow River Conservancy Contributions*, special *Regulations for Maritime Border Defense Contribution* (*Haijiang Juanshu Zhangcheng* 奏定海疆捐輸章程) were issued in December 1841. Contributions were accepted until 1843, in some coastal provinces until 1845. According to Mao Haijian's calculation, it yielded a silver income of at least over 13 million *liang*, of which 42% was directly used by the provinces to cover their costs of participating in the First Opium War, and 11% went into river conservancy. The appropriation of 32% of the income is not accounted for according to Mao Haijian.[37]

35 Xu 1968, 54–56. For the Grand Canal crisis see: Leonard 1996 and Jane Kate Leonard's paper in this volume.

36 Xu 1968, 56–57; For the Khoja revolts see: Newby 2005.

37 Mao 1996, 34–80.

At least part of this latter portion might have been used to replenish the treasury of the Board of Revenue, which in 1842 derived almost 60% of its income from contributions. From the two diagrams below it becomes clear that in fact only the grand campaigns, but not the regular sale of *jiansheng* degrees, were able substantially to relieve the pressure on the treasury of the Board of revenue:[38]

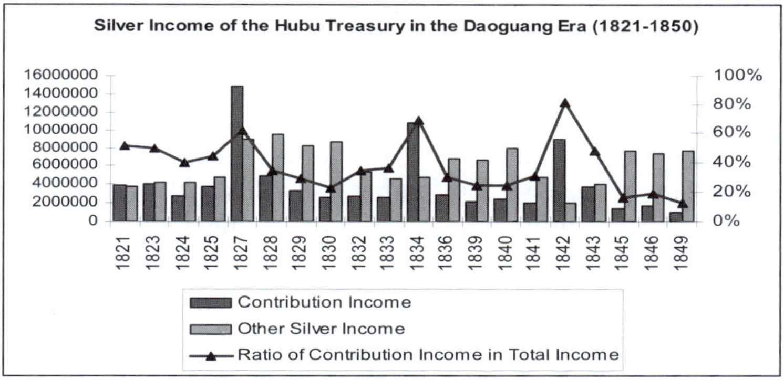

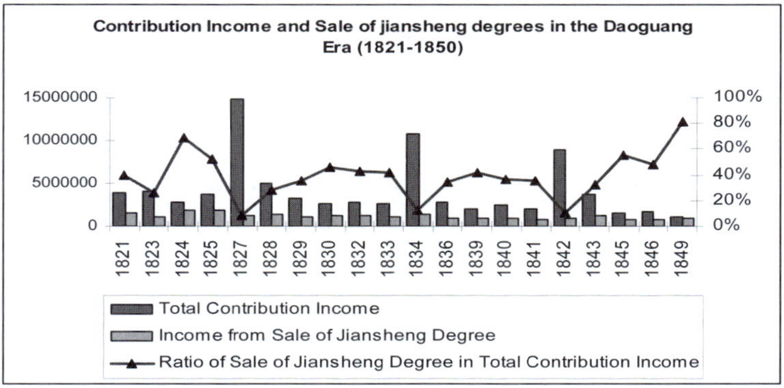

Thus, even though the total revenue yielded from the sale of offices was small compared with the regular revenue of the empire, contributions were

38 Compiled from: "Linian Hubu yinku dajin ce" (see note 33; in the original source as quoted by Luo Yudong, the total income of the Board Treasury consists of both silver and copper cash income. These diagrams are – as is Iwai's (2004, 89) – calculated on the basis of the silver income only); Tang 1931, 439–441.

indispensable as long as no alternative modes of deficit reduction (such as government loans) could be found.

The Price of an Office

The actual price of an office is not easy to determine, because to obtain an office patent did not automatically lead to appointment. Moreover, depending on the time and circumstances, one could choose between various options to proceed to eventual office-holding. Of course, the price and procedures changed over time. In order to better understand the process of obtaining an office through a contribution during the first half of the 19th century, a hypothetical case is constructed here. Given a commoner wanted to purchase an office, his options would have been the following. The potential purchaser would have first to buy a *jiansheng* degree; until the 1850s the price for this was generally 108 *liang*.[39] This could be done at any time according to the Regular Precedents, but the candidate then had to travel to Beijing or to commission a Beijing bank to handle his contribution. To purchase an office, one had to wait for a grand campaign. Many bought the degree together with the office patent. If it was a regular seal-holder office (*zhengyinguan* 正印官) such as the post of a magistrate (rank 7a), the purchaser would also have to buy an exemption from recommendation (*mian baoju* 免保舉). In the Military Supply Contribution (*Chouxiang Shili* 籌餉事例) promulgated in 1851, the prices for the office of magistrate and exemption from recommendation were 3,330 and 600 *liang* respectively.[40]

There are detailed pricelists for each office and item, but it is not clear, how the pricing system was originally constructed. There were no market prices or bidding for offices as in Europe, the only thing that happened when market forces were beginning to operate in the chaos of the post-Taiping era was that prices plunged. Until that time prices were fixed in the *Precedents*

39 Chang 1955, 104–105.

40 I have chosen the example of the Military Supply Contribution here, because this is the most complete set of regulations available to me at the moment, see: *Chouxiang Shili* 籌餉事例, in: *Qinding hubu haifang zhenggong xinli zhangcheng* (1968), vol. 2, 627ff. The *Yugong Ermao Shili Tiaokuan* 豫工二卯事例條款 (1843) seen at Beijing University Library does not include the *Regular Precedents*.

(tables of prices formed their main contents), with one such list being deducted from the last, mostly with a slight price reduction. Prices for single offices usually corresponded to the rank system with a steep curve from ranks 4a (the highest available provincial rank) to 6a, but quite a flat curve from 6b to non-commissioned officials; only the offices of magistrates (7a), salt administrators (e.g. the sub-assistant salt controller, *yanyunsi yunpan* 鹽運司運判 who is ranked 6b) and treasurers (8a) were priced above their rank, obviously in tacit acknowledgement of the irregular income these positions could yield.[41]

If no grand campaign was available at the time, the candidate could also simply purchase a degree and a brevet title, and then wait for the next better opportunity. For non-seal-holding offices, the brevet title could be the stepping stone for a regular office patent, although this was not the case for sealholders and some other important offices such as the above-mentioned salt administrators and treasurers. In the *Military Supply Contribution* (*Chouxiang Shili* 籌餉事例) promulgated in 1851 the brevet title of a second class sub-prefect (*tongpan* 通判, 6a) was specified as costing 1,600 *liang*. The title-holder paid 1,314 *liang* for the office diploma as compared with 2,460 *liang* paid by the *jiansheng* degree holder. This means that almost three-quarters (1,146 *liang*) of the price already paid for the brevet title (1,600 *liang*) could be deducted from the price of the substantive office.[42]

The office patent thus obtained entitled its holder to take part in the appointment procedures of the Board of Appointment (*buxuan* 部選). Upon registration at the Board, the purchaser became a candidate for office (*houxuan guan* 候選官). However, this was no guarantee of an actual appointment. The Board had to balance the interests of various types of candidates eligible for appointment including officials returning from the mourning or sick leave, new graduates from the civil service examinations, contributors (purchasers) and others; each of these types was grouped into an appoint-

41 See tables in Xu 1968, 111. The differences between metropolitan offices are less obvious.

42 "Chouxiang Shili 籌餉事例," p. 678; "Zengxiu xianxing changli 增修現行常例," in: *Qinding hubu haifang zhenggong xinli zhangcheng* (1968), pp. 896, 898. That these regulations were indeed applied is revealed in a memorial of the governor-general of Hunan and Hubei Cheng Qicai 程齊采 and governor of Hubei Xiyu 襲裕 (XF 1/12/19), cited in: Chen Kuanqiang 1968, 39–40.

ment class (*ban* 班).[43] Appointment took place on specified days of the month. For every vacancy which became available, a candidate was chosen from an appointment class. The sequence of classes was fixed by regulations, and this differed in odd and even months. With regards to the appointment of magistrates, purchasers did not have the best prospects, because this was the preferred employment for newly graduated *jinshi* and *juren*. Following the Daoguang era, the purchasers' class (*juanban* 捐班) occupied only four positions in a sequence of 23 (nos. 16–20 in the odd months and 7–11 in the even months, and there were never 23 vacancies available in any one month).[44] The appointment of the second-class subprefect was somewhat simpler and more favorable for purchasers. One selection cycle comprised six vacancies, and in odd months every second went to a purchaser.[45] Therefore, this office was very popular with purchasers.

Theoretically, holders of office patents had not only purchased the qualification for office, but were also eligible to being appointed. However their default appointment was only in odd months. Therefore, in practice, their chance of being appointed was very low. A purchaser thus needed to secure a better place in the appointment sequence. There were two ways to do this: first, one had to pay an additional fee in order to be eligible to appointment in both odd and even months. After this route also became congested, the Daoguang era introduced the priority (*banci* 班次, also called "*huayang* 花樣"). A candidate who purchased the highest priority – actually this meant that he had to pay double price for his office – would always be preferred once it was his class's turn in the appointment sequence.

The next available option was informal assignment (*fenfa* 分發). This meant that a candidate was sent as additional personnel – sometimes designated as "trainee" (*xuexi* 學習) at one of the Boards or as "intern" (*shiyong* 試用) at the provincial governments – to the post of his choice (initially the province or government office he was sent to was chosen by lot, later one could choose by paying an extra fee). Thereby, he became an expectant official (*houbuguan* 候補官) and was eligible to act as a substitute if the official in charge was temporarily absent (*shushi* 署事) or to do commissary work

43 The appointment procedures have been described in detail in: Wu 2004, 361–412.

44 *Guangxu Daqing Huidian Shili*, *juan* 9, cited from Wu 2004, 378.

45 *Guangxu Daqing Huidian Shili* 1991, *juan* 44: 1, 560.

in the informal bureaucracy (*chaiwei* 差委).[46] Informal assignment was also a way to familiarize oneself with the highest authorities in the hope of being recommended to regular office. Since the Yongzheng era there had been two kinds of official posts: only some of the vacancies were eligible to be filled through appointment by the Board (*xuanque* 選缺) in the process described above, and in many cases the provincial governor would select a candidate of his own choice (*tibu que* 題補缺).[47] Recommendation to office could thus provide an alternative route to office-holding.

Added together, the price of the various options in 1851 was as follows (in *liang*):

	Magistrate, 7a	Second class sub-prefect, 6a
Jiansheng degree	108	108
Basic price	3,330	2,460
Basic price including the purchase of a brevet title	--	2,914
Appointment both in even and odd months (*sanban* 三班, *bulun shuangdanyue xuanyong* 不論雙單月選用)	1,431	1,026
Exemption from recommendation (*juanmian baoju* 捐免保舉)	600	--
Informal assignment to province of choice (*zhisheng fenfa* 指省分發)	1,920	1,280
Highest priority group (*fenque xianyong* 分缺先用)	4,761	3,492
Total	12,150	8,366
Total including the purchase of a brevet title	--	8,820

These prices do not include the dues and fees that accompanied the purchase of an office, most notably the identity confirmations required at every step of the procedure (*yinjiefei* 印結費), patent fees (*zhaofei* 照費) and handling fee of the Boards (*fanshiyin* 飯食銀).[48] Together these fees could also amount to several hundred *liang*. They were an important source of extra income for the Beijing officials who did not receive the anti-corruption allowance, but they did not relate directly to government finances.

46 Wu 2004, 393–394.

47 This is also described in Skinner 1978, 1–77.

48 For the identity confirmation, see: Wu 2003, 1–32. According to one source the Board fee in the *Chouxiang Shili* was 8 *qian* for every 100 *liang*, see: "Minsheng chouban juanshu bingxiang zhuoyi tiaokuan 閩省籌辦捐輸兵餉酌議條款," in: *Fujian Shengli* 1964, 1062–1068.

Compared with the price of an office, the annual income situation of officials in Taiyuan prefecture, Shanxi province – not one of the "fattest posts" – in the 1880s appeared low:[49]

	Magistrate, 7a	Second class sub-prefect, 6a
1. Nominal basic salary	45	60
Actual amount paid (rounded)	14	42
2. Nominal allowance ("silver to nourish honesty")	1,000	1,200
Actual amount paid	900	1,080

On the purchaser's side, amortization of the purchase would take 7–13 years, given that only regular income was obtained. However, even though there was always the risk of being sent to a poor place (*kuque* 苦缺), contributors might speculate for much higher gain given that many offices had substantial irregular income from tax surcharges, handling fees and other sources which, as Chang Chung-li has shown, could by far exceed their combined earnings from regular salary and the anti-corruption allowance.[50]

From the standpoint of the central government, which according to the regulations received the lion's share if not all of the contributed silver, the sale of offices was a bargain. Only the basic salary was paid out of the regular tax income of the central government. The anti-corruption allowance came from the "meltage fee" (*haoxian* 耗羡), a surcharge paid by tax payers. This would mean that the central government could take as much as 270 resp. 139 years to repay its debt to the magistrate resp. second class sub-prefect in question (but only if full salary was paid). According to Chang Chung-li's estimate, the statutory basic salary of all civil and military officials (excluding the eight banners) was 1,398,303 *liang* (based on the number of regular officials employed in 1880).[51] According to the statistics published by Luo Yudong, the average annual income obtained by the Board of Revenue from contributions between 1724 and 1853 was about 3 million *liang*. In the 19th century, it surpassed 1 million even in meager years.[52] This would mean that the sale of offices fully paid the official salaries of the cen-

49 Gangyi 2002, 80–81, 107–108.
50 Chang Chung-li 1962, 15–34.
51 Ibid., 35–37.
52 Luo 1979, 6–7.

tral government. As in the European case, it was the subjects who had to pay the bill (see above).

Following the Xianfeng era (1851–1861), the nominal price for the office patent, appointment and informal assignment was no longer paid in full, and payment in kind and even in promissory notes became more common. According to an estimate of the Board of Revenue, the actual payment rate was 20–40% of the basic price and about 60% of the appointment mode and priority by 1869.[53] Moreover, contribution campaigns were organized by contribution bureaus (*juanju* 捐局) in the provinces and people did no longer have to travel to Beijing to receive an office patent. The income from the sale of office patents was used in the provinces instead of being remitted to Beijing. Thus, the central government lost an important source of revenue, and its role was reduced to issuing blank office patents and collecting patent and handling fees.

However, the Board of Revenue, keen to secure its income, in the same year created a new priority group above all others (called "*xinban yuque xian* 新班遇缺先"). Purchasers for this group had first to purchase the appointment in odd and even months and the highest of the old priority groups and above that again deliver 80% of the combined nominal price of the two in hard silver to the Board of Revenue.[54] Consequently, even though the sale of office patents surged because of the price discounts, many contributors opted to purchase the cheaper informal assignment without priority. With almost all available vacancies occupied by the expensive high priority groups and the growing pile-up of applicants in all available selection classes, there was a growing number of expectant officials with no hope of actually ever holding office. Expectancy thus became more and more divorced from regular

53 "Tongzhi ba nian Hubu zouding Dabacheng xuanbu zhangcheng 同治八年戶部奏定大八成選補章程," in: *Qinding hubu haifang zhenggong xinli zhangcheng* 1968, 130–131. The new priority group had apparently been necessary, because a struggle for dividing the shares from the contribution income was underway between the central government and the provinces during these years. In 1867, for example, Zuo Zongtang started a new provincial contribution campaign for supplying the troops in the fight against the Muslim rebellion in Gansu. He requested to collect the priority fees, originally reserved for Beijing, on behalf of the province and to have half of the stipulated silver price commuted into rice to be delivered directly to the military camps (Zuo Zongtang, "Tuiguang mijuan zhangcheng 推廣米捐章程" (23. 9. 1867), in: Zuo 1986: 465–6).

54 Ibid., 129–145; Xu 1968, 120.

office-holding. Simultaneously, the income of these expectants was also increasingly earned not from occasional appointment as substitute for absent regular office-holders (paid for by the central government) but from employment in the informal bureaucracy of the provinces such as Lijin tax bureaus, foreign offices, state enterprises, and the contribution bureaus themselves. The increase of government functions in the 19th century was not compensated for by an expansion of the regular bureaucracy, but by an increasing role of informal bureaus staffed with expectant officials, many if not most of whom had obtained their office patent through purchase.[55] This might have been the reason why office patents put on sale by the government continued to attract purchasers despite the fact that regular appointment became more and more difficult to attain.

Examinations vs. Purchase: The Family of Zhang Jixin

On the purchasers' side, the contribution system was not only directed at commoners seeking employment, however. Active officials themselves were also a continuous source for contribution revenue. Robert Marsh, who analyzed a sample of directories of provincial officials (*tongguanlu* 同官錄), has found out that young men from official families were most inclined to purchase their office by means of contributing. He assumed that this was due to the fact that "they were, on the average, the wealthiest stratum in the society."[56] But their access to resources was probably not the main reason for this phenomenon. Rather, family traditions might have played an important role. In France, once you bought an office, this secured your family position for generations, as offices were inheritable and sometimes even linked to nobility. In China, in order to maintain a family tradition, constant success in the civil service examinations was necessary. If the sons did not do well in the exams, this was a reason for grave concern for the fathers. Purchasing offices was the natural alternative. Moreover, as stated above, the system of

55 Xie 2001, 50–61; Leung 2002, 61–78. Zhou Xun in his *Shuhai Congtan* 蜀海叢談 (1903) lists 24 such bureaus in Sichuan, of which at least six had been established as early as the 1870s (Iwai 2004: 143–145). See also Jane Kate Leonard's paper in this volume.

56 Marsh 1962, 461.

punishments and the absence of appointment security compelled any official to invest continually in his own promotion and the promotion of his family members.

Zhang Jixin's 张集馨 (1800–1878) diary, which records the history of his family between 1800 and 1865, may serve as an example. Zhang's family came from Yizheng 儀征 county in Yangzhou prefecture, Jiangsu province. His father, Zhang Shifeng 張式封 (–1820), was a *shengyuan* and made his living from the family landholdings and as a teacher.[57] The family was active in competing for official posts by every means available including purchase and participation in the civil examinations. In Jixin's youth, the family fortunes were almost ruined, because Zhang Shifeng had to repay a debt of several thousand *liang* left by his younger brother who had borrowed money to purchase the post of a magistrate but died before he could be appointed. Nevertheless, the myth of the riches earned by officials made their elder brother assume that he had been cheated by Zhang Shifeng when the inheritance was divided (in fact only boxes with cloths). This led to a family feud.[58]

Zhang Jixin's biological elder brother Zhang Jicheng 張集成 did not succeed in his studies. In 1814, the relatives of his wife urged him to purchase a military post as a lieutenant at a Grand Canal transport station (*wei qianzong* 衛千總) in order to feed his family. Later in 1840 when Zhang Jixin was prefect of Taiyuanfu he supported his brother and planned to purchase a promotion in office for him. In 1843, Zhang Jicheng was removed from office for failing the transfer of navy boats to Beijing (the boats were stuck in shallow water). Zhang helped him to purchase a return to office (*juanfu* 捐復) whereafter he was transferred to Zhejiang.[59]

Zhang Jixin himself was ill when the licentiate exam (*yuanshi* 院士) took place in his home county in 1814. He went to Beijing and purchased a *jiansheng* degree in 1822 in order to take part in the Shuntian examination, where he was successful and became a *juren*. He took the entry test as a teacher in one of the Banner schools in Beijing (*jiaoxi* 教習), which allowed him to stay in the capital to prepare for the metropolitan examination. At that

57 Zhan 1981, 475.

58 Zhang 1981, 6.

59 Zhang 1981, 51, 72.

time, four members of the Zhang family competed in the exams. Finally, Zhang became a *jinshi* in 1828 at the second attempt.[60] Advancing on the regular path in various provincial offices, Zhang obtained several promotions in sub-rank due to contributions to military or relief campaigns. In 1848, as judicial commissioner of Sichuan (rank 3a), he received five sub-ranks and two recorded merits for contributing 5000 *liang* for famine relief after flooding in Jiangsu. This donation was not voluntary but had been ordered by Imperial decree.[61]

In 1851, Zhang was removed from his post as financial commissioner of Henan (rank 2b) and punished with military exile for allegedly having failed to prevent his subordinates from killing innocent Tibetans in his previous post as financial commissioner of Gansu. Theoretically, elevations of sub-rank could be used to cancel out punishments, but this held only for minor "public offenses" (*gongzui* 公罪) punished with suspension of salary or demotion in sub-rank. In this case they were useless. A year later, in late 1852, Zhang was given the 4th rank and appointed judicial commissioner of Henan (actually a 3a position).[62] This year is missing from Zhang's diary, so it is not clear whether Zhang made a contribution in order to accelerate his return to office (*juanfu* 捐復).[63] One year later, Zhang was removed from office again (this time from the post of a financial commissioner of Zhili, rank 2b) and restored to the 5th rank only in 1855.[64] In 1857, he was financial commissioner of Gansu again but only with the 4th rank. In the same year, he contributed 6000 *liang* for a military campaign against the Tibetans in Gansu hoping to obtain a plume decoration (*hualing* 花翎). However, at this time the price for a plume decoration was increased to 7000 *liang* and an Imperial edict urged him to send another 1000.[65]

60 Zhan 1981, 478; Zhang 1981, 13.

61 Zhang 1981, 106. Other promotions reported: Promotion of one permanent sub-rank in 1846, promotion of three sub-ranks in 1860 for contributing 3000 liang for military supplies (Zhang 1981, 84; Zhan 1981, 485).

62 Zhan 1981, 483.

63 This was possible according to "Zengxiu chouxiang shili tiaokuan", in: *Qinding hubu haifang zhenggong xinli zhangcheng* 1968, 345–436). Although I used a later edition of 1889, the paragraph is marked as having been part of the original regulations promulgated in 1851.

64 Zhan 1981, 484

65 Zhang 1981, 220.

Zhang's cousin and younger brother by adoption, Zhang Jisheng 張集聲 (1837–1869), probably was a *jiansheng*. He purchased a post of an assistant department director (*yuanwailang* 員外郎, rank 5b) in the metropolitan bureaucracy, but was rejected and obtained only the patent of a secretary in the Supervisorate of Imperial Instruction (*zhanshifu zhubu* 詹事府主簿, rank 7b). In 1863, he used the opportunity provided by the Shaanxi Rice Contribution Campaign, a military contribution campaign whose proceeds went towards troop provisioning during the campaigns against the Muslim uprising in Shaanxi and Gansu. Zhang Jisheng now made his contribution from a better position. He was successful and added informal assignment (*fenfa* 分發) to the Board of Revenue where he worked in 1863. The reason why he was interested in such a low-paid metropolitan position was that this provided him with the opportunity to take part in the Shuntian prefectural examination, which he passed as a *juren* in 1867. Unfortunately, he died two years later.[66]

Zhang Jixin's only son Zhang Languan 張蘭官 (1843–?) made a similar career as his uncle. Due to the position of his father, he was registered at the Imperial Academy as a privilege student (*enyin* 恩蔭) in 1850 aged just 8 *sui*. Later he purchased the post of a department director (*langzhong* 郎中), with rank 5a the highest available metropolitan position by contribution, but was also rejected and given only the post of a secretary (*zhushi* 主事, rank 6a). He had to make an additional contribution (*jiajuan* 加捐) of 1,000 liang in Beijing in order to obtain the office patent of an assistant department director (*yuanwailang* 員外郎, rank 5b). Only in 1866, Languan finally succeeded in purchasing the office of a *langzhong* 郎中 with informal assignment to the Board of War. By paying an additional sum, he also obtained a rise in sub-rank by six grades (*jia liu ji* 加六級), and for his father the honorary title of the 2nd rank (*fengdian* 封典). In 1870, he finally became a *juren* in the Shuntian examination.[67]

Zhang Jixin also supported the two sons of his elder brother, Quanguan 張全官 (1825–?, called Daquan 大全) and Erquan 二全 (1827–?), by purchasing offices for them. In 1860, as financial commissioner of Fujian, Zhang purchased the post of a magistrate (*zhixian* 知縣, 7a) for Daquan

66 Zhang 1981, 376; Zhan 1981, 486.

67 Zhang 1981, 129, 376; Zhan 1981, 487–488.

with the brevet rank of an assistant prefect (*tongzhi* 同知, 5a) and informal assignment to Zhejiang. Unfortunately, the local contribution campaign was closed after the 25th registration period (*mao* 卯). Thus Daquan, who was in the 26th registration period, only obtained the post of an assistant magistrate (*xiancheng* 縣丞, 8a). In late 1864, when Zhang Jixin was judicial commissioner of Shaanxi, but accompanied Shaanxi troops to Gansu to quell the Muslim rebellion, he contributed 1,600 *shi* of grain with a nominal value of over 5,000 *liang* (in fact, Zhang had used only 2,000 *liang* of *Kuping* silver) for Lei Zhengwan 雷正綰's starving troops. In this way, Daquan was included in the recommendation list for military merits and at the same time was in the highest priority cohort available (called "*yuque jinxian jixuan* 遇缺儘先即選"). Zhang believed that in this way his nephew might not face the problems that his cousin and son had encountered, but would surely be appointed assistant magistrate.[68] With Erquan, Zhang asked another military commander, Cao Kezhong 曹克忠, for help in purchasing the post of an assistant department director (*yuanwailang* 員外郎, 5b) in the metropolitan bureaucracy with informal assignment to a board.[69]

Zhang actually thought that his two nephews, both in their early forties, were good for nothing and he had grave doubts that they would make good officials. His main motivation in purchasing offices for them was the future of the family:

> The brothers are both in their forties, but have not achieved anything. Left in their home county their intellectual horizon will narrow even further. If they are given offices, [at least] they will have social intercourse with offical circles and be influenced by them. This will probably broaden [their horizon] and in the future will save us from having their children and grandchildren growing up and marrying only in Sanjiacun village with no one who [is able to] make the family prosper.[70]

This example shows three characteristics of the "social market"[71] for office patents in the 19th century. First, an official career was still highly attractive,

68 Zhang 1981, 376, 382.

69 Zhang 1981, 404.

70 Ibid.

71 The term was contributed by Harald Witthöft during the discussion at the October 2006 workshop of the project.

even if only as an expectant official. Second, to purchase an office was a family business, and the stability of the family occupation beyond the life span of one generation was as important for the Chinese purchaser as it was for the French. Third, the widespread sale of offices did not fundamentally devaluate meritocracy (the civil service examinations), rather the one would be used to supplement the other. Moreover, the example of Zhang Daquan's military contribution and Zhang Jixin's purchase of a plume decoration shows that the idea of merit was not completely absent from the purchase system.

Conclusions

In European history, venality of office was largely made illegal in the course of the late 18th and early 19th century. Two aspects were crucial for this development: first, the introduction of meritocracy in public employment, which, at least indirectly, was influenced by the Chinese example;[72] and second, the introduction of more efficient means of public finance, in which Prussia led the way.[73] By designating the conferment of an office for the delivery of money or assets as a reward for a contribution and subjecting it to strict legal regulations, the Qing government solved the contradiction between the sale of offices and the selection of officials by meritocratic examinations. At the same time, being unable to adapt its financial system to the permanent crisis of dike breaks, war, and foreign aggression, it became increasingly dependent on the sale of offices as a means of anti-deficit policy. From the point of view of the purchasers, the purchase system never replaced the examination system as an important way to regular office, as Kondō Hideki has shown for the position of the *xian* and *zhou* magistrate.[74] On the other hand, the sale of office patents became increasingly divorced from regular appointment to office. Divorcing the sale of office patents from the sale of a favorable place in the appointment procedures, not only channeled a larger portion of the income from venality to the provinces instead of

72 Chang 1942; Teng 1943; Menzel 1956; Guy 1963; Wunder 1993.

73 Möller 1980.

74 Kondō 1963.

the Board of Revenue, it also created an abundance of expectant officials who could staff the burgeoning local sub-bureaucracies which offered favorable alternatives to regular employment. Thus, we may ask the question whether the successful sale of offices prevented necessary reforms of the financial system and the structure of the bureaucracy. A comparison of European and Chinese venality may lead us to a better understanding of China's diverging development in the 19th century. Therefore, more research on the actual functioning of the Chinese purchase system and its social and political implications is necessary.

Bibliography

"The Sale of Official Rank, Adopted by the Government of China for Increasing its Revenue; Translation of a Proclamation Calling on the People to Come Forward and Make Purchases." *The Chinese Repository* XIII (1849): 207–209.

Bruce, Anthony (1980). *The Purchase System in the British Army, 1660–1871*. London: Royal Historical Society.

Ch'ü, T'ung-tsu (1962). *Local Government in China under the Ch'ing*. Cambridge, MA: Harvard University.

Chang, Chung-li (1955). *The Chinese Gentry: Studies on Their Role in Ninteenth-Century Chinese Society*. Seattle, WA: University of Washington Press.

Chang, Chung-li (1962). *The Income of the Chinese Gentry*. Seattle, WA: University of Washington Press.

Chang, Y. Z. (1942). "China and English Civil Service Reform." *The American Historical Review* 47.3 (Apr.): 539–544.

Chen Kuanqiang 陳寬強 (1968). *Qingdai juanna zhidu* 清代捐納制度 (The Qing Contribution System). Taipei: n.p.

Doyle, William (1996). *Venality: The Sale of Offices in Eighteenth-century France*. Oxford: Clarendon Press.

Elman, Benjamin A. (1999). *A Cultural History of Civil Examinations in Late Imperial China*. Berkeley, CA: University of California Press.

Fujian Shengli 福建省例 (Provincial Regulations of Fujian), ed. by Taiwan yinhang jingji yanjiushi 臺灣銀行經濟研究室. Taibei: Taiwan yinhang, 1964 (*Taiwan wenxian congkan* 臺灣文獻叢刊, 199), cit. from: http://www.sinica.edu.tw/ftms-bin/ftmsw3.

Gangyi 剛毅 et al. (eds.) (2002). *Jinzheng jiyao* 晉政輯要 (Elements of the Administration of Shanxi Province). In *Xuxiu siku quanshu* 續修四庫全書. Shanghai: Shanghai guji, vol. 883–884.

Guy, Basil J. (1963). "The Chinese Examination System and France, 1569–1847." *Studies on Voltaire and the Eighteenth Century* 25: 741–778.

Ho Ping-ti (1962). *The Ladder of Success in Imperial China*. New York, NY: Columbia University Press.

Hsieh, Pao Chao (1925). *The Government of China (1644–1911)*. Baltimore: John Hopkins University Press.

Iwai Shigeki 岩井茂樹 (2004). *Chûgoku kinsei zaiseishi no kenkyû* 中国近世財政史の研究 (A Study of the Fiscal System in Early Modern China). Kyoto: Kyoto daigaku gakujutsukai.

Kondō Hideki 近藤秀樹 (1963). "Shindai no ennō to kanryō shakai no shūmatsu 清代の捐納と官僚社会の終末" (The Qing Contribution System and the End of the Bureacratic Society). *Shirin* 史林 46.2: 82–110; 46.3: 77–100; 46.4: 60–85.

Leban, Carl (1990). "Sale of Office or Fines in the Later Han: A Matter of Interpretation." In Albert E. Dien (ed.). *State and Society in Early Medieval China*. Stanford, CA: Stanford University Press, pp. 31–47.

Leonard, Jane Kate (1996). *Controlling from Afar: The Daoguang Emperor's Management of the Grand Canal Crisis, 1824–1826*. Ann Arbor, MI: University of Michigan.

Leung, Philip Yuen-sang (2002). "Crisis Management and Institutional Reform: The Expectant Official in the Late Qing." In R. J. Antony and J. K. Leonard (eds.). *Dragons, Tigers, and Dogs: Qing Crisis Management and the Boundaries of State Power in Late Imperial China*. Ithaca, NY: Cornell University Press, pp. 61–78.

Lin Man-houng (2006). *China Upside Down: Currency, Society, and Ideologies, 1808–1856*. Cambridge, Mass.: Harvard University Asia Center.

Luo Yudong 羅玉東 (1979). *Zhongguo lijin shi* 中國釐金史 (History of the Likin Tax). *Jindai Zhonguo shiliao congkanxubian*, vol. 612. Taibei: Wenhai.

Malettke, Klaus (ed.) (1980). *Ämterkäuflichkeit: Aspekte Sozialer Mobilität im Europäischen Vergleich (17. und 18. Jahrhundert)*. West Berlin: Colloquium.

Mao Haijian 茅海建 (1996). "Yapian zhanzheng qingchao junfei kao 鴉片戰爭清朝軍費考" (Investigation of the Military Expenditures of the Qing Dynasty during the First Opium War). *Jindaishi Yanjiu* 6: 34–80.

Marsh, Robert M. (1962). "The Venality of Provincial Office in China and in Comparative Perspective." *Comparative Studies in Society and History* 4.4: 454–466.

Menzel, Johanna M. (1956). "The Sinophilism of J. H. G. Justi." *Journal of the History of Ideas* 17.3 (June): 300–310.

Miyazaki, Ichisada (1976). *China's Examination Hell: The Civil Service Examinations of Imperial China*. Translated by Conrad Schirokauer. New York, NY: Weatherhill.

Möller, Horst (1980). "Ämterkäuflichkeit in Brandenburg-Preußen im 17. und 19. Jahrhundert." In Klaus Malettke (ed.). *Ämterkäuflichkeit: Aspekte Sozialer Mobilität im Europäischen Vergleich (17. und 18. Jahrhundert)*. West Berlin: Colloquium, pp. 156–176.

Montesquieu, Charles de. *The Spirit of the Laws*. New York, NY: Hafner, 1949.

Mote, Frederick W. (1974). "The T'u-Mu Incident of 1449." In Edward L. Dreyer, Frank Algerton Kierman and John King Fairbank (eds.). *Chinese Ways in Warfare*. Cambridge, MA: Harvard University Press, pp. 243–272.

Mousnier, Roland (1971). *La venalité des offices sous Henri IV et Louis XIII*. Paris: Université de France.

Newby, Laura J. (2005). *The Empire and the Khanate: A Political History of Qing Relations with Khoqand c. 1760 – 1860*. Leiden: Brill.

Parry, John Horace (1953). *The Sale of Public Office in the Spanish Indies under the Hapsburgs*. Berkeley, CA: University of California.

Qian Bocheng 錢伯城 (ed.) (1990). *Guwen guanzhi xinbian* 古文觀止新編 (A New Edition of the Anthology of Classical Prose). Shanghai: Shanghai Guji.

Qinding hubu haifang zhenggong xinli zhangcheng 钦定户部海防郑工新例章程 (New Imperial Precedents and Regulations for the Maritime Defence and Zhengzhou Yellow River Conservancy Contributions, 1889). Taibei: Chengwen, 1968.

Guangxu Daqing Huidian Shili 光緒大清會典事例 (Guangxu 25 nian 光緒二十五年 [1899]). Beijing: Zhonghua shuju, 1991.

Reinhard, Wolfgang (1974). "Staatsmacht als Kreditproblem: Zur Struktur und Funktion des frühneuzeitlichen Ämterhandels." *Vierteljahrschrift für Sozial- und Wirtschaftsgeschichte* 61: 289–319.

Schuller, Wolfgang (1994). "Kaiser Julian und der Ämterkauf." In Rosmarie Günther (ed.). *E fontibus haurire: Beiträge zur römischen Geschichte und zu ihren Hilfswissenschaften*. Paderborn: Schöningh, pp. 197–202.

Shang Yang (1928). *Book of the Lord Shang: A Classic of the Chinese School of Law*. Translated by Jan Julius Duyvendak. London: Probsthain.

Skinner, G. W. (1978). "Cities and the Hierarchy of Local Systems." In A. P. Wolf (ed.). *Studies in Chinese Society*. Stanford, CA: Stanford University Press, pp. 1–77.

Swart, Koenraad Walter (1949). *Sale of Offices in the Seventeenth Century*. S'Gravenhage: Martinus Nijhoff.

Tang Xianglong 湯象龍 (1931). "Daoguangchao juanjian zhi tongji 道光朝捐監之統計" (A Statistics of the Sale of *jiansheng* Degrees during the Daoguang Era). *Shehui Kexue Zazhi* 社會科學雜志 2.4: 432–444.

Tanii Toshihito 谷井俊仁 (2004). "Shichō gengaku shugi zaisei no ronri 清朝原額主義財政の論理" (The Logic of the Principle of Fixed Quota in the Fiscal System of the Qing Dynasty). In Iwai Shigeki 岩井茂樹 (ed.). *Chūgoku kinsei shakai no chitsujo keisei* 中国近世社会の秩序形成 (The Formation of Social Order in Early Modern China). Kyoto: Kyoto daigaku, pp. 414–440.

Teng, Ssu-yu (1943). "Chinese Influence on The Western Examination System: I. Introduction." *Harvard Journal of Asiatic Studies* 7.4 (Sep.): 267–312.

Watari Masuhiro 渡昌弘 (1986). "Mindai ennō nyūkan gaikō 明代捐納入監概観" (Entering the *Guozijian* by Contribution during the Ming Dynasty). *Shūkan Tōyōgaku* 集刊東洋學 56 (Nov.): 20–35.

Wu Yue 伍躍 (2003). "Ennō to inketsu ni tsuite: Shin dai ennō seido ronkō 捐納と印結について：清代捐納制度論考（二）" (On Contributions and the Identity Confirmations: Explorations of the Qing Contribution System (2)) *Shirin* 史林 86.1: 1–32.

Wu Yue 伍躍 (2004). "Shindai no ennō seido to kōho seido ni tsuite 清代の捐納制度と候補制度について" (The Qing Contribution System and the Expectancy System). In Iwai Shigeki 岩井茂樹 (ed.). *Chūgoku kinsei shakai no chitsujo keisei* 中国近世社会の秩序形成 (The Formation of Social Order in Early Modern China). Kyoto: Kyoto daigaku, pp. 361–412.

Wu Yue 伍躍 (2006). "Mingdai juanna zhidu shitan 明代捐納試探" (Preliminary Notes on Ming Contributions). In Zhu Chengru 朱誠如, Wang Tianyou 王天有 (eds.). *Ming Qing Luncong* 明清論叢. Beijing: Zijincheng chubanshe, 7: 55–80.

Wunder, Bernd (1993). "Das Prüfungsprinzip und die Entstehung der Beamtenschaft in Deutschland." *Jahrbuch für Wirtschaftsgeschichte* 1: 11–26.

Xie Junmei 謝俊美 (2001). "Wanqing maiguan yujue xintan: jianlun juanna zhidu yu Qingchao miewang 晚清賣官鬻爵新探：兼論捐納制度與清朝滅亡" (New Explorations of the Sale of Offices during Qing Dynasty: The Contribution System and the Decline of the Qing Dynasty). *Huadong Shifan Daxue Xuebao (Zhexue shehui kexue ban)* 33.5 (Sept.): 50–61.

Xu Daling 許大齡 (1968). *Qingdai juanna zhidu* 清代捐納制度 (The Qing Contribution System). Hong Kong: Longmen Shudian.

Yugong Ermao Shili Tiaokuan 豫工二卯事例條款. Printed by Xu Xia Xuan ji 徐霞軒記. Daoguang 23 [1843] (Beijing University library).

Zhan Sixian 詹嗣賢 (1981). "Shiqingzhai zhuren nianpu 時晴齋主人年譜" (Chronological Biography of Zhang Jixin). In Zhang Jixin 张集馨 (1981). *Daoxian huanhai jianwenlu* 道咸宦海見聞錄 (Experiences in Official

Circles during the Daguang and Xianfeng Eras). Beijing: Zhonghua Shuju, 475–488.

Zhang Jixin 张集馨 (1981). *Daoxian huanhai jianwenlu* 道咸宦海見聞錄 (Experiences in Official Circles during the Daguang and Xianfeng Eras). Beijing: Zhonghua Shuju.

Zhongguo diyi lishi danganguan, ed. (1992). *Yapian zhanzheng dang'an shiliao* 鴉片戰爭檔案史料 (Archival Material of the Opium Wars). Tianjin: Tianjin Guji.

Zhou Yumin 周育民 (2000). *Wanqing caizheng yu shehui bianqian* 晚清財政與社會變遷 (Late Qing Fiscal Policy and Social Change). Shanghai: Renmin.

Zuo Zongtang (1986). *Zuo Zongtang quanji* 左宗棠全集 (Collected Works of Zuo Zongtang). Shanghai: Shanghai Shudian, vol. 3.

Layers of Deception: Counterfeiting Cases in the Mid-Qing

Roger Greatrex

Introduction

Currency-based economies, as opposed to straightforward bartering, rely on the belief of those who use the currencies, be they coinage or paper currency, in the validity and value attributed to the currency instruments they have at their disposal. For this reason, the crime of counterfeiting strikes at the very heart of a country's economic prosperity. Distrust in the validity or value of a currency questions its perceived purchasing power and thus impedes its intended use as an instrument to facilitate commerce. Today crimes linked to the illegal manipulation of credit card information and digital banking information send significant tremors through the hearts of private citizens and banking institutions alike; in former times anxiety as to the genuineness and convertibility of the currency that citizens had at their disposal aroused similar feelings. In the west, since early times golden, silver and copper currencies, usually but not always round in shape, have carried the images of rulers and various information in a multiplicity of shapes and styles, making use of both sides of the coin. Chinese coinage, at least from the seventh century until the end of the eighteenth century followed one principal pattern. Coins were round with a square central hole, and they never carried the images of rulers. On the obverse of the coin there were four Chinese characters. These were the name of the reign-period during which the coin was minted and a word signifying 'coinage' (usually *tongbao*), with one Chinese character each in the four quadrants of the coin. On the coin's reverse in early times there may, but not necessarily, be found marks identifying where it was minted. From the Ming dynasty onward greater use was made of the reverse of coins, with information as to the value of the coin being shown, a trend that continued and developed in the Qing dynasty, to the extent that we may say that currency become genuinely double-sided from the seventeenth century onwards. This rendered counterfeiting more difficult, but does not seem to have deterred those intent on doing do.

With regard to the question of what Chinese coins themselves were actually made of, in this paper the expression *tongqian* will be translated throughout as 'copper coinage', although to be more precise *tong* was a general designation for the raw material used in the making of cash, which due to the introduction of other metals in the production process was, in fact, bronze. Scientific tests of the composition of coins have revealed that Tang dynasty coins minted in the early eighth century contained between 57% - 80% copper, 10% - 34% lead, 4% - 9% tin and small amounts of iron.[1] The percentage of copper rarely rose above 80%, and more usually hovered around 65% on average over the following centuries. In the early fifteenth century, coins were composed of approximately 74% copper, 17% lead, 7% tin and traces of zinc and iron, and in the early seventeenth century 60% copper, 6% lead, 2% tin and 32% zinc. During the reign of the Qianlong Emperor, the period that this paper focuses on, the composition of coins was roughly 56% copper, 4% lead, 37% zinc and a trace of tin.[2]

As in all countries, from early times there have existed in China laws and administrative regulations stipulating dire punishment for those who counterfeited silver or copper coinage, and later falsified paper currency, debased coinage by clipping so as to obtain copper or silver, or destroyed copper coinage to produce household or religious items. A decree of 729 forbade the unauthorised production and circulation of all copper products, which is explained in the text of the decree as expressly referring to coins[3], and paragraph 391 of the *Tang Legal Code* of 737 punished counterfeiting with life exile at a distance of three thousand *li*. The commentary stipulates that if the arrest was made before the actual production of coins had begun, the punishment would be reduced to two years of penal servitude, and further that if the tools themselves were not as yet fully prepared the punishment would be further reduced to one hundred blows with the heavy rod.[4]

1 Liu Jun and Liu Jianmin 1999, 138.

2 Ibid., 146.

3 *Tang da zhaoling ji* 112, 533.

4 *Tanglü shuyi* 26, 480.

Tang legislation was continued in the Song dynasty where it is repeated in the *Song Penal Conspectus* of 962, with the addition of two appendices, one of which is a decree of 931 of Li Dan of the Later Tang prohibiting the production and circulation of iron and tin alloy coins.[5] With regard to administrative regulations, an edict promulgated early in the reign of the first emperor of the Song dynasty, Zhao Kuangyin, in 967 forbids the production of counterfeit coinage, and the debasement of coins through clipping.[6] In 971 a further edict prohibited the production of false gold.[7] In the reign of Zhao Kuangyin's successor Zhao Jiong another edict was promulgated in 982 forbidding the production of counterfeit coinage of lead or tin, or of substandard copper cash, which resulted in the total weight of one thousand cash being less than the standard four *jin* of copper.[8] With regard to the misuse of coinage, in 991 a decree expressly forbade "illegally melting down copper coinage to produce household articles."[9] That this problem remained unresolved is demonstrated by edicts later in the Song dynasty, such as that promulgated by Zhao Ji in 1111 forbidding the use of two types of counterfeit currency, one of tin and the other of iron, in the north-west region.[10] In the Southern Song dynasty, the *Classified Legal Clauses Effective in the Qingyuan period* of 1202 states that the punishment for counterfeiting was strangulation, and goes on to itemize the various degrees of lenience permitted those who informed the authorities regarding the crime.[11]

In the Ming dynasty the stipulations of the *Tang Legal Code* were perpetuated, but the problem of counterfeiting was equally perpetual. Dong Gu (*jinshi* 1516) writes that when he first visited the capital, he found that all the traders used debased currency, and were only willing therefore to accept coins at half their nominal value.[12] A few years later counterfeiting was so rife that the value of coins could, on occasion, sink to only one quarter of

5 *Song xingtong* 26, 462f.

6 *Song da zhaoling ji* 198, 730.

7 Ibid. 198, 731.

8 Ibid. 183, 664.

9 *Songchao yanyi yimou lu* 2, 13; Greatrex 1996, 95.

10 *Song da zhaoling ji* 184, 669.

11 *Qingyuan tiaofa shilei* 29, 278.

12 *Bili zacun* A, 58.

their nominal value.[13] The Ming Code continued the stringent punishment of counterfeiters, stipulating death by strangulation for both the instigators and the artisans who carried out the actual production, and a reduction by one grade for those who knew of the production but failed to inform the authorities. The mere use of one string of counterfeited cash in a commercial transaction was punishable by one month bearing the cangue.[14]

A measure repeatedly attempted to bring about an end to the problem of counterfeit copper cash was the forbidding of the usage of copper coinage in commercial transactions altogether, and the enforcement of the use of paper currency. Such interdictions were promulgated from time to time throughout the Ming dynasty, for example in 1394 when the surrender of all copper cash to the authorities was required[15], and in 1448 when the Wardens' Offices of the Five Wards of the capital were instructed to fine offenders ten times the value of the copper coinage that they had in their possession.[16] However such orders were powerless to hinder the use of copper cash by the populace for any great length of time.

One reason is that copper cash remained in usage for centuries after their minting. Lu Shen (1477–1544) writes that in his youth people still used coins dating from the Song dynasty, and that even Tang and Yuan dynasty coins were still in circulation.[17] Gu Yanwu (1613–82) echoes Lu's words, writing that in his youth, one hundred and fifty years later, in the marketplace one encountered various sorts of Northern and Southern Song copper cash, and even coins dating from the Tang.[18]

The fundamental problem, as clearly expressed by Hans Ulrich Vogel, is that in imperial China the economic mechanisms for counterfeiting came into play when the nominal value of coinage was higher than its intrinsic value; in this case counterfeiting occurred. When the nominal value was lower than its intrinsic value, coins would be melted down to produce everyday articles, or even eventually for further counterfeiting.[19] The latter case is

13 *Ming Wuzong shilu* 83, 6b.
14 *Da Ming huidian* 170, 12a.
15 *Ming Taizu shilu* 234, 2a.
16 *Ming Yingzong shilu* 166, 2a.
17 *Yanxian lu* 10.
18 *Rizhi lu jishi* 11, 29a.
19 Vogel 1989.

exemplified by the following passage in an official administrative record: "These days one can obtain more than eight *jin* of copper by destroying one thousand cash; the value of copper is greater than that of the coins themselves. People can obtain double the profit. If legal measures are not stringent, it will be impossible to prohibit such behaviour."[20] During the reign of the Qianlong Emperor, so as to prevent the destruction of copper cash and the production of counterfeit debased coinage, a suggestion was made by the Zhejiang Provincial Administration Commissioner Zhang Zhenruo that tin should be introduced into the copper at the time of minting rendering the coinage brittle and unsuitable for use in the production of other copper items. However this proposal failed to receive imperial support, and the Qianlong Emperor instead favoured a return to the use of silver for commercial transactions.

The problem of the nominal and intrinsic value of copper coinage became increasingly acute in the reign of the Qianlong Emperor, and at times each province minted its own cash. The value of copper increased significantly and, directly related to the inferior quality of official cash, the production of counterfeit coinage flourished. Eventually a departure from the traditional relationship between the nominal and intrinsic value of coinage was proposed by Liang Zhangju (1775–1849) who wrote in his '*Proposal to mint large denomination coins* (*Qing zhu daqian*)': "It is not necessary to use ten cash worth of copper for a large denomination ten-coin or one hundred cash worth of copper for a hundred-coin [...] This will result by itself in the end of the use of counterfeit coinage and foreign currency that people are hoarding."[21] However, his suggestion found opponents, and the de-linking of the nominal and the intrinsic value of cash would remain an unresolved issue for years to come.

Published historical materials dealing with counterfeiting cases

The study of counterfeiting in practice is necessarily undertaken principally through the examination of official documents and legal proceedings, al-

20 *Qingchao wenxian tongkao* 14, 4972b.

21 *Langji congtan.*

though anecdotal materials, as I have shown above, can be of value. For the pre-Song period, for example, four accounts of the private casting of metal objects, two of which concern counterfeiting, are recounted in an early Song encyclopedia. Each of them is connected in some way to Buddhism, either to monks or by being set in the precincts of a Buddhist temple.[22] The connection is clear. Buddhist temples contained metal religious statuary and possessed copper bells, and thus attracted miscreants who received their just retribution. While these stories are probably apocryphal, they nevertheless bear witness to a common crime.

Legal codes and administrative regulations for each dynasty are readily available. However, with regard to case materials, which can provide us information regarding the social status and economic conditions of the counterfeiters themselves, the situation is less promising. The late-Southern Song *Collection of Enlightened Judgments by Celebrated Judges* takes up the problem of counterfeit products, such as foodstuffs and medicine, in the market-place,[23] and makes mention on several occasions to cases involving forged seals and documents,[24] but only gives one example of a judgment concerning counterfeit currency.[25] The situation regarding the Ming dynasty is a little better. The *Collection of Classified Legal Clauses Effective during the August Ming Dynasty* includes six cases between 1476 and 1491, which occurred in Suzhou, Henan, Shanxi and Yunnan. The cases provide us with a good account of the authorities' view of counterfeiting, but do not go into the details of each case sufficiently to allow us to understand the social and economic ramifications of the crimes.[26]

For the Qing dynasty, the situation is altogether different. Two collections of legal cases, the well-known *Xing'an huilan* or *Conspectus of Penal Cases* of 1834, and the rather less well-studied *Bo'an xinbian* or *New Collection of Revised Cases* of 1781 provide us with more than twenty cases to study; these and other cases in legal compendia will be mentioned again below. However, it is the single case in the *Bo'an xinbian* that tells us the

22 *Taiping guangji* 113, 784, 116, 807–809.

23 *Minggong shupan qingming ji* 14, 528.

24 Ibid. 2, 52 and 11, 422.

25 Ibid. 12, 466.

26 *Huang Ming tiaofa shilei zuan* 42, vol 2, 250–255.

most about counterfeiting and legal intricacies of assigning guilt and sentencing involved. The events of the case of Chen Xiao from Qingyang County in Anhui that unfolded in 1768 and 1769 are remarkable reading, and adumbrate the widespread economic consequences of his crime.[27]

If our detailed knowledge of counterfeiting in the Qing dynasty were limited to this case, little more could be known. However, preliminary research in the Number One Historical Archive in Beijing on cases handled by the Court of Judicial Review (*dali si*) in 1767, the year preceding Chen Xiao's malfeasance, revealed an unexpectedly large number of cases concerning counterfeiting. The cases mentioned in the following pages originate in part from research in these archival materials. Taken cumulatively, something beyond the scope of this short paper but which will be presented in a proposed monograph, the cases allow us to obtain a clear understanding of counterfeiting, the social and economic conditions of its perpetrators, and permit us to draw well-founded conclusions regarding its significance in the Qing dynasty economy. The following three cases are drawn from three different sources. The first and richest case, that occurred in 1751, is found in the *Weijin* section of the *tiben* documents held in the National Archives in Beijing, the second case, that occurred in 1768, from the published Ba County Archives, and the third a short version of the *Bo'an xinbian* case from 1769.

Case 1 (1751): Layers of deception in small-town counterfeiting

Zhang Zhengkun, 46 *sui*, from Guangji County (60 km north-west of the modern Jiujiang City) in Huangzhou Prefecture (mod. Echeng City, Hubei Province) lived nearby Cai Liangshi, 43 *sui*, who was a guardsman in the Transport Command in Qizhou (*Qizhou weijun ding*). On 3 February 1751 (Qianlong 16.01.08) Cai returned to his home after a grain transport and the following day visited Zhang to make his New Year's greeting. The two men got talking and Zhang, whose business was slack, came up with the idea of counterfeiting coinage. He offered Cai two mace (*qian*) of silver a day as

27 *Bo'an xinbian* 28, 22a–26b.

wages. Cai agreed and a third associate Hu Shengwan put up the capital; Zhang and Cai asked Hu Shengwan to put a capital of 6,400 cash.

On 16 February Zhang visited a man by the name of Zhang Xiannan to purchase 50 catties (*jin*) of discarded copper (*fei tong*), and paid 3,200 large coins for it. Zhang Zhengkun asked Zhang Xiannan to buy in a further 50 catties, wherewith he would make a further payment of 3,200 cash and agreed to return within 5 days to collect the copper. At this point, Zhang Xiannan came up with the idea of clipping government cash to produce the discarded copper, and over a period of from 10 days from 16 February onwards he clipped 11,300 coins and obtained the 50 catties. Cai has also sought out a man by the name of Qin Yuancan and obtained 30 catties of discarded copper from him, for which he paid 1,920 cash. Zhang Xiannan in the meantime muddled 6,300 clipped coins among government cash and sold them on to boat travellers, whose identities have not been established. In this way he obtained 3 taels (*liang*) 5 mace of silver.

Cai Liangshi asked Qin Yuancan to obtain more copper for him, and Qin in turn asked a man called Rao Kunhou to get his associates to buy in 100 catties of discarded copper. By 1 March Rao had only obtained 1 catty, so he and his wife Ms Zhang came up with the idea of clipping coins. Over eleven days until March 12 they clipped 22,520 coins and thus obtained 99 catties of copper. With the 1 catty they already had, the amount was 100 catties. They gave it to Qin Yuancan, who gave it in turn to Cai Liangshi, who in turn passed it on to Zhang Zhekun! Rao and his wife passed off 8,520 coins by mixing them among government cash.

Zhang Zhekun now went to a certain Liu Tiansheng who had a shop in Han City (Han zhen), i.e. Hankou, and purchased 50 catties of zinc, and employed two men – Zhu Xizi (otherwise known as Zhu Dezhao) and Zhang Shilin – as labourers. On March 28 and 29 Cai Liangshi built an oven in the rear premises of Zhang Zhengkun's house, made a coin mould, and on 30 March they began to cast coins.

To recapitulate, the accomplices had by this time secured 230 catties of copper and purchased 50 catties of zinc, built an oven and a mould, employed labourers and taken nearly two months to get this far. A side-effect of the preparations was that 33,820 coins had been clipped, and 14,920 debased coins had been introduced into circulation. And along the way, Zhang Xiannan had got his hands on 3 taels 5 mace of silver.

Casting the coins

There seems to have been a strict division of labour. Cai Liangshi "wielded the tongs" (*chang qian*) and watched the fire; Hu Shengwan "plucked the coins" (*zhai qian*); Zhu Xizi tramped down the [moulding] board (*ci ban*) and scraped the [moulding] sand (*gua sha*); Zhang Shilin carried water (*tiao shui*) and did odd jobs (*da za*); and Zhang Zhengkun assisted by finishing the middles and circumferences of the coins. Working until 9 April they made 105,000 coins. Zhang Zhengkun and Hu Shengwan each received a share of 4,750 coins. Cai Liangshi received his wage which amounted to 3,000 coins, Zhu Xizi received 1,500 coins, and Zhang Shilin just 1,000 coins. In all these five men's share amounted to 15,000 coins.

Putting the coins into circulation

The remaining 90,000 coins were looked after by Qin Yuancan who on two occasions, in the fourth month and the intercalary fifth month, sold the counterfeit coins to a certain Wang Yanzhang (also known as Wang san, or Number Three Wang) who lived in Huanggang County, the county town which lay eighty km north-west of Guangji County. In all Wang paid 63,900 cash for the counterfeit coins, of which Qin received a commission (*huishouqian*) of 3,600 cash.

Up to this point in time, everything had gone well for the counterfeiters. They had sold their counterfeit cash for roughly two-thirds of their face value, and not been discovered. This was probably due in part to Guangji County being a rather out-of-the-way sort of a little place. They had paid roughly 64 cash for each catty of copper, and produced 105,000 coins out of 230 catties of copper and 50 catties of zinc, or a total raw materials cost of about 17,000 cash. After paying wages, commissions and also, while unmentioned, repaying Hu Shengwan's capital, they had made a profit of 36,900 cash, or approximately 20 taels of silver. Greed now definitely got the better of their senses.

Doing it all again, and getting caught

After making the necessary preparations, on 27 June (Qianlong 16.intercalary 05.05) Zhang Zhengkun began to do it all again, and Cai Liangshi and Hu Shengwan agreed to be his accomplices. They went once again to Liu Tiansheng in Han City and bought a total of 150 catties of copper and zinc. Then they went to a certain Wang Dehong, who was a Student by Purchase Fourth Class (*jiansheng*), also known as Wang Hanye, and he agreed to rent them a room. They promised him five mace of silver a day as rent. On this occasion Zhu Xizi was not willing to work for them, so they hired another two labourers, Zhu Mingjie and Guo Guan'er. On 29 June Cai built the oven in Wang Dehong's rear rooms (*hou chong fang*) and made the mould, and the following day they started casting. There was the same division of labour. By the end of 14 July they had cast 92,000 coins. It was at this point that Wang Dehong burst in and told them they had to leave. To make his point clear he pushed over the oven! Cai Liangshi and his associates took everything (equipment, counterfeit coins, remaining copper and zinc, etc.), and returned to Zhang Zhengkun's house.

On 20 July (Qianlong 16.intercalary 05.28) Qing Yuancan sold 75,000 counterfeit coins to Cao Qishan of Qingyang County in Jiangnan and obtained 45 taels of silver. Two days later when Cao Qishan and his paternal nephew Cao Shengcheng were carrying the coins to a boat, they were apprehended by a county resident called Zhang Quanyi. The crime had come to light when they had been discovered trying to trade in (*fanmai*) counterfeit coins. When they were questioned, Cao Qishan stated that he and his nephew sold fans to make their livelihood. They had come to Wuxue to sell their products but lost their capital. They had met Qin Yuancan who had told them that he had "cheap money" for sale. So, they paid 45 taels of silver for 75,000 coins, but when they were carrying them down to load onto a boat, they had been apprehended. Cao Shengcheng said that it was all his uncle's doing, and that he knew nothing of the matter!

A careful search of Qin Yuancan's lodgings failed to reveal any oven for forging or any implements, to any counterfeit coins. Qin testified that Cai Liangshi and Zhang Zhengkun had made the coins in Wang Dehong's house. All Qin had done was to sell on the coins for them. In the fourth month, Wang san, i.e. Wang Yanzhang, was selling pigs at Xiong Mingchen's yard (*xing*) (Xiong Mingchen was arrested on 9 August), and Wang had come to Qing to buy 50,000 coins from him. The following month Wang san had come again, and bought a further 40,000 coins from Qing. Qing received a commission of 40 coins per thousand for his involvement. Qing further stated that Cao Qishen had come to him and bought 75,000 coins at a price of 6 mace of silver per thousand. It was first now with these arrests, writes the Guangji County magistrate Yu Xuehao, that he and his District Jailor (*dianshi*) He Changmao understood where all the accused resided, i.e. in Wuxue.

Supplementary evidence

When Zhang Zhengkun's house was searched, everything was found:

i. One destroyed oven
ii. Three earthenware cauldrons
iii. Two pairs of small iron tongs
iv. One file
v. One pair of iron scissors

Zhang Zhengkun's wife Ms. Lu said in her statement, "My husband absconded in the first month of this year (Qianlong 16.01), and I don't know where he is!" Similarly Cai Liangshi's wife Ms. Wang said, "My husband went out of the door early on the first day of the New Year and I haven't seen him since then. I don't know where he is!"

In his evidence, Zhang Zhengkun explained that they stopped making coins on (Qianlong 16.03.14) because they heard a rumour, that they obtained more than 110 catties of discarded and clipped copper though Qin Yuancan, that they obtained 50 catties of discarded copper and 50 catties of clipped copper from Zhang Xiannan, and that the remainder was purchased in Hankou by Cai Liangshi. Regarding working conditions, Zhang Shilin stated that when he worked as a water carrier, he was paid 7 candarins (*fen*) of silver a day. Xiong Mingchen, we learn, ran a shop selling pigs in Wuxue.

Hu Shengwan stated that Zhang Zhengkun and Cai Liangshi came to his house and asked him to put up the capital and be an accomplice. "I did not want to engage in counterfeiting and was afraid, so I didn't agree. Zhang said that we could do just for a few days, and that if we heard any rumours we could stop!"

Cai Liangshi said that when he was in Zhang Zhengkun's house, he asked Zhang how his business selling cotton was going, and Zhang just said "Lousy! (*bu hao*)" Zhang knew that Cai had worked previously in the Jiangxi Provincial Mint and knew how to cast coins. Cai admitted that he knew, but that capital was needed.

When Cai Liangshi wondered where one could obtain copper and zinc, Zhang Zhengkun said that Zhang Xiannan bought up discarded copper, and "Of course there are sellers!" Zhang Zhengkun further explained that between 6–14 February (Qianlong 16.01.11–19) he did not go anywhere because his daughter was sick. On 15 February he went to Zhang Xiannan's house and said that there was someone who wanted to buy a load of discarded copper. Zhang Xiannan said that he only had 50 catties at a cost of 8 candarins of silver per catty. "I went home and calculated that we had to pay four taels of silver for 3,200 coins." When Zhang Zhengkun carried the copper home in baskets, he laid clothing over the top to hide it. Someone told Zhang Zhengkun that if he added zinc to the copper he could make a bit more profit. So he decided to go to Hankou to buy it. Then he came to think of the cotton that he had at home, so he took forty catties of cotton when he travelled by boat to Hankou, and managed to sell his entire load within four days (Qianlong 16.02.23–27). On 21 March he bought twenty-five catties of zinc at the Liu Family Copper Store at the Four Officials Hall (*Siguandian*) for one tael of silver, and four days later he bought a further twenty-five catties at the same shop. He carried the zinc home in the bags he had used for the cotton. Zhang also purchased 300 catties of charcoal for nine mace of silver. In the third month they cast 105,000 coins, and each thousand coins weighed two catties and 10 taels. The wages that the workers received were as follows:

Cai Liangshi	3,000 coins = 2 taels of silver
Zhu Longzi	1,500 coins = 1 tael of silver
Zhang Shilin	1,000 coins = 7 mace of silver
Zhang Zhengkun	4,750 coins
Hu Shengwan	4,750 coins

Wang San sold on 50,000 coins. Each thousand coins netted 670 government cash (*dazhi qian*), so all in all Zhang Zhengkun and Hu Shengwan received a total of 33,500 government cash. Hu took 3,000 and Zhang 3,500, which left 27,000 cash over. And Qin Yuancan received a commission of coins for each one thousand. And there were still 40,000 counterfeit coins left at Zhang's house!

On 29 May (Qianlong 16.05.05) Zhang and Cai decided to repeat their enterprise. Cai said that they should go to Hankou and buy 150 catties each of copper and zinc, so they converted their 27,000 cash into 34 taels of silver, and on 10 June (Qianlong 16.05.17) they took a boat to Hankou, arriving four days later. Zhang went once again to the Liu Family Copper Store and bought fifty catties each of copper and zinc for ten taels. The next day, 15 June, he went back to the store and bought a further one hundred catties each of copper and zinc for twenty taels. Copper was one mace six candarins per catty, and zinc was four candarins per catty. Thereafter Zhang fell sick and had to stay in Hankou for a few days to recover. On 22 June Zhang bought six oil baskets (*lou*), into which he put the three hundred catties of copper and zinc, which made three carrying loads. In all for his food during his stay in Hankou he used three taels and eight or nine mace of silver.

When on 27 June (Qianlong 16.intercalary 05.05) Zhang Zhengkun went to Wang Dehong to rent lodgings, Wang said, "You have a room now at your own home, why do you want to rent a room?" Zhang said he intended to cast some objects. Wang asked what they were, but Zhang was unwilling to reply. Zhang returned the following day and Wang asked directly, "Just what are you making?" The only thing that Zhang could do was to admit that it was counterfeiting. Wang said that it was a crime, and burst out "How can you do it?" Zhang said that it would only take a few days, and if there were any inspection they would stop. Furthermore when he promised Wang Dehong five mace of silver a day as rent, Wang agreed.

Zhang bought three hundred catties of charcoal for nine mace of silver. By 14 July they had made 92,000 coins and still had between fifty and catties of copper and zinc left. It was then that Wang came into the room, pushed over the oven, cursed Zhang for what they were doing, and told them to stop. So, they all left the same night and went back to Zhang's house.

Qin Yuancan sold on 75,000 coins to Cao Qishan for six mace of silver for each thousand, which makes forty-five taels of silver. Zhang tells us that as soon as he heard that Cao Qishan had been arrested by Zhang Quanyi, he threw seven thousand counterfeit coins and more than fifty catties of copper and zinc into the river. Finally, Zhang emphasized that he had promised to Cai to purchase the necessary copper and zinc, and that they had not destroyed or defaced official coinage.

Verdicts and punishments

The punishment for the principal and workers involved in counterfeiting was decapitation, for clipping copper cash the punishment was strangulation, and for being aware of the prosecution of the crime but failing to inform the authorities the punishment was being sent into slavery. Accessories after the crime were punished with one hundred blows of the heavy rod and three years penal servitude, and landlords who failed to ascertain that counterfeiting was taking place received one hundred blows, but were not sent into penal servitude.

In this case the punishments were as follows:

Zhang Zhengkun	decapitation
Cai Liangshi	decapitation
Hu Shengwan	slavery
Zhu Longzi	slavery
Zhu Mingjie	slavery
Guo Guan'er	slavery
Wang Yuanzhang	slavery
Zhang Shilin	100 blows, 3 years penal servitude, 40 board cangue
Cao Qishan	100 blows, 3 years penal servitude, 40 board cangue
Wang Dehong	100 blows, 3 years penal servitude, 40 board cangue

Wang Yuanzhang's wife Ms. Feng begged to be allowed to follow her husband into slavery, but her wish was refused. When it came to the local police, nobody knew anything! The Security Group Head (*baozheng*) Yu Liren and the Neighbourhood Chief (*jiazhang*) Zhang Zhenyi in Zhang Xiannan's district both said that they lived one *li* away so they had no idea anything untoward was going on. His neighbours knew nothing, and Rao Kunhou's Security Group Head knew nothing. The situation was a bit worse for those living near to Zhang Zhengkun. The Security Group Head Wang Sizheng and Zhang's neighbour Zhang Tingxian and Wang Dehong's Neighbourhood Chief Yu Qifeng all were sentenced to one hundred blows and the forty board cangue. Furthermore, all the Security Group Heads and Neighbourhood Chiefs were dismissed from their positions. The only individuals who escaped without investigation or punishment were the unknown boat passengers who bought the counterfeit coins; the relatives of Zhang and Cai who already lived apart from them; Xiong Mingchen, the pig-ship owner and Xu Wenlu, the pig-seller; Cao Shengcheng, the fan seller; Liu Tiansheng, the copper shop owner; and He Xiushan, the carrier.

Discussion

I suggest that, given the typical richness of information in the above case, investigation of the archives is the only means to understand the problem of counterfeiting in the Qianlong dynasty. Published works do not carry sufficient or sufficiently detailed materials to obtain any understanding of the problem and its intricacies. For example, the excellent *Xiang'an huilan* includes twelve briefly stated cases, but not one of them refers to a crime perpetrated during the reign of the Qianlong Emperor. The *Bo'an xinbian* carries only one case of counterfeiting, albeit a fascinating one, that of Chen Xiao from Qingyang County in Anhui which occurred in 1768 and 1769, to which we shall return. The *Cheng'an huibian* includes four cases from the reign of the Yongzheng Emperor and two cases from the reign of the Qianlong Emperor,[28] but they are of an exemplary nature and the emphasis principally is the treatment of official mismanagement of the case, rather than the counterfeiting itself. Among its lengthy legal explanations, the *Lie'an quanji* includes only one case,[29] and this only to provide an example of the tricky question of how to proceed when the counterfeiters had not managed to produce any coins by the time of their arrest. The *Duli cunyi* is invaluable for its mention of many memorials submitted during the reign of the Qianlong Emperor concerning counterfeiting (in Qianlong 8, 9, 16, 18, 24, 25,

28 Li Maofa: Yongzheng 13.09.03; Li Guang'en: Yongzheng 12.05; Suo Yiding and Liu Ran: Qianlong 08.07.19; Wang Han: Qianlong 10.04.17; Ru Yaonian: Yongzheng 11.11; and Zhu Qishan: Yongzheng 03.28.

29 Wang Junning: Kangxi 37.08.16.

26, 30, 32, and 37) but obviously does not provide any cases. The two collections published by the Ba County Archives (*Qingdai Baxian dang'an huibian: Qianlong juan* and *Qingdai Qian-Jia-Dao Baxian dang'an xuanbian*) include only one case dating from the reign of the Qianlong Emperor, although sixteen later cases are given. If we look back to earlier times, while the six entries in the *Huang Ming tiaofa shilei zuan* do make passing mention of cases between 1476 and 1491, the principal discussion is of legal issues rather than the facts of the crimes, so even for earlier times we lack any detailed information on the crimes and the criminals. Our only recourse is to the archive cases in the Number One Historical Archive.

The *Weijin* section of *tiben* documents stretches from box 9779 to 10019, or a total of 240 boxes. With each box containing an average of 10 cases, we have a large but not impossibly large source of potential materials. Of course, not all *weijin* cases deal with counterfeiting. In our research Wang Xianguo and I have already made one or two hitherto inexplicable discoveries. We have looked at a random sample of years to begin with, namely Qianlong 2, 12, 22, 32, 41, 52 and 58, and failed to discover a single counterfeiting case in Qianlong 2, 41, 52, and 58. Although further research must refine our finding, it appears that counterfeiting cases are concentrated to Qianlong 10 to Qianlong 40, with a peak between Qianlong 18–32. This is not the situation, by way of comparison, with gambling, where we have twelve cases in Qianlong 2, nine in Qianlong 22, twenty-six in Qianlong 32, twenty-six in Qianlong 41, and twenty-two in Qianlong 58. Gambling cases are spread throughout the reign of the Qianlong Emperor. One explanation could be that this is simply a result of the incomplete nature of the holdings. Another is that all the early Qianlong and late Qianlong counterfeiting cases are presently found in the National Palace Museum in Taipei. A third possibility is that the counterfeiting cases are stored in another section of the archives, but this we have been assured is not the case. A fourth explanation would be that the submission of *tiben* concerning counterfeiting changed around Qianlong 10 and then changed again around Qianlong 40, but this seems very unlikely. A fifth explanation is that counterfeiting was no longer viewed as an important crime, which it was necessary to submit in *tiben* form, after Qianlong 40, but the wealth of later *tiben* mitigates this attempted explanation. All that I can say at present is that further research will hopefully bring us to a solution.

Another interesting discovery we have made when reading cases in full, and please note that an average case runs to over one hundred pages, is that two of my own theories have been thus far shown to be unsupported by evidence. The first theory was that we would find evidence of county level officials, and possibly even higher, in some way involved in counterfeiting, either through providing capital, protection of some sort, or assistance in distribution of counterfeit coinage. My idea was supported, I felt, by a case in the *Huang Ming tiaofa shilei zuan* where we read that Xuzhou counterfeiters in 1478 transported counterfeit copper coinage to the capital planning to put it into circulation there, and stored their hoard in the residence of an official's relative.[30] However, this sort of involvement has not been found to exist, although one case contains an account of allegations of involvement in counterfeiting which are later revealed to be totally unfounded. The second theory was that counterfeiting, including as it often does the destruction or defacement of coinage, would, almost inevitably, be connected with gambling and other even more serious crimes. This idea came to my mind as a result of a linkage that I perceived in imperial comments recorded by Wang Yong (fl. 1227) concerning a decree issued in 991:

> These days there are evil, young good-for-nothings who engage in wanton ill deeds. Their lesser crimes include gambling, while the greater crimes are slaughtering cattle and horses and destroying copper coinage [...] If a gang becomes rather large in size, then its members engage in theft and robbery, arson (*zonghuo*), rape (*xingjian*) and murder. If we do not curb this onslaught, it will certainly be a great disaster.
>
> In the intercalary second month of 991 it was decreed concerning all those who congregate to gamble, open gambling shops, butcher cattle, horses, mules, and dogs [to sell] as foodstuffs, or illegally melt down copper coinage to produce household articles, that the Kaifeng Superior Prefecture authorities would be rigorously on the alert for them in the city's markets, and arrest them. Those who were convicted would be executed by decapitation. Those who concealed them and were not forthcoming with information would be similarly punished.[31]

30 *Huang Ming tiaofa shilei zuan* 42, 702.

31 *Songchao yanyi moulu* 2, 13; *Xu Zizhi tongjian changbian* 32, 713.

So my thinking went, what holds good for the Song probably holds good for the Ming and probably for the Qing. My supposition was strengthened when I read in a proposal dated to the end of 1477:

> The stupid populace is ignorant; every day there is widespread counterfeiting. I humbly submit that if in the imperial capital itself counterfeiters do not know fear, how can we wonder that throughout the vast empire counterfeiters are scarcely apprehensive? If we do not rigorously forbid counterfeiting we shall find ourselves in terrible straits. In truth, each catty of copper is only worth five or six candarins, and one can cast one hundred and fifty or sixty coins from it, giving in one day a one hundred per cent or two hundred per cent profit; this is the reason for counterfeiting.[32]

However, thus far in our research we have not found any mention of counterfeiting directly leading to more serious crimes. There have been indirect connections, for example when counterfeiters have got into drunken brawls and someone has been badly injured or killed, but there does not seem to be any progression from counterfeiting to more serious crimes, or any evidence for stating that gambling rings spread counterfeit currency.

Case 2 (1768): Getting caught in Sichuan

The Ba County Archives have published the case of Wang Gao, 38 *sui*, from Guizhou,[33] who had come to Ba County with his family and found lodgings in the vicinity of the Education Hall (*bencheng jiaochang guan jingxiang*). In his evidence, given on 19 August 1768 (Qianlong 33.7.8), Wang stated that when he came to Ba County he saw that small cash (*maoqian*) were widely in circulation. Wang asked his friend Xu Binran where he could lay his hands on some small cash, since there were people who wanted to exchange cash, and Xu said that he had a few thousand coins. When Wang tried to pass on 2,000 coins, his customer was a yamen runner who promptly arrested him on 17 August 1768 (Qianlong 33.07.06)!

Xu Binran was 50 *sui* and came from Ba County; his only relations were his wife Ms. Yu and a daughter who was 7 *sui*. Xu was a tinsmith, and very poor, so he came up with the idea on 20 September 1768 (Qianlong

32 *Huang Ming tiaofa shilei zuan* 42, 700.

33 *Qingdai Baxian dang'an huibian: Qianlong juan* 1991, 332–333.

33.08.10) of counterfeiting coinage. He bought eighteen catties of zinc for a few hundred cash, made a wooden frame, and using the iron oven that the family cooked their food on and a clay cauldron (*sha guan*), every evening he cast a hundred or so coins. Many of them broke because the zinc became too dry and brittle, so he only managed to produce … (here the text is unclear) coins, and still had not managed to put them into circulation. Xu stated that he did not have any associates, and that his neighbours knew nothing of his crime at all. Xu explained that he had learnt the casting method when he was a worker at the Provincial Mint, but that since he was not very practised in the craft he had not been able to make many coins successfully. When Xu was arrested on 6 October 1768 (Qianlong 33.08.26), he stated it was the first time that had attempted to counterfeit coinage. The equipment he used was:

i. One iron rake (?) (*bagen*)
ii. One pair of iron pincers
iii. One clay cauldron
iv. 2,000 zinc coins
v. Two wooden frames
vi. One coin mould
vii. ….. [text unclear] coins used to make imprints
viii. One bag of copper fragments
ix. Two lumps of zinc
x. Six coin branches (*qianzhi*)
xi. Four incomplete zinc coins

In the verdict, the county authorities note that since Xu's lodgings were cramped and he was afraid of being discovered, he waited till the dead of night to make the counterfeit coins, that he worked alone, and that he melted the zinc in the clay cauldron. The county authorities further noted that he had not made copper coins but only zinc coins (2,000 in total), and that he had not damaged government coins. The verdict was that since the number of coins did not exceed the set limit of ten thousand, Xu should not be executed but should be sent into slavery in Heilongjiang.

Case 3 (1769): Turning informant in Anhui

How did a counterfeiter get caught? One way, as we have seen above, is when he is caught in the act, either of putting coins into circulation or actually making them, or when a customer for his goods turned informant. This is the case found in the *Bo'an xinbian*. In brief, Chen Xiao from Qingyang County in Anhui, studied to become a coppersmith in his youth. Falling on hard times he came upon the idea of counterfeiting copper coins and asked his uncle Chen Lun to be his partner in crime. Chen Lun agreed and they each put up two thousand cash as capital. Chen Xiao purchased some discarded copper, and set up a clay cauldron and a wooden box, etc. He used [crushed] black bricks and spring ash (?) which he mixed into mud, and then pressed down into the box. Taking some small coins, he made impressions in the mud thus producing a coin mould. Between the beginning of December 1768 to the end of June 1769 (Qianlong 33.11–Qianlong 34.5), Chen Xiao and Chen Lun made, all in all, 48,500 coins. Chen Xiao managed the oven, while Chen Lun scraped out the charcoal and carried water. When Chen Xiao and Chen Lun heard that, in another case, Xu Fu had been arrested, they became scared and stopped casting coins, and destroyed their apparatus.

In the December 1768 Zha Daozhou told his son-on-law (*yi xu*) Bi Juhua to purchase on his behalf (*daimai*) small cash (*xiaoqian*). Bi in turn asked a certain Wang Long to purchase on his behalf 8,000 coins from Chen Xiao. In March 1769 (Qianlong 34.2), Bi Juhua again entrusted Wang Long to purchase 12,000 coins from Chen Xiao. In all Bi gave Wang Long 8,400 government cash (*da zhiqian*), but Wang Long only gave Chen Xiao six thousand and hid the other 2,400 cash for himself! Chen Xiao also sold on 5,000 coins to passing merchants, for which he obtained 1,950 government cash (*daqian*), and also sold 16,000 coins to boat passengers, for which he obtained 5,600 government cash. Chen Xiao shared all the proceeds with Chen Lun. They hid away the remaining counterfeit coins when official inspections for counterfeit cash were enforced.

To recapitulate, Chen Xiao and Chen Lun made a total of 48,500 counterfeit coins. 41,500 of these were converted into 15,950 government cash, of which Wang Long cheated them out of 2,400 cash. Counterfeit currency was thus worth a little more than one third of its face value, and the profit was thus between one hundred and two hundred per cent, or the same figures as given in 1477.

In January 1770 (Qianlong 34.12), when the Bureau of Inspectorate (*Duyuan*) sent inspectors (*weiyingyuan*) to gather up counterfeit cash, Zha Daozhou turned in 4,600 coins that he still had to the authorities and made a confession, with the result that Chen Xiao and Chen Lun were apprehended. Chen Lun fell sick in gaol, leaving a number of unclear legal points, for example, who precisely was the principal culprit who should be executed and who the accessory to the crime who should be sent into slavery, and what should be done with Zha Daozhou who had waited until the brink of investigation before coming forward and confessing. To cut short a very lengthy legal discussion, Chen Xiao was executed, Chen Lun was sent into slavery and Zhao Daohua received ninety blows of the heavy stick and two and a half years penal servitude.[34]

Conclusion

A few preliminary conclusions can be drawn from the above three cases. Firstly, that at the heart of any counterfeiting operation there will be probably be found an impoverished coppersmith, tinsmith or someone who has laboured in a provincial mint. Secondly, that the idea of counterfeiting was commonplace and the possible penalties far from sufficient to act as an inhibition. Thirdly, that the authorities only discovered counterfeiting when they came upon it red-handed, or when too many people got involved in the prosecution of the crime; someone was bound to make a mistake eventually. Fourthly, in the production of counterfeit coins, the acquisition of all the materials and tools necessary was not particularly risky. What was difficult was the actual casting of the coins, and then introducing them into circulation. Fifthly, and finally at this stage of the research highly tentatively, the impact of the crime on the financial state of the Qing Empire appears to have been negligible, since the sums involved were derisorily small, particularly when compared to crimes of official corruption.

34 *Bo'an xinbian* 38, 22A–26B.

Yet, it is evident that the crime of counterfeiting was taken extremely seriously by the authorities. Vast administrative resources in terms of effort and time were spent on punishing offenders, even those who had not managed to produce a single counterfeit coin. Public opinion and the marketplace vendors believed counterfeiting was extremely widespread and even official coinage was traded below face value. In other words, there was an atmosphere of unease that negatively affected commercial activities and which the authorities, increasingly sensitive to perceived social disaffection, attempted to curtail with remarkable tenacity. To conclude with a trace of exaggeration, it almost appears as if the existence of one counterfeit coin was thought to be enough to rock the economic foundations of the empire.

Bibliography

Bili zacun. Dong Gu (*jinshi* 1516). Congshu jicheng chubian.

Bo'an xinbian. Quan Shichao et al. *1781, repr. Chengwen chubanshe*, 1968.

Cheng'an huibian. Zhou Xuejian (preface 1746). Naikaku bunko copy.

Da Ming huidian. 1587 ed. Jiangsu Guangling guji keyinshe, 1989.

Duli cunyi dianzhu.. Xue Yunsheng (*jinshi* 1856); Hu Xingqiao et al., eds. Zhongguo renmin gong'an daxue chubanshe, 1994.

Greatrex, Roger (1996). "Song Dynasty Legislation Concerning Gambling." In *Florilegium Japonicum,* Copenhagen.

Huang Ming tiofa shilei zuan. Dai Jin (1484–1548). Koten kenkyûkai, 1966.

Langji congtan. Liang Zhangju (1775–1849). Biji xiaoshuo daguan.

Lie'an quanji Zhang Guangyue (printed 1733). Naikaku bunko copy.

Liu Jun and Liu Jianmin (1999). *Zhongguo gu qianbi zhenwei jianbie*. Guangdong keji chubanshe.

Ming Wuzong shilu, *Ming Taizu shilu, Ming Yingzong shilu*. Taipei: Chung-yang yen-chiu-yüan li-shih yü-yen yen-chiu-so, 1966.

Minggong shupan qingming ji. Anon (ca. 1262). Zhonghua shuju, 1987.

Qingchao wenxian tongkao. Zhejiang guji chubanshe, 1988.

Qingdai Baxian dang'an huibian: Qianlong juan. Dang'an chubanshe, 1991.

Qingyuan tiaofa shilei. Xie Shenfu (fl. 1160–1202). Seikadô bunko copy, repr. Xinwenfeng chuban gongsi, 1976.

Rizhi lu jishi. Wang Niansun (1613–82). Shanghai guji chubanshe, 1985.

Song xingtong. Dou Yi (914–996). Falü chubanshe, 1999.

Songchao yanyi yimou lu. Wang Yong (fl. 1227). Congshu jicheng chubian.

Song da zhaoling ji. Anon. Zhonghua shuju, 1962.

Taiping guangji. Li Fang (925–996). Zhonghua shuju, 1981.

Tang da zhaoling ji. Song Minqiu (1019–79). Xuelin chubanshe, 1992.

Tanglü shuyi. Changsun Wuji (d. 659). Zhonghua shuju, 1983.
Vogel, Hans Ulrich (1987). "Chinese central monetary policy." In *Late Imperial China* 8: 2.
Xing'an huilan. Zhu Qingqi. 1834, repr. Chengwen chubanshe, 1968.
Xu Zizhi tongjian changbian. Li Tao (1115–1184). Zhonghua shuju, 2004.
Yanxian lu. Lu Shen (1477–1544). Congshu jicheng chubian.

Local Demographic Variations in the Lower Yangzi Valley during Mid-Qing Times

Mark Elvin and Josephine Fox

Many years ago, I overheard Bill Skinner remark that in social and economic research the basic question that we have to ask, and keep asking, was 'What covaries with what?' His words, brief, penetrating, and apposite, have remained at the back of my mind ever since; and, from my personal perspective, our present essay is a belated tribute to this observation and the man who made it.[1] We use new data and partially new methods to show the extent of variations in age-patterns of marriages, births, and deaths in thirteen counties and a prefecture in the lower Yangzi valley region, and suggest that it is now becoming important, as the next step, to try to determine the likely differences—environmental, social, and economic—that lay behind these variations. We also provide a basic toolkit, linked to our project website, with which sinologists and demographers with new lower Yangzi-valley data of the kind we have used can in the future extract further evidence of such local demographic variations for themselves, simply by running the two programs *logit.match.search.* and *life.table*.[2]

We have postponed to another occasion the discussion of how our findings relate to the now quite extensive recent scholarly work on the dynamics of the Qing population. Before we embark on this we need to have a better idea of how well our results stand up technically to further criticism, or fail to. If, however, their general tenor had to be encapsulated in a phrase we would say that, loosely, the mid-Qing population that emerges through the mists of analysis is both 'non-Malthusian', because of the indirect evidence that it gives of a significant limitation of births within marriage, and 'non-modern' because of the high level of infant mortality.

1 The date was probably some time around 1968–1969, and the occasion most probably one of the two conferences that Bill organized in these years on the city in China (M.E.).

2 URL http://gis.sinica.edu.tw/QingDemography/. Designer: Tzai-Hung Wen. Location: Center for Geographic Information Science, Academia Sinica, Taipei. It contains data, coding conventions, and programs in PERL, all freely downloadable.

1. The background to the analysis

In our paper, "Marriages, births, and deaths in the lower Yangzi valley during the later eighteenth century,"[3] we presented a reconstruction of population dynamics based on the consistent interlocking of eight different types of demographic information. All but two of them were extracted from the short and relatively systematic biographies of virtuous women in local gazetteers.[4] The main method used was the *modelling* of a given pattern of data relating to a certain demographic phenomenon by using *other* data in our dataset, plus consistent assumptions as necessary, as the input into the model. An example is the frequency of female bereavements by age. Modelling this needed the schedule of age-specific marriage rates for females from the data, the distribution of age-differences between spouses from some of our earlier data, and reconstructed schedules of age-specific male and female mortality. The interrelationships of the totality of these modelling operations are visually summarized in Figure 2.1 (p. 371).

The sources are symbolized by the rectangles with heavy black, blue, or green borders and light-beige coloured backgrounds.[5] Seven of them were generated by our own research on the brief biographies of virtuous women in Qing dynasty gazetteers and a lineage genealogy from Hu'nan.[6] The last item, on the percentages of rural widows in age-groups in the early twentieth century, was borrowed from the work of Notestein and Chiao on farming families in the late 1920s as part of the Buck farm-family survey.[7] Though anachronistic, it was needed to complete the interlocking. Modelling procedures, most of them probabilistic, are shown in round-cornered cartouches

3 "Marriages, Births, and Deaths in the Lower Yangzi Valley during the Later Eighteenth Century," in Clara Wing-chung Ho 何劉詠聰, ed., *Five Windows on the Chinese World* (Lexington Books (Rowman and Littlefield): forthcoming 2008/09).

4 See the bibliography of sources at the end.

5 Black borders refer to deaths, blue borders to marriages, green borders to births.

6 *Zengshi sixiu zupu* 曾氏四修族譜 [Zeng Family Lineage Register, Fourth Recension]. Compiled by Zeng Chuan 曾傳. Revised by Zeng Huailiu 曾懷柳 et al.; re-edited by Zeng Yuxu 曾毓緒, and Zeng Guangzuo 曾廣祚 (Xiang xiang 湘鄉 in Hengyang, [Hu'nan], 1900).

7 Frank Notestein and Chi-ming Chiao, "Population". Chap. 13 in J. Buck, ed., *Land Utilization in China* (Nanjing: University of Nanjing, 1937. Reprinted, New York, NY: Paragon Book Reprint Corp., New York, NY, 1964).

with orange-beige coloured backgrounds. The analysis presented here is best read in conjunction with our earlier paper, though we have done our best to make it clear on its own terms.

The first paper dealt with regional aggregates. In the present paper we tackle disaggregation: that is, establishing and analyzing the *variations* in the measures of local populations within the overall region. Our core findings are summarized in three tables presented below: 2.1 on mortality (p. 347), 2.2 on female first marriages (p. 351), and 2.3 on the gross reproduction rate (GRR) for females (p. 355). These are the visible tops of what one might think of as computational icebergs.

The central pillars of our reconstruction are two standard life tables, one for females and the other for males, which we take as applying to our data for the lower Yangzi region as a whole.[8] Our initial sample of 14 localities was, however, selected on the basis of picking areas where the gazetteers had the best quality of data we could find, and not of searching for representative quality or geographical balance. The key concern at this stage was simply to have good enough materials to let us develop a methodology. In general, individual gazetteers, on their own, do not contain a sufficient quantity of data in their biographies of 'virtuous' women, to allow locally independent analyses other than those of rates of female deaths at ages above 50 Chinese calendrical years (*sui* 歲)[9] and of the age-specific frequencies of female first marriages. We have been able to do other analyses by interweaving,

8 As of January 2007. For the figures, see Appendix 1 (p. 360). Subsequent small additions to the database have not shifted the findings for the death rate for the region as a whole outside the level of precision to which we have been working for the expectancy of life at birth, namely years measured to 1 place of decimals. Large additions to the database will undoubtedly shift them more in the future. Consistency requires retaining the standard life tables as stable benchmarks for reference, hence distinct from the empirical regional pattern as this is from time to time refined.

9 For the details of the conversion of the calendar-based *sui* with integer intervals to exact western years of age, see our chapter in Ho (forthcoming). Briefly, a *sui* value of s years ranges from $w = s - 1.5$ to $w = s - 0.5$ *exact* western years of age, with a mean of $w = s - 1$, assuming an equal distribution of births through each year, and ignoring mortality within each year.

where needed, the relationships established for the larger sample in our full regional database.[10]

Calculation of most demographic rates has been indirect. For example, we used the differential survival of widowed mothers-in-law and of complete couples of parents-in-law, by the age of their daughter-in-law when she was bereaved, to determine the approximate relationship between the male and female life tables (the first of these applying to the father-in-law and the dying husband and the second to the mother-in-law). In addition to several other parameters derived from the data, this also required supplying 'by hand' the values for the age-differences between fathers-in-law and mothers-in-law. There were empirical constraints on the permissible mean size of this last gap, but it was useful for fine-tuning so as to produce an exact fit of the model to the data.[11] We also used (after some intermediate manipulations) the data on a mother's age-specific possession of a given number of *surviving* sons to test that they fitted with our reconstructed birth rates and death rates for *males*, since we already had a schedule of female ages at first marriage from the data; and this latter let us simulate the proportions of the marriages of a given length there were for mothers widowed at a given age. Almost every item had to be interlocked in this way with several others; and the entire structure is not unlike a Buckminster Fuller geodesic dome, in which every piece must be tightly in place for it to be stable.

A so far unsolved methodological question remains. We reached approximate stabilization by a process of experimental adjustments applied 'by hand' using the separate programs shown in Figure 2.1, rather than via a

10 How this was done for life tables for both sexes over the full span of ages and of birth rates is analyzed in detail in our first paper.

11 We kept the mean interspousal age difference within the plausible historical limits defined by those derived for lineages in south China by Liu Ts'ui-jung [Liu Cuirong] 劉翠溶, « 明清時期家族人口與社會經濟變遷 » [Lineage Populations and Socio-economic Changes in the Ming and Qing Periods], 2 vols. (Taibei: Academia Sinica, 1992). In the end, without any forcing, our best-fitting +3.22 years (the plus sign indicating that the husbands were older than their wives) only differed from her South China mean of +3.47 by approximately -3 months. The two reconstructed life tables have the dominant role in determining the closeness of data and model survival rates as measured by M/B, 'M' indicating mothers-in-law only, and B, for 'both' parents-in-law, indicating complete couples. Work done subsequent to the computing for this paper has shifted the mean interspousal age-gap to +3.1791 years.

single master algorithm systematically searching a multi-dimensional solution space. So, is this stabilization in a rough-and-ready sense both approximately optimal and essentially 'unique'? Or does there exist a radically different way of assembling the data into another internally consistent, demographically plausible, stabilized cross-linked pattern? We are inclined from our explorations to think that there is no other substantially better solution accessible through continuous incremental improvements on our present solution, but should stress that we lack the intellectual tools to prove this. About the possible existence of a clearly separate island of higher overall optimality we are for the moment unable to have a useful opinion. Our challenge to any critic here would be to ask him or her to devise a significantly better fitting overall reconstruction using the data and coding conventions provided on our website.

The two most obvious uncertainties in our reconstruction are the death rates for males above about 60, and the death rates for young and teenage women. The first are reconstructed by giving them the same pattern as the older-age female deaths, which is very solid, but starting at a slightly higher absolute level of survival, so that they fit smoothly with the male pattern for the preceding ages. Our guess, on general grounds, would be that the male standard increasingly overestimates old-age male survival rates as age rises, but we have no way of knowing by how much. At the other end of life, our reconstructed standard for females shows female survival in the first year as lower than that for males (specifically, $l(1)_f$ = 0.68787 versus $l(1)_m$ = 0.7200).[12] This is a backward extension from the calculated female young-adult rates relative to those of males. For the males, in contrast to the females, we do have early-age data, but the female deficit just mentioned seems unlikely in terms of general human experience, which shows baby girls as tougher survivors when they compete on equal terms.[13] We would therefore suggest that our female standard (summing up what we think is to be found in the data) suggests *female infanticide* at a level such that *at least*

12 The symbolism $l(x)$ indicates the proportion of a birth cohort born at the same time that still survives at the age of *x* years. The 'l' stands for 'living'.

13 Lazarus, John, "Human Sex Ratios: Adaptations and Mechanism, Problems and Aspects," in Ian Hardy, ed., *Sex Ratios. Concepts and Research Methods* (Cambridge: Cambridge University Press, 2002).

10.4 per cent of all female deaths in the first year of life were due to deliberate killing. The justification for this is that setting the first-year 'intrinsic' female survival rate at approximately the same as that of the males[14] seems the lowest level that is warranted. If anything, it may have been higher still. The implied 'intrinsic' expectation of life at birth is 28.5 years, essentially the same e(0) as that for males.[15] We have however retained the reconstructed lower female first-year survival rate for all analytical purposes, as this seems to be closer to what was probably happening in real life.

Finally, at the heart of the reconstruction lie the parent-in-law survival data. These join the patterns for the two sexes at adult ages; and there is no doubt that the reconstruction would be more secure if we had *directly usable* cases that amounted to three or four times the 5,056 that we currently have in the database for the lower Yangzi valley during the Qing dynasty.[16]

1. Applying the regional template

By using the locality data for female mortality at or above 50 *sui*,[17] which are available in the majority of the lower Yangzi valley (LYV) gazetteers for the Qing dynasty, we can determine the degree, and direction, in which a locality varied from the corresponding truncated higher-age part of the pat-

14 Note that to obtain a smoother comparable year-by-year q(x), that is, the mortality rate following age x, in the early years, we actually need to put it 0.02128 higher than the male rate. A sample of the qualitative evidence for female infanticide during the mid-Qing is given in M. Elvin, "Unseen Lives. The Emotions of Everyday Existence Mirrored in Chinese Popular Poetry of the Mid-Seventeenth to the Mid-Nineteenth Century" in R. Ames et al., eds., *The Self as Image in Asian Theory and Practice* (Albany, NY: SUNY, 1998), 144–146. We use 'infanticide' to include differential neglect of girls, since we have no practical way of discriminating quantitatively between the two phenomena.

15 The symbolism e(0) indicates the mean number of person-years lived after the age of exactly 0 (the moment of birth) by a member of a given population.

16 Directly usable' here means cases with information on *either* the survival of a widowed mother-in-law *or* the survival of the complete parents-in-law couple as these appear to have the most nearly systematic coverage. The M/B ratio by the age of the daughter-in-law at bereavement is the most reliable guide to the in-laws survival pattern that is being modelled. There are no usable data on cases where *both* parents-in-law had died.

17 Our programs do all their calculations in *exact western years*, but here we are only describing the principles of the matching process. The mean value of 50 *sui* is 49 years.

tern in the LYV regional template. Specifically, this is done by (1) expressing $l'(x)$, the *proportion* of the locality population, which is already de facto truncated,[18] surviving to a given age x[19] in terms of logit $l'(x)$, the value of the *logit* function of this proportion,[20] and (2) finding two parameters, α (an amount added on or subtracted from *all* the logit values), and β (an amount by which *all* the logit values are first multiplied before the adding or subtracting of α), that would *transform* the $l(x)$ in the section of the regional model with ages above 50 so that its logits match as closely as possible the logits for the equivalent local data for ages above 50. The sequence from (2) on is applying the logit transformation to the $l(x)$ of the *whole* standard table first, then *antilogiting* back to $l_t(x)$,[21] then truncating the transformed proportions to the truncated $l'_t(x)$ with the radix at 50, taking logits *again*, *but* this time of the $l'_t(x)$ with the first logit value at 51, and, finally, matching these with the logits of the locality data $l'(x)$, to determine the closeness of fit. Put slightly differently, these operations are as follows:

(1) determine the values of logit $l'(x)$ for the $l'(x)$, the proportions surviving at age x in the *locality* data from 51 through 85, taking $l'(50)$ as 1.0, the starting-point or 'radix' of the truncated life table after which the proportion of the locality population that has survived to this age gradually diminishes towards 0, due to deaths;

(2) transform the $l(x)$ of the all-ages standard life table over ages $x = 1$ through 85 to logit $l(x)$;

18 We use the primed form $l'(x)$ when the population is *truncated*, in the sense that a range of ages between 0 and r (for 'radix') is missing, or has been removed. The plain $l(x)$ always refers here to the proportion of a *full-age-range* population still living at age x. The radix becomes the $l'(0)$ of the truncated life table. In general, only virtuous widows who had survived to 50 *sui* or over were qualified to have their biographical particulars recorded in the local gazetteer, hence their 'life table' was 'truncated'.

19 The proportion is expressed as a decimal fraction from 1.0 (that is, all) at the first age being considered (the radix) down to 0.0 (that is, none) at the last age. Note, though, that the logit function is minus infinity when $x = 0$ and $l(x) = 1$, so the logit curve starts at the first proportion surviving that is less than 1. See the formula given later.

20 See formula on p. 341. Logit-system terms are henceforth in Arial type.

21 Turning the logits back into proportions by the inverse formula. The explicit formula for the antilogit is also given at the end of this section.

(3) use the computer program *logit.match.search*[22] to look systematically, to the degree of precision desired, for the values of α and β, over their permitted ranges,[23] to find the pair of values that most precisely transform the regional standard life-table logits[24] over the full span of ages in the form

$\text{logit}_t\, l(x) = \beta.\text{logit}\, l(x) + \alpha$, to give the closest match to the data logits when

i. The transformed standard logits have been turned by the anti-logit function back into $l_t(x)$ for all ages;

ii. This full age-span table of $l_t(x)$ has been truncated at age 50, and new $l'_t(x)$ with their starting-point of 1.0 at 50 calculated; and the logits of these, namely $\text{logit}\, l'_t(x)$, taken with a radix of 50, hence starting at the age of 51; and

iii. The nearest closeness of fit has been determined by *summing the squares of the differences* between the data $\text{logit}\, l'(x)$ and the regional $\text{logit}\, l'_t(x)$, after its survivorship proportions have been truncated and transformed, for selected values of x,[25] and the α and β selected that produce smallest of these sums.

With a computer these tedious routine operations are no problem to perform repeatedly under the guidance of a search algorithm.

In this way, by determining the transformation parameters α and β that produce the best fit between the transformed regional values and the locality values for the higher ages, the age-by-age proportions surviving, and hence the mortalities, can be found from an α,β-transformed version of the standard table for both sexes in that locality for *all* ages. The relative reliability of the outcome of this procedure depends on two conditions, however. The first is that we are prepared to apply the same transformation parameters to the males as we have found work best for the females, and the second is that we

22 Available on the project website.

23 About -0.5 .. 0.5 for α, and about 0.5 .. 1.5 for β.

24 The subscript t in $\text{logit}_t\, l(x)$ indicates that the logit of the standard has been *transformed* by multiplying it by β and then adding α.

25 We have used $x = 55, 60, \dots 75, 80$. One could use all the ages in the truncated span, but this 6-age set seems adequate here.

are confident that the locality is very likely to have a pattern of survivorship by age that is structurally 'close' to the regional pattern.

The operational sense of the term 'close' is simply that such a standard-to-local transformation of the life-table pattern can be done with a high degree of *precision*. *Not all* local populations can be closely matched by *any* standard population transformed by these two parameters with values lying within the range of acceptability. This is why the selection of a suitable standard life table, or the *de novo* creation of a new standard, as we have done for the LYV, matters crucially when we are attempting a from-part-to-whole reconstruction of this kind.[26] Examples of what we see as, in some cases, extremely and, in other cases, sufficiently close matching are given in Table 2.1. Ultimately, though, the maximum 'acceptable' size of a sum of squared differences between the logits of the data and those of the transformed standard values, over 6 or more representative ages, depends on the judgement of the investigators. In the present case, we found that none of the currently ready-made and widely used model standard tables would cover the range of *all* our localities acceptably, though we could easily find some that would cover any given *subset* well enough. This was why we created a separate standard for the LYV.[27]

It only remains now to give the explicit forms for the logit and antilogit transformations. These are as follows:

$$\text{logit } l(x) = 0.5 \ln ((1 - l(x)) / l(x)) \qquad (1),$$

in other words, half of the natural (or base *e*) logarithm ln of the ratio of the proportion of a population cohort[28] that is *dead* by age *x* to the proportion that is still *alive* at this age; and

$$\text{antilogit}(\text{logit } l(x)) = 1 / (\exp(2.\text{logit } l(x)) + 1) = l(x) \qquad (2).$$

26 I.e., using the survivorship proportions at ages of and over 50 *sui* as the guide to reconstructing those for the ages under 50.

27 As detailed in Mark Elvin and Josephine Fox, "Marriages, Births, and Deaths in the Lower Yangzi Valley during the Later Eighteenth Century," in Clara Wing-chung. Ho, ed., *Five Windows on the Chinese World* (forthcoming).

28 A 'cohort' is a group that has been born at the same time.

The term 'exp' stands for the exponential function found on any good hand calculator. It raises *e* to the power of the index supplied, and is the inverse of the natural logarithm function.

A few further points need to be noted about the logit system at this point. The first is that at the age when the proportion deceased equals the proportion surviving, the logit's value will be 0.5 ln (0.5/0.5), that is 0.5 (ln 1) = 0. The second and third relate to the effects of α and β. Alpha raises or lowers the *height* of the logit line according to whether the parameter is greater or lesser than 0, its 'neutral' or identity value. A higher logit value for a given age means a higher mortality, and conversely a lower one a lower mortality. Beta puts opposing *twists* at the lower and higher ends of the line, either in one pair of opposed directions or the other, depending on whether it is greater or less than its identity value of 1. Multiplying by a β that is greater than 1 will increase rates of survival at *earlier ages* (hence lower mortality), when the logits have negative values, and, conversely, reduce them at *higher ages* (hence increase mortality), when the logit values are positive. The reverse holds if β is less than 1. The fourth point is that, although the logit curve is not a straight line, especially toward its extreme points, it can be handled in many ways like one. This is why the adding and subtracting of a single value of α, and the multiplying by a single value of β, for all values, work to a good approximation. It should also be remembered that the use of the logit system in rough-data demography as here was pioneered by the late William Brass, and his works still often make the best first point of reference in case of problems.[29]

This is the logic behind the conceptual tool we use for approximating death rates in the LYV region's localities with which we are concerned. Those doing such work on a new county or prefecture will of course have to take the time to extract and encode the data, which is the time-consuming part of the operation. There is, however, no need for a sinologist or demographer to master the details of even the relatively simple mathematics provided here. All that is required is that he or she can find the computing facili-

29 William Brass, "On the Scale of Mortality," in W. Brass, ed., *Biological Aspects of Demography* (London: Taylor and Francis, 1971), and William Brass, *Methods for Estimating Fertility and Mortality from Limited and Defective Data* (Chapel Hill, NC: Laboratories for Population Statistics, 1975.)

ties to run the the website program *logit.match.search*, to identify the α and β wanted for a locality when one is working with a particular model or standard life table, and to insert them in the program *life.table*, to generate the l(x), q(x), and e(x)[30] for the full age-span in the locality concerned.

2. The lower Yangzi valley standard tables

Figure 2.2 shows the age-specific mortalities from our reconstructed LYV standard tables. The female curve includes what we suspect is female infanticide, as already indicated. They are compared with the analogous curves for (1) a *real* population, that of Taiwan under Japanese rule for 1909–1911,[31] and (2) a *model* population, that of the widely used revised Coale and Demeny 'west' family.[32] (See p. 372.)

In the basic untransformed Coale and Demeny model one curve is for females in their 'west' pattern with the expectation of life at birth set at 25 years, and the other for males with the expectation of life at birth at 22.9. We have used the alpha and beta parameter values, using the LYV female standard as a reference, that give the best higher-age match for the females, with a sum of squared errors of 0.0075, to transform the Coale and Demeny tables, for both sexes. This brings the Coale and Demeny 'error' for the female expectation of life at birth down to 1.3 years. The 4.8 year 'error' for males is not meaningful, since if we had been working with the Coale and Demeny model we would have recalibrated the male rates against the female ones using our *parents.in.law.model*. But the upper levels of the female rates are

30 Respectively, the proportion surviving at age x, the mortality at age x, and the expectation of life at age x.

31 Data from Li Zenglu [Li Tseng Lu] 李增祿, *Abridged Life Tables for Males and Females in Taiwan, 1906/ 62* (The Historical Research Commission of Taiwan Province: Taibei, 1965). The help of Dr Zhao Zhongwei in providing photocopies of these is gratefully acknowledged. Note that in the middle seventies the curves for the Taiwan males and females merge to the point of being indistinguishable. The e(0) for Taiwan calculated here would seem to differ slightly from those given by Liu Shiyong [Liu Shi-yung] 劉士永 in his "Differential Mortality in Colonial Taiwan (1895–1945)," *Annales de Démographie Historique* 2004.1, Table 2. The years 1911–1914 were however a period of rapidly seesawing mortality (Liu's Figure 2).

32 Coale, Ansley, and Paul Demeny, *Regional Model Life Tables and Stable Populations*, 2nd ed. (London and New York, NY: Academic Press, 1983).

fixed by the data at this part of the curve, and they cannot be changed in this way.

A look at the details of the data for Figure 2.2 in the appendix shows that the Taiwan female babies have a slightly lower mortality in their first year than the male ones, and the possible adjustment that we have already suggested[33] to the LYV standard on the grounds that infanticide obscured a lower 'intrinsic' rate brings the female:male ratios for the first year of life in the LYV and in Taiwan quite close. Thus the LYV $q_f(0)' = 0.2787$[34] and $q_m(0) = 0.2800$ have a ratio of 0.995 (as compared with that for Taiwan's $q_f(0) = 0.2305$ and $q_m(0) = 0.2404$, which is 0.959), rather than the wide divergence shown in the appendix data used for this first point in Figure 2.2. The comparison gives some modest support to the view that the efforts of the Japanese colonial government to suppress infanticide in Taiwan had some effect.[35]

This point apart, the general similarity of the three pairs of tables up to around age 35 is evident. After this point, the LYV Standard becomes slightly distinctive. The males appear to live more years than females, for reasons already mentioned, and are in this unlike the other two cases shown. More interestingly, the LYV curves for the two sexes stay close together. This proximity is forced on our reconstruction by the parents-in-law survival data, which can only be modelled in a reasonable way if this feature is built into their standard tables. Mortality for both sexes in the LYV Standard after ages 60 to 65 also rises less sharply than in the Coale and Demeny 'west' model. It is natural to ask if perhaps the faithful widows in our sample, who had to survive to at least 50 *sui* to qualify for recognition and recording, were not to some extent selected by this requirement for a modest degree of extra potential for longevity. For females, this suggestion seems to run into the obstacle of the very close correspondence between the LYV Standard and the Taiwan 1909–1911 female pattern until well into the seventies. The divergence between Taiwan males and females from about 35 to 70 (the male data for the ages after this being fairly clearly to some extent implausi-

33 Though not used in our calculations.

34 The prime here indicates that the figure has been adjusted to remove female infanticide.

35 K. B. Olds, "Female Productivity and Mortality in Early-Twentieth-Century Taiwan," *Economics and Human Biology* 2006 2.4 (June).

ble) starts too soon, however, for it to be concluded that the LYV male-female ratio should have followed a similar pattern. Parents-in-law data rule this out for most of these ages for the LYV.

3. Reconstructed local rates for proportions surviving by age

Let us look now at our method in action. The next three Figures cover a selection of localities in the LYV region, and also of some on its edge or outside it. The *relative* rankings established here with regard to mortality, nuptiality, and fertility for the LYV region are the core of the paper, and the most robust part of its findings. Figure 2.3 shows that the fitting of the data and the α,β-transformed female standard can be done in the best cases with a sum of the squares of the errors for each point going as low as 0.0001, as in the case of Shexian. Jiaxing and Shangrao are almost as tight. Details are given in Table 2.1. For a few localities the fit is comparatively poor. Figure 2.4 shows Tongshan at a reasonable 0.0016, but Qianshan is an order of magnitude worse but within limits at 0.0161. The worst-matching case we have found in the LYV is Rugao at 0.0585. Note that it is not the *distance* from the Standard that is the focus of interest here, but the degree of *precision* with which a transformation can be effected. Figures 2.3, 2.4, and 2.5 represent this by pairs of lines, one for the data and the other for the appropriately α,β-transformed model. As noted, our working hypothesis is that, if the transformation is close to precise, and the lines all but coincide, then the local population that is being matched is likely to belong, if obviously within the same geographical region, to something like the same 'family' as that defined by the LYV Standard, and that if not, then we should keep the possibility open but come to no conclusions until additional relevant evidence is available. (See pp. 373–375.)

But where does a demographic 'region' in this sense start or stop? The definition of a 'region' can vary radically according to the criteria used. Figure 2.5 shows the close fits for three areas that are *not* in the lower Yangzi valley: Guiyang in the southwest, Dingzhou in the north China plain, and Zunhua to the northeast of Beijing and close to being outside the historical area thought of as being culturally 'Han' Chinese.[36] These all may be part of one connected zone, perhaps with 'demographic islands' like Rugao within it. At the moment we are still at the stage of posing such questions, rather than answering them. Equally, the small size of the Rugao sample (366 cases) suggests that we should not be too concerned about its poor fit. Clarifying the frontiers of what we have called the 'LYV region' is an important task for the future.

36 The historical, social, and economic backgrounds of Guiyang and Zunhua are described in Mark Elvin, "Blood and Statistics: Reconstructing the Population Dynamics of Late Imperial China from the Biographies of Virtuous Women in Local Gazetteers," in H. Zurndorfer, ed., *Chinese Women in the Imperial Past: New Perspectives*. Leiden: Brill, 1999. The mortality estimates in this piece should be regarded as outdated, especially those for Zunhua. See also Mark Elvin, *The Retreat of the Elephants. An Environmental History of China* (New Haven and London: Yale University Press, 2004), chap. 8 and 9.

Table 2.1

Key female mortality measures from selected localities in the lower Yangzi valley, and three localities outside it

(underlying data smoothed by rolling 3-year means)

Locality	*Sample Size*	*Fit*	*Alpha*	*Beta*	*e(0)f*	*e(10)f*
All LYV	12588	0.00011	-0.001	1.005	27.2	41.1
Shexian	5018	0.00014	-0.077	1.005	29.6	42.0
Jiaxing	2784	0.00071	0.160	1.049	22.1	38.6
Shangrao	317	0.00091	-0.234	0.952	35.1	45.1
Tongshan	1367	0.00159	0.045	1.065	25.1	39.4
Xuancheng	523	0.00383	-0.054	1.026	28.7	41.3
Xingguo	564	0.00429	0.025	0.983	26.6	41.2
Yixian	260	0.00452	-0.078	1.068	29.1	40.8
Leping	374	0.00539	-0.063	0.962	29.6	42.6
De'an	184	0.00567	0.169	0.987	22.3	39.6
Wuyuan	329	0.01224	-0.046	1.022	28.5	41.3
Qianshan	413	0.01609	-0.062	1.000	29.2	41.9
Le'an	54	0.05303	-0.256	1.110	34.3	42.3
Rugao	366	0.05852	-0.206	1.061	33.2	42.5
Dingzhou	263	0.00083	-0.167	0.929	33.3	44.7
Guiyang	819	0.00157	-0.006	0.977	27.6	44.7
Zunhua	448	0.00697	-0.005	1.036	27.1	40.5

NOTE: Poyang, with only 35 cases, has been omitted from the LYV section. The 'fit' is the sum of the squares of the errors with respect to the transformed lower Yangzi region values.
DATE COMPUTED: January 2007.

Table 2.1 shows the use of the program *logit.match.search* to determine (1) the values of alpha and beta that must be used to create the best match between locality data and an appropriately transformed LYV female Standard for proportions of females surviving at ages above 50 *sui*, (2) the closeness of the fit, expressed in terms of the sums of the squares of the errors, and (3) the results of using these values in the program *life.table* to transform the

LYV Standard female table for *all ages*, and determine expectations of life at various ages (here at birth, e(0), and at age 10, e(10)).

Three conclusions emerge. (1) The régimes of childhood and adult mortality are markedly different, as revealed by the last two columns. The lowest levels of the first are approaching the calamitous for a population that cannot draw in fresh recruits through in-migration. The latter is quite reasonable for a pre-modern population. Any serious easing of early childhood death rates (including a reduction in female infanticide), especially in the localities with the worst e(0), looks as if it would have triggered a population explosion; and we would guess that in modern times it did. (2) The range of expectancies of life at birth is significantly different as between different localities. A girl born in Jiaxing had an e(0) of 22.1 years; her sister born in Shangrao had an e(0) of 35.1 years, a difference of 13 years. Any study of China's late-imperial population thus needs to be cautious about framing its conclusions in terms based only on aggregate measures. The e(10) are also markedly closer together than the e(0). Local variation, assuming our reconstruction is not too far wrong, is mainly a matter of differential survival in childhood, which thus assumes crucial importance for the analysis of the demographic history of this period. (3) Although death rates at older ages are not the best guide to variations in mortality over the full span of life, within the LYV region the underlying older-age pattern seems steady. The LYV value of alpha only ranges from -0.234 to +0.169, and that of beta from 0.952 to 1.11. If in the future we are to talk about a demographically typical core 'Chinese' population in this period it will have to be defined at least in part by its adherence to a basic pattern such as this one from which most individual local population patterns can be reasonably precisely reproduced by a logit transformation using a restricted range of parameters, though probably not as tight as those shown here for a single region. For the moment, of course, it is too soon to say whether we will find that we need a single pattern, or several, for a satisfactory description of at least most of the Han population of late-imperial China as a whole. And, indeed, we may never know, as not every region is equally well supplied with suitable gazetteers.

When we turn to particular localities, an interesting question is what environmental, social, economic, and cultural reasons lay behind Jiaxing's high mortality. For the moment, we have only tentative answers. Jiaxing was one of the most economically developed areas of late-imperial China (even though it also suffered exceptionally severely from epidemics.) If further investigation shows that, at least for a number of important cases, the positive correlation between a high level of pre-modern economic development and the high level of mortality revealed by the demographic data for Jiaxing can be sustained, then the idea, which is sometimes found, that such a kind of extremely intensive economic development, with its elevated ratio of of labour to land, and widespread symbiotic peasant handcraft industry, was a possible path to some sort of 'modern' economic breakthrough becomes, not impossible to believe—seeing that some early modern European cities seem to have been 'sinks of mortality'—but certainly harder to entertain.[37]

4. Marriage

The mean age of first marriage for women, and its spread about the mean, did not differ between counties in the LYV to anything like the same degree as did the expectation of life at birth. The variations are shown in Table 2.2 for those counties where the size of the sample is large enough to justify recording them. It is desirable to use the locality rather than the regional marriage schedule, if possible, in estimating the locality birth rates, which is done in the next section. The question therefore arises as to the reliability of the smaller samples.

Figure 2.6 gives an illustration of the problem of judging the adequacy of the size of a sample of data. (We say 'illustration' because only one run, which has been randomly selected, is shown for each set of a given number of trials.) If we assume, solely for the sake of argument, that the proportions of women marrying at each age shown in the data from Wuyuan, our largest locality sample, are actually correct, then we can use these frequencies as the basis of probabilistic simulations on the computer using varying numbers of trials. Each trial is the conceptual equivalent of a data point. It is clear from the Figure 2.6 that at 50,000 and even at 5,000 trials the replication of the

37 Mark Elvin, *The Retreat of the Elephants,* chap. 7, "Richness to Riches: The Story of Jiaxing." There is a *prima facie* case for suspecting that increased population density increases early childhood mortality. See R. Woods and N. Shelton, *An Atlas of Victorian Mortality* (Liverpool: Liverpool University Press, 1997), 69. In our view economic 'modernity' is indissolubly linked with modern science, but that is a separate issue.

pattern is virtually perfect. There is, after all, only one use of a pseudo-random number required, unlike our more complex models used for the reconstruction of the life tables where random-number usage is three or more times greater. The run with 500 trials is also clearly not seriously misleading; nor even is that with 250. The pattern only begins to break down at 100 trials, and even then not in such a way as to be seriously misleading. This method, given here in its simplest form, can be used in most other cases to establish an approximate notion of how likely a limited number of datapoints are to have captured the facts to a degree that makes it reasonable to use them. (See p. 376.)

Two of our most important localities, Shexian and Jiaxing, have samples of data on age at marriage of 176 and 174 cases respectively. There is therefore a certain risk in setting up calculations that incorporate their locality marriage rates. However, for trials with 175 cases per run, using the Wuyuan data as before, the mean error[38] in the mean age at marriage over 30 runs was only 0.133 of a year. This is about 48.5 days, over a range of double that, and not enough to deter us from using them.

38 Ignoring ± signs.

Table 2.2

Females' ages at first marriage in selected localities in the lower Yangzi valley and three localities outside it

Area	*Sample Size*	*Mean*	*Sample Std. Dev.*
Lower Yangzi Valley	3582	17.33	2.000
Wuyuan	840	16.71	1.786
Tongshan	558	17.61	1.575
Qianshan	541	17.11	2.058
Yixian	536	17.04	1.514
Xuancheng	278	17.64	1.604
Shangrao	249	17.82	2.432
Shexian	176	17.99	2.196
Jiaxing	174	19.00	2.996
Rugao	54	17.87	2.092
Guiyang	672	17.01	2.072
Zunhua	203	17.27	2.123
Dingzhou	38	16.40	2.013

NOTE: None of the other LYV counties, namely De'an, Le'an, Leping, Poyang, and Xingguo had more than 17 cases, and have therefore been omitted.

Table 2.2 shows the mean ages of women at their first marriage, and the 'sample' standard deviation.[39] The standard deviation ('sigma' or 'σ') is a measure of the spread of a distribution around its mean. Essentially what happens is that the difference between the mean and each case in the sample of data is squared; the sum of these squares is divided by the number of cases minus 1; and the square root taken of the result. When a curve is a basic 'Gaussian', or 'normal', about 68% of the values lie within one standard deviation to each side of the mean. If we use the LYV regional weighted mean of

39 So called to distinguish it from the deviation from the mean of a population as a whole.

mean of 17.33 and the σ of 2.000 in Table 2.2, it takes only a moment to use the output from the program *marriage.count* for the LYV as a whole to find that slightly more than 71 per cent of the ages of marriage fall within the 4-year range from 15.33 to 19.33. The distribution is thus marginally more sharply peaked than for a basic Gaussian curve.

The most interesting feature of this table is the way that Jiaxing prefecture stands out as an exception to the otherwise broadly consistent pattern of most first female marriages, which are tightly compressed into a restricted band of ages around either side of 17. Jiaxing marriage came on average a year later than in any other locality, and the main group of marriages was spaced out over a longer period than those of the others. Its nearest rival was Shangrao. Compare Jiaxing's $2\sigma \approx 6$ with Shangrao's $2\sigma \approx 4.9$.

5. Fertility

Using the *birth.distribution* program, with locality male and female life tables and locality age-specific marriage schedules inserted, makes it comparatively straightforward to determine the levels of births of girls needed in the localities of the lower Yangzi valley region for the exact replacement of a cohort of the population. We determine the corresponding boy births by adopting what we judge to be a suitable sex ratio. We have used a mid-range 105.5 on this occasion, but some specialists think it may have been higher in China.[40] The gross reproduction rates for females (GRR), plus the implied male rates, for places with a sufficient quantity of local figures for independent calculation, are given in Table 2.3.

The basis for this procedure is a general empirically based year-by-year schedule of the the most common pattern of (fractional) female births that a *notional undying and constantly reproducing single female* would have had over the ages of 10 through 49 to exactly replace herself. This schedule was originally determined by Heather Booth, working with William Brass. We

40 William James, "The Sex Ratio of Oriental Births," *Annals of Human Biology* 12.5, 1985.

have used the convenient version published later by Basia Zaba.[41] Under the conditions of real life, and in addition under the social conventions of late-imperial China, allowance has to be made for the curtailment of the biological reproductive years in a female cohort by (1) female *mortality* at all ages from 0 up to 49, (2) the as yet *unmarried status* of a proportion of women at each age, (3) the proportions of formerly married women at each age who are *widowed* (as the result of male mortality), and (4) the readjustment to (3) required for the effects of *widow remarriage* by age. The simplifying assumptions behind the overall calculations are of universal marriage of females, and of no extramarital children, as well as no second or higher-order remarriages of widows. These assumptions are all, in the strict sense, inaccurate, but broadly correct for analyzing Chinese society at this time in aggregate. Hence the task of the program *birth.distribution* is to identify the *multiplier* that, when applied to the modified year-by-year fractional female births will bring back the sum of these to unity.

The level of widow remarriage is set to match the Notestein and Chiao levels of the proportions of (non-remarried) rural widows in south China by each female age-group in the late 1920s. There seems to be no other available way of calibrating probable widow age-specific remarriages, even though the procedure evidently introduces an anachronism.[42]

We have in all cases in our calculations here left the age-difference between spouses at the regional mean of 3.221 years,[43] since the data on parents-in-law survival that are our only access to this information are too sparse to yield reliable results for individual localities. Since our information on the frequency distribution of the interspousal age-gap comes from another source, a Hu'nan lineage genealogy,[44] we have also just used this as a

41 Basia Zaba, "The Demographic Impact of AIDS: Some Stable Population Simulation Results," (London: Centre for Population Studies, London School of Hygiene and Tropical Medicine, 1994), appendix.

42 Frank Notestein, and Chi-ming Chiao, "Population", chap. 13 in John Buck, ed., *Land Utilization in China* (Nanjing: University of Nanjing, 1937. Reprinted, New York, NY: Paragon Book Reprint Corp., New York, NY, 1964).

43 As already stated, work done subsequent to the computing for this paper has shifted the mean interspousal age-gap to +3.1791 years. This should make little difference to the results in most cases.

44 *Zengshi sixiu zupu* 曾氏四修族譜 [Zeng Family Lineage Register, Fourth Recension], compiled by Zeng Chuan 曾傳. Revised by Zeng Huailiu 曾懷柳 et al.; re-edited by

straightforward regional distribution pattern. If the relevant locality genealogies were available, it would be possible to remedy both these oversimplifications. We have also had to use the values for α and β that have been found for the females of each locality by *logit.match.search* for the males as well; but they are of course applied to the male Standard table. All of these unavoidable procedures are likely, on balance, to have reduced the individual differences between the localities more than to have increased them, though this will not necessarily always have been the case. They also point to directions for a future sharpening of our results.

Zeng Yuxu 曾毓緒, and Zeng Guangzuo 曾廣祚. Xiang xiang 湘鄉 in Hengyang, [Hu'nan], 1900.

Table 2.3

Gross Reproduction Rates for females in selected localities of the lower Yangzi region in mid-Qing times

Locality	*Female GRR*	*Boy births*	*Total child births per lifelong reproducing woman*
LYV	2.4587	2.5939	5.0526
Shangrao	1.9644	2.0724	4.0368
Jiaxing	3.2353	3.4132	6.6485
Yixian	2.2515	2.3753	4.6268
Qianshan	2.2888	2.4147	4.7035
Wuyuan	2.3077	2.4346	4.7423
Shexian	2.3112	2.4383	4.7495
Xuancheng	2.3332	2.4615	4.7947
Tongshan	2.6229	2.7672	5.3901
Guiyang	2.4180	2.5510	4.9690
Zunhua	2.4556	2.5907	5.0463

NOTE: this table only includes localities with a sufficient quantity of data for an independent estimate of female marriage rates. The calculations are based on the assumption of a stationary population. Guiyang and Zunhua, which are not in the LYV, are included for purposes of comparison.

The findings for Shangrao and Jiaxing appear together at the head of this table, after the regional figures, as relatively extreme instances that dramatize its main message. Jiaxing, with a female life expectancy at birth of 22 years and a female gross reproduction rate of 3.2 girls and of over 6.6 children of both sexes per woman, was in a different demographic world from Shangrao, with a female expectancy of life at birth of 35 and a female gross reproduction rate of 1.96 girls, or 4 children, per woman. We need to avoid thinking in terms of either extreme as characteristic of this large part of

China, and form a conception, rather, of *a wide range of demographic behaviours* that embraced them both, with a greater number of cases located somewhere in-between, as well as, quite possibly, a handful of outliers still further removed from the majority, but as yet unidentified.

Finally we have to ask if the smooth measures that we have used for our reconstruction are misleading to the extent that they conceal what might be called certain 'regular irregularities'. Figure 2.7 shows the proportions in the data of sons *recorded as* surviving to mothers widowed after from 1 to 12 *years of marriage*. In our previous paper, where we used the ages at *bereavement* rather than the length of the marriage, we discarded the direct figures for the ratios of surviving sons to widows by age at bereavement as misleading because of what was the apparently strong influence of the presence of a living son on a widow's opting for fidelity (rather than remarriage), and hence becoming eligible for recording as an exemplar of virtue, and so, given survival to 50 *sui*, entering our data. The result was an upward bias being imparted to the proportion of new widows with surviving sons as opposed to those without. In place of the direct measure we therefore used a less distorting Bayesian measure, namely the probability of a woman who had *at least* one surviving son having *exactly* 2 surviving sons when she was bereaved at a given age. (See p. 377.)

Here we present this earlier Figure again for convenience, labelled as Figure 2.8.[45] We will, however, only discuss one of its aspects on the present occasion. This aspect is the striking deceleration and then reacceleration in the solid red line showing the data measure for the presence of exactly 2 sons, when contrasted with the modelled reconstruction, which latter is represented by the solid black line that for more than half the time runs along with the solid red one. If we take 17 as the mean age of marriage, it would appear that after 5 to 6 years from the probable onset of childbearing, which would have mostly been at between 18 to 19 years of age, there was a period of about 4 years in which the bearing of sons (and presumably of female

45 Some of the terms used in it will be unfamiliar to those who have not read the first paper. Briefly, 'EWA' stands for 'exact western years of age', and 'fuzzy' cases are those where the data indicate the presence of at least one surviving son when a widow was bereaved but leave open the possibility of more. Adjustments, in the form of weights on a linear gradient, have to be made to capture this latter effect, which increases, as one would expect, with the age at which the mother was bereaved.

children as well) dropped away before coming back to the modelled at level around the age of 28. In other words, we are probably looking at prima facie evidence of the *spacing* of births. Note the black arrow. This should now be compared with Figure 2.7, which has a similar arrow in approximately the same place. (See pp. 377–378.)

For simplicity of presentation, in 2.7 we have modelled cases sorted by the lengths of marriages only for data entries where the age of the wife at marriage was 18. Since the interest here lies in *the trend lines*, nothing much would be gained by adding the other ages, especially given the very low dispersion of ages at marriage around the mean. In the case of marriages of only a few years' duration, the *modelled* ratio of surviving sons per new widow[46] is only about *half* that of the *sons*-per-widow ratio in the *data*. It seems that the same selection bias caused by the presence of sons that we detected in the data based on the mother's ages at bereavement is also (as one would expect) at work here. By a duration of 6 years, though, the model-to-data ratio roughly stabilizes at around two-thirds.[47] Like their counterparts based on age at bereavement, these data are thus of little or no use for a direct reconstruction of the *absolute level* of birth-rates.

But the *trends*, rather than the improbably high levels, are interesting. It would seem likely, unless very special effects had a unique effect on the recording of very short marriages,[48] which can in general serve as a proxy for the early years of any typical marriage, that childbearing got off to a *rapid start*. After a first year so biassed that it exceeds the modelled rate for children of *both* sexes, the solid red line of the surviving-sons-per-new-widow data rises in close synchrony with the modelled curve for the birth-rates for children of *both* sexes for the durations of marriage from 2 through 4 years. On the reasonable assumption of a broadly constant son-induced bias to 'virtue' over these first 4 years, the age-specific proportion of surviv-

46 Or mothers having had a given duration of married life.

47 As shown by the brownish-green curve in Figure 2.7. See the numerical appendix for details. Note that the values for this ratio are shown by the vertical axis on the *right*-hand side of the Figure.

48 Normally the couples would not have known in advance that their time together was destined to be short and therefore accelerated reproduction, but those recording the wife's virtue might, afterwards, have been disproportionately moved emotionally by the extremely short duration of the marriage.

ing sons to widows who were recorded because of virtuous fidelity rises, as can be seen, at close to the rate of the modelled proportion of surviving children of *both sexes* to mothers.

But then its rate of increase starts to fall. By between marriage durations of 6 and 7 years its rate of increase is momentarily zero. After this it picks up again, and rises thereafter at a rate only slightly slower than that between marriage-durations of 2 and 4 years. This is another version of the support we found earlier in Figure 2.8 for the hypothesis that there was *birth-limitation during marriage*, in the form of *spacing*. Here we have the same phenomenon but measured against a slightly different index of time—length of marriage (from age 18) rather than age at bereavement. It should be noted that in this second case (that of Figure 2.7) approximately the same linear gradient of weights increasing with marriage length has been used for adjusting 'fuzzy' items in the data as is the case in Figure 2.8.[49] This matters, as in Figure 2.8 the 'dip' is *not* visible in the data curve that has *not* had adjustment for fuzzy cases (as shown in this Figure by the *dotted* red line).[50] Appropriate adjustment is thus crucial to the suggestion that we are making. The justification of the linearly increasing gradient of weights used in Figure 2.8 is that it is the one that brings the adjusted data closest to the model.[51] With due caution under these circumstances, our guess would be, taking Figures 2.7 and 2.8 together, that married couples tended to pause once they had one surviving son who was at least 5 years old, and so likely to make it through to adulthood. The LYV male e(5) is 43.4 years. From durations of 7 years onwards, however, the tempo picks up again.

6. Discussion

Apart from the final set of points made at the end of section 5 above we have focussed on the nature of the data for *localities* within the lower Yangzi region in mid-Qing times, and on the techniques needed to use the regional pattern, established from a larger regional sample, to provide a framework

49 Given the different types of time-measure it is technically impossible to make the two gradients match exactly.

50 In other words, 2.7 inversely helps confirm that the adjustment process is correct.

51 For a more detailed discussion see Elvin and Fox (forthcoming).

into which it is possible to fit the information from the localities at the prefectural and county level. These normally create problems because they provide smaller samples and are at times poorly documented in some specific respect. What has emerged from our work is a picture of *microvariation* that is extremely marked as regards mortality, very limited as regards ages at marriage and their distribution, and significantly marked as regards the gross reproduction rate (GRR), which has been calculated on the basis of an assumed stationary population, and which can be seen, in general terms, as a rough proxy for the average rate of fertility over the long run.

In summary, we have found (1) relatively high infant and relatively low adult mortalities for the mid-Qing lower Yangzi valley, (2) a wide range of 13 years in the $e(0)_f$ for the different LYV localities in our sample, and (3) a relatively restricted range required for the Brass α and β parameters needed to modify our new multi-age-based LYV standard to give the closest match to the female older-age data from these localities (specifically, α: -0.234 to +0.169; β: 0.925 to 1.110).

Some important analytical issues have been left for a future paper, especially that of how best to adapt the methods and data used here to a historical population that was probably rising between 1700 and 1850 at a rate near 0.43 per cent annually.[52]

Finally, we should like to return to the theme with which we opened: how is it that in the same region of China, the lower Yangzi valley, and around the same time, the later eighteenth century, different counties (plus one prefecture) could have such large differences in expectation of life at birth, ranging over 13 years? We have tried a number of the obvious hypotheses, and they do not seem to work.

March 2007

52 The pattern of the late-imperial increase in population remains a matter of debate. The figure in the text is based on the calculation, thinking in terms of millions of people, and taking the two dates given in the main text as termini, that 410/215 = 1.91 = 1.00432^150. For the debate see the summary by Robert Marks, "China's Population Size during the Ming and Qing: A Comment on the Mote Revision," (delivered at the AAS annual meeting of 2002) on the Whittier College website, and reachable directly via entering "C ' P S D M Q : A C M R" into Google for searching (August 28, 2007).

Appendix: selected numerical data

Figure 2.1 Standard Life Tables for the Lower Yangzi Valley: age-specific survival, expectancy, mortality with ω (omega) = 85

Age	*l(x) F*	*e(x) F*	*q(x) F*	*l(x) M*	*e(x) M*	*q(x) M*
0	1.00000	27.2263	0.31213	1.00000	28.4327	0.28000
1	0.68787	38.4317	0.17149	0.72000	38.3496	0.20000
5	0.56991	41.9638	0.09605	0.57600	43.4221	0.08681
10	0.51517	41.1562	0.01974	0.52600	42.3112	0.01901
15	0.50500	36.9347	0.02444	0.51600	38.0828	0.02907
20	0.49266	32.7972	0.05763	0.50100	34.1481	0.05190
25	0.46427	29.6500	0.07980	0.47500	30.8805	0.07368
30	0.42722	27.0051	0.09089	0.44000	28.1384	0.08564
35	0.38839	24.4563	0.09650	0.40232	25.5405	0.09154
40	0.35091	21.8032	0.10518	0.36549	22.8637	0.09598
45	0.31400	19.0749	0.12350	0.33041	20.0278	0.11301
50	0.27522	16.4147	0.14814	0.29307	17.2643	0.13533
55	0.23445	13.8417	0.19795	0.25341	14.5807	0.18141
60	0.18804	11.6569	0.23777	0.20744	12.2703	0.21862
65	0.14333	9.54044	0.27412	0.16209	10.0252	0.25313
70	0.10404	7.24077	0.39206	0.12106	7.60874	0.36560
75	0.06325	5.41451	0.46530	0.07680	5.64618	0.43750
80	0.03382	3.15647	0.63779	0.04320	3.26015	0.60856
85	0.01225			0.01691		

NOTE: The l(x) figures are the proportions surviving of a notional birth cohort of 1.0. The q(x) are the proportions of the surviving proportions dying in a given period of 5 years. The e(x) figures are years of remaining life. 'F' = 'Females', and 'M' = 'Males'. Omega ω is the cut-off age at which calculations terminate. Mortality here is shown for 5-year intervals after age 5. It has not been smoothed.

Figure 2.2 Mortalities compared: LYV female and male Standards; Taiwan 1909–11, and Coale and Demeny 'west' model with basic e(0) female = 25 and e(0) male = 22.9 transformed with logit system parameters alpha a = 0.01 and beta b = 0.9 for the closest match with LYV females at ages over 50 *sui*.

Age	*LYV f*	*LYV m*	*TW f*	*TW m*	*C & D f*	*C & D m*
0	0.3121	0.2800	0.2305	0.2404	0.3276	0.3705
1	0.1628	0.1524	0.1248	0.1270	0.1746	0.1934
2	0.0747	0.0781	0.0633	0.0604	0.0846	0.0887
3	0.0437	0.0513	0.0409	0.0364	0.0515	0.0504
4	0.0390	0.0450	0.0352	0.0311	0.0433	0.0419
5	0.0296	0.0319	0.0236	0.0207	0.0278	0.0266
6	0.0232	0.0227	0.0154	0.0134	0.0170	0.0159
7	0.0200	0.0180	0.0111	0.0097	0.0114	0.0105
8	0.0185	0.0167	0.0107	0.0093	0.0112	0.0102
9	0.0151	0.0136	0.0095	0.0085	0.0106	0.0095
10	0.0096	0.0088	0.0076	0.0072	0.0097	0.0085
11	0.0059	0.0055	0.0064	0.0063	0.0091	0.0078
12	0.0040	0.0038	0.0058	0.0059	0.0088	0.0074
13	0.0041	0.0041	0.0060	0.0061	0.0091	0.0077
14	0.0043	0.0045	0.0065	0.0063	0.0097	0.0083
15	0.0046	0.0052	0.0071	0.0067	0.0105	0.0091
16	0.0048	0.0056	0.0076	0.0070	0.0111	0.0097
17	0.0049	0.0059	0.0079	0.0071	0.0114	0.0101
18	0.0057	0.0064	0.0082	0.0076	0.0118	0.0106
19	0.0072	0.0074	0.0089	0.0085	0.0124	0.0115
20	0.0094	0.0090	0.0098	0.0099	0.0132	0.0128
21	0.0110	0.0100	0.0105	0.0109	0.0138	0.0138
22	0.0118	0.0106	0.0109	0.0114	0.0142	0.0143
23	0.0124	0.0111	0.0114	0.0122	0.0145	0.0146
24	0.0134	0.0121	0.0120	0.0135	0.0148	0.0149
25	0.0148	0.0135	0.0130	0.0155	0.0153	0.0154
26	0.0159	0.0146	0.0138	0.0169	0.0156	0.0158
27	0.0165	0.0152	0.0142	0.0178	0.0159	0.0160
28	0.0169	0.0156	0.0146	0.0184	0.0162	0.0164
29	0.0173	0.0161	0.0150	0.0193	0.0166	0.0169
30	0.0180	0.0168	0.0155	0.0205	0.0171	0.0176
31	0.0185	0.0174	0.0160	0.0215	0.0176	0.0182
32	0.0189	0.0177	0.0163	0.0222	0.0179	0.0185
33	0.0191	0.0180	0.0169	0.0232	0.0181	0.0190
34	0.0194	0.0182	0.0178	0.0249	0.0185	0.0196
35	0.0196	0.0185	0.0191	0.0271	0.0189	0.0206
36	0.0199	0.0188	0.0201	0.0289	0.0193	0.0212
37	0.0201	0.0190	0.0207	0.0301	0.0195	0.0217
38	0.0204	0.0192	0.0209	0.0310	0.0198	0.0223
39	0.0208	0.0194	0.0209	0.0323	0.0200	0.0232

40	0.0213	0.0196	0.0207	0.0340	0.0203	0.0245
41	0.0217	0.0198	0.0207	0.0353	0.0206	0.0255
42	0.0220	0.0200	0.0208	0.0364	0.0208	0.0261
43	0.0225	0.0205	0.0209	0.0368	0.0210	0.0267
44	0.0234	0.0213	0.0207	0.0371	0.0213	0.0275
45	0.0246	0.0224	0.0202	0.0370	0.0217	0.0287
46	0.0254	0.0232	0.0200	0.0371	0.0219	0.0295
47	0.0260	0.0237	0.0200	0.0375	0.0222	0.0301
48	0.0267	0.0244	0.0210	0.0390	0.0230	0.0311
49	0.0279	0.0254	0.0228	0.0416	0.0244	0.0328
50	0.0296	0.0269	0.0255	0.0452	0.0264	0.0352
51	0.0308	0.0280	0.0274	0.0478	0.0279	0.0369
52	0.0316	0.0287	0.0285	0.0495	0.0287	0.0380
53	0.0330	0.0299	0.0296	0.0513	0.0297	0.0391
54	0.0354	0.0322	0.0314	0.0541	0.0314	0.0408
55	0.0390	0.0355	0.0340	0.0579	0.0338	0.0432
56	0.0416	0.0378	0.0359	0.0607	0.0355	0.0450
57	0.0432	0.0392	0.0371	0.0626	0.0366	0.0461
58	0.0444	0.0404	0.0384	0.0642	0.0386	0.0481
59	0.0465	0.0423	0.0405	0.0666	0.0424	0.0518
60	0.0494	0.0450	0.0435	0.0699	0.0479	0.0571
61	0.0515	0.0469	0.0457	0.0723	0.0519	0.0608
62	0.0529	0.0481	0.0471	0.0739	0.0541	0.0630
63	0.0541	0.0493	0.0491	0.0765	0.0564	0.0656
64	0.0561	0.0512	0.0526	0.0809	0.0604	0.0702
65	0.0588	0.0537	0.0577	0.0871	0.0662	0.0768
66	0.0608	0.0555	0.0613	0.0916	0.0703	0.0815
67	0.0621	0.0567	0.0635	0.0942	0.0727	0.0842
68	0.0659	0.0602	0.0671	0.0974	0.0767	0.0881
69	0.0730	0.0668	0.0736	0.1030	0.0841	0.0953
70	0.0834	0.0765	0.0831	0.1112	0.0949	0.1058
71	0.0907	0.0832	0.0898	0.1168	0.1025	0.1131
72	0.0948	0.0870	0.0937	0.1200	0.1067	0.1171
73	0.0977	0.0898	0.0977	0.1210	0.1121	0.1234
74	0.1027	0.0945	0.1046	0.1221	0.1220	0.1352
75	0.1099	0.1012	0.1144	0.1236	0.1364	0.1527
76	0.1149	0.1060	0.1214	0.1247	0.1464	0.1645
77	0.1177	0.1087	0.1254	0.1254	0.1518	0.1708
78	0.1253	0.1159	0.1286	0.1283	0.1591	0.1774
79	0.1399	0.1296	0.1340	0.1337	0.1727	0.1899
80	0.1615	0.1499	0.1416	0.1416	0.1927	0.2082
81	0.1762	0.1637	0.1470	0.1470	0.2062	0.2205
82	0.1839	0.1711	0.1499	0.1498	0.2133	0.2269

NOTE: Mortality is the $q(x)$ defined in the note to Figure 2.2, namely the frequency or probability of dying over the following year. All these figures have been *smoothed twice* with a rolling 3-year average, to produce a smooth gradient between successive points. No adjustment has been made to the LYV figures for females to allow for the effects of a probable female first-year infanticide of at least 10.4 per cent.

Figure 2.3 Transforming Standard female truncated logits to match data female truncated logits: selected cases

Age	*LYV Std*	*Shexian D*	*Shexian T*	*Jiaxing D*	*Jiaxing T*	*Shangrao D*	*Shangrao T*
55	-0.87465	-0.98132	-0.97500	-0.67953	-0.68317	-1.16410	-1.17350
60	-0.38434	-0.47293	-0.48185	-0.15919	-0.16481	-0.71827	-0.71027
65	-0.04159	-0.13598	-0.13689	0.19775	0.19983	-0.40934	-0.38847
70	0.24897	0.15474	0.15573	0.51123	0.51087	-0.10039	-0.11734
75	0.60467	0.50961	0.51420	0.87377	0.89419	0.21682	0.21235
80	0.98270	0.89580	0.89544	1.32000	1.30430	0.55683	0.56030

NOTE: Values are logits. 'D' indicates data logits with radix at 50. 'T' indicates LYV Standard after transformation for optimal Brass α and β by logit and antilogit procedures, truncation of years below 50, and calculation of truncated-value logits for radix = 50.

Figure 2.4 Transforming Standard female truncated logits to match data female truncated logits: further selected LYV cases

Age	*LYV Std*	*Tongshan D*	*Tongshan T*	*Qianshan D*	*Qianshan T*	*Rugao D*	*Rugao T*
55	-0.87465	-0.83686	-0.81657	-0.89001	-0.95449	-1.31320	-1.15740
60	-0.38434	-0.28568	-0.28896	-0.56314	-0.46418	-0.57002	-0.63215
65	-0.04159	0.09384	0.08294	-0.13845	-0.12144	-0.16156	-0.26206
70	0.24897	0.41885	0.40081	0.20519	0.16913	0.13622	0.05409
75	0.60467	0.80693	0.79339	0.54623	0.52483	0.47123	0.44434
80	0.98270	1.19100	1.21430	0.89343	0.90286	0.74924	0.86258

NOTE: Values are logits. 'D' indicates data logits with radix at 50. 'T' indicates LYV Standard after transformation for optimal Brass α and β by logit and antilogit procedures, truncation of years below 50, and calculation of truncated-value logits for radix = 50.

Figure 2.5 Transforming Standard female truncated logits to match data female truncated logits: selected cases from outside the LYV

Age	*LYV Std*	*Guiyang D*	*Guiyang T*	*Zunhua D*	*Zunhua T*	*Dingzhou D*	*Dingzhou T*
55	-0.87465	-0.89439	-0.87781	-0.92299	-0.88722	-1.06010	-1.07690
60	-0.38434	-0.40181	-0.40054	-0.35744	-0.37635	-0.63435	-0.62649
65	-0.04159	-0.05846	-0.06789	-0.00874	-0.01756	-0.33252	-0.31455
70	0.24897	0.23168	0.21329	0.34458	0.28798	-0.05981	-0.05253
75	0.60467	0.57114	0.55640	0.61884	0.66387	0.27420	0.26506
80	0.98270	0.89439	0.91985	1.06030	1.06540	0.60452	0.59909

NOTE: Values are logits. 'D' indicates data logits with radix at 50. 'T' indicates LYV Standard after transformation for optimal Brass α and β by logit and antilogit procedures, truncation of years below 50, and calculation of truncated-value logits for radix = 50.

Figure 2.6 Probabilistic simulation of the effects of decreasing sample size: distribution of proportions of ages of first marriages of women using Wuyuan county as a 'standard' (840 data cases)

		Numbers of runs				
Age	*Wuyuan data*	*50,000*	*5,000*	*500*	*250*	*100*
9	0.000595	0.00064	0.0006	0.000	0.000	0.00
10	0.002976	0.00276	0.0030	0.000	0.000	0.00
11	0.005952	0.00542	0.0056	0.002	0.008	0.00
12	0.014881	0.01552	0.0114	0.020	0.008	0.00
13	0.044048	0.04548	0.0460	0.052	0.040	0.05
14	0.108330	0.10914	0.1094	0.114	0.132	0.06
15	0.170830	0.17052	0.1718	0.178	0.164	0.20
16	0.213690	0.21182	0.2152	0.216	0.220	0.23
17	0.205360	0.20468	0.2072	0.190	0.208	0.24
18	0.135710	0.13652	0.1314	0.138	0.112	0.15
19	0.063690	0.06360	0.0650	0.064	0.056	0.06
20	0.018452	0.01874	0.0174	0.012	0.032	0.01
21	0.005357	0.00574	0.0068	0.002	0.008	0.00
22	0.004762	0.00458	0.0058	0.004	0.000	0.00
23	0.004167	0.00362	0.0026	0.004	0.008	0.00
24	0.001190	0.00122	0.0008	0.000	0.004	0.00

Figure 2.7 Mean proportions of sons surviving to widowed mothers by length of marriage data adjusted for 'fuzz', and converted to western measure of duration

Length of marriage	*Ssons per widow D: A,C*	*Ssons per widow M married at 18*	*Ratio Ssons in M/ Ssons in D*	*SKids per widow M married at 18*
1	0.4325	0.199	0.47966	0.335
2	0.4765	0.260	0.52019	0.501
3	0.6403	0.347	0.54379	0.667
4	0.7675	0.430	0.54464	0.826
5	0.8365	0.508	0.57285	0.977
6	0.9040	0.582	0.66324	1.120
7	0.9034	0.651	0.68148	1.255
8	1.0350	0.718	0.67396	1.383
9	1.1436	0.780	0.64773	1.503
10	1.2544	0.838	0.65020	1.617
11	1.3351	0.894	0.64990	1.724
12	1.4391	0.948	0.64946	1.827

NOTE: 'D' indicates 'data', 'M' indicates 'model'. 'Ssons' stands for 'surviving sons', and 'Skids' stands for 'children of *both sexes* surviving', after the length of marriage shown.

'A' indicates 'adjusted' for fuzzy cases. 'C' indicates that *sui* data have been converted to exact western years of age prior to calculating other figures. The model only uses marriages at 18 in order to simplify the presentation of the pattern.

Figure 2.8 Age-specific probability of a widow, given that she has at *least* 1 surviving son, having *exactly* 2 surviving sons

Age at bereave-ment	*Model ssons/age*	*Unadjusted Data ssons.age*	*Adjusted Data ssons/age*	*'fuzzy' cases*	*Total cases in EWA*
18	0.04612	0.03073	0.06145	129.0	355.5
19	0.07007	0.04252	0.07823	182.0	529.5
20	0.09946	0.05433	0.10479	240.5	645.0
21	0.13138	0.07262	0.13346	280.5	798.0
22	0.16240	0.08290	0.16321	358.5	864.5
23	0.18955	0.08288	0.17808	419.0	1030.5
24	0.21358	0.09417	0.18712	410.0	1139.5
25	0.23388	0.10622	0.20207	451.5	1042.5
26	0.25192	0.11222	0.22092	506.5	1092.5
27	0.26590	0.12235	0.25194	558.5	1210.0
28	0.27835	0.13479	0.27527	415.0	1301.0
29	0.28808	0.13470	0.28893	118.5	916.0

NOTE: Fuller details in this Figure may be found in Elvin and Fox (forthcoming).

Bibliography

A. Sources used for the Lower Yangzi Valley Region

'CW (date):' is used throughout to indicate a photographic facsimile reprint published by the Chengwen company in Taibei, Taiwan, in their series *Zhongguo fangzhi congshu* [Compendium of Chinese local gazetteers]. The letters 'HZ:' stand for 'Huazhong' (Mid China). The number that follows the second colon indicates the publication number in that series.

We do not normally list more than two of those who compiled (*zuan* 纂) or revised (*xiu* 修)—or, in some respects, 'edited'—the gazetteer. In general we use *only* the names found on the title page of the Chengwen reprint, where there is one. The rationale for this limitation is that the main purpose of a bibliographic entry is unambiguous identification of the item. Usually these names are followed by *deng* 等, which indicates that there was one or more other person involved, analogously to our 'et al.' We have not indicated this in the entries. In all but a few cases its presence can be assumed.

Within a gazetteer, 'LN' stands for *lie nü* 列女, the biographies of exemplary women; ' j.', plural ' jj.' indicates the *juan* 卷 or traditional 'chapter(s)' in the original work. After a solidus ' / ', capital Roman numerals in front of a ' : ' give the volume(s), and the ordinary Arabic numerals that follow list the relevant pages in the reprinted version, where this exists.

The final item in each entry, when it is appropriate, is the call number of the work for the National Library of Australia (indicated by 'NLA'). All of these numbers for the gazetteers begin with 'OC 3110.3 5604 ser.', and we have therefore omitted this, entering only '...' and the variable part, which consists of the series number and the work number in the series. This last is the same as the Chengwen series publication number.

We have westernized the imperial reign-title dates, using the western solar year within which the greater part of the relevant traditional Chinese lunar year fell. Details may be found in Xue Zhongsan 薛仲三 and Ouyang Yi 歐陽頤 eds., *Liangqian-nian Zhong-Xi-li duizhao-biao* 兩千年中西曆對照表 [Corresponding Sino-Western calendars for the two thousand years 1–2000 C.E.], Hong Kong: Shangwu, 1961.

De'an xianzhi 德安縣志 (De'an County Gazetteer). 1871. Cheng Jingzhou 程景周 (comp.), Shen Jianxun 沈建勳 (rev.). LN: j. 12. CW (1989): HZ: 922 / III:767–854. NLA: … 1. v. 922.

Jiaxing fuzhi 嘉興府志 (Jiaxing Prefectural Gazetteer). 1879. Wu Yangxian 吳仰賢 (comp.), Xu Yaoguang 許瑤光 (rev.). LN: jj. 64–79. CW (1970): HZ: 53 / IV–V:1907–2437. NLA: … 1 v. 53.

Le'an xianzhi 樂安縣志 (Le'an County Gazetteer). 1684. Compiled and revised by Fang Shen 方甚 (comp. and rev.). LN: j. 7. CW (1989): HZ: 931 / II:528–529. NLA: … 1 v. 931.

Leping xianzhi 樂平縣志 (Leping County Gazetteer). 1870. Wang Yuanxiang 汪元祥 (comp.), Dong Ece 董萼策 (rev.). LN: j. 8. CW (1989): HZ: 930 / V:1979–2205. NLA: ... 1 v. 930.

Poyang xianzhi 鄱陽縣志 (Poyang County Gazetteer). 1824. Zhang Qiongying 張瓊英 (comp.), Chen Xiang 陳驤 (rev.). LN: j. 24. CW (1989): HZ: 933 / IV:1295–1610. NLA: … 1 v. 933.

Qianshan xianzhi 鉛山縣志 (Qianshan xianzhi). 1873. Hua Zhusan 華祝三 (comp.), Zhang Jianheng 張建珩 (rev.). LN: jj. 19–21. CW (1989): HZ: 911 / IV–V: 1587–1863. NLA: … 1 v. 911.

Rugao xianzhi 如皋縣志 (Rugao County Gazetteer). 1808. Ma Ruzhou 馬汝舟

(comp.), Yang Shouyan 楊受延 (rev.). LN: j. 9. CW (1989): HZ: 9 / III:1551–1772. NLA: … 1 v.9.

Shangrao xianzhi 上饒縣志 (Shangrao County Gazetteer). 1872. Li Shufan 李樹藩 (comp.), Wang Sipu 王思蒲 (rev.). LN: j. 21. CW (1989): HZ: 744 / VI–VII:1827–2241. NLA: … 1 v.744.

Shexian zhi 歙縣志 (Shexian County Gazetteer). 1828. Lao Fengyuan 勞逢源 and Shen Botang 沈伯棠 (comp. and rev.). LN: j. 8, section 11. CW (1985): HZ: 714 / V:1379–1969. NLA: … 1 v. 714.

Tongshan xianzhi 銅山縣志 (Tongshan Country Gazetteer). 1926. Wang Jiashen 王嘉詵 (comp.), Yu Jiamo 余家謨 (rev.). LN: jj. 68–69. CW (1970): HZ: 32 / IV:1693–2022. NLA: … 1 v. 32.

Wuyuan xianzhi 婺源縣志 (Wuyuan County Gazetteer). 1826. Huang Yingyun 黃應昀 and Zhu Yuanli 朱元理 (comp. and rev.). LN: jj. 28–33. CW (1985): HZ: 679 / VII–VIII:2443–3051. NLA: … 1 v. 679.

Xingguo xianzhi 興國縣志 (Xingguo County Gazetteer). 1872. Jin Yiqian 金益謙 (comp.), Cui Guobang 崔國榜 (rev.). LN: jj. 27–28. CW (1989): HZ: 939 / III:1025–1199. NLA: … 1 v. 939.

Xuancheng xianzhi 宣城縣志 (Xuancheng County Gazetteer). 1888. Zhang Shou 章綬 (comp.), Li Yingtai 李應泰 (rev.). LN: jj, 20–25. CW (1985): HZ: 654 / V–VI:1853–2433. NLA: … 1 v. 654.

Yixian zhi 黟縣志 (Yixian County Gazetteer). 1822. Wu Dianhua 吳甸華 (original rev.). Wu Zijue 吳子玨 (further rev.). LN: j. 8. CW (1983): HZ: 725 / III:999–1237. NLA: … 1 v. 725.

Zengshi sixiu zupu 曾氏四修族譜 (Zeng Family Lineage Register, Fourth Recension). Zeng Chuan 曾傳 (comp.), 1900. Zeng Huailiu 曾懷柳 et al. (rev.); Zeng Yuxu 曾毓緒 and Zeng Guangzuo 曾廣祚 (re-ed.). Xiang xiang 湘鄉 in Hengyang [Hu'nan].

B. Selected secondary works directly used in the reconstruction and analysis

Brass, William (1971). "On the Scale of Mortality." In W. Brass, ed., *Biological Aspects of Demography*. London: Taylor and Francis.

Brass, William (1975). *Methods for Estimating Fertility and Mortality from Limited and Defective Data*. Chapel Hill, NC: Laboratories for Population Statistics.

Coale, Ansley, and Paul Demeny (1983). *Regional Model Life Tables and Stable Populations*. 2nd ed. London and New York, NY: Academic Press.

Elvin, Mark. (1998) "Unseen Lives. The Emotions of Everyday Existence Mirrored in Chinese Popular Poetry of the Mid-Seventeenth to the Mid-Nineteenth Century." In Roger Ames et al., eds., *The Self as Image in Asian Theory and Practice*. Albany, NY: State University Press of New York.

Elvin, Mark (1999). "Blood and Statistics: Reconstructing the Population Dynamics of Late Imperial China from the Biographies of Virtuous Women in Local Gazetteers." In Harriet Zurndorfer, ed., *Chinese Women in the Imperial Past: New Perspectives*. Leiden: Brill.

Elvin, Mark (2004). *The Retreat of the Elephants. An Environmental History of China*. New Haven and London: Yale University Press.

Elvin, Mark, and Josephine Fox. Forthcoming "Marriages, Births, and Deaths in the Lower Yangzi Valley during the Later Eighteenth Century." In Ho (forthcoming).

Harrell, Stevan (1995). Ed. *Chinese Historical Microdemography*. Berkeley, Los Angeles, and London: University of California Press.

Hardy (2002). See Lazarus, J.

Ho, Clara (He Liu Yongcong 何劉詠聰) (Forthcoming: Lexington Books [Rowman and Littlefield]). Ed. *Five Windows on the Chinese World*.

James, William (1985). "The Sex Ratio of Oriental Births." *Annals of Human Biology* 12.5.

Lazarus, John (2002). "Human Sex Ratios: Adaptations and Mechanism, Problems and Aspects." In Ian Hardy, ed., *Sex Ratios. Concepts and Research Methods*. Cambridge: Cambridge University Press.

Li Zenglu [Li Tseng Lu] 李增祿 (1965) *Abridged Life Tables for Males and Females in Taiwan, 1906/62*. The Historical Research Commission of Taiwan Province: Taibei.

Liu Shiyong [Liu Shi-yung] 劉士永 (2004). "Differential Mortality in Colonial Taiwan (1895–1945)," *Annales de Démographie Historique* 2004.1.

Liu Ts'ui-jung [Liu Cuirong] 劉翠溶 (1992). "Ming Qing shiqi jiazu renkou yu shehui jingji bianqian" 明清時期家族人口與社會經濟變遷 (Lineage Populations and Socio-economic Changes in the Ming and Qing Periods). 2 vols. Taibei: Academia Sinica.

Marks, Robert (2002). "China's Population Size during the Ming and Qing: A Comment on the Mote Revision." (Comment delivered at the AAS annual meeting of 2002.) Whittier College website, reachable by entering "C ' P S D M Q : A C M R" into Google (downloaded, 28 August, 2007).

Notestein, Frank, and Chi-ming Chiao (1937). "Population". Chap. 13 in J. Buck, ed., *Land Utilization in China*. Nanjing: University of Nanjing. Reprinted, New York, NY: Paragon Book Reprint Corp., New York, NY, 1964.

United Nations (1982). *Model Life Tables for Developing Nations*. New York, NY: United Nations Organization.

Wolf, Arthur, and Chieh-shan Huang (1980). *Marriage and Adoption in China, 1845–1945*. Stanford CA: Stanford University Press.

Woods, Robert, and Nicola Shelton (1997). *An Atlas of Victorian Mortality*. Liverpool: Liverpool University Press.

Zaba, Basia (1994). "The Demographic Impact of AIDS: Some Stable Population Simulation Results." London: Centre for Population Studies, London School of Hygiene and Tropical Medicine.

Acknowledgements

We should like to thank the Chiang Ching-Kuo Foundation for International Scholarly Exchange and the Australian Research Council for grants that made much of this work possible. Judith Pabian, the Research Grants Officer of the Research School of Pacific and Asian Studies in the Australian National University, and Dorothy McIntosh, the Administrator of the Division of Pacific and Asian History, took as much as possible of the bureaucratic burden off our shoulders. Our foremost intellectual debt is to Dr Basia Zaba of the London School of Hygiene and Tropical Medicine, and we should also like to thank Dr Zhao Zhongwei of the Research School of Social Sciences in the Australian National University, as well as Dr Gigi Santow and Dr Michael Bracher for their help and inspiration. We hope that many other colleagues will forgive us not mentioning them individually. We are extremely grateful for their assistance.

M.E. and J.F

March 2007

Illustrations

Figure 2.1

The interlocking of the data and other measures used for the reconstruction of the population dynamics of the lower Yangzi valley region in the later eighteenth century. See the text for the meaning of the coding embodied in the shapes of the cartouches and in the colours.

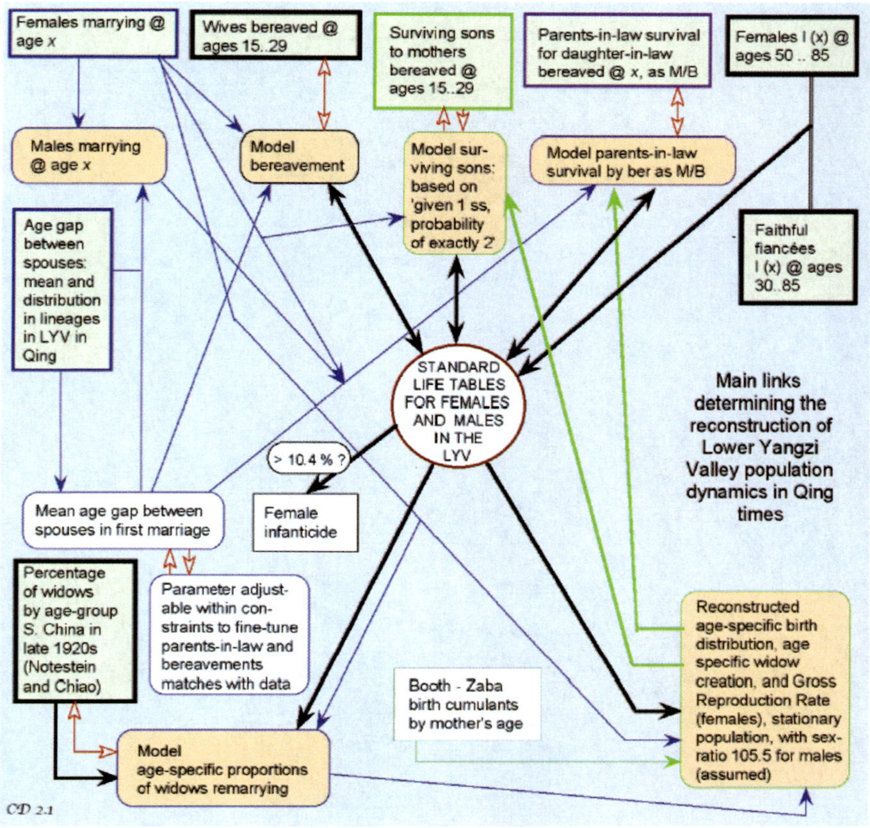

Figure 2.2

Annual mortality of females and males in the lower Yangzi valley during the middle of Qing dynasty compared with those calculated from the unadjusted life tables for Taiwan 1909–1911, and and from the Coale and Demeny 'west' family of life tables, here taken at at e(0)f 25 and adjusted to the closest fit with the lower Yangzi valley standard. *Sui* measure converted to exact western years of age.

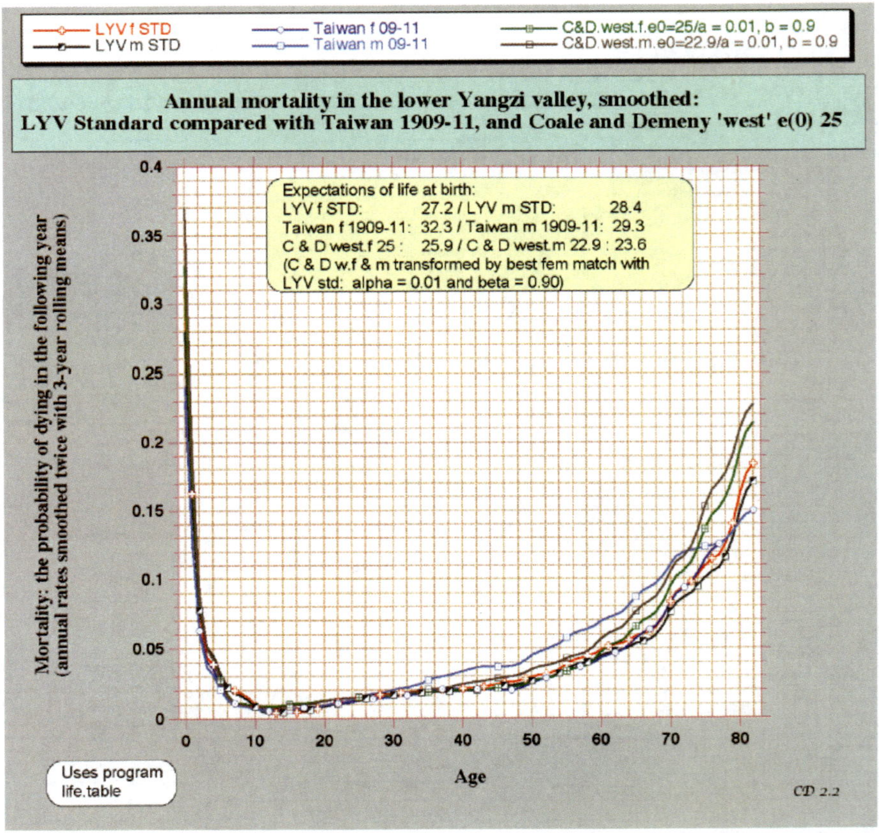

Figure 2.3

Transforming LYV Standard female logits for all ages to truncated logits for matching with logits from data for deaths at ages above 50 *sui* in Jiaxing prefecture, and the counties of Shexian and Shangrao, with *sui* converted to western exact ages.

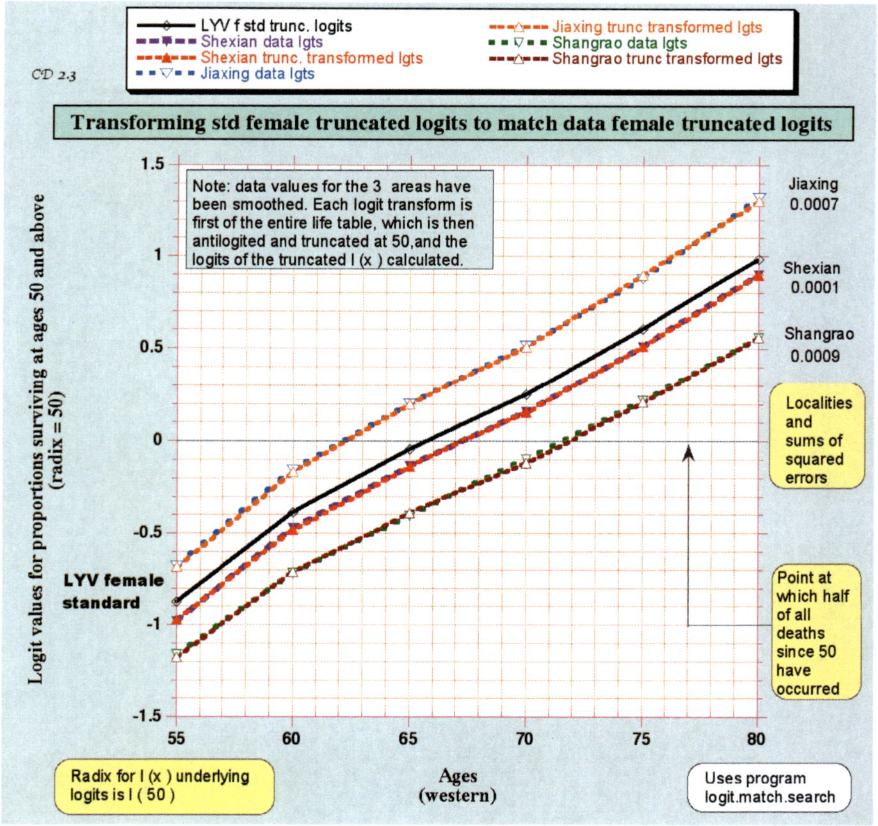

Figure 2.4

Transforming LYV Standard female logits for all ages to truncated logits for matching with logits from data for deaths at ages above 50 *sui* in the counties of Tongshan, Qianshan, and Rugao, to show good, adequate, and marginal closeness of fit, with *sui* converted to western exact ages.

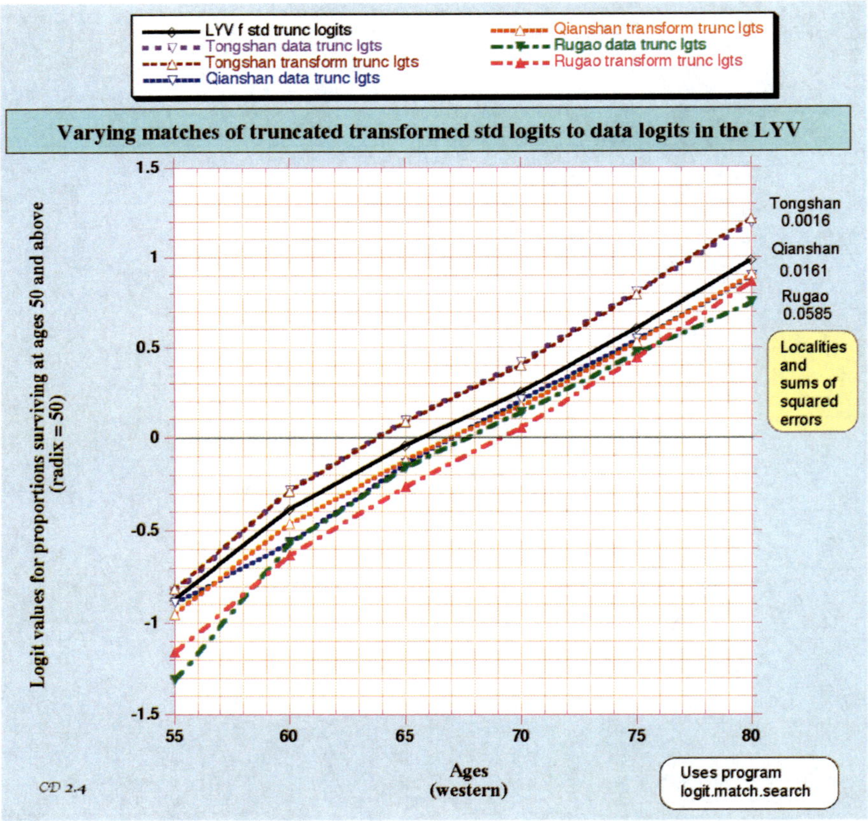

Figure 2.5

Transforming LYV Standard female logits for all ages to truncated logits for matching with logits from data for deaths at ages above 50 *sui* in Dingzhou, Guiyang, and Zunhua, localities not in the lower Yangzi valley region, with *sui* converted to western exact ages.

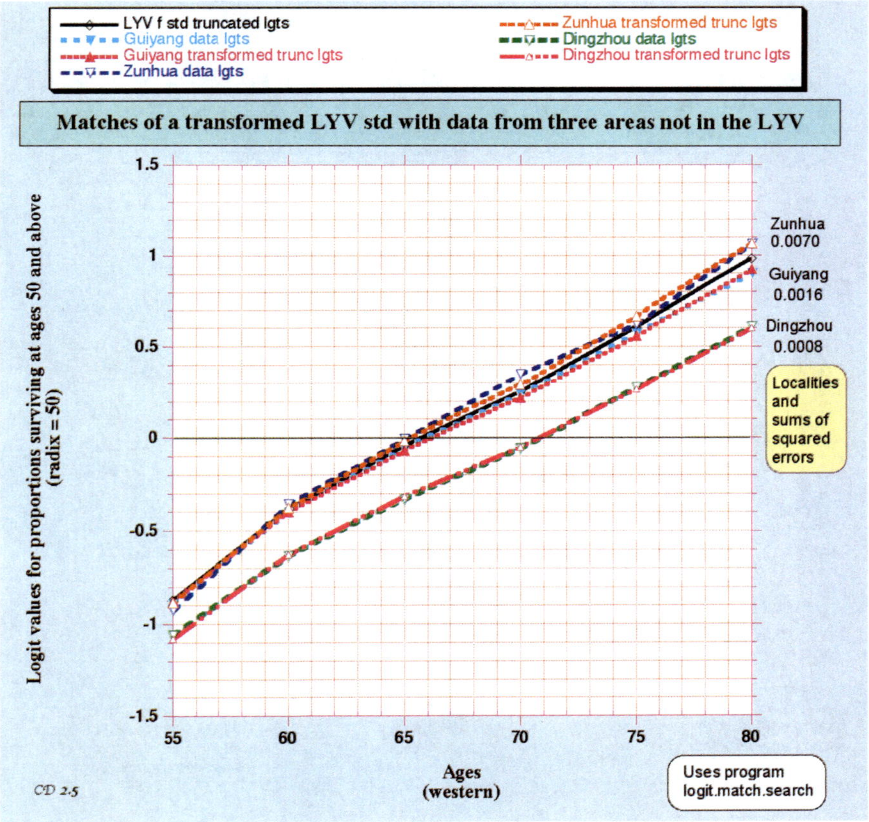

Figure 2.6

Tests on the degradation of the pattern of the distribution of ages at first marriage for females with the diminution of sample size, using the data from Wuyuan county as an example for simulations. See the text for a discussion.

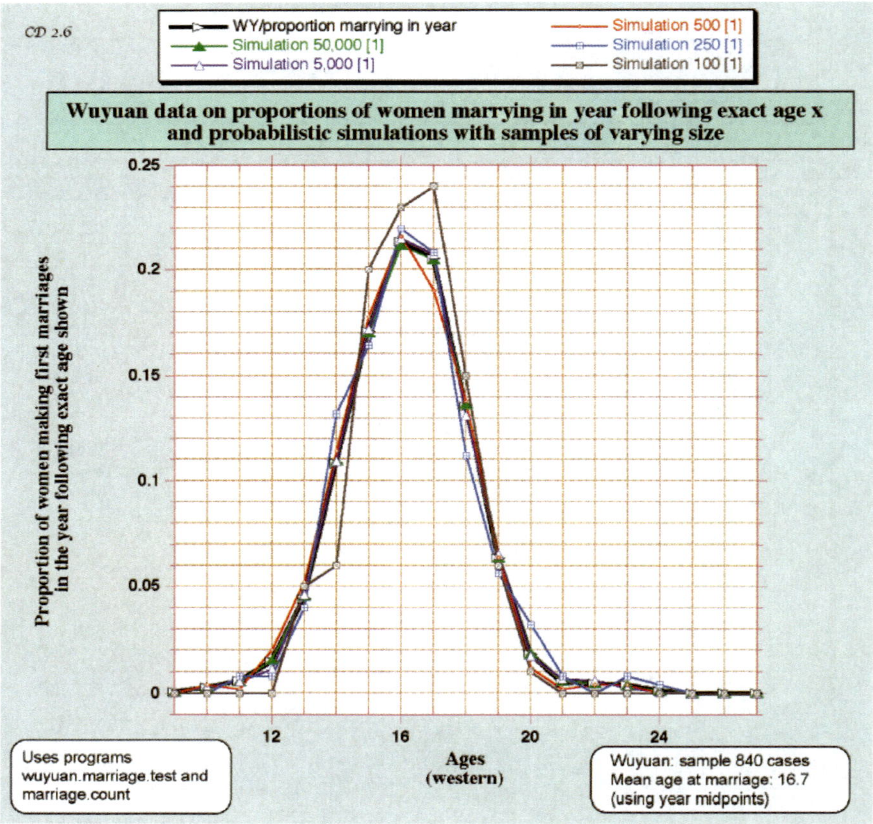

Figure 2.7

Proportions of sons recorded as surviving to mothers widowed after varying lengths of marriage in the mid-Qing lower Yangzi valley region, using data adjusted by weights increasing in a linear manner with age to allow for ambiguous cases of ‘at least one but possibly more surviving sons', and converted to exact western years, accompanied by modelled curves for surviving sons and surviving children of both sexes for comparison. The black arrow indicates the probable pause in childbearing after 5 to 7 years of marriage. Only cases of females aged 18 at marriage are included, hence a fairly short duration of pause. See text on the selection bias in these data.

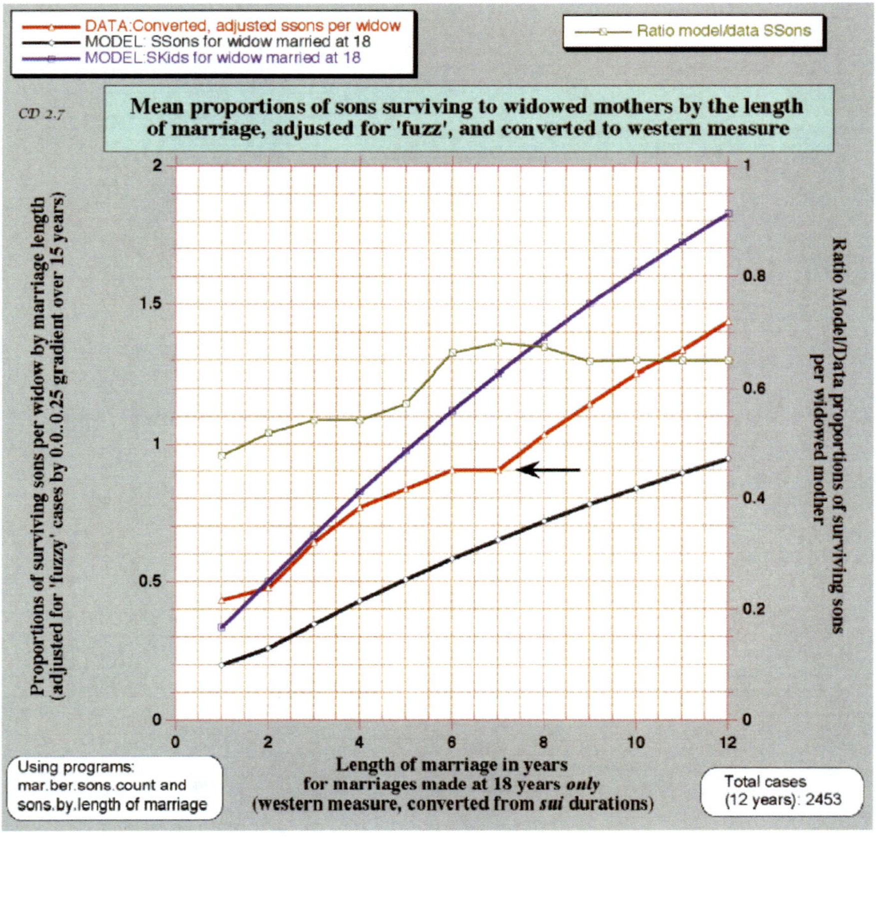

Figure 2.8

Age-specific probability of a wife widowed at a given age who has at least 1 surviving son in fact having exactly 2 surviving sons, for the mid-Qing lower Yangzi valley region, with *sui* converted to exact western years of age, and curves showing both data adjusted by weights increasing in a linear manner with age to allow for ambiguous cases of 'at least one but possibly more surviving sons', and non-adjusted data. Accompanied by a modelled equivalent. The black arrow indicates the probable pause in childbearing between ages 23 and 27. Cases of women married at all ages < 30 included, hence a wider spread of the pause than in Figure 2.7. See text on the selection bias in these data.

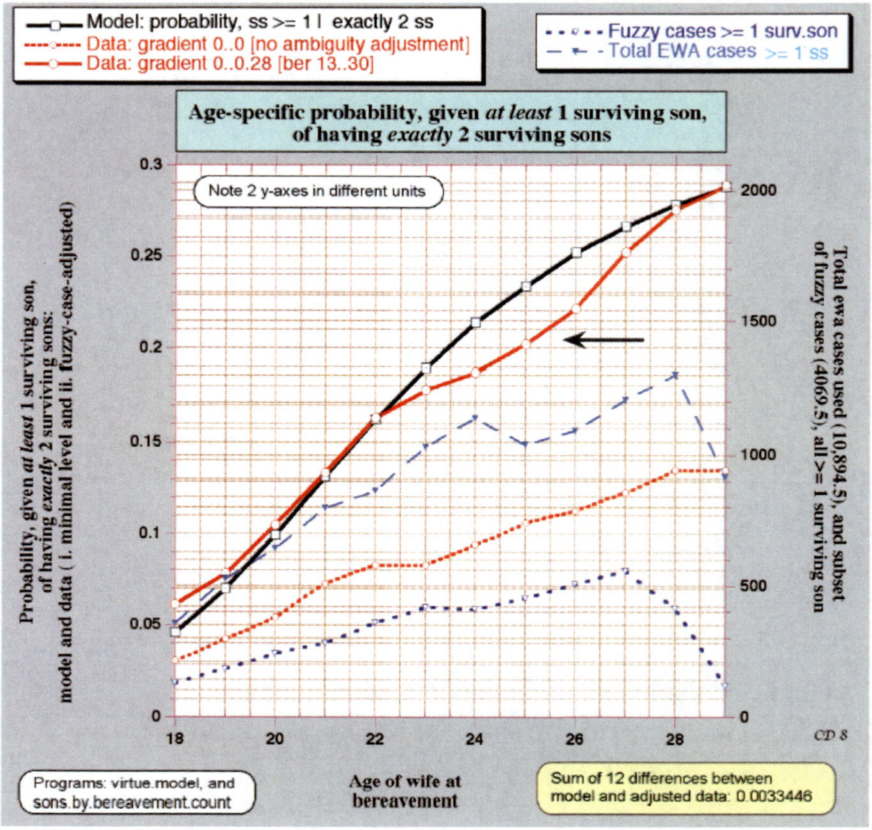